# PAKISTAN'S FOREIGN POLICY

# PAKISTAN'S FOREIGN POLICY

Sudhansu Kumar Patnaik

KALPAZ

*Published by*

Kalpaz Publications
C-30, Satyawati Nagar,
Delhi – 110052
Ph.: 011-47034999, 9811692060
www.kalpazpublications.com
E-mail: kalpaz@hotmail.com

*Distribution Network*
gyanbooks.com
India, USA, Canada, UK, Australia, France



ISBN: 978-93-5722-856-5 (PB)

First Published, 2024

*Printed at:* Gyan Press, Delhi.



**Pakistan's Foreign Policy**
Author: Sudhansu Kumar Patnaik

*To*
*My Mother*

# Contents

# List of Tables

# Preface

This book is a revised version of my thesis presented to the Centre for International Politics, Organisation and Disarmament, School of International Studies, Jawaharlal Nehru University, New Delhi for the award of Ph. D. Degree in International Relations in 1987. This was done under the supervision of the late Professor K.P. Misra.

Basically a formal document with a rigid theoretical structure cast in the conceptual framework of systems, the thesis was written in academic prose to carry conviction among a few examiners that the system approach is valid for the analysis of the foreign policy behaviour of a State in the modern International System. The impulse to develop it into a book form came predominantly from my teachers, students and friends which became difficult for me to resist. After long hesitancy, I took up the task and decided to publish it.

In the course of my revision of the thesis, I have tried to make it accessible to the world of both academic and non-academic elites with a wider spectrum of interests. This itself presented me a challenge of highest intellectual order at multiple levels. The treatment of the material is done in such a way that it will not only preserve the theoretical thrust of the analysis so essential to emerging theorists but also open the historical panorama that will satisfy the salacious curiosity of a common elite interested to know the dynamics of foreign policy behaviour of Pakistan even if the analysis is limited to the period from 1947 to 1971.

To bring the bacon home, I have opened out the topic beyond the narrow confines of my thesis by providing a background chapter on Pakistan's political profile since 1947 which gives the reader an insight into main matrix of Pakistan's foreign policy. At the same time, the objective of the book is reflected in the Introductory pages in such a way that it will logically lead the readers to the heart of the topic and at the same time provide a raison d'etre for a scientific analysis. I have also endeavoured in my own inimitable style to develop a sense of direct communion with the readers by taking great care to see that it should impart to the readers my deep commitment to the subject which is something that is worth writing and reading about. In the process, I have also tried to maintain directness and simplicity and retained only those jargons without which the book lose its analytical utility and intellectual rigor. In the same vein, I have drastically cut down many irrelevant footnotes so that the book keeps the readers absorbing to the end.

In the preparation of this book, I am indebted to a host of individuals and institutions. To all of them I owe an word of apology, as it is not possible to mention their names individually, even if, I love to do so. But I will be committing an act of sacrilege if I do not mention a few of them who loom large in the contribution they have made to my development as a student of politics. Of all, I am beholden in bounteous gratitude to my revered supervisor Professor Late K.P. Misra for my intellectual growth and emotional sustenance without whom I could not have become what I am today. I am also immensely grateful to my old teachers of J.N.U., Professor M.S. Rajan, Professor M.S. Venkataramani, Professor A.K. Damodaran, Professor M. Zuberi and Professor A.K. Ray whose love, guidance and moral support lifted me out of morass when I was struggling in J.N.U. to eke out a niche for me in the academic world. Beyond this, lie my unsolicited indebtness to a great scholar whom I have never seen, Professor James N. Rosenau of the George Washington University, United States whose inspiring words will always remain a beacon light for me in my life.

However, an intellectual enterprise of this nature is always an intensely personal one, so do mine. The views expressed herein are entirely mine for which, I, alone, am responsible.

February, 2005 *Sudhansu Kumar Patnaik*

# Introduction

The study of Pakistan's foreign policy has fascinated scholars since its inception in 1947. The trauma of its birth, its search for an identity, its ancient religion, its historical legacy, its cultural antipathy, its state-structure, its societal cohesion, its ruling elites, its failure in democracy, its military dictatorship, its alliance with the West and above all its relation with India have received varied treatment by scholars in the analysis of its foreign policy. Underlying all their studies, two points emerge most prominently that leave the analysis much to be desired.

In the first place, most of their analyses are value-laden, reflective of being culture-bound and geographically circumscribed. Barring a few, many analysts view Pakistan from narrow perspectives which are embedded in the moors of their nationality, class, race and ideology. As a result, certain cultural assumptions and values blur their vision not to view the dynamics of foreign policy in the broader spectrum of international relations. The same phenomenon is interpreted in different ways by different analysts as it filters through their culture-biased spectacles. While the sociology of knowledge argues cross-cultural perspective to inform the analyses, this is missing in this generic type of ethno-centric research. This is, as a matter of fact, more pronounced in the case of Indian and Pakistani scholars. Caught up in the web of "Anti-Pak-Anti-India" syndrome, their analyses are pervaded with, "I am essentially good but am occasionally forced by circumstances to behave badly, whereas you are bad but are occasionally forced by circumstances to behave well". Like the attribution theorists each has a tendency to overemphasize the dispositional factors when explaining the behaviour of others while stressing situational factors to account for their own. This is a truism in any social science research which, in the nature of things, can hardly be value-free. But what is imperative for any analyst is to make his values explicit, since value willy-nilly underlies the selection of social problems for investigation. Then it becomes easier for other analysts to determine the extent to which data shape results because data are identified on the basis of explicitly elaborated values.

Secondly, while making conceptual concession that different kinds of truth answering myriad questions that stem from diverse scholarly concerns are possible, it must be stressed without any fear of contradiction that analysis in any approach whether traditional or behavioural must observe its own rules. This is singularly lacking in these analyses. Despite their stress on single country study and tracing the behaviour of identifiable actors in particular situation at specific moment in time, nowhere the challenge is accepted to show that their problems are adequately revealed by the richness of their data and the clarity of their descriptions and explanations and the ascertainment of how and why the events happened as they did. Similarly, none of their accounts are coherent and insightful that will render their findings independent of the very coherence and insight with which they organise and analyse their data. It is hardly revealed from where they have procured each component of their data and it leaves much room for misrepresentation of them. So, one is tempted perforce to tell that their findings can only be accepted or rejected on the basis of the strength of their arguments or their standing in the academic world, because they have failed to observe the true canons of the non-scientific approach. However, this should not be misconstrued as making out an "evangelical" plea for the superiority of scientific approach. To posit this is to accept the view that an "objective reality" is only discoverable by one method rather than the other. Even if such a reality exists it can be never known. But nothing prevents and it won't be out of context to postulate here the canons of scientific approach which its practitioners observe in the analysis of foreign policy.

In a scientific analysis of foreign policy, the analyst structures the phenomena of foreign policy in terms of recurring patterns that transcend generations and particular situation. He looks for the number of times a pattern of behaviour is likely to reoccur. And the greater probability of its occurrence, there is more of revealing of the phenomena in all its dimensions. So, he engages in probabilistic statements on the basis of isolating the patterns of occurrence. As a result, he builds up certain nomothetic generalisations which clarify the relationship between two or more variables, specifies the conditions under which relationship holds, and explicates why the relationship should be expected to hold. This leads him to build upon a general theory that encompasses and explains more and more of the foreign policy phenomena. He elaborately states his values, assumptions, concepts and procedures that underlie his selection of phenomena in such a way that other analysts reach the same conclusion by gathering the same data and processing them in the same manner. He clarifies the rules that he follows in processing and interpreting data. He specifies each operation carried on in gathering data, lays down the categories used for the classification of data, defines precisely the concepts for operationalization and statistical analysis taken for isolating the patterns in data. He follows the exact rules of interpretation which if not properly followed will make the same set of data reveal different meanings to different analysts. Similarly, different sets will be produced by different researchers if each step in the data-making operation is not meticulously taken. However, one major advantage of this approach lies in the fact that the analyst links together a coherent and insightful account of his data in such a way that the truth of his findings can be verified independent of himself.

The present research on Pakistan's foreign policy is innovative in the sense that it makes a departure in the mode of analysis. In its attitude to enquiry, it is quite scientific though it adopts a unified approach by marrying empirical description with cogent analysis that will yield an easy comprehension of why Pakistan acts and interacts as it does. In our study the time dimension is vast, covering roughly a quarter century of Pakistan's functioning in the arena of the international system. This is a formidable canvas to trace and uncover myriad forces acting upon its policy makers entrusted with the task of formulating foreign policy decisions. In the nature of things, they never lend themselves so easily amenable to systematic analysis. Partly the difficulty stems from a lack of free access to data and partly from its very absence itself. Even where data are available there still remains the baffling problem for the student to integrate facts to explain past decisions and to build up general prepositions. To overcome this haunting problem and to bring the vast array of data into a semblance of order, an attempt has been made to identity, describe and assses the sources of its foreign policy in both substantively through and methodologically rigorous way in a cross-level perspective. This is sought to be done within the framework of an analytical model based on the systems approach.

The model is built upon a host of assumptions. In the first place, if foreign policy comprises the external behaviour of states, it is this behaviour which is treated as the unit of analysis. In foreign policy analysis, it means one focuses on the acts of the state. And by adopting the foreign policy acts as the unit of analysis, the study of foreign policy is placed with the philosophical and theoretical tradition of Talcott Parsons, Edward Shils and others. Secondly, there is no levels of analysis problem if one adopts this perspective of action theory. While one cannot analyse both national subsystem and international system as comparable units, there is hardly any analytical problem when one deals simultaneously with variables at various levels of aggregation. An explanatory model of foreign policy requires inclusion of independent variables at all levels of aggregation. Once it is recognized, the indicators of foreign policy behaviour of states can be put in a clear format for data analysis. This enables the analyst to make useful references about the relative strength of variables at multiple levels and to trace the interaction effects among these variables. Thirdly, if regular behaviour defines a system, it is legitimate to view the state as a subsystem in all encompassing international system or a system composed of a network of subsystems, comprising an environment, a group of actors, structures, through which actors initiate actions to respond to challenges of events at home and abroad. They all occur continuously in a circular flow of demands on policy, policy processes and products of policy. The decision feeds back into the system. Fourthly, if the concept of system is used as a distinct method of analysis, some of its characteristics like boundaries, internal elements and others need to be delineated. In sum, it is argued that this will enhance a scientific comprehension of the external behaviour of states as a system model facilitates an analytical construction of properties of action shared by all specific states. The model is a fictional state permitting analysis about the real states regardless of their actual differentiations. It also solves the perplexing problem of goals, motivations in national policy, for the behaviours of the decision-makers are treated as the unit of analysis. Further, the phenomenological issue is resolved as it permits focus on the phenomenal field of policy-makers, since it is assumed that cognitive process and belief system of key decision-makers are central to the study of decisional output.

The model contains a broad conceptualisation of variables at their highest level of abstractions both internal and external which subsume different types of specific inputs. Each variable commences with a sub-varibale that contains an enumeration of the empirical questions that it seeks to answer and an explanation of why questions are viewed as salient. Thus, historical description is accompanied by analytical perspective that underlies each subvariable, and they are provided and developed in an explicit context designed to illustrate or affirm an analytical point.

Relationship between all the variables considered relevant to the attitude, behaviour and event which they seek to explain are specified. So, it is clearly explicated how the dynamics of Pakistan foreign policy system shapes its external behaviour. Similarly, it is clearly indicated how variations in one set of variables may be linked to variations in another set. There is a plethora of evidence used to delineate the relationship among the variables, to assert the interpretations about particular phenomenon and to reach general conclusions about the central pattern. A set of hypothesis is developed embracing each variable which will project the analysis into future and it should be explicit and of "if then" variety which will link a particular variable with an aspect of Pakistan's external policies. And the goal of hypothesis testing is to determine the relative potencies of independent variable and to trace the distortion, if any, brought about by intervening variables. And in the process to find out the impact of intervening variable in particular decision-making situation, and how it has become decisive that has shaped the resultant output.

In our enquiry into Pakistan's foreign policy behaviour, the following seven hypotheses are taken up for empirical validity.

(a) A society which is unified by a common culture and historical experience can more effectively pursue its foreign policy goals than one which is rent with cultural dissension and lacked a shared historical experience.

(b) The resources and attribute dimensions of a State affect its capabilities that condition its foreign policy behaviour.

(c) The continuity and change in the foreign policy behaviour of a State are correlated with systemic requirements and changes from time to time.

(d) The regional systemic variable is quite potent in influencing the foreign policy behaviour of a state.

(e) The basic arrangements that organize the structure of authority among different agencies of government constitute a significant variable affecting the foreign policy behaviour of a State.

(f) The personality characteristics of the decision makers are potent in influencing the foreign policy decision-makers under certain conditions when :

  (i) the more dramatic are the means of assuming power;
  (ii) the more charismatic is the head of state;
  (iii) the more general interest the head of state has in foreign policy; and
  (iv) the more authority a head of state has over foreign policy.

(g) In the decision-making the cognitive beliefs are central to the decisional output.

While cross-national studies are the main bases for building up general theory of foreign policy, it is hoped that a research of spatio-temporal dimension involving variables at different levels of aggregation is equally rewarding because substantive knowledge is important. As Sidney Verba sums up the dilemma. "Reality seems to demand a configurative approach; generalizability seems to demand a more analytical approach". While comparative study of foreign policy has clearly been more amenable to the demands of generalizability, reality should now be given more of a chance. So, it would be good if research is undertaken to do country, and perhaps region-based cross-level studies. This line of argument finds adequate support from James N. Rosenau, Ole. R. Holsti, Nazli Choucri and Robert C. North.

Now coming to the diagrammatic representation of the model, we have posited that the decision-making process passes through two distinct stages: first, policy preference leading to decision and, second, action or output. In the first place, the key policy-makers, represented as a, b and c, perform broad intellectual task of policy-making and reach a particular policy preference. And the manner in which they accomplish this task determines the boundary of the decision to which their policy preference leads. The impact of the key decision-maker's cognitive beliefs predominates on policy preference though it is also influenced by other variables, and this leads to the final decision which is equally prone to influences of other variables. Precisely for this the policy preference is chosen as the dependent variable in place of the decision. Secondly, between the decision and the action or the output, the bureaucratic and the organizational dynamics distort the process that shape the resultant action, or the output.

The major cluster of societal variables which shapes Pakistan's foreign policy subsumes distinct dimensions. They are categorized as "culture and history" and "capabilities". "Culture and history" are defined as the norms and traditions that underlie the relationship among a society's members, their interpretations of their common heritage, and all other means by which they sustain the ties of the community. So it is hypothesized that a society which is unified by a common culture and historical experience can more effectively pursue its foreign policy goals than one which is rent with cultural dissension and lacked a shared historical experience. Our enquiry into Pakistani society revealed that it was socially fragmented, ethnically diverse and its people spoke differing languages and dialectics for which the pattern of social and political development, the Muslim response to the British rule and the colonial policy and the character and timing of the Pakistani Movement were primarily responsible. They also did not share a common historical perspective. These factors also hindered the process of national integration in Pakistan as it heightened, within a short time, the subaltern group consciousness pioneered by the East Pakistan whose demand for the recognition of Bengali as one of the national languages of Pakistan became strident with each passing day. The end of the rule of Hindustanis also eliminated the fantasy of Indo-Islamic identity of the Pakistani society. The rise of the Bengali vernacular elites coincided with the premature demise of the Parliamentary democracy in Pakistan. As a result, they were denied of any effective channel to make their numerical voice felt in the political system which was completely monopolised by the Civil-Military bureaucracy manned by people drawn from the main stratum of West Pakistan to the complete exclusion of the Bengalis. With the disintegration of the Muslim Legue, Pakistan lost an all-Pakistani political party which alone could have aggregated the interests of all sections of Pakistani society. Things worsened during the Ayub era. Political elites, mainly Bengalis, were totally alienated as it established an administrative state controlled by civil-military elites. Regionalism reared its ugly head which was gradually exacerbated.

However, it affected the foreign policy of Pakistan in three distinct ways. In the first place, to promote national integration, they looked for an Islamic identity which fanned Bengali chauvinism and its ruling elites stressed on anti-Indian component of Indo-Islamic identity which ultimately shaped their policy towards India. As a result, India became a major factor in its domestic and foreign policy. Secondly, in the name of Islamic ideology, Pakistan weaved a world of grandeur of Islamic solidarity which influenced its policy towards the Muslim countries and assumed the role of a self-appointed conscience-keeper of Muslims living in India. Thirdly, as the numerically majority Bengalis threatened the political survival of the ruling junta and their social and political hierarchy, they increasingly turned to the external powers to invoke their support for its preservation. Lastly, it led to the sad demise of the territorial state of Pakistan in 1971.

In our treatment of the subvariable "capabilities" we have adopted James N. Rosenau's conceptualization which denotes the resource and attribute dimension of a state. So, we deal with geography, size, military capability and economic development as relational variables of "capabilities". In this connection, it is hypothesized that each of these relational variables shape the capabilities of a state which has conditioned its foreign policy behaviour. In our enquiry into the capabilities of Pakistan during the period 1947 to 1971 the following findings are in order. In the first place, the unremitting sorrow of Pakistan is geography. Pakistan is derisively called a geographical monstrosity as its two wings were separated by thousand miles of Indian territory depriving it of a compact territorial personality, and their vastly differing geographical features perpetuating an uneven economic growth and social mobilization. Besides, it has the unique distinction of being flanked by three great powers—China, the Soviet Union and India. Interestingly while its eastern wing was opening out to the countries of Southeast Asia, its western wing joined the peninsula of the West Asia. This peculiar geographical location weighed enormously on its policy-planners, given the Russian traditional quest for the warm waters of Arabian Sea, and its unhappy relation with India with whom it shared long borders and all its major towns and industrial establishments were literally part of India's frontier zones. This was further honed by Afganistan's continued hostility which was manifested in its repudiation of the Durand Line as their common border and in its espousal of the cause of fictitious "Pakhtoonistan". It was really a herculean task on the part of a small country to defend its eight boundaries which compounded its geo-strategic problems. This was clearly highlighted during the 1965 war when East Pakistan was practically left defenceless that served to heighten Bengali sense of negligence on the part of the central authority. As revealed in our analysis, Pakistani ruling elites though predominantly Punjabis had a unified geo-strategic thinking—as India posed the only threat to its territorial integrity. They never feared any aggression from China, though Ayub's offer of joint defence of the subcontinent was made only in the context of the cultural revolution in China as he was deeply unnerved about its final outcome. But their fear of Soviet advance was deep-seated and genuine as was revealed after the U-2 incident. However, geography certainly constrained Pakistan's capabilities in three ways: on the geo-military plane; in the uniform economic development of its two wings and in greater social mobilization.

With regard to size, our enquiry reveals that Pakistan being perched on the rendezvous of Asia and Europe with a population of 80,000,000 was deemed to be one of the bigger nations of the world in terms of demography and geopolitical significance, hence destined to play a potential role in the post-war politics of Asia. A synoptic survey of its size as defined by present day theorist to include both human and non-human resource dimension, showed that it lacked basic ingredients of power—coal, petroleum, hydro-electricity, natural gas and also of minerals—iron-ores, chromite, and manganese. Nature was not bounteous, nor government has made any appreciable effort to explore what it possessed. Similarly, despite governmental effort, human resources have not been fully tapped, despite big strides made in the field of education. Pakistan still has to go a long way to catch up with the developed world to become a big power. It has entered only threshold of the scientific, technological and space age. To that extent, it has impressed upon the policy-makers the problems and possibilities of their state to function in a broader operational environment of the world in which both the human and non-human resources set definite limits to any effort at enhancing its capabilities that indirectly affects the formulation and prosecution of foreign policy goals. Further, functioning in the context of the South Asia, this problem was compounded as India was the major component of its operational environment. Besides, it is further exacerbated as the operational environment of its successive decision-makers got converged on their psychological environment as their struggling present, enlivened by the fears wrapped in the mantle of the bitter past, projected the hopes of a rosy future. This partly explained why Pakistan never got reconciled to the status of a smaller nation vis-a-vis India in post-independence era. This was itself a reflection of the attitude of its founding father who never agreed to any constitutional formula in undivided India which would have denoted a lesser status for the Muslim League. Hence, Pakistan's continued predicament was to outbid India in all spheres in the world politics.

What gives the factor of geography and size of a state its actual importance is its military preparedness and the dependence of the national power upon it is too obvious to need much elaboration. Our enquiry into the military capability of Pakistan showed that it started its military establishment almost from a scratch as the Joint Defence Council failed to make a fair and equitable distribution of the military and material assets of the British Indian Army between India and Pakistan in the ratio of by 36 to Pakistan to 64 to India because of lack of cooperation from India. However, Pakistan moved beyond this as its military establishment grew phenomenally over the years, though it adopted voluntary military service. Its defence expenditure sheds enough light on this. In 1947-48, it was less than one per cent of G.N.P. In 1971, it rose to 6.9 per cent. In absolute terms it increased from 32.4 million to 719 million. To strengthen its military establishment it first turned to the United States which became its principal supplier from 1954 to 1965, though it received weapons from the United Kingdom and Germany. Since 1965, when the United States imposed embargo, China has replaced the United States as the major arms supplier, though it has possessed a modest amount of arms from the Soviet Union too. Now, the point that is germane to our analysis is how far it enhanced the capabilities of Pakistan. The answer seems to be in the negative, even if, it is admitted that its military establishment was capable enough to throw off any challenge from any quarter to its territorial integrity.

It should be borne in mind that the subject of military capability is in itself very complex. One cannot account for all the relational variables bearing upon its capabilities. But there are certain built-in structural and functional constraints affecting its operational efficiency. In the first category, it is pointed out that in the specific condition of Pakistan, impact of defence burden on its economy, the retention of the Junior Commissioned Officer in the military command structure, the exclusive representation of four districts of Punjab to the exclusion of Bengalis and above all their constant involvement in politics and their view of guardianship have militated against its enhanced capabilities. With it was coupled the functional problems which emanated from Pakistan's complete dependence upon outside sources for supply, problems of coordination of diverse system of weapons, their servicing, lack of friends for finance for their repairs, and replenishment of share parts were the most inhibiting factors. So, it can be said that though it did not significantly spruced up its capabilities, its desperate drive for acquisition of American military aid forced it to shed off its initial policy of non-alignment.

In our examination of the economic capability of Pakistan, we found that being an underdevelopment economy whose mainstay was agriculture, it adopted a capitalist mode of development to enhance its industrial growth. It adopted a developmental strategy which was a product of the interactive influences of a congeries of economic actors to subserve the interests of its ruling elites. As a result it did not contribute significantly to its capabilities. Besides, the philosophy of growth and the developmental strategy underlying it had high economic contents. And to underwrite it, it was compelled to depend upon the United States which was in a position to render large-scale economic aid. We also noted that its policy shifts towards the communist bloc which occurred in 1960's had no correlation with its actual procurement of foreign aid.

With regard to the systemic sources, it is agreed that one cannot study the external behaviour of states independently of the larger international system in which it occurs and toward which it is precisely directed. And for conceptualizing international political system, we have adopted Rosenau's view that international politics is differentiated from other types of politics on the basis of much greater functional distance that separates its actors. If the international system is defined in this way, the most important systemic variables are the Great Power structure and alliances. While Great Power structure refers to the pattern of relationship prevailing among great powers in any era of human history, the alliances are also derivative from them.

In our enquiry we found that Pakistan achieved its statehood in 1947 under the shadow of Cold War which assumed the form of a relentless struggle between communist and western political ideas each embodied in powerful coalition of states that tended to divide the world into two distinct blocs. There was no demand on Pakistan either from the Soviet Union or the United States, the two pioneers of the alternative systems, to toe their line in foreign policy, for which it adopted a policy of nonalignment. Though Pakistan was more keen to foster its relationship with the United States, India received greater attention. Between 1952-61, the Soviet Union became keen to get a foothold in South Asia and decided to favour India against Pakistan. And as regards the United States, with the ushering in of the Republican administration, Pakistan loomed large in its global strategic perspective. As a result, Pakistan's long desire to join the Western alliance system, particularly of the United States, was fulfilled. Here we find that its alignment with the United States was a product of systemic compulsions.

In the early 1960's the prevailing configuration of power changed in international politics which became a loose bipolar system, because of intra-bloc conflicts. It was accompanied by a change in the location and technique of conflicts between the two Super Powers, and the emergence of the Third World, which was caught up more intensely in the vortex of Super Power politics. The central power balance became immune from the contagious effects of the Third World conflicts. With the edvent of Kennedy era, the need for a modus operandi with the Soviets received top priority. Johnson went a step further by making East-West detente the basis for an European settlement which would eventually lead to the solution of the German problem. In this backdrop, the policy of the Super Powrs changed towards Pakistan. The non-aligned states were cultivated with understanding and sympathy by the United States and were given considerable economic aid to enable them to foster a stable political order and rapid economic development. Correspondingly, the value of 'allies' dwindled, as the development of ICMB and Polarish submarine reduced the strategic importance of military bases around the periphery of the Soviet Union and after the Sino-Soviet rift, China became the common enemy of both the Super Powers. In its global policy of containment of China, India was expected by the United States to play a major role. But this did not minimise the strategic importance of Pakistan in its over-all global strategy. Kennedy made efforts to keep both Ayub and Nehru in good humour. But, the Sino-Indian war of 1962 altered the equation. The United States gave substantial military aid to India which was too much for Ayub to stomach. As the military balance was drastically tilted against Pakistan, Ayub bitterly complained but to no avail. As a result, Ayub felt ditched. This gave him a spacious plea to reorient the country's foreign policy. First, he viewed that it would not incur the American hostilities, because of the ongoing process of detente, second, China would be forced to come to terms with its neighbour whose strategic value would be cashed in once Pakistan came out of the American embrace. Now, Ayub reformulated his foreign policy which he termed as the policy of "bilateralism" which meant setting as bilateral equation with the Soviet Union, the United States and China, so it can be said that while Ayub justified it as a product of geographical compulsion, as a matter of fact it was a mere rhetorical rationalization. The real reason which compelled the rethinking seems to be the political constraint emanating from a multipolar international system that made untenable a policy conceived in the era of Cold War to serve the national interest.

In the mid-Sixties, the American attitude and involvement in subcontinental affairs underwent radical change when it encouraged the Soviet Union to mediate in Indo-Pakistani disputes. Taskent was in all probability a manifestation of this phenomena. It maintained complete neutrality in the Indo-Pakistani war of 1965 and instead imposed the embargo on military aid to both the countries. Its relation with Pakistan remained at the lowest ebb. But the Soviet Union made considerable headway. There was a perceptible shift from its earlier stand on Kashmir when it called for a peaceful settlement of the Kashmir dispute by the two interested parties. There was further progress after the exit of Khrushchev from power.

In the period following 1969 the United States was following a policy of detente with the Soviet Union in a radically different situation in which the latter had erased its strategic superiority. So its success depended upon a balanced relationship with China that would shore up its bargaining position for striking a strategic deal with the Soviet Union. Khruschev's successors were pursuing a selective strategy for concentrating on the Eurasian continent. Its main plain planks were isolation of China in the East, and flirtation with Japan, and consolidation of their position in South Asia and presence in the West Asia and the Mediterranean. In this backdrop, the growing Sino-Soviet cleavage opened a new vista for the United States to pursue a triangular pattern of global politics. So the main thrust of Nixon's foreign policy was the reinstatement of the Soviet Union as the main rival of the United States and the reduction of the American engagement against China.

This phase coincided with the onset of the Bangladesh crisis which gave a rare opportunity for the United States, China and the Soviet Union to settle their respective accounts. On the one hand, the United States was keen to consummate the Moscow summit and without China trip, it would not have a Moscow trip, and on the other hand, it wanted to discover and sustain an area of agreement where both China and the United States would supplement each other's power to limit the Soviet influence and Indian hegemonism. As India's involvement in the crisis engaged the subcontinent in a wider pattern of conflict, the major power got involved because the crisis threatened the very existence of Pakistan. As a result, Yahya's response to crisis was shaped by the impact of the systemic influences.

Regarding the impact of alliance system on its foreign-policy, our analysis highlights that Pakistan was associated with the Western Powers through an interlocking membership in four mutual security arrangements. Its basic objectives were to procure American military aid and the Western Powers' political and diplomatic support in its dispute with India, particularly Kashmir. But the Pakistani policy-makers were unaware of the objectives and the motivations of the Western Powers, particularly of the United States. Their basic objective was to acquire the bases in Pakistan and to enlist its political support for their policy in Asia. Once the importance of bases declined, Pakistan fell from their grace. But it served to make Pakistan the American Trojan Horse in Asia, alienated it from the Muslim World, antagonised the Soviet Union, made it suspect in the eyes of the Afro-Asian world and embittered its relationship with India.

Our enquiry into the impact of regional systemic source shows that India, China and the West Asian countries have deeply influenced its foreign policy behaviour. India remained its principal enemy from which threat is perceived by its successive policy-makers to emanate to its territorial integrity. As a necessary corollary it was Kashmir with which it was primarily interested, for the Indian control of Kashmir stood as a denial of the Two-Nation theory, the main basis of Pakistan and its continued raison d'etre. As a result, since its birth, the search for security and independence from India and the solution of the Kashmir dispute to its satisfaction had led to an agonising quest for augmenting its capabilities in terms of procuring the military aid and diplomatic support from the Big Powers especially the United States. Kashmir became the litmus test for judging the cordiality or hostility of any country or an individual for Pakistan over the years. Its growing affinity and consequent disillusionment with the Western Powers particularly the United States stemed mainly from this issue, so also its declining faith in the efficacy of the United Nations. Its policy shift in early 1960's towards the Communist world was also dictated by this consideration. The issue still continued to be the main stumbling block for Indo-Pakistan rapprochement, even if the bases of hostility were wider than Kashmir.

With regard to China, our enquiry reveals that China's policy towards Pakistan in the years 1947-53 was in keeping with its general pattern of policy towards Asia as a whole. It was one of militantly revolutionary policy marked by open hostility and contempt towards Asian leaders branding them as the hirelings of imperialism. But Pakistanis have responded with a measure of shrewd diplomacy; they have recognised China, advocated its admission into the United Nations and refused to brand it as the aggressor in the Korean war. It showed that Pakistan was very sensitive on issues hurting Chinese susceptibility. Perhaps this laid down the foundation for future cordiality. Interestingly enough, China on its part has never endorsed India's claim to Kashmir in the hey-day of Sino-Indian relationship, even it played cool, Pakistan's membership of the SEATO, because in the Bandung Conference, Bogra, Pakistan's Premier assured him that it was not directed against them as the real enemy of Pakistan was India.

In the aftermath of Indo-Chinese war of 1962, China courted Pakistan and the vice-versa. And both discovered in the Indian subcontinent an area of agreement as a clear perception of their interest resulted in the coincidence of their objective to contain India which was their common enemy. Henceforward, they followed a cooperative policy which led to the endorsement of Pakistan's view regarding Kashmir by China, and it eventuated in the Indo-Pakistani wars of 1965 which was even terminated at the behest of the Chinese authorities. This was also repeated in 1971 war. China has become a major factor in Indo-Pakistani relation and would continue so till such time unless India and Pakistan composed their differences or Sino-Soviet rift is dissolved or Indo-Soviet relation is weakened.

With regard to the West Asian subordinate system, it is found that Pakistan acquired independent statehood with a growing awareness of its belonging to a community of Muslims that dwelled all over the globe. It also discovered its leanage to a past which was pristine in glory, for long tarnished by the machination of the Western imperialist powers. As its leadership viewed the successful fruition of their freedom struggle as a manifestation of a renewed sense of Islamic belonging made resurgent in the aftermath of the Second World War, they made a fervent plea for reviving this world spirit. So, they stressed their natural and religious links, common culture, and identity of economic interests. With this objective, they hosted numerous international conferences to discuss problems of mutual security and economic interests for promoting world Islamic Solidarity. Underlying this, was their desire to bear the mantle of leadership of the Muslim World, and to enlist their support in its dispute with India.

Pakistan's intentions were revealed and became suspect when it joined the Western alliance system orchestrated by the United States which was directed to divide the Arab world. Its stand on the Suez crisis was deplored by the Muslim countries. As it encountered increasing opposition, it gave up its pet idea of promoting economic integration as a prelude to political integration of the Muslim World. It progressively discovered its pluralistic character, and as there was no reverse flow of stimuli from them, it abandoned the idea of treating them as an organic entity and instead followed policy at the level of individual countries with the acceptance of the concomitant compulsions of international diplomacy.

Now coming to our enquiry into the governmental structure, it is found that Pakistan adopted a domestic system of the Westminster variety from 1947 to 1958 and functioned as an open society. But the parliamentary democracy had a sad demise in October 1958, when Mohammad Ayub Khan imposed martial law, ruled for four years without a Constitution. He completely depoliticised the political system by banning political activities and proscribing political parties. In 1962, he promulgated a new constitution, established presidential democracy with all the trappings of the

Parliamentary system. He called it "guided democracy" best suited to the Pakistani genius. He also revived political parties, who were permitted to carry on political activities under stringent laws. In 1965 he himself contested for the office of Presidency from a political party owing its origin to his inspiration. After his fall, in 1968, Pakistan again reverted to Martial Law administration under Yahya Khan who held a general election on the basis of universal adult suffrage in 1970 but it was still-born as civil war broke out leading to the break-up of the country.

Now, it is revealed that various legislators of Pakistan have taken keen interests to debate policy issues, though it was the preserve of the executive. The debate ranged from broad policy goals to specific details of the foreign policy.

The first Constituent Assembly (1947-54) debated many vital policy matters which included Pakistan's membership of the United Nations, Kashmir,' China's recognition, Pakistan's policy towards the Arab world, its stand on Korea, Liaquat Ali's proposed visit to Russia and above all its relation with India. It showed that the fundamentals of foreign policy laid down by Jinnah had a broad national consensus and the legislature gave a support to the executive. It also continued during the tenure of Liaquat Ali Khan. However, his India policy was bitterly assailed, while his policy towards the Muslim world received enthusiastic endorsement. But this broad national consensus broke down during the tenure of Khawaja Nazimuddin with the split in the Muslim League and its disintegration in the East Pakistan and it was further eroded during the premiership of Mohammad Ali Bogra with Pakistan's conclusion of mutual security treaty with the United States. The Second Constituent Assembly (1954-56) never debated any important foreign policy issue. It was rechristened as the First National Assembly of Pakistan when election to the new House took place under the first republican constitution of 1956. During the term of Suhrawardy who became the Prime Minister on 12 September 1956 the first major foreign policy debate was initiated. The pent-up feelings of the legislators gave way in a blistering attack on every facets of Pakistan's pro-Western foreign policy. Though Suhrawardy made a spirited defence of the policy of the previous government, and the House approved it, its government fell subsequently when the pro-Chinese Maulana Bhasani withdrew support and formed a new political party. It revealed the lack of consensual basis in Pakistan's foreign policy.

During the tenure of the Second National Assembly, debates generated much heat and passion. This period coincided with the large-scale supply of Western arms to India in the wake of the Sino-Indian war of 1962. Indian policy of non-alignment was bitterly assailed. Pakistan's membership with the Western alliance system came under heavy fire and members argued for a more realistic policy. The pro-Chinese sentiment of the nation came to sharper focus. In the debate that started in the aftermath of the Indo-Pakistani war of 1965, members profusely praised China and condemned the role of the United Kingdom and the United States. And the relationship with the Soviet Union found a responsive chord. This certainly served Ayub's objective to underwrite his policy of bilateralism. On the whole, it can be said that legislative debate in Pakistan has reflected the national consensus or its absence in different times. Even in the Ayub era it has not abdicated its moral responsibility despite the fact that it was not truly representative of the nation as a whole. However, like all countries, whether democratic or authoritarian, open or closed, foreign policy remains the preserve of the executive.

In our focus on personality characteristics of Pakistani decision-makers, we have chosen only Mohammad Ali Jinnah and Mohammad Ayub Khan out of a host of many, as these two figures provided strong leadership in Pakistan during the period 1947-71. In this connection, we have delineated the specific conditions (in the form of a few empirically tested propositions) present in Pakistan during 1947 to 1971 which have provided enough stimuli to these key decision-makers to bring their idiosyncratic traits to bear upon their policy decisions. In the first place, we have proved that though Jinnah never assumed political power in a dramatic way, the movement for Pakistan of which he was the author and architect had all the dimensions of a revolution. But in case of Ayub Khan he assumed power in a dramatic way. Secondly, Jinnah was a charismatic leader while Ayub had never the appeal of a charisma, though he enjoyed the obedience of his followers and secured their loyalty. Thirdly, both Jinnah and Ayub had general interests in foreign policy. Lastly, both dominated the decision-making structures and held complete sway over the policy-making.

In the concluding part of our enquiry, our main objective was to prove that of all the personality traits, the cognitive beliefs is central to the decisional phenomena, while the bureaucratic and organizational variables are not without potency.

It is hypothesized that the foreign-policy decision-making in every political system proceeds in two distinct stages: policy preference leading to decision and action or output. The cognitive beliefs of the decision-makers become weighty on policy preference, while decision that is arrived at is again subject to the vagaries of the bureaucratic and the organizational variables. We have taken Pakistan's decision to conclude the Mutual Security Assistance Agreement with the United States in May 1954 for empirical testing. On exploration, it is found that Jinnah's cognitive traits dominated the policy preference which was reached by himself even before 1947. And it led to a decision when he formally decided to send his special emissary to the United States to present his case before its Government. Jinnah did not live long. So it was left to his successors to implement his decisions. Mohammad Ayub Khan, the Commander-in-Chief of Pakistan armed forces, who enjoyed complete trust of Liaquat Ali and subsequently of Ghulam Mohammad was intimately associated with the task of negotiating with the United States as the agreement had more of military dimensions. In the process, Ayub distorted it to subserve his political ambitions.

Now, all our seven hypotheses taken up in seven chapters are happily proved. It can be asserted that Pakistan's foreign policy behaviour during the last span of twenty-four years had been deeply influenced by domestic, systemic, regional, systemic, governmental and idiosyncratic variables. As revealed, it has sometimes been affected by a combination of one or more of these variables and the presumed interaction among them. In some situations, we have successfully isolated them though taking recourse to historical facts. In one particular decision, we have found that the cognitive beliefs of Jinnah affected the policy preference, and the decision that was taken by him was subsequently distorted after his death by Ayub Khan out of sheer personal motivations. This clearly validates our •model. But we have not attempted to build up these seven hypotheses into nomothetic generalizations as the model was applied only to Pakistan, not to any cross-nation comparison which is required in a theory-building enterprise. It is now left for the future students to apply the model for the analysis of foreign policy of states in a cross-level perspective to reap its theoretical pay-offs.

In conclusion, it can be said that India continued to be the main bugbear of the policy-makers' perceptual world. For this, responsibility partly lies with India. Being a powerful neighbour, larger in size and greater in resource, it needs to adopt a more benign attitude towards Pakistan by a sympathetic understanding of its predicaments and plights that emanate from the travail of its nation-building efforts and its psychological persecution to elevate itself as a dignified member of the international community carrying some political clout commensurate with its capabilities. Pakistan on its part, should bear in mind that it has to function in the complex politics of Asia in general and the South Asia in particular, where the interventionary pressures of Great Powers in the nature of the situation cannot be eliminated for which it must sooner or latter, come to terms with India, however, its hostilities are implacable. This is an inescapable reality which the policy-makers of Pakistan will take in their stride, either to modify the South Asian environment or to live with it. Our findings clearly showed that Pakistani policy-makers have no qualms to stoke anti-Indian sentiments, perpetuated in the form of Kashmir dispute and ideological cleavage between the two religions, among the masses to preserve their own dominance in the political system right from 1947. The new generations of politicians and peoples have come upon the scene in both the countries of the subcontinent. But unfortunately, the policies followed by the respective governments over the years unmistakably reflect that they have been blinders in the old perceptual prisms of the past. But what is the desideratum of the present is a quantum jump on the part of the policy-makers of both countries from the psychological environment of their predecessors who have brought untold misery to three generations of Indo-Pakistanis by their blighted policies resulting in three otherwise avoidable wars.

# 1
# Political Development in Pakistan

It is a well known fact of history that Islam came to India largely as a religious force during eighth century. A product of Arab-Persian civilization and culture, it came from Bagdad—the intellectual hub of the civilized world—combining the spirit of rationalism and scientific enquiry of Arabs with the graces of life and art of the Persians. The Arabs, being epitome of these cultures, became the true standard—bearers of early Islam which was highly gracious and benign. It is these cultured Arabs, who, in their political conquest, brought their dominant faith Islam to the Indian soil with the invasion of Sind in the 712 A.D. Sind was made a part of the Arab Empire for half a century till it fell away from the Empire and became the first independent Muslim State on the West Coast of India. Though there was no further invasion of Arabs, contact with the Arab world grew apace as a result of increasing cultural and commercial interaction of medieval India. Islam, within a period of 300 years, gradually and imperceptively, with its messages of 'humanism and egalitarianism, captivated Indian heart and peacefully took its place among many religions of India (Jainism, Budhism, Christianity, Zoroastrianism) without any conflict or rancour.

With the decline of Bagdad, Central Asia became the main intellectual centre of the Arab-Persian Civilisation whose new standard bearers became the various war-mongering tribes; the Turks; the Mongols (latter called Moguls in India), and to a large extent, the Afgans of Indian borderland. Suffused with tribal ethos and culture, Islam lost its earlier elan and became a rigid faith suited to its expansion by political conquest of the marauding chieftains. Enthroned as a militant religious creed of these conquering tribes, it reappeared in India in its new garb as a political force in fresh waves of invasion commencing from 1000 A.C. of Mahmud of Ghazni who made Punjab an outlying province of the famous, Ghaznavite Kingdom to be followed by Shahab-Ud-Din Ghori who ultimately sat on the throne of Delhi in 1192. Ghori's conquest marked the emergence of a new political order in India even if his writ never run the whole of India. It was further consolidated, when Babar (a Turko-Mongol of Timurid line of the Central Asia) established the historic Mogul Empire in India in 1526 and within a brief span of a century and a half, the rest of India came under his subjugation.

Unlike earlier invasions, the Afgan conquest had two contradictory developments[1]. While it produced powerful reactions among the people leading to vast exodus of many Hindus to the South who perceived a threat to their religious way of life, there was a mellowing of Indian Society which absorbed Islam for various reasons. First, the new Afgans were basically of the Indo-Arayan race linked to the Indian people as Afganisthan was a part of India for a long stretch of time. Its language Pusto was a derivative of Sanskrit and its numerous monuments of ancient times bore ample testimony to the impact of Indian culture, chiefly of Buddhist period. Second, the Afgans adopted India as their home land and had no other connections. The Afgan dynasties became real Indian dynasties by a great deal of racial fusion brought about by war and dynastic marriages. Besides, by their conscious and deliberate administrative and religious policies, the Turko-Mongol dynasties became more Indian than Turks or Mongols. The Afgan ruler made special efforts not to interfere with the old customs and traditions of Indian society. No fundamental change was introduced in the economic life of the Indian people. So, life continued as of old, placid and serene as ever. Third, the idea of brotherhood of Islam and the theoretical equality of its adherents made a powerful appeal, especially to the downtrodden Hindus, who were denied for centuries any semblance of equality of treatment because of rigid caste structure and stratification of the Indian society. Individual and group conversions first started in Bengal. Even people belonging to higher castes also adopted this new faith for purely political and economic reasons, as Islam was the religion of the ruling class. The Hindu society known for its age-old tolerance attached no importance to it. It only reacted adversely during Aurangzeb period which systematically followed the policy of defiling Hinduism and resorted to forced conversion of Hindus on a mass scale. Fourth, Persian became the court language and naturally many Persian words and idioms crept into popular use and many people, with the passage of time, eagerly learnt the language, including Hindus, to enhance their job prospects and to curry royal favour. As a result, Indian culture and learning was in a state of intellectual ferment. A synthesis worked out itself which resulted in a new syncretic culture as vividly reflected over time in the contemporaneous Indian art, architecture, sculpture, painting, music and language too. Gradually but imperceptively, the Hindus and Muslims developed numerous common traits, habits, ways of life, artistic taste, because of long contact and of peaceful coexistence and also because a vast majority of Muslims were converts from Hinduism. They lived together as one people in villages and towns, spoke the same languages, even participated in many traditional festivals and rituals, faced the same agonies, problems of life and shared the same political destinies. Despite this cultural assimilation, India retained its pristine identity and Hinduism, in all its varieties, remained the dominant faith of the land and Islam flourished peacefully unhindered and sure of itself, its possibilities and limitations. No racial question ever troubled the Indians who developed with the passage of centuries, a tolerant, humane but stubborn Indianness. The Muslims remained spread all along the heartland of the Indo-Gangetic plain reflecting the course of Muslim conquests even though a vast majority of them was concentrated at its Western and North-Western end due to the early penetration of Islam there and at the eastern belt of Bengal and Assam for the large-scale conversion of low-caste Hindus and impact of Buddhism there.

But this harmonious and composite existence with Hindus, however, did not blur the deep division that marked the Indian Muslims as a class. Besides, being an odd amalgam of diverse racial stocks, the Indian Muslims were splitted in matters caste and creed, even though they believed in Holy Koran, rituals of priesthood, religious dogmas, common social practices and habits. Doctrinal differences, also divided them broadly into Sunnis and Shias, while a number of Sufis and Ahmediyas existed among them .[2] There was also a distinct pattern of social stratification based on a tradition of descent, ethnicity, and occupational specialization for which Muslims were categorized as Ashraf (nobility) and Aslaf (commoner), even if, the class structure was fluid and allowed upward mobility in social hierarchy. The Muslims who came from outside India were basically feudal in outlook and considered themselves as part of the ruling class, the nobility and functioned as state officials in military and administration, they also enjoyed the right to collect land-revenue in Punjab and United Provinces. They also enjoyed the grant of land as Jagirs and Muafi land for personal use and endowments for running educational institutions especially in Bengal and Bihar. They were also attached to the Mogul

Courts as scholars. This class also developed a highly intricate and sophisticated culture taking the cue from the Mogul Courts. In the gradual evolution of the Indian social structures, they became the major administrative and military elites in urban centres and feudal lords in the country side. A vast majority of the landlords in Punjab and the United Provinces were these Muslims of alien blood. Very few of them were converts from Hinduism. They set themselves apart from the vast majority of Muslims who were either converts from Hinduism or scions of those humble servants whom the Great Moguls brought with them for personal attendance at court. In Bengal and Bihar, especially in the former, 98 per cent Muslims were converts. Barring a few Muslim landed gentry, rest were marginal farmers, butlers , bakers, weavers, shoe-makers, and tailors like their counterparts scattered in the rest of India. In the western coast of India like Kutch, Kathiawar, Gujrat, the traditional trading Hindu community like Khojas, Memons and Bhoras clung to their traditional occupation even after conversion to Islam and dominated industry and commerce in India and retained many Hindu customs and practices. Interestingly, there was little difference between Muslims and Hindus. A Bengali Muslim was more nearer to a Bengali Hindu, than to a Punjabi Muslim, similarly a Punjabi Muslim was more nearer to Punjabi Hindu than to a Sindhi Muslim. So the differences between Hindus and Muslims in Mogul India was more geographic than religious while differences between Muslims was predominantly economics and not sectarian. This social composition of Hindus and Muslims did not alter the traditional economic structure of the Indian Society.

The new sovereign state of Pakistan which came into existence on August, 14, 1947 was carved out of the undivided Indian subcontinent to provide a home land for the Indian Muslims. It marked the culmination of the movement for Pakistan which was anchored on the two-nation theory whose protagonists advocated the establishment of a new nation-state on the precise plea that Indian Muslims, though formed twenty-five per cent of the Indian population, constitute a dominant ethnographic category distinct from the Hindus. The new state, it was ardently hoped, would be territorially compact, socially cohesive, emotionally integrative and economically vibrant. The new land of Islam being home to all the Muslims of the sub-continent will fulfill their long cherished dreams as they would be free to order their ways of life according to the canons of Islam untrammelled by the cultural contamination of the Hindu religious order. Besides, it will open up new vistas of opportunities for growth and development as the Muslims will be liberated from economic exploitation and political hegemony of the dominant Hindu elites. But when freedom came, the new state was born in such a conjecture of circumstances that all their calculations went haywire and all their dreams fractured which prompted Quaid-i-Azam to tell that what he got was a moth-eaten Pakistan.

First, it is one of the ironies of history of modern state system that a nation born precisely on the basis of national self-determination, lacked a territorial personality of its own as its eastern and western wings were separated by thousand miles of sprawling Indian territory. Second, the concept of a separate Muslim state to be called Pakistan and the very raison d'etre of its continued existence could not be fulfilled as a vast majority of Indian Muslims were still left over in the subcontinent. Third, its endeavour to define the ideology of state in terms of Islamic identity has failed to resolve the continuing controversy regarding the precise role of religion in politics, a controversy that has mirred the Pakistani state in deep crisis ever since. Third, it became a polyglot nation and one of the least developed states in the Third World. The Muslim majority areas which comprised the modem state were socially, politically and economically the least developed regions of the British India. Besides, the population inhabiting these areas were overwhelmingly poor, illiterate and rural, and tribal. They were also socially fragmented, ethnically diverse, spoke myriad dialects and languages and came to be disproportionately divided in its various regions and wings. However, comprising a total area of 364,737 squares miles with a population of 80,000,000[3], Pakistan, being perched on the bridge-head between Asia and Europe, was deemed to be one of the bigger nations of the world in terms of its population and geo-strategic significance. As a matter of fact, it was a second largest muslim nation and the fifth country of the world when it commenced its career with a glorious vision of its future.

The Muslim majority areas which constituted the modern State of Pakistan contained migrations of refugees of two different streams, the urban Muslims from the province of Madhya Pradesh, Uttar Pradesh, Bombay, Gujarat and the rural Muslims from the eastern districts of Punjab and Bengal. It added elements of flux and fluidity to a society that was not only ethnically diverse and fragmented with different language and dialectics but also politically volatile in its most formative years. The Mujahir-refugee-culture and political outlook were radically different from the indigenous segments of the Pakistani society. While the former believed in secularism, liberal political and Laissez-faire economy, the latter sought to establish an Islamic State founded in conformity with the dictates of the Quaran and the Sunnah and a State-managed economy. Being a product of two divergent culture, a clash was bound to occur between those two groups which profoundly influenced not only the character of Pakistani society but also the future profile of its political development.[4]

Pakistan opted for a democratic polity with the attainment of its statehood and became a federal State comprising two provinces of "East Pakistan" and "West Pakistan". The first federal legislature, known as the First Constituent Assembly, was the product of transfer of power in August 1947.[5] It was endowed with dual functions, to prepare a new Constitution and to act as the federal legislature till a new Constitution was framed and put into operation. Mohammad Ali Jinnah, the author of the Pakistani movement, became the first Governor-General of Pakistan and chose Liaquat Ali to be its first Prime Minister. Though Jinnah lived for a brief span, the concentration and personalization of all authority and power enabled him not only to establish a unitarian pattern of leadership that brooked no dissent but also showed that he alone was the source of legitimacy of the government as he had been of the Pakistani Movement[6]. As Governor-General, he was able to control the deliberation of the Constituent Assembly and the functioning of the federal and provincial governments from outside the Parliament.[7] It led to the emergence of what has been described as the Viceregal system in Pakistan.[8] With the death of Jinnah in September 11, 1946, Khwaza Nazimuddin became the Governor-General which was practically offered by Liaquat who became the real centre of authority clearly establishing Prime-Ministerial dictatorship in Pakistan. But it was short-lived as Liaquat was assassinated on October 16, 1951.

Within hours of his death, Ghulam Mohammad became the new Governor-General and Nazimuddin was made to step down to adore the Office of the Prime Minister. Unfortunately, Nazimuddin now became a victim of the Objectives Resolution of Liaquat. As it changed the Qualdi-i-Azam's conception of a secular Pakistan it triggered off anti-Ahmedia riot in Lahore in 1953 which came under Martial Law. Ghulam found this a convenient plea to dismiss Nazimuddin and appointed Mohammad Ali Bogra, Pakistan's Ambassador to the United States, the new Prime Minister. Close on the heels, came the termination of the United Front Ministry of A.K. Fazlul Haq in East Pakistan on May 30, 1954 followed by the dissolution of the Constituent Assembly on October 24, 1954 and proclamation of state of Emergency in Pakistan. Armed with the decision of the Federal Court which validated his action on grounds of State necessity[9], he formed a new Cabinet headed by Bogra which included his henchmen Iskander Mirza, Mohammad Ayub Khan and Chaudhuri Mohammad Ali. With this, ended the dominance of the "Hindustani" in Pakistani public life[10] and the military bureaucratic elite came to monopolize the decision-making structure of Pakistan during the period 1951-58.[11]

But the decision of the Federal Court in Yusuf Patel's case forced Ghulam to hold election on June 20 and 21, 1965 to the Second Constituent Assembly on the lines on which the dissolved Assembly was chosen. On August 7, 1955 Mirza was sworn in as the new Governor-General of Pakistan and Ghulam was forced to tender his resignation on September 19. Mirza now reconstituted his new coalition Cabinet under the Prime Ministership of Chaudhury Mohammad Ali which adopted the first Constitution of Pakistan on March 2, 1956. On March 23, Mirza was indirectly elected the President of the new Islamic Republic of Pakistan.

The new Constitution provided for a Parliamentary form of government. The Parliament consisted of President and one House, the National Assembly of Pakistan. The head of the State, the President, was to be a Muslim and to be indirectly elected by a simple majority of the National Assembly. He would function as a titular head and the real power was to be exercised by the Cabinet headed by the Prime Minister responsible to the legislature. The Preamble to the Constitution accepted Allaha's sovereignty over man. All laws in Pakistan were to conform to the holy Quaran and Sunnah. The State will not place any law on the statute book that was repugnant to either to the Holy Book or to the accepted practice of the Prophet Mohammad[12]. On September 18, 1956, Choudhury resigned followed in quick succession by H.S.Suhrawardy, I.I.Chandrigar and Feroz Khan Noon. Speaking of coalition politics in Pakistan during this period, Keith Callard remarks:[13]

> "The general pattern of politics of Pakistan has been for individual leaders to attempt to establish their personal leadership while those who have been left out of office or became disappointed with their share of power and prestige form together in a temporary alliance to dislodge the ministry. Thus, no basis for a lasting consolidation of political groups has emerged or seems likely to emerge".

The first National Assembly was dissolved on the night of October 7, 1958 when Mirza issued a proclamation abrogating the Constitution, dismissing the central and provincial governments and declaring Martial Law throughout Pakistan and appointing Ayub Khan as the Chief Martial

Law Administrator and Supreme Commander of the Armed Forces. On October 27, Mirza was forced to resign and Ayub proclaimed himself to be the President of Pakistan. A new era of one-man rule began in Pakistan. On the following day, Ayub promulgated Presidential Cabinet Order Leaving Mirza's Cabinet intact but abolishing the Office of the Prime Minister. It was incorporated with the President's Office, paving the way for the emergence of Presidential form of government. The coup detat was greeted with a sense of relief by a large segment of population who were tired of politician's machination. Ayub ruled the country without a Constitution for almost four years. Pakistani society slided gradually on the path of praetorianism and became truely a garrison State.

Things looked up, when Ayub presented a Constitution on March 1, 1962. The Constitution established a Presidential form of Government with a novel dispensation of making the head of the State an integral part of the legislature which comprised only one house known as the National Assembly of Pakistan. The National Assembly consisted of 150 members equally divided between its two wings and to be elected by 80,000 basic democrats who were also equally divided between its two wings. All political parties were proscribed. Elections were held on non-party basis to the Second National Assembly which functioned for long four years until its dissolution in 1965 following Presidential elections. Though, Ayub justified the system of Basic Democracy by asserting that his Constitution was a blending of democracy with discipline,[14] soon he discovered that a political system could not be run without political parties. This compelled him to reshape the old Muslim League for accommodating various elements of his constituency with the avowed purpose of perpetuating his political dominance. In the elections held to the National Assembly in 1966, Ayub's Pakistan Muslim League got a steam-roller majority of 125 out of 156 seats. But unfortunately, Ayub's political fortune dwindled following the resignation of Z.A. Bhutto from the Cabinet. The Assembly had a stormy career as is reflected in the political upheavals of the time. In February 1967, it was prorogued marking the end of seven years of legislative life in Pakistan. With the resignation of Ayub in March 1969, another bout of military rule followed with the installation of General Yahya Khan as the Chief Martial Law Administrator of Pakistan.[15]

But Yahya unlike others held election in December 1970 on the basis of universal adult suffrage for the first time in the history of Pakistan under the procedure set by the Legal Framework Order issued by him on March 30, 1970. In pursuance with this, the National Assembly was to consist of

300 members, 162 was to be chosen by East Pakistan and 138 by the West Pakistan which was now dissolved into four provinces of Beluchistan, North-West Frontier Province, Punjab and Sind. These provinces along with East Pakistan constituted the five federating units which would share power with the federal government under the new Constitution to be framed within 120 days of the election. The election was held on December 7, 1970, the Awami League of Sheikh Mujibur Rahman bagged all 160 seats in East Pakistan and the People's Party of Pakistan of Z.A. Bhutto got 81 seats from the West Pakistan[16]. The National Assembly was to act as the Constitution-making body and then convert itself into federal legislature. But it was still-born as it never met. Mujib's demand for provincial autonomy and Bhutto's refusal to share power with Mujib on his terms created a political impasse which forced Yahya a military crackdown on the East Bengalis secessionist movement that ultimately led to the dismemberment of Pakistan and birth of the new sovereign State of Bangladesh on December 16, 1971.

It can be fairly said that politicians in the Pakistani experience with the possible exception of Jinnah, Liaquat and Suhrawardy were unfamiliar with the essentials of political office. Nazimuddin, Bogra, Chundrigar and Noon were rank amateurs and innocent in a world dominated by the civil and military administrators like Ghulam, Miraza, Ayub and Yahya who were real rulers. Their imprint, less than made by Jinnah, Liaquat or Surhawardy, identifies Pakistan's first half-century. Vice-regalism rather than accountable politics predated Pakistan's independence. It was perpetuated by Jinnah and Liaquat following the transfer of power. It could not be successfully neutralized by subsequent politicians of limited vision whose crave for political power made them to thrive on the Civil-Military bureaucracy. Summing up the political development marking the end of old Pakistan, Lawrence Ziring remarks:[17]

"Pakistani political life was consumed by the forces of necessity, not by the promise of democratic development. Instabilities from within and threats from without set the rhythm for government policy and authoritarian controls prevailed over libertarian urges. Strong, centralized government was the perceived need as the country moved from one crisis to another. It is now more evident that the turning-point came in 1971 with the secession of East Bengal and its metamorphosis as the independent State of Bangladesh. Although a centre comprising civil-military officials had dominated the Pakistani political process in the years following the death of Jinnah in September 1948, they could not prevent, and in fact their policies and programmes set in train the dissolution of the union between East and West Pakistan. An institution, the civil-military bureaucracy, predicating its right to rule on its supposed capacity to safeguard the integrity of the State, ignominously presided over its dismemberment. In so doing the lie was cast to the claim that the higher bureaucracy was preferable to governance by politicians".

Zulfikir Ali Bhutto came to power as the President and Chief Martial Law Administrator of a vivisected Pakistan. The Pakistan that emerged in 1971 contained four unequal parts, Punjab, Sind, Beluchistan and North-Western Frontier Province. It was a colourful mosaic of many diverse people, who spoke different languages and belonged to diverse cultures. These differences remained submerged as long as Bengal was a part of Pakistan. The question of finding a solution to the sharing of power between the two wings had occupied all political attention. The principle of parity between two wings was the basis of the Constitutions of 1956 and 1962. With East Bengal no more and the West Pakistan divided into four unequal parts the focus now shifted to Pakistan's internal plight. Irreconcilable differences arose on a number of issues between its polyglot nationalities, especially the problem of power sharing between the Centre and provinces became once more crucially central.

The trauma of defeat in East Pakistan had a salutary effect on the behaviour of politicians of West Pakistan who readily agreed to a new Constitution. It came into operation on August 14, 1973 as a result of a Constitutional consensus reached with political leaders of diverse hues. The Constitution of 1973 represented a consensus on three crucial subjects: the role of Islam in politics; the sharing of power between the Central Government and the federating provinces and the division of responsibility between the President and the Prime Minister.[18] First, the Constitution introduced a modified Parliamentary system. Article 90 made it very clear that the Prime Minister is the key decision-maker as it reads: "The executive authority of the Federation shall be exercised in the name of the President by the Federal Government consisting of the Prime Minister and the Federal Ministers which shall act through the Prime Minister who shall be the Chief Executive of the Federation". This modification was intended to protect the Prime Minister from the fickleness of changes in party loyalty that virtually paralysed previous Governments before Ayub. Secondly, the fear of small provinces about Punjabi domination was sought to be removed by the creation of a bicameral legislature consisting of two houses, a Senate with equal provincial representation and a national assembly with seats distributed according to population. Thirdly, Islam was made the "State religion of Pakistan", a phrase that had never been mentioned in the previous Constitutions of 1956 and 1962. It had a profound impact as it required that the State "shall endeavour to preserve and strengthen fraternal relations among the Muslim countries based on Islamic unity". It was truely a novel feature. What was left of Pakistan was truely Islamic.

The operation of the Constitution clearly revealed that Bhutto did not really intend to abide by the consensus he has reached with the opposition. On February 12, 1974, the government in Beluchistan was dismissed on charges of incitement to rebellion against the Central Government, closely followed the resignation of the Government of the North-West Frontier Province in sympathy with the Government of Beluchistan. On May 24 Bhutto made an amendment to the Constitution which endowed the executive with authority to declare any political party illegal if found operating in a manner prejudicial to the sovereignty or integrity of the country. Though this power was conditioned to be exercised with the approval of the Supreme Court, it was mere a eye-wash. Later event demonstrated that the court was very keen to oblige the Government in power. To cap it all, he took the final step of turning Pakistan into one-party State when he ordered another election to the National Assembly on March 7, and for the provincial Assemblies on March 10, 1977. In the elections that followed, combined opposition called Pakistan National Alliance which contained Jamat-i-Islami on the right and the National Democratic Party previously known as the National Awami Party on the left bagged only 36 out of 192 seats. Stated differently, they polled only 18.8 per cent total votes cast which made it suspect in the eye of the public of indiscriminate rigging. This sparked off widespread movement which generated tensions that government found impossible to cope with. In order to restore law and order, General Zia-ul-Haq ordered army's operation called "fair-play" and finally took Bhutto and leader of the PNA into protective custody. To soothe the ruffled feeling of the masses, Zia-ul-Haq announced that fresh election will be held within 90 days.

Subsequently, Bhutto was released but was accused of participating in a conspiracy to murder a political rival named Ahmad Raja Kasuri, his one time political protege turned opponent. A case was lodged in the Lahore High Court which not only heard a criminal case but also dwelt at length in the manner Bhutto had administered Pakistan during his years of stewardship as revealed in a number of White Papers published by the Government. Finally, the Lahore High Court delivered its verdict on March

19, 1978 finding him to be an "arch culprit" in the ambush of Mr. Kasuri with the sole objective of killing him and ordered his execution. It was upheld by the Supreme Court, in its historic verdict declared on March 31, 1979. In the small hours of the night of April 4, 1979 Bhutto was hanged in the Rawalpindi Jail.

In his first speech after assuming power and declaring martial law, General Zia-ul-Haq declared: "It proves that Pakistan which has been created in the name of Islam will continue to survive only if it sticks to Islam, that is why I considered the introduction of an Islamic system as an essential pre-requisite for the country".[19] However, this question begs an answer: the raison-d'etre of the creation of Pakistan. The question could not be resolved in the life time of Jinnah and remained unanswered. But Zia like all his predecessors understood the inherent contradiction of the Pakistani society when he said, "Take out Judaism from Israel and it would collapse like a house of cards. Take Islam out of Pakistan and make it a secular State, it would collapse".[20] While its immensity prevented others to grapple, Zia tried to come to terms with it by interfacing Islam with democracy. He introduced many innovative measures to bring about the process of Islamization of the political and social structure of Pakistan by the marriage of Islamic politics with parliamentarianism.

A system of Islamic code was introduced to reinforce a set of Shariat Laws. The Political Parties Act of 1962 was amended on August 30, 1979 making it binding on the part of all existing political parties not only to register with the Election Commission but also to bring out formal manifestoes explicitly containing Islamic provisions. A twelve member committee of scholars and ulemas was appointed to make recommendation for the introduction of Islamic structure of the governmental system. On March 20, 1981, he promulgated a Provisional Constitutional Order setting up a Federal Council (Majilis-e-Shura), consisting of such persons as the President may by order determine to perform such functions as may be specified by him. It also empowered him to dissolve any organisation or group that in his opinion has been found or is operating in a manner prejudicial to the sovereignty, integrity or security of Pakistan. It also permitted only those parties which had previously registered with the Election Commission to participate in the political activity. As a result, Pakistan People's Party was debarred from participating in the political activities. It also sought to invalidate retroactively all the judgements of the court against the earlier orders of the government.

But all these efforts ran counter to the temper of the time and the emerging texture of the Pakistani society. Zia now confronted the dialectical aspect of the Pakistani society which he tried to resolve but it only resulted in the synthesis of new ideas and experiences, hopes and aspirations that placed the country on the threshold of a new era of political development. He promised election twice, once in October 1977 and again deferred it to October 1979. But as it drew near, the victory of pro-PPP elements in the polls of local bodies of September 1979 made Zia postpone national election indefinitely. His Islamisation measures were looked upon by the opposition political leaders as a delatory tactics for the restoration of democracy in Pakistan. Now, time seemed to be running out for him when political leaders cobbled together an odd assortment of eleven parties including PPP and Jamat-i-Islami under a common banner called the Movement for Restoration of Democracy. It launched its struggle on August 14, 1983 to restore democracy.

Realising its potential mischief and being prodded by the Western donors,[21] Zia took the wind out of the opposition sails by announcing on August 12, 1983 his blue print for holding election and restoring democracy. He set March 23, 1985 as the dead-line for holding the national election. But undeterred by this, the MRD appealed to masses to launch a popular struggle for restoration of democracy. Though it started with a lot of promise, the movement failed for two specific reasons. First, it did not spread to rural areas excepting Sind where it was effectively controlled by the government. Second, at an fairly early date, it acquired a narrow objective other than the restoration of democracy which eroded progressively its mass appeal. In particular, it sought to redress the provincial grievances held by the Sindhis against the Punjabi dominated decision-making structure of Pakistan. But it did serve a purpose for Zia. He was convinced that his plan must include some safeguards for ensuring that the restoration of democratic process did not undermine his authority. To ensure this he held a referendum on December 19, 1989 which confirmed his election to the Office of Presidency for five years by 98 per cent of affirmative votes and ensured his election before the elections of National and Provincial Assemblies. The referendum had the merit of obviating the necessities of holding elections under 1973 Constitution which would have resurrected the Assemblies elected in 1977 and posed legal problems regarding the tenure of his Presidential Office. However, with this, a hesitant and halting process of civilianization of military regime started in Pakistan.

Close on the heels, Zia held elections on February 25, 1985 for 217 National Assembly seats and on 27 for 483 seats in the four National Assemblies. It is a significant milestone in Pakistan electoral history for a number of reasons. First, it destroyed the organisational politics in the country and effectively localized it within the confines of electoral constituencies. Second, his policy of Islamisation suffered an irreversible set-back as reflected in the poor performances of the candidates backed by Jamat-i-Islami. Third, there was a pronounced swing to the right which brought the rural aristocracy to the centre of Pakistani politics. It was made possible by the absence of discipline normally exercised by the political parties for which voters choice was polarised. The same lack of discipline produced an entirely different result in cities. A new set of urban politicians were elected to the Assemblies with no mandate other than to criticize the government. They were politically volatile and adrift as issues and policies never figured in their election planks. This significantly affected the functioning of the National Assemblies which became chaotic which convinced Zia that political parties have to be restored some way or the other for the smooth transaction of the House. The MRD boycotted the elections. However, 53.69 per cent of registered voters did vote, and for Zia's martial law regime, the 1985 elections shored up its bargaining position with the emergent Parliament on the future constitutional framework.

On March 2, 1985 Zia promulgated the Restoration of the Constitution Order that introduced sweeping changes in the Constitution of 1973. A new provision was added to article 90 which stipulated, "The executive authority of the Federal Government shall vest in the President and shall be exercised by him either directly or through officers subordinate to him". It further said: "if any question areas whether any matter is or is not a matter in respect of which the President is by the Constitution empowered to act in his discretion, the decision of the President in his discretion will be final, and the validity of anything done by the President shall not be called into question on the ground that he ought or ought not to have acted in his discretion". The new order in a number of ways created a supra-parliamentary institution of the Presidency which was imposed on both the federal and provincial legislatures and governments. Such an imbalance enabled the President to do away with the ruling government either of his own accord or in conjunction with other centres of power. In actuality, the Amendment has enabled the military to use Presidential powers to retain its preeminent position within Pakistan. During the 1985-88 period, the Eighth Amendment created an "unbalanced diarchy" in Pakistan.[22]

Now, Zia formed the new Cabinet under the stewardship of a veteran politician from Sind, Mahammed Khan Junejo, Junejo displayed considerable independence which was tolerated by Zia and his military generals. It led the National Assembly to pass a vote of confidence unanimously in his favour in its first formal session. The new Parliament passed an Indemnity Bill to pave the way for lifting martial law. But it took months of hard bargaining with the President to come to an understanding on the contents of the Bill which included a number of compromises with regards to the sharing power between the President and the Prime Minister which became the substance of the 8th Amendment to the Constitution. President Zia continued to be COS despite the opposition's demand that he shed his uniform. Thus 8th Amendment bestowed a position on the Army Chief Superior to that of the elected Government of Prime Minister Junejo who only provided legitimacy to Zia's military government. Beyond all this, the Indemnity Bill provided legal protection to Zia's administration for all acts during eight years of martial law. The Parliament also passed the Political Parties Act which stipulated that a political party could function only if it is registered with the Election Commission and accept Pakistan's. Islamic ideology and undertake not to carry on any activity that would defame or bring into disrepute the army or the judiciary.

Having armed with this executive power Zia sent the army to barrack on December 30, 1985, thus ending the third phase of Military rule in Pakistan. A new pattern of civil-military relationship emerged following Junejo's decision to revive the Pakistan Muslim League which ushered in a new Cabinet comprising new faces of Junejo's imprint. It acted with relative independence from Zia who watched now the flow of politics from the barracks of Pakistan as the opposition reiterated their determination to restore the 1973 Constitution in its unamended form.

Benazir Bhutto came to power after the death of General Zia-ul-Haq in a plane crash. In November 1988,Benazir's Pakistan's People's Party bagged 92 of the 207 National Assembly seats. Lack of a clear majority gave President Ghulam Ishaq Khan and the army ample scope for political manouevring. But within fifteen days. PPP succeeded in forging an alliance with Mohajir Qaumi Movement which gave it a clear majority in the Assembly to form the government. It was only made possible after making compromises with the military and with the intervention of the United States Ambassador.[23] Now, Pakistani politics came to be dominated by three centres of power, the President, the COAS and the Prime Minister. Of these the President and the COAS had more powers than the Prime Minister for reasons already mentioned. In the changed situation, Ishaq revised his view of Presidential power and came to regard himself as the conscience-keeper of the nation, which was manifested in his views on a number of issues like Afghanistan and Pakistan's nuclear problem. This was resisted by the Bhutto Government. As a result, relationship with the President became so tense, that the dissolution of National Assembly was anticipated long before it actually happened. She also failed to establish a viable working relationship with the provinces. Her relationship with Beluchistan and Nawaz Sharif's Government in Punjab remained in a state of constant confrontation which had an unsettling effect on the working of federal government. Besides, she challenged frequently the military. Matter came to a climax when General Hamid Gul, head of ISI was replaced by a retired General and she preemptied the President by announcing that Chairman of the Joint Chiefs of Staff, Admiral Sirohey was due to retire. These challenges prompted the military to implicitely support no-confidence motion against the government in November 1989. Though it failed, military looked for an opportunity to play its dirty game.

Events moved very first, Bhutto lost her lusture among the masses. In the first seven months of 1990 ethnic clashes in native provinces of Sindh snowballed into mass protest against her government. Altaf Hussain, leader of the mass movement, passionately opposed her. A total and unprecedented strike gripped Karachi which resulted in indiscriminate violence. A reluctant army was forced to take action to quell down the domestic turbulence. Nor General Baig remained a silent spectator when the Kashmir issue surfaced in early 90's and subsequent exchanges between India and Pakistan made the prospect of the war imminent. But the Iraqi invasion of Kuwait provided an opportunity to remove Benazir, because the army could not trust to leave the matter in the hands of a young women, perceived to be a lady with limited vision and capability.[24] Ghulam Ishaq's declaration of state of emergency underlined gravity of the problems confronting the nation. However, these events gave Ishaq a convenient plea to dismiss Bhutto's government on August 6, 1990 and dissolve the National Assembly. According to the President, the country needed new leadership and he called on the leader of the opposition Ghulam Mustafa Jatoi to form a care-taker government until new election was held. The Presidential authority to terminate Benazir's rule was derived from Presidential extraordinary power granted in Article 58(2)(b) of the 8th Amendment to the Constitution of 1973. President promised that new election will be held on October 24. Benazir cried foul, insisting that the

President had acted illegally and was merely doing the bidding of the army but she could not reverse the decision.

The years following Benazir's dismissal was marked by usual pattern of mud-slinging and political witch-hunting. PPP became the object of elaborate criticism. Benazir was charged, with committing many administrative improprieties. Ishaq promulgated the Special Courts for Speedy Trials Ordinance, 1990 and implemented the Parliament and Provincial Assemblies (Disqualification for Membership) Rules and Holders of Representative Offices (Prevention of the Misconduct) Act which were promulgated during the regime of Mr. Bhutto. These ordinances and laws were profitably utilized by Jatoi for political vendetta. At the same time Jatoi started his coalition-building effort for a broad-based electoral alliance of his National People's Party with Jamat Ulama-1-Islami of Hussain Ahmad and Mumtaz Ali Bhutto's. Sindh National front and the Mohajir Qaumi Movement of Altaf Hussain's to form Islam Jamhoori Ittad. Mian Afgal Khan was elected-President of IJI.

The general elections were held on October 24, 1990. As anticipated, the coalition headed by IJI won a clear majority, by taking 105 seats in the new National Assembly. Other parties aligned with IJI won another 50 seats. The PPP and its partners in the People's Democratic Alliance won 45 seats. PPP lost support in every province and its greatest defeat was in Punjab. For the first time in Pakistani history, the ruling party enjoyed two-third majority in National Assembly. The nation-wide rejection of PPP meant that Nawaz Sharif, the lead of the IJI would be called upon to form the new government and also that Punjab was again in the centre of national politics. Benazir's initial reaction to defeat was bitter and critical. The elections for provincial Assembly produced the same pattern. Sharif declared that his IJI would form government in all four Provinces.

Sharif was inducted as the Prime Minister on November 6, 1990. Pledging an administration that would rise above confrontation, he declared his intention of working with opposition on domestic and foreign issues.[25] "All the major issues", he declared "would be confronted on the basis of cooperation"[26]. In response, Benazir declared "the opposition would stand with the government when it stands by the people"[27]. He promised to streamline the government which will work efficiently and economically. One of the spin-offs was polarization of political forces in Pakistan. The ideological confrontation of 70's and 80's was over. Both agreed on domestic agenda of liberal democracy and market economy. The provincial government and the opposition also developed a working relationship, despite differences on various issues. In fact, the relative ease with which the Sharif government operated with the four provinces enabled him to settle long standing 26 inter-state disputes. Even on foreign policy issues, the position of IJI and PDA became identical, after the former gave up its anti-India and anti-US policies and veered round to a political settlement in Afghanistan.

Initially, Sharif government did not operate against the backdrop of a hostile military. The military continued to support him, as a counterbalance to Bhutto's popularity and with the help of General Gul, IJI came to power in 1988 election.[28] But, once in power, Sharif's relations, with armed forces was far from cordial. Though, army differed on his Gulf War policy, he was careful not to question openly the role of the armed forces or that of the COAS. This precluded a chance for the army to make a common cause with Ishaq to play his power game. Once he took over Prime Ministership, it was expected that his relationship with the President would improve. These expectation stemmed from the fact that not only Ishaq and Nawaz were the product of Zia era but also that in the political game President had always supported Nawaz against Benażir.

But now emboldened by a clear majority in the National Assembly, Sharif began to take independent initiatives for counter balancing the Presidential power against the army. Aware that the military would continue to play a significant role in Pakistan politics, Sharif wanted a "pro-Prime Minister" COAS to replace General Beg on August 1991. He failed in this attempt when President Khan appointed General Asif Nawaz Janjua to the position. Although unhappy with the selection, Sharif reportedly tried to entice Janjua by "offers and opportunities"[29]. Even the President ignored Sharif's recommedation of the COAS appointment of General Waheed Kakar, whom Ishaq named after superseding senior Generals. The relationship became so sour, Isaq was looking for an alternative to Sharif. Benazir offered, such an alternative. But after the failure of the long march which Benazir threatened to launch in December 1992 with Presidential blessing and the manner in which Sharif foiled it, forced her for a rapprochement with him. Now the events unfolded in such a way that it inexorably led to fall of Sharif government. Benazir's departure to London coincided with General Janjua's death and installation of Abdul Waheed Kakar, whose apolitical disposition changed the troika, into a "semi-diarchy" again.[30] It prompted Sharif to initiate, a review of 8th Amendment. Meanwhile, he refused to declare his support for Ishaq's reelection at the end of 1993 despite indications from the President that he wanted another term. Sharif's attitude caused apprehension among the legislators who feared that an open test of wills may force Isaq to dismiss the government before Presidential election. To prevent this, they declared support for Ishaq but he was not convinced.

In 1992 Sharif furtune declined. The IJI coalition, an unholy marriage solemnized by the military's ISI agency began to disintegrate. The National People's Party, the Jammat-i-Islami, the Mohajir Qaumi Movement at different times and for different reasons, broke ranks with the alliance. The twelve MQM members of the National Assembly also resigned. These desertions did not pose a threat to Sharif's government but eroded the two-thirds Assembly majority needed for any constitutional amendment. The formation of a Conscience Group in the Senate by some IJI senators weakened Sharif's hold over the upper house as well. The IJI coalition now consisted mainly of the Muslim League and the Awami National Party, strange bedfellows given their historic animosities and hatred.

By the end of March the resignation of a third of Sharif's Cabinet and the claim of Janjua's wife that her husband has been poisoned created a near crisis situation in the midst of which Ishaq dissolved the National Assembly on April 18 and dismissed Sharif's government on charges of corruption, mal-administration and failure to work effectively with provincial governments. Balkhsher Mazari, a dissident from the Sharif government was appointed caretaker Prime Minister with PPP as the major partner.

But it lasted barely six weeks, when Supreme Court on a writ petition filed by Sharif against the dissolution of National Assembly declared a historic judgment quashing the Presidential order as illegal and unconstitutional and restoring both the Prime Minister and the National Assembly.[30] It was a great blow to Isaq and now he shuffled his cards more adroitly. A new power equation crystallized in the provinces. Isaq got Punjab Assembly dissolved within minutes of the Court's decision in a pre-emptive bid to foil Sharif's attempt to regain his home base. Simultaneously, North West Frontier Province Assembly was dissolved and a no-confidence motion was placed against the Chief Minister of Sindh. By manipulating provincial politics, Isaq isolated the Central Government, queering the pitch for Sharif to regain initiatives in the provincial politics. Sharif's effort to pass the controversial Article 234 in the Parliament to regain control of Punjab was foiled by Ishaq when he refused to sign the proclamation. It assumed crisis proportion when the armly decided to stay neutral and refused to obey the order of Central

Government without Presidential assent. However, General Waheed Kakar brought about a compromise under which Ishaq and Sharif jointly stepped down on July 18. A new caretaker administration was formed led by Senate Chairman Wasim Sajjad, as acting President and Moeen Qureshi, a former Vice-President of World Bank, as Prime Minister and new mid-term elections were announced for October 6, 1993.

The mid-term general elections, held on October 6 for the National Assembly and October 9 for provincial Assemblies, were remarkably free and fair. Although the Muslim League charged the caretaker government of pre-engineering the outcome, it was careful to declare that rigging had not taken place. It was something unusual in the electoral history of Pakistan. The elections resulted in a hung Parliament, even if the PPP and the PML emerged as two leading parties capturing 86 and 72 seats respectively in the National Assembly of 207 seats. The PML (Chatha group) secured 6 seats and the Pakistan Islamic Front won only 3. Interestingly, independent candidates won 15 seats. A similar situation prevailed in provinces, the PPP won 93 seats in Punjab, 56 in Sindh, 22 in North West Frontier Province (NWFP) and 6 in Beluchistan. Significantly, it managed 8 seats in Sindh,establishing itself as a truely national party. In the popular vote PML (Nawaz) had an edge by securing 39.7 per cent of vote over the PPP which got 38.1 per cent. Islamic parties suffered a humiliating defeat capturing even less than the minorities in the National Assembly. The regional parties line NAP in NWEP and the confideral party in Sindh and ethno-nationalist elements in Beluchistan also suffered stunning defeats. At the same time, PML and PPP made significant inroads into the provinces. The MQM which had been a strongest party in urban Sindh, boycotted the National Assembly election on the assumption that the voter should stay away, but it marginally affected, making the PML and the PPP the major beneficiaries of the boycott.

This distribution of power created an impression that no single party would be able to form a government and it would prompt the armed forces to intervene. The problem was solved when the PPP captured the position of Speaker and Deputy Speaker of the National Assembly. Benazir Bhutto was elected Prime Minister on October 19 and the PPP succeeded in establishing provincial governments in Punjab and Sindh. PML(Nawaz), on the other hand, only managed to form a coalition government in NWEP with the help of NAP. His PPP's major success, however, was getting Benazir's close confident, Farooq Leghari elected President on November 13. The 1993 elections saw the emergence of two genuinely national Political

Parties led by two charismatic leaders with firm roots in the provinces. After taking the oath of office, Benazir declared it the moment of reconciliation and pledged to work to strengthen democracy and promote tolerance. Sharif, reciprocating the gesture,remarked: "We will not indulge in negative politics. We will cooperate with the government for the cause of democracy. Pakistan cannot afford crisis after crisis. We will work to end this".[32]

This is precisely because, both of them had been tested in high office and had developed an appreciation for the limits of the power. Bhutto made it clear that the time has come when the country demanded efficient and effective government and there was no need to check-mate opposition in political games. It would simply produce bitter consequences, waste resources, time and create political impasse that was the bane of Pakistani political life. On the one side, opposition was too popular, too deep rooted and disciplined to be taken for a cool ride. The imperative of the situation demanded the institutional subordinations of the civil-military bureaucracy to the elected government for the crystallization and consolidation of democratic political forces in the country. Sharif appeared to share this conclusion with Benazir. This was reflected in their approach to repeal the 8th Amendment. With Leghari as the President, Bhutto has nothing to gain from attenuating the scope of Presidential power set forth in the amendment. Indeed, as indicated in the dismissal of the NWEP Assembly in February 1994, she could gain from the utilization of these powers. Nor did the opposition now benefit from any change as that could strengthen Bhutto's control.

The outgoing Prime Minister Moeen Qureshi, has curved out a new path for the nation, when he introduced multiple reforms programmes to address the economic malaise and dismantle the higher bureaucracy. Before leaving office, he ordered significant changes in the federal government, which received popular approval. True to his commitment to serve in a selfless, non-partition way, Qureshi not only retired from political scene, but also left Pakistan. This demonstration of political statesmanship was not lost on the articulative public, nor it was slighted by Pakistan's leading personalities. This became the touch-stone for measuring the performances of the Sharif government. The subsequent election of President Leghari reflected the environment of reconciliation permeating the country. Leghari's election seemed to promise that for the first time in Pakistani history, an elected government would serve its full term. The politicians not only demonstrated that they were responsive to the public demand for unity, they also got a President who conformed to the wishes of Prime Minister, Parliament and the party in power. Reciprocating the gesture of the nation, Leghari declared, "the time has come for stability, for political unity and economic development".[33]

## References


1. Jawaharlal Nehru, *The Discovery of India* (New Delhi; 1981), pp. 227-88.
2. Anil Seal, *The Emergence of Indian Nationalism* (Cambridge, 1976), pp. 298-340.
3. Mohammad Ayub Khan, *Friends Not Masters: A Political Autobiography* (London, 1967), p. 547.
4. Shahid Javed Burki, *Pakistani Nation in Making* (London, 1986), p. 46.
5. G.W. Chaudhury, *The Constitutional Development in Pakistan* (London, 1959), pp. 6-22.
6. Saleem M.M. Quereshi, "Iqbal and Jinnah: Personalities, Perceptions and Politics" in C.M. Naim, ed., *Iqbal, Jinnah and Pakistan: The Vision and Reality* (Syracuse, 1979), pp.11-41.
7. K.B. Sayeed "Political Leadership and Institution-Building Under Jinnah, Ayub and Bhutto" in Lawrence Ziring, Ralph Braibanti and Howard Wrigging eds., *Pakistan: The Long View* (Durham,1977), pp. 251-52.
8. Mohammad Waseem, "Pakistan's Lingering Crisis of Dyrachy" in *Asian Survey* (Berkeley), Vol. XXXII, no.7, July 1992, p. 623.
9. Leslie Wolf-Phillips, *Constitutional Legitimacy: A Study of the Doctrine of Necessity* (London, 1979), p.7.
10. Sisir Gupta, Pakistan's Domestic Crisis and Foreign Policy in M.S. Rajan and Sivaji Ganguly eds., *Sisir Gupta: India and the International system* (New Delhi, 1981), pp. 192-202.
11. M.S. Venkataramani, *The American Role in Pakistan* (New Delhi, 1982), p.171.
12. Burki, n. 4, p. 48.
13. Keith Callard, "The Political Stability in Pakistan" in *Pacific Affairs* (Vancouver), Vol. 29, no.1, March 1956, pp.5-21.
14. Chaudhury, n. 5, pp. 6-22.
15. Burki, n. 4, p.55.
16. *The Dawn* (Karachi), December 8, 1970.
17. Lawrence Ziring, "The Second Stage in Pakistani Politics" in *Asian Survey* (Berkeley), Vol. XXXIII, no.12, December 1993, p. 1176.
18. Burki, n. 4, p. 71.

19. Zia-ul-Haq, *The Pakistan Times* (Lahore), July 8, 1977.
20. Tariq All, *Can Pakistan Survive* (New York, 1983), p.133.
21. Samina Yasmeen, "Democracy in Pakistan" in *Asian Survey* (Berkeley), Vol. XXXIV, no. 6, June 1994, p. 575.
22. *Ibid.*, p. 574.
23. *Ibid.*, p. 573.
24. Lawrence Ziring, "Pakistan in 1990:The Fall of Benazir Bhutto" in *Asian Survey*, Vol. XXXI, no. 2, February 1991,p. 114.
25. *Ibid.*, p.122.
26. *Ibid.*, p. 122.
27. *Ibid.*, p. 122.
28. Christina Lamb, *Waiting for Allah* (New York, 1991), p. 36.
29. Ahmad Rashid, "Death of a Pragmatist", *The Herald* (Karachi) January 1993, p. 56a.
30. Yasmeen, n.21, p.578.
31. Tahir Amin, "Pakistan in 1993: Some Dramatic Changes" in *Asian Survey*, Vol. XXXIV, no. 2, February 1994, p. 193.
32. Ziring, no. 17, p. 1182.
33. *Ibid.*, p. 1185.

# Part-I

# Model-Oriented Analysis

**A Model for the Analysis of Foreign Policy**

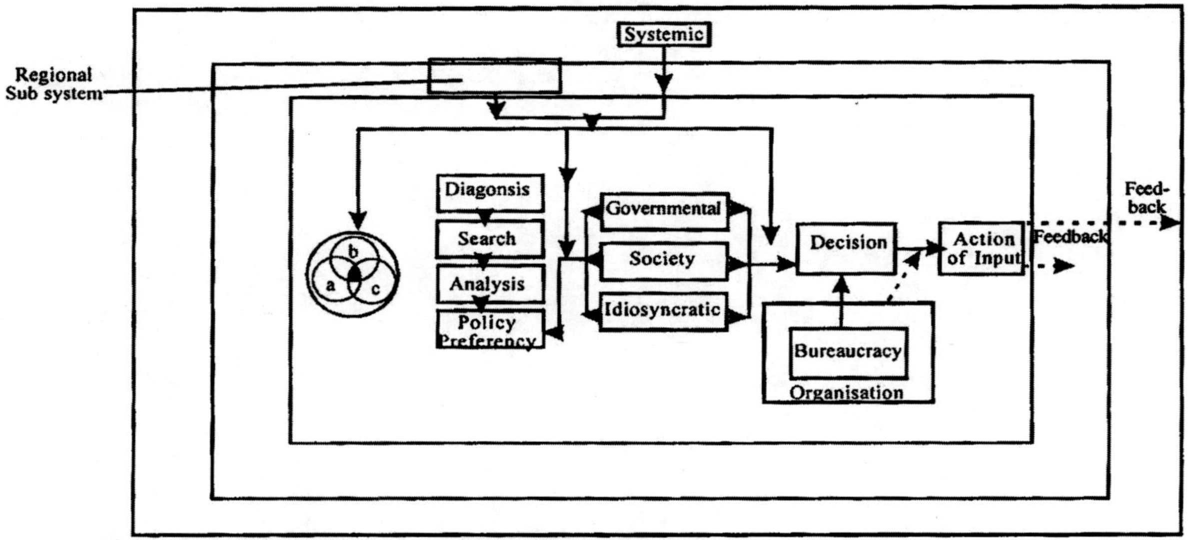


1. The Shaded area is the shared beliefs, among the collective decision makers.
2. Level of the Aggregation–Idiosynratic, Societal, Governmental, Regional Systemic and Systemic
3. Collective decision makers–(a) President, (b) Prime Minister, (c) Foreign Minister.
4. Gognitive style and belief system of the top dicision-makers becomes weighty at policy preference stage.
5. In rational model, the decision is arrived at only after diagonsis, search, analysis and policy preference, they may not proceed in a heat sequence as provided in the diagram, one or more stages of the process may be bypassed.
6. At decision stage, bureaucracy and organisational variables act as intervening variables rather than indepent variables.

# 2

# A Model for the Analysis of Pakistan's Foreign Policy

## (a) The Case for an Analytical Model

It is a truism that when one conjures up the world of foreign policy analysis from the vintage position of the discipline in the mid-1950's, one is just amazed by a plethora of new concepts, categories, theories, approaches, models, that have been spawned over the years. These efforts marked the end of the halcyon days of the traditional analysts. These analysts viewed the state as an undifferentiated abstraction possessing all the anthropomorphic attributes of will, personality and perception. They also looked upon the state as pursuing its goals abroad in the light of its geographic, political, historical, economic and strategic interests. And these goals are derivative from the objective situations in which nations find themselves at various periods of history. So these assumptions of reification of the State and objectification of its situation came under challenge from the scientific analysts. They recognized that ambiguous formulation, reified entities, and undisciplined modes of enquiry could never reveal the dynamics of the external behaviour of a state. Once the state is stripped off its veneer of reification, it becomes a visible embodiment of a set of interacting human officials who speak and act in the name of the state and allocate its values for realization of its goals by appropriate course of action in the realm of international system.

These human officials are known as decision-makers. They are concrete and identifiable actors. Their behavioural manifestations are not abstract or mystical and can be observed by any observer. Their behaviour is the product of causal processes and exhibit regularities and pattern of flows. So they can be measured and quantified. But explicit theory and operationalized concepts are necessary for any attempt at quantification and measurement. Hence, an unending quest started among scientific analysts to build models which serve this objective admirably well. The rationale is that an analytical model offers a host of advantages in the analysis of foreign policy.

As a matter of fact, a model denotes an orderly and logically integrated set of concepts, categories and propositions designed to show how some institution or process functions. All explanations and predictions are based on images regarding the way the things are arranged and how they function in the real world. Such images, even though never set down in ink or print, are models. That is, certain aspects of reality are abstracted from the totality and form the basis of description of how things work, how people behave or what will happen. So, it makes possible to have an accurate description of the phenomenon under consideration which coincides with empirical referent to a considerable extent. As a result, it renders the data meaningful without which data will not fall into place. It also functionally identifies how the component of behaviour can be structured and how they relate to each other. It has also the capability to explain the relationship among the phenomena under investigation, as it is composed of a number of assumptions from which conclusions are derived. Besides, it treates causal relationship in such a fashion that it enables analysts not only to prove validity of explanation but also to achieve parsimony whose implications for any research strategy is considerable.[1] However, to posit these merits, is not to argue that an observer is a prescient individual who can discover the "objective reality" of world politics through the simplification of his analytical model. The reality is always captured and designed in terms of the observer's mental model of the most relevant and distinguishing features of the phenomena. An eminent scholar cogently observes:[2]

> "Unable to perceive and depict the universe of international phenomena in its entirety, the observer is forced to select some of its dimensions as important and in need of close examination, while dismissing others as trivial and unworthy of further analysis...Use of the diagrammatic technique serves as a reminder that though there may be an objective truth about world politics, the observer can never know it. He must select in order to know reality, and in so doing he must distort it".

So, it has been argued that as the students of foreign policy cannot validly break reality down into its simplest, most basic relationships, he should instead work with more complex and thus, hopefully less unrealistic analytical model. However, the fact that no model takes into account all possibly relevant factors does not make these intellectual tools less useless.

As two Scholars observe:[3]

> "On the contrary, the abstraction of similar limited aspects from different concrete units that are unique in their respective totalities and the derivation of general descriptions from such abstractions form one of the most powerful techniques by which modern man reduces his complicated universe to some kind of intelligible and increasingly manageable order".

**(b) The Postulation of the Model**

The present model is delineated in the form of a diagram. Like all analytical models, it contains a set of inter-related concepts and assumptions. Hence, it is imperative to clarify the assumptions underlying it.

In the first place, if foreign policy can be defined as consisting of the external behaviour of states then it becomes legitimate to assume that it is this behaviour which can be treated as the fundamental unit of analysis—the phenomena one is primarily concerned for description and explanation. Consequently, what one studies are acts or behavioural activities and in foreign policy analysis this means one focuses on the things the states say and do abroad. So, by adopting the foreign policy acts as the unit of analysis, the study of foreign policy is placed within the philosophical and theoretical tradition of those scholars such as Margaret Mead (1938), Talcott Parsons and Edward A. Shils (1960) and William H. Ricker (1957), who emphasise the acts in the scientific analysis of foreign policy, even if, primary actor remains the nation-state.

As a necessary corollary to the adoption of foreign policy acts as the unit of analysis, it can be argued that there is no level of analysis problem involved in foreign policy research. It was J. David Singer who was the earliest to recognise that there is such a problem. However, the main thrust of Singer's argument does not refer to analysis problem at all[4]. It refers to what are commonly called "Units of analysis", that is the units or cases across which one compares. What Singer is saying correctly is that an analyst cannot analyse both national subsystem and international system as though they are comparable units. But he never argues that one necessarily encounters an analytical problem when dealing simultaneously with variables at different levels of aggregation. Singer does not deny the possibility of cross-level relationship. It is analytically legitimate to relate a state's foreign policy to both national characteristics and aspects of international system. To be sure, the levels of these variables are different but there is certainly no logical fallacy and presumably some.theoretical merit in positing such relationship. An explanatory model of foreign policy necessarily requires inclusion of independent variables at all levels of aggregation, if it is to be valid and cogent. It is intuitively obvious that both national and systemic factors condition the kind of behaviour emanating from the national actor.[5] Once it is recognised, the empirical investigator can perform his conceptual task in such a manner in which the indicators of foreign policy behaviour of states are put in a clear format for data analysis, and will enable him not only to make useful inferences about the relative strengths of variables at multiple levels but also to trace the interaction effects among these variables. There are, however, very few quantitative studies in which variations in national behaviour are related to domestic factors and to factors arising in the international system. Even if, there is no level of analysis problem involved, the tendencies persist. Two researchers, who have developed and tested such multi-level models are Nazli Choucri and Robert C. North who observe[6]:

> "A model focusing either on national or on international effects is likely to be vulnerable on theoretical terms (by reducing everything to internal factors or to considerations external to the system) and incomplete in operational terms... What we are suggesting, therefore, is that optimum specifications would, by necessity, include both internal and external variables. A mixed model of this sort is likely to yield greater pay-offs in the long run".

The second assumption is that if the category of system can be used as a distinct unit of analysis for foreign policy of states, then certain characteristics usually associated with it need to be postulated:

(a) the system to be investigated must be explicitly distinguished from its environment;

(b) the internal elements of the system are explicitly stated;

(c) the relationships between the system and its environment are to be explicitly stated;

(d) where these relationships involve deductions, the canons of logical reasoning are employed; and assertions concerning relationships between the system and the real world are confirmed according to the canons of scientific method.

Since regular behaviour defines a system, it is legitimate to view the nation-state as a subsystem in an all encompassing international system, or a system composed of a network of subsystems, comprising an environment, a group of actors, and structures through which actors initiate actions to respond to challenges for preserving or modifying conditions in the environment and processes which sustain the flow of demands and the product of the system as a whole. They all occur continuously in a circular flow of demands on policy (inputs), policy processes and product of policy (outputs). The decision (outputs) feeds back into the system. As a result, the substance of inter-state relations becomes a flow of interactions. There is a continued circular flow of policy and action both within and between nations in a complex pattern. So, the relations are always established and disestablished by sequential occurrence of events. Since relations of nations, most of the time, find an ordinary level of operation in a kind of steady state of exchange and interaction, then it becomes easier to argue that changes in the state of relations between nations become the focus of analysis because of the dynamics of state's external behaviour.

Thirdly, it is further assumed that the most perplexing questions, of goals, motivations and purposes in national policy can be answered if the behaviour of officials of the states is treated as the unit of analysis. Here another problem crops up as to whethe. they pursue goals consciously or not. Although there is no consensus on this, it is generally viewed that they move towards outcome of which they have little knowledge, and over which they have less control. But nevertheless they do prefer and therefore select particular outcome and attempt to realise it by conscious formulation of strategies. Similarly, if it is asked why specific goals are preferred, one can answer it by assuming identical goals of all the national actors. But different conclusions can be arrived at if one investigates the processes by which national goals are selected, the internal and external factors that impinge on the processes, and institutional matrix from which they emanate. As a matter of fact, if the analyst intends to explain a nation's foreign policy he cannot settle for the mere postulation of these goals. He is compelled to go back a step and enquire into their genesis, and the processes by which they become the crucial variables. Another significant implication of this is that it is only within this particular framework that one can expect any useful application of the decision-making approach. It is true, the decision-making variables should not be conceived as synonymous with the foreign policy behaviour itself. Its main merit is to relate the variable attributes of the decision-making units and processes to foreign policy outputs.[7]

Fourthly, it is also assumed that the most intractable phenomenological issue is resolved. The phenomenologists contend that the individual or groups are not influenced by the objective forces of their milieu but by the fashion in which these forces are viewed, perceived and evaluated by them, however distorted such perceptions may be. So, if one embraces a phenomenological view of causation, then he is compelled to adopt a phenomenological model for explanatory purposes. It is precisely because the analyst's concern extends beyond the description of "what happens" to the realm of explanation and the omission of "cognitive and perceptual linkages" would be "ontologically disastrous". The analyst may observe correlation between all sorts of forces in the international system and the behaviour of nations but their causal relationship must remain "strictly deductive and hypothetical" in the absence of empirical investigation of its causal chain which links the two. Since nation-state is seen as a group of individuals operating within an institutional framework, it makes perfect sense to focus on the phenomenal field of those individuals who allocate values for the state in the policy-making process.

The earliest in the field of international politics to recognize this was Snyder whose decision-making approach was based on the core premise that foreign policy choices would be fruitfully analysed from the decision-maker's perspective and his "definition of the situation". It received greater support after the publication of one book and an article by Kenneth E. Boulding entitled 'Image' and 'National Images and International System' in 1956 and 1959 respectively.[8] The initial stimulus was also provided by Harold and Margret Sprout with their distinction of the psychological and operational environment.[9] So, the earlier assumptions that foreign and defence policies could be best understood and formulated exclusively on the basis of unitary and rational actor model as manifested in the works of Raymond A. Bauer in 1961 and Charles E. Osgood in 1959 were thrown overboard.[10] Even Graham T. Allison in his study of the Cuban missile crisis within the framework of organizational model did not consider the cognitive process model but the potential value of it was clearly admitted by him in his conclusion, since no significant correlation between the bureaucratic role and the decision-making was revealed. This suggested at least some limitation to the core premise of the bureaucratic model: "Where you stand depends on where you sit". Similarly, John D. Steinbruner's study of the proposed multilateral force (MLF) for NATO tested four alternative conceptions of decision-making: rational, adaptive rational, bargaining, and cognitive process models and reached the same conclusion[11]. However, research made tremendous strides after Alexander L. George's reconceptualization of the Operational Code which offered an approach regarding the role of belief systems in decision-making that spurred an impressive array of case studies in recent years, pioneered first by Ole R. Holsti, Michael I, Shapiro and G. Mathew Bonham and Robert Axelrod.[12] Holsti argues that for some decisions a cognitive process perspective is fundamental and should be the starting point of the analysis. It shares an assumption which differentiates belief system and cognitive process from mere ideology and policy preference. Substantively belief system refers to a more or less integrated set of beliefs about man's physical and social environment. In case of political leaders, beliefs about history and the nature of politics may be especially important. Cognitive processes refer to various activities associated with problem solving—perception, appraisal, interpretation and information-processing strategies for coping with ambiguity, decision-rules and the like. These cognitive activities assumed to be in interactive relationship with individual belief systems as well as with the environment.

Lastly, it is assumed that although the cognitive process model is central to the study of decision outputs other three alternative conceptions of decision-making like unitary rational model, organizational model and bureaucratic politics are also not without potency. So, the research on belief system should be embedded in a broader context and the problems of linking and interrelating theories and concepts that are oriented to the individual decision-maker and to the behaviour of dynamics of group and organization need to be addressed simultaneously taking into account variables at different levels of aggregation.[13] Such is the rationale of the present model which will enable the analyst to perform the task of establishing the linkages in the various situational contexts of the decision-making.

In the foregoing, the analytical model is delineated containing some orderly and logically integrated set of categories and broad assumptions. But the main purpose of a model is to throw up some theoretical propositions about the behaviour of the decision-maker which is bound to be as diverse as the targets of his behaviour and the circumstances under which he makes his choice So, the model should be provided with materials out of which such propositions can be fashioned. It is the political environment, with respect to which decisions are made, constitutes the material. As we know, political environment which lies outside the decision-making organization serves as the matrix from which internal and external stimuli emanate for the decision-maker. So any attempt at theorising decisions must include an effort to have some notion about the nature of stimuli and its levels of aggregations to which the decision-maker is exposed. It is a much explored idea that the processes comprising political environment is as crucial as those occurring in the mind of the decision-maker. To reconstruct the objective world from the perspective of the decision-maker the analyst must first, examine the world itself so that he can comprehend the dynamics and limits of the decision-maker's perspective. Even if the decision-maker serves as the organizing focus for enquiry, and the variables within the decision-making organization are crucial, it should not be forgotten that they vary depending upon the events outside it. Therefore, in the first place, a systematic segregation of stimuli at their various levels of aggregation is essential to identify and establish the major variable clusters affecting foreign policy choice. Again these major variable clusters need to be elaborated for all the inputs which each of them subsume. Because, the analyst must know how to proceed with the line of enquiry for a comparative analysis. So, what is most imperative is to suggest the relative strength of these major variable clusters under varying conditions, and to outline a method for comparing them. Added to this, the inputs subsumed under each major cluster is to be elaborated in detail for the analyst needs "if-then" proposition that will enable him to process data in terms of the interactions presumed to take place within and among the major variable clusters.

Now, the major variable clusters can be segregated in the systemic aggregation continue. The systemic aggregation continue distinguishes between those that originate in the idiosyncracies of the decision-maker himself, those that arise out of the procedures and the institutions of the government, those that emanate outside the government but within the society, those that derive from circumstances external to the society in the regional subsystem and those that arise from situations external to the region but within the international system. In the model, they are termed as idiosyncratic, governmental, societal, regional sub-systemic and system variables.[14]

Each of these major cluster of variables subsume a number of relational variables which are distinctly elaborated for conceptualization.

Secondly, it is observed that the process of interaction occur in specified locales and through concrete actors; namely in the agencies of government and through the actions and relationship of those officials charged with the formulation and conduct of foreign policy. It should be borne in mind that whether inputs emanate from the national system or the international system or idiosyncratic sources, they are converted into decision and action or only output as they are experienced, evaluated and reconciled by identifiable decision-makers. And this conversion of inputs occurs, interestingly, both within and among individual decision-makers. At the intra-individual level, the analyst must focus on the belief system and cognitive process that act as the filter through which policy-planners identify, gather, shift and evaluate information and alternative choices to reach a particular policy preference which leads to formal decision. At the interindividual level, the analyst must also concentrate on the pulls and pressures of the organizational and the bureaucratic dynamics that operate between the decision and action or output. This will enable the analyst not only to comprehend the dynamics of decision-making of a particular state but also for a cross-country comparison.

Now, coming to the diagrammatic representation of the model, one finds that in the national system usually the top decision-makers along with lesser policy-makers take the decision. As outlined in this model, a,b, and c represent President, Prime Minister, and Foreign Minister. They, first of all, engage themselves in the broad intellectual and interactive task of diagnosis, search and analysis of the situations abroad to which they must respond and make a policy preference. The manner in which these policy-making tasks are performed is likely to establish the boundaries within which decisions are made. For example, the definition of the situation, or the extent of search and analysis may eliminate certain policy options from considerations or may focus on others. They may have shared beliefs or intellectual differences. But in both cases, it is very saliently crucial even if at policy preference stage, other variables do influence. In the former case, the central belief systems of all the collective leaders predominate while in the latter case, the top decision-maker's belief system and cognitive style not only prevails, but he also bypasses the hierarchy. But it should be assumed that belief system and cognitive style do not unilaterally determine the individual's choice of action, as decisions may also be sensitive to other variables as outlined in the model. The influence of an actor's beliefs is more likely to be weighty in his policy preference, the option he prefers than in determining the option he finally chooses. Hence, it is essential and useful to regard the decision-maker's policy preference rather than his final choice of action as the dependent variable.[15] But in the model, it is shown that the policy preference which results in decision is again subject to the pulls and pressures of dynamics of the organizational and the bureaucratic politics which are likely to be operative between decision and action and what finally emerges is termed as the foreign policy action or behaviour of the state. It is important, in this connection, to recognize here the distinction between decision and action, because the literature on the bureaucratic politics tends to gloss over many potential sources of slippage between executive decisions and the implementation of policy in the form of foreign policy actions.[16]

Coming to the methodology for constructing the belief systems and cognitive style of the decision-makers, it would be very useful and relevant to adopt the "Operational Code"(OC) approach of Alexander L. George who formulated ten questions, of which the first five concern "philosophical issues" while the rest five are most specifically oriented towards the instrumental or policy questions, having to do with goals-means relations.[17]

In designing a model of this kind, no originality is claimed, as its basic categories and concepts are formulated and operationalized and assumptions explored by scholars long back. Nor it originated as a reaction against deficiencies of earlier ones. The variables are simply incorporated into the model, which are arrayed according to the levels of analysis. Such levels are usually associated with the levels of aggregation so that units at a lower level of analysis such as the behaviour of the state can be combined to form a higher level of analysis. Although the state and international system level of analysis are most common in the foreign policy analysis, it may be useful to consider the intermediate level of analysis such as the international region. This multi-level analysis, is its only merit and its theoretical pay-offs will be judged to the extent it throws up certain testable hypothesis when successfully applied to the analysis of the foreign policy of states.[18]

**(c) The Applicability of the Model to Pakistan**

The analysis of foreign policy of Pakistan is to be based on this model which will incorporate Pakistani contents into its skeletal forms. So, it is an empirical challenge to relate the categories, concepts and assumptions underlying the model to comprehend dynamics of its external behaviour.

The State of Pakistan can be designated as a national sub-system in the subordinate system of the South Asia in the all encompassing international system. If regular behaviour defines a system, an analyst can well explore how the subsystem of Pakistan since 1947 is engaged in continuous interaction with other subordinate systems of the South Asia and the West Asia in the international system. So, there will be no difficulty to delineate its manifest political boundary which is a prime requisite for the existence and operation of a system. It is within this boundary, that it has been exposed to stimuli and in turn responded to challenges of events in the international system.

Like all systems, it has core elements. It has a group of actors identified as its strategic decision-makers, like Mohammad Ali Jinnah, Liaquat Ali Khan, Ghulam Mohammad, Ikander Ali Mirza, Mohammad Ayub Khan, Zulfikar Ali Bhutto, Zia-ul-Huq, Benazir Bhutto, and Nawaz Sharif. The analyst can trace their pattern of interactions with other actors in the international system through their manifold actions. It has a structure to perform certain functions which includes Parliament, and the Cabinet, and such decision-implementing agencies like the Foreign and Defence Ministries and other related Ministries and Services.

Like all decision-makers, the Pakistani leadership was subjected to stimuli emanating from five major sources: systemic, regional systemic, societal, governmental and idiosyncratic. Before responding to any challenges of events unfolding within the boundary, they receive the stimuli from all these sources and get engaged in the intellectual task of diagnosis, search, analysis and policy preference, and reach a decision. At the policy preference stage their belief systems and cognitive style predominate and act as the prism through which policy preference leads to decision. Between the decision and the output, the organizational interests and the bureaucratic bargaining of the Military Services, the Defence and the External Affairs Ministries act as the intervening variables, which shape the external behaviour of Pakistan. And there has been a continuous flow of demands on policy inputs, policy processes and product of policy (outputs). The relationship was always established and disestablished by a sequential occurrence of events that has been vibrating its international life since 1947.

As its outputs, which constitute its external behaviour, are products of interactions among the inputs being filtered through the prism of the cognitive beliefs of its decision-makers and again subject to the vagaries of the organizational and the bureaucratic dynamics, the analytical challenge remains to empirically trace how its decision ranging from joining the Western alliance system by concluding a military security agreement with the United States in 1954 to becoming a nuclear state can be systematically explained through a model based on a systems approach as a distinct unit of analysis of the foreign policy of a state.

## References

1. J. David Singer, "The Level of Analysis Problem in International Relations" in Klaus Knorr and Sidney Verba, eds., *The International System : Theoretical Essays* (Princeton, 1961), pp. 77-92.
2. James N. Rosenau, *The Scientific Study of Foreign Policy* (New York, 1971), pp. 11-12.
3. Harold and Margaret Sprout, *Foundations of International Politics* (New York, 1962), p. 39.
4. Don Munton, "Comparative Foreign Policy : Fads, Fantasies, Orthodoxies, Perversities" in James N. Rosenau, ed., In Search of Global Patterns (New York, 1976), pp. 257-71.
5. The simulation-based study by Crow and Noel is perhaps unique in its multiple focus on personality, organizational and situational factors, set Wayman J. Crow, and Robert C. Noel, *The Valid Use of Simulation Results* (Mimeo, 1965), Western Behavioural Sciences Institute, Ohio, U.S.A.
6. Nazli Choucri and Robert C. North "The Determinants of International Violence",Papers Peace Research Society (International),Vol. 12,1969, pp. 33-63.
7. Patrick I. MaGowan, "The Future of Comparative Studies: An Evangelical Plea" in James N. Rosenau, ed., *In Search of Global Patterns* (New York, 1976), pp. 217-35.
8. K.S. Boulding, *The Image* Michigan,1956), and "National Images and International Systems", *Journal of Conflict Resolution* (New Haven), Vol. 3, no. 2, June 1959, pp. 120-31.
9. Harold & Margaret Sprout," Environmental Factors in the Study of International Politics", *Journal of Conflict Resolution* (New Haven),Vol. 1, no. 4, December 1957, pp. 309-28.
10. See, for details, Raymond A. Bauer, "Problems of Perception and the Relations between the United States and the Soviet Union". *Journal of Conflict Resolutlon* (New Haven), Vol.5, no.3, September 1961, pp. 223-29; Charles E. Osgood, "Suggestions for Winning the Real War with Communism", Journal of Conflict Resolution (New Haven), Vol. 3, no. 4, December 1959, pp. 311-25; Harvey Wheeler, "The Role of Myth System in American Soviet Relations", *Journal of Conflict Resolution* (New Haven), Vol.4, no.2, June 1960, pp.179-84; and Sidney Verba, "Assumptions of Rationality and Non-Rationality in Models of the International System", *World Politics* (Princeton),Vol. 14, no. 1, October 1961, pp. 93-117.
11. He concludes that "the handling of multiple objectives and the response to the structural uncertainty required explanations at the level of the individual decision-maker and it was the cognitive process model which provided the

best fit with the phenomena observed"; see John D. Steinburner, "The Mind and the Milieu of Policy Makers: A Case History of the MLF" (Ph.D. dissertation, Massachusetts Institute of Technology, Massachusettes, U.S.A. 1968), pp. 538.

12. For details, see Ole R. Holsti, "The Belief System and National Images: A Case Study". *Journal of Conflict Resolution* (New Haven), Vol. 6, no. 3, September 1962, pp. 244-52; Michael I. Shapiro and G. Mathew Bonham, "Cognitive Processes and Foreign Policy Decision-making", *International Studies Quarterly* (Michigon). Vol.17. no.2, June 1973. pp. 147-74, and Robert Axelrod, *Structure of Decision: The Cognitive Maps of Political Elites* (Princeton,1976); Alexander L. George, "The 'Operational Code': A Neglected Approach to the Study of Political Leaders and Decision-making", .*International Studies Quarterly* (Michigan). Vol.13. no. 2, June 1969, pp. 190-222.
13. Ole. R. Holsti, "Foreign Policy Decision-makers view Psychologically: Cognitive process Approaches" in James N. Rosenau, ed., *In Search of Global Patterns* (New York, 1976), pp.120-43.
14. This is based on Rosenau's classification of the major cluster of variables constituting the main sources of foreign policy. For elaboration, see his article "The Study of Foreign Policy" in James N. Rosenau, Kenneth Thompson and Govin Boyd, eds., *World Politics: An Introduction* (New York, 1976), pp.15-35. The regional sub-systemic variables which is added is based on Michael Brecher's model set out in his article, "The Subordinate State System of Southern Asia", *World Politics* (Princeton). Vol.15, no.2, January 1963, pp. 213-35, where he indicates that comprehension of the global system cannot be achieved unless analysis proceeds at the regional sub-systemic level. Rosenau claims that his categorization schema contained in this article is designed out of his pre-theories and theories of foreign policy. But in this article he observed, "...all foreign policy analysts either explain the external behaviour of the societies in terms of five sets of variables or proceed in such a way that their explanations can be recast in terms of the five sets... the five sets are what we shall call the individual, role, governmental, societal and systemic variables", see his book The *Scientific Study of Foreign Policy* (New York, 1971), pp. 95-150. What made him to revise his earlier opinion to drop "role" variable in his later categorization schema in 1976 is quite intriguing. Because he was the first scholar to have tested the relative potency of role and individual variables, see his article, "Private Preferences and Political Responsibilities: The Relative Potency of Individual and Role Variables in the Behaviour of US Senators" in J.

David Singer, ed., *Quantitative International Politics* (New York, 1968), pp. 17-50.

15. Alexander L. George, "The Causal Nexus between Operational Code Beliefs and Decision-making Behaviour: Problems of Theory and Methodology" in L. S. Falkowski, ed., *Psychological Models in International Politics* (Colorado, 1979), p. 104.
16. Ole R. Holsti, "Foreign Policy viewed Cognitively" in Robert Axelrod ed., *Structure of Decision: The Cognitive Maps of Political Elites* (Princeton, 1976) pp. 15-55.
17. Alexander L. George, The Operational Code: A Neglected Approach to the Study of Political Leaders and Decision-Making", *International Studies Quarterly* (Michigan), Vol.13, no.2, June 1969, pp. 190-222.
18. James N. Rosenau once remarked in 1972: "In the long run, if not in the short run as well, the course of international history seems likely to be shaped by the convergence of forces in which talents, aspirations and prospectives of particular individuals are of relatively minor importance", see his book review in *American Historical Review* (Washington), Vol. 77, no. 5, December 1972,pp.1415-16. But in 1976 in his article, "The Study of Foreign Policy", cited earlier, he implicitly refutes this by admitting the fact that "intra-individual variable distorts the rational model of policy-making. This "intra-individual variable" is nothing but can be termed as the other name of belief system and cognitive style of the decision-maker.

    Of late, in a seminal work, both James N. Rosenau and Ole R. Holsti have come together and recognized how the foreign policy perceptions, belief systems and orientations of American leaders are central to the role played by the United States in the World. In the same vein, both of them have clearly admitted: "Thus reader will not find exhaustive discussions of the pressures and constraints within the international and domestic arenas nor of all the ways by which these make themselves felt or ignored in foreign policy process". See Ole R. Holsti and James N. Rosenau, *American Leadership in World Affairs: Vietnam and the Breakdown of Consensus* (Boston, 1984), Introduction, p. (XIV).

# Part-II

# Major Inputs

# 3
# Societal Sources

In the initial years of scientific enquiry, it was clearly recognised that actions of a state are undertaken by concrete and identifiable actors known as its decision-makers. But, there was a pervasive tendency among the scientific analysts to assume that the decision-makers broadly formulate policy in response to emerging events at home and developments abroad without consideration of the fact that the composition, structure and functioning of the society were equally valid to the formulation and conduct of its foreign policy.[1] However, this perspective changed with the advent of capability analysis and decision-making approach in the field of foreign policy that marked an increasing sophistication in the mode of scientific enquiry when it became crystal clear that what transpires within the society has a definite bearing, affecting not only the content of policies of a state but also its capacity to implement them. Thanks to these fortuitous developments it is now no longer a conjecture that the ability of a state to achieve its goal and to underwrite its policies is dependent upon intangible aspects of societal organisation and tangible factors as well. The analyst now has to probe into social, economic and political structures of the society in order to isolate the factors in the internal setting that affect the choice of the decision-makers. And the analyst is free to assume that a society's economic institution, social structure, educational system and its major value-orientation condition the actions of its policy-makers. But, it should be borne in mind that the analyst who focuses on the societal sources of foreign policy must identify and conceptualize the linkages that bind the decision-makers to their internal settings. As a matter of fact, the societal cluster subsumes many distinct dimensions which are categorised in framework as "culture and history" and "capabilities". The analytical challenge is meant to discern the effects of these variables on the plans and courses of action of the decision-makers.

**Culture and History**

It is assumed by the foreign policy theorist that one of the most important cluster of societal variables involves the norms and traditions that underlie the relationships among a society's members, their interpretations of their common heritage and all other means by which they sustain the ties of the community.[2] So, it is argued that a society which is unified by a common culture and historical experience can more effectively pursue its foreign policy goals than one which is rent with cultural dissensions among its diverse groups. It is precisely because the foreign policy officials need societal support and the extent of this support is significantly affected by the degree to which basic values are shared by all members of the society. Besides, the major value-orientation of a society also serve as the foundation for the policy-makers to fashion its foreign policy goals and to choose the means to underwrite them. This partly explains why a business oriented state is more likely to accord a greater priority to economic policies to achieve its foreign policy goals than one in which the dominant value-orientation is military. These cultural values get translated into foreign policy plans through a variety of ways ranging from the impact of public opinion on policy-making to the effects, of socialization of policy-makers on their official behaviour, as they are the bearers and perpetuators of the societal culture.

The new sovereign state of Pakistan which came into existence on 14 August 1947 was carved out of the Indian Subcontinent to provide a homeland for the Indian Muslims. It was one of the rare instances in the history of modern state-system that a nation which gained independence on the basis of the national self-determination lacked a unified territorial personality of its own as its eastern and western wings were separated by thousand miles of sprawling Indian territory. The Muslim majority areas which formed the State of Pakistan were socially, economically, and politically the least developed regions of undivided India. Its population which was socially fragmented, ethnically diverse, and spoke different languages and dialects, came to be unequally divided in its two wings. Basically poor, illiterate and overwhelmingly rural, they represented a congeries of groups and interests in Pakistani society. In sum, the social structure of Pakistan on the eve of its independence was a mosaic of diversities marked by cultural dissensions. This prevented Pakistan to evolve a consensual basis of its major value orientations among its policy-planners to fashion foreign policy goals and select means to underwrite them effectively.

Before isolating the impact of this variable, an attempt is being made here to understand the historical dynamics of this fragmentation for which one is forced to dwell upon three primary contributory factors out of a welter of many : first, the pattern of social and political development of the Muslims in the Indian Subcontinent, second, the Muslim response to the British rule and its colonial policy and third, the character, nature and the timing of the Pakistan movement.[3]

While it is not easy to delineate them in their details, suffice it to note that the Indians Muslims were splitted in matters of caste and creed even through they believed in holy Koran, rituals of priesthood, religious dogmas, and common social practices.[4] Doctrinal differences divided them broadly into Sunnis and Shias, while a large number of Sufis existed among them. There was also a distinct pattern of social stratification based on the tradition of descent, ethnicity and occupational specialization, for which the Muslims were categorized as Ashraf (nobility) and Ajlaf (commoner), even if the class structure was fluid and allowed upward mobility in social hierarchy. Besides, the caste-like communities like Bhoras, Khoja Ismailis, and Memons, converts of the traditional Hindu traders, existed among them in Western India[5]. The Muslim population in undivided India was also unevenly distributed. While they were spread all along the heartland of the Indo-Gangetic plain reflecting the course of Muslim conquest, a major chunk of them was concentrated at its western end due to the early penetration of Islam there and at the eastern end of Assam and Bengal for the strong impact of Buddhism and large scale conversion of low-caste Hindus[6]. British rule hard hit these eastern Muslims who were in a majority, as its revenue policy reduced them to poor peasants, making the Hindus the landlords, while replaced the old Muslim elites by newly emerging elites of Bengali Hindus, as Persian and Urdu were replaced by English as the official language of the British Government. But their coreligionists in Western India who were in a minority maintained their status and power as they were highly educated and urbanized.[7]

These diverse Muslim groups pulled in different directions as they responded differently to the British rule during Indian freedom struggle. The traditionalists led by Ulemas, who responded by retreating to orthodoxy and resistance, set up a theological academy at Deoband in 1867 which became the main hub of their anti-British nationalistic fervour and later on joined the Indian National Congress to fight against the Britishers.[8] The secular modernists led by Sir Syed Ahmed Khan responded by making an appeal to the Muslims to shed off their religious obscurantism, to eschew politics and cooperate with the Britishers for the economic and educational advancement of their community.[9] In 1906, these emerging educated middle class Muslim elites of the minority provinces set up under his leadership the Muslim League Party for expousing the cause of Indian Muslims. The third response was primarily political and also reflected attempts by regional Muslim elites in the Muslim majority provinces of Punjab[10] and Bengal to protect their personal and community interests in the complex communal politics of their region after inauguration of the self-government commencing from 1919 onwards.

These diverse forces eventually became merged for the time being in the Pakistan Movement spearheaded by the Muslim League. The League, which acted primarily as an instrument of the dominant upper class elites and landlords drawn exclusively from the Muslim minority areas of north India, was captured by young nationalist Mohammad Ali Jinnah in 1913. He aligned himself with the Indian National Congress which was the only political party in India espousing the nationalist cause. He was convinced that he could advance Muslim cause by acting as a sort of pressure group from within the Congress. He could visualize that the end of colonial rule in India required solidarity between the Hindus and the Muslims. They were the twin sister communities in India. They should cooperate with each other for the welfare of the motherland. But this solidarity must be based on the separateness of the Muslims and not on their merger in an Indian conglomerate. So, to preserve this and organize Muslims for a distinct share in political power, he fiercely advocated the provision of separate electorate for them in central and provincial legislatures. He made this demand clear as early as October 1916—three months before the conclusion of the Lucknow Pact—when he presided over the 16th Bombay Provincial Conference which was attended perhaps more by the Hindus than the Muslims. He said:[11]

"The Mahammedans want proper, adequate and effective representation....But (they) further require that representation should be secured to them by means of separate electorates. The question of separate electorates has been before the country since 1909 and rightly or wrongly the Mussalman community is absolutely determined for the present to insist upon separate electorates. To most of us the question is no more open to further discussion or argument, as it has become a mandate of the community."

Jinnah being a liberal constitutionalist did not approve Gandhiji's method of direct action and call for civil disobedience movement for the realization of the nationalist aspiration. But he failed to prevail as the organization was in the firm grip of Gandhiji's leadership. So he resigned from Congress. But his resignation did not materially affect the League-Congress cooperation which reached its zenith in the Khilafat Movement in which the use of religious symbols by the Ulemas to mobilize the Muslims in favour of Khalifat and the use of Hindu religious symbols by Gandhiji to mobilize the Hindu masses brought an unprecedented upsurge of anti-British sentiments. In the entire drama, the League was isolated as its President Jinnah refused to associate himself because of his distrust, not of the Khilafat cause but of the methods adopted to promote that cause.[12] The League continued to remain an elite organization devoid of mass support among the Muslims. It remained dormant and divided. When the All Parties Conference was convened in Calcutta in 1928 in response to the appointment of the Simon Commission to formulate their own proposals for constitutional reform, Jinnah presented the demands of the Muslim League for separate electorates. He was hooted down, his scheme was rejected. This was a frustrating experience for him as his dissent was ignored because he had no right to speak on behalf of the Muslims.[13] He did not represent them and the League was not a force to be reckoned with in the Indian politics.[14] In utter humiliation, he resigned from the League and repaired to England.

While Jinnah was in London, the King gave his Royal Assent to the Government of India Act of 1935 which was a big step towards self-government in India. In the provinces, responsible government was established over virtually the entire field of subjects ordinarlily falling to a province in a federation. The provinces now increased to eleven. Each was to have its own elected ministry. In the structure of such elections, the several minorities—whether Muslim, Christian, Parsees or Hindus—were to be safeguarded by the just apportioning of seats, voted for in separate communal electorates. It was in the new constitution that as far as possible each provincial ministry should include ministers selected from the minority parties. The pattern of representation, described as the Communal Award, had been devised by the British premier Ramsay MacDonald after the Round Table Conference to satisfy the minorities, particularly the Muslims. The elections were to be held in the first week of 1937. Early in 1936, the Muslim League met in Bombay and decided to form its own Central Election Board, with Jinnah as President.[15] But in the election that followed, the League though narrowly based and improvised, won only 104 of 489 Muslim votes and most of these were in the Muslim minority areas of north India where it had no prospect of forming a government. It cut a sorry figure in the Muslim majority provinces where Muslim seats were captured by regional Muslim elites. Jawaharlal Nehru was naturally confident after this heartening victory in which the Muslim League got less than five per cent of the Muslim votes that were cast. Early in March 1937, shortly after the election, he said that there were only two parties in the country—"Congress and the British". To this, Jinnah replied, "There is a third party... the Muslims" and added:[16]

> "We are not going to be dictated to by anybody. We are willing to cooperate with any group of a progressive and independent character, provided its programme and its policy correspond to our own. We are not going to be camp-followers of any party. We are ready to work as equal partners for the welfare of India."

Nehru and the Congress spurned Jinnah's offer to work as equal partners. Commenting on this, Sir Percival Griffiths, a former leader of the European Group in Indian Central Legislature wrote:[17]

> "The Congress High Command refused to sanction Congress-League coalitions and in the Hindu majority provinces ministries consisting only of Congressmen were formed. In the United Provinces, for example, Muslim representatives were invited to join the Ministry, but only on the condition that they become members of the Congress party and the Muslim League ceased to exist. In other provinces, similar conditions were imposed, and with one exception, members of the Muslim League were rigorously excluded from office.
>
> The Congress party was fully within its rights in adopting this exclusive policy and may even have felt that it was following normal parliamentary practice. There can be little doubt, however, that it made a grave tactical blunder. There was no difference in social or economic policy serious enough to make Congress-League coalitions unnatural or unworkable and the Muslims therefore felt, rightly or wrongly, that they were excluded from office merely because the Congress was essentially a Hindu body."

This period of misfortune of the League coincided with the earlier decision of the Congress to embark upon a movement of mass Muslim contact in order to bring them within the Congress fold on the basis of a socialist programme and thus wipe out the League out of existence.[18] Muhammad Iqbal in his letters to Jinnah had clearly pointed out, during this period, the poverty of the Muslim masses and the need to concentrate on the economic aspect in order to enlist their adherence to the League causes. He had also before the election of 1937 spelt out the strategy that the League should adopt to ensure the compliance of the regional Muslim League parties with the principles and policies of the All India Muslim League.[19]

> "Indirect election to the Central Assembly had made.it absolutely essential that the Muslim representatives returned to the Provincial Assemblies should be bound by an All India Muslim policy and programme, so that they should return to the Central Assembly only those Muslims who would be pledged to support the specific Muslim questions connected with the Central subjects and arising out of their position as the Second Great Nation of India".

Jinnah never heeded them. But now it was grimly realized that the League must embark upon a massive mobilization effort to organize the Muslim community lest it would not only be alienated from the masses but also in the process would be left out of the political game. Till then, it had not evolved any strategy to integrate the regional political elites into its central structure nor any economic programme for the uplift of the Muslim masses. In his melancholy loneliness, Jinnah, once discovered Iqbal's letters. In a letter, dated 28 May 1937, Iqbal had recorded his firm belief that "to make it possible for Muslim India" to solve its problems, it would be "necessary to redistribute the country and to provide one or more Muslim states with absolute majorities."[20] In an another letter dated 21 June 1937, Iqbal wrote: "... You are the only Muslim in India today to whom the community has a right to look up for safe guidance through the storm which is coming." Jinnah acted upon the suggestions offered in these letters: In a speech at Lucknow on 15 October 1937, he declared "... the majority community have clearly shown their hand that Hindustan is for Hindus." He warned that the present Congress party policy would result in "class bitterness" and "communal war." As Belitho wrote:[21]

> "With the speech at Lucknow, Mohammad Ali Jinnah began his final ascent towards power. There was no longer any confusion in his mind as to the aims of Congress, or the possible fate of the Muslims in India. He talked of the 'sufferings' and 'sacrifice' and the fire of persecution through which deliverance would come; of the nation that would 'emerge' ...Then the characteristic sentence, 'Think on hundred times before you take a decision but once a decision is taken, stand by it as one man."

Now, Jinnah came fully under the captivating spell of Iqbal's ideas and ideologies. Iqbal had earlier suggested him the idea of a separate state as the only rational solution for the Hindu-Muslim problem. Speaking in his presidential address at the Allahabad Annual session of the All India Muslim Legue, Iqbal declared:[22]

> "I would like to see the Punjab, North-West Frontier province, Sind, and Baluchistan amalgamated into a single state. Self-Government within the British empire or without the British empire, the formation of a consolidated North-West Indian Muslim state appears to me the final destiny of the Muslims at least of North-West India".

As a theoretical justification, Iqbal expounded his theory of Muslim communalism. Islam was the sole basis of communal integration which necessarily implied a categorical rejection of any other bases of group cohesion such as culture, language, territory or region. These twin concepts were then harnessed by Jinnah to the service of his political strategy which gave him a bargaining counter in the constitutional tussle going on in India in 1940s. Impelled by these ideological feedback, Jinnah felt emboldened to propound his famous "Two-Nation" theory. India was not a country but a continent. It was inhabited by many communities but Muslims and Hindus were dominant ones. They constituted two distinct nations according to any prevailing conception of nationhood. Muslim's claim to self-determination was an inherent right. So, in expounding his 'Two-Nation' theory, he redefined Iqbal's theory of Muslim communalism as Muslim nationalism and Iqbal's idea of communal autonomy was resurrected as the right to national self-determination for Muslims.[23] The influence of Iqbal on the thinking of Jinnah was evident from his following speech:[24]

> "Hindus and Muslims belong to two different religious philosophies, social customs, literatures. They neither intermarry, nor interdine together and, indeed, they belong to two different civilisations which are based mainly on conflicting ideas and conceptions... It is quite clear that Hindus and Mussalmans derive their inspiration from different sources of history. They have different epics, their heroes are different and different episodes. Very often the hero of one is foe of the other and, likewise, their victories and defeats overlap. To yoke together two such nations under a single state, one as a numerical minority and the other as a majority, must lead to growing discontent, and final destruction of any fabric that may be built up for the government of such a state... Mussalmans are a nation according to any definition of a nation and they must have their homeland, their territory and their state."

Jinnah also took up the earlier suggestion of Iqbal. He launched massive campaign to organise the Muslims in which the major plank became the separate Muslim identity. The League was transformed within a short time from a tenous grouping of middle class elites and landlords into a unified organisation representing the diversities of Indian Islam and together with the integration of the regional Muslim political elites in Bengal and Punjab into its fold it profoundly affected the course of development of Muslim nationalism in India from 1938 to 1947.

On 23 March, 1940 at Lahore Annual Session, the All India Muslim League adopted the famous resolution, popularly known as the Pakistan Resolution demanding the creation of "Independent States" in the North-Western and North-Eastern zones of India which constituted predominantly Muslim majority areas.[25] Henceforth, Jinnah's only mission was to propagate the concept of 'Two-Nations', thereby demolishing the popular myth of a United India nation in order to establish the positive elements of a separate Muslim nationality. The League, led by Jinnah promising a Muslim homeland won a landslide victory in 1945-46 election, capturing ninety per cent of all Muslim seats in India. It won all Muslim seats in the Central Assembly and 428 out of 492 seats in the Provincial Assemblies. He clearly established League's right to speak on the behalf of the Muslim community. The League demanded Pakistan and was finally granted. But what Jinnah said, it was a moth-eaten Pakistan as the two largest provinces of Punjab and Bengal were partitioned to form the new state.

Pakistani nationalism which led to the establishment of Pakistan in 1947 was utterly a pre-modern concept as its proponents never occupied the land they demanded nor they ever lived together in recent or distant past. Its bases were, in fact, community separatism and religion derived nationality. In this sense, it was purely Muslim nationalism or as its critics viewed, Muslim communalism, which became the vehicle for the achievement of Pakistan. The Muslim League used the notion of a separate Muslim identity in forms of Islamic ideology and the "Two-Nations" theory to cut across the diversities of the Muslim community and succeeded temporarily in uniting the fragmented Indian Muslims. It was accomplished at the level of elites through their incorporation into the All-Indian Muslim League and the movement for Pakistan and at the level of masses, through the charismatic leadership of Jinnah and his symbolic appeal of a Muslim homeland.

That Islamic ideology and the "Two-Nations" theory were no more than tools of political expediency sold skillfully to the Muslim masses during the movement became glaringly evident the moment Pakistan started its innings as an independent nation in August 1947. Jinnah forthwith rejected the notion of religious politics.[26] As time rolled by, Pakistani political leadership faced the most formidable task of defining Pakistan's national identity in a manner which would help them to reintegrate Pakistani society at a level that would transcend the mosaic character of the Indian Muslim community. That little thought had gone into this aspect of the problem, of how a Pakistani nation could find its fulfilment in a separate statehood, was itself reflected in the famous Lahore Resolution of March 1940 recallng for some kind of Pakistan.[27] Conceived in the midst of the World War when events were fast occurring, it gave little time for the Muslim League to think of any modern ideas of Pakistani nationhood for which many of its provisions were vague and deliberately kept undefined. For one thing, the nation that was born was not a Pakistani nation as such but an Indo-Islamic nation which would find its homeland in those parts of India where the Muslims were in a majority. and the nature of future relationship between the two Muslim majority areas in the sub-continent was kept purposefully ambiguous. Interestingly enough, the call for Pakistan was given in the name of 'Muslim India', not in the name of the people living in the two Muslim-majority regions. Lastly, most intriguing was the fact that the people in these two parts were to constitute themselves to independent states and not to emerge as a single political entity. To present these facts, is to belabour the point that the dilemma of defining the identity of Pakistani nation was of their own making. It appeared simple to its early leaders and did not pose any problem for the following reasons. In the first place, Pakistan was itself a fulfilment of the political aspiration of the Indo-Islamic community. Secondly, the political elites who presided over the decision-making structure of the government in Pakistan after independence were Indo-Islamic in origin.[28]

Thirdly, the Muslim League, which was controlled mainly by the Hindustanis, dominated the political life of the country to the exclusion of all other organisations. Lastly, the geographically isolated, and politically ineffective, the East Pakistanis could not challenge the Indo-Islamic group of refugee providing leadership in the country. When their first rumbling was heard in Dacca in March 1948, over the language issue, Jinnah was alive and he firmly declared that Urdu would be the national language of Pakistan and there could be no other basis for Pakistani nationhood except the Islamic consciousness of the people in both wings of the country. These helped to sustain the myth of Indo-Islamic unity in the formative years.

Jinnah died in 1948, Liaquat was assassinated in 1951 and with them the domination of the Hindustani, in Pakistan's political life ended. Hereafter, the problem of aggregating the interests of peoples of different regions, specially of the two dominant provinces of Punjab and East Pakistan, became the major problem of Pakistani politics. Though it was grimly realised that Pakistan was a jerry-built state structure reflecting the diversities of its social order, it never appeared to Pakistani leadership that there was a basic contradiction between the manner it was conceived and the measures they have adopted after 1947 to keep it going. In retrospect, it seemed that Pakistani leadership should have adopted the following measures. In the first place, they should have admitted that the most important organic nexus between them was their Indianness. If the idea of subcontinental unity would have been trotted out to feed the masses instead of force-feeding them on an ideational and situational diet of "Islam in danger" and "Down with Hindu India", the integration of Pakistan would have definitely appeared feasible. Secondly, they should have otherwise provided Pakistan an ideology or creed with clear-cut definition with a broad-based domestic consensus. And this should have been reflected in the national polity which alone could have provided major building-blocks for its society. Lastly, this ideology should have been territorially anchored and symbolized by a national organization aggregating interests of the diverse segments of the Pakistani society, particularly of East Pakistanis[29].

Now, with regard to the first, the Pakistani leaders for various reasons stressed their differences with India and adopted many measures, economic and political, to break the ancient cultural and organic links, thereby weakening the concept of an Indo-Islamic Unity. It was only the negative anti-India aspect of this identity that found expression in unfriendly relations between the two countries. Coming to the second, when they stressed the Islamic character of Pakistan as the basis of its national identity, a variety of problems cropped up with the Pakistani elites which was itself divided over the precise meaning of Pakistan's Islamic identity. The mixed character of Pakistani elites' political culture came to the fore in their attempts to define the character of the Muslim nationhood. There was no consensus between the modernists and secularists on the one hand and the traditional religious leadership on the other. While the first group comprised the political elites of the League and the civilian and military bureaucracy, the traditionalists were represented by the Ulemas. The magnitude of their internecine conflict could be easily judged in the manner the Constitution of 1956 tried to effect a compromise between their contending claims.

With regard to the last, it was expected that the Muslim League would fulfil the need, but it belied the expectation because, the exclusively Muslim sectarian character of the League could not be immediately discarded as it had been basis of the League's foundation, and its rejection would have alienated the powerful religious elements. Besides, with the passage of time, the Muslim League came to be dominated by the Punjabi landed gentry whose values and interests ran counter to those of emerging class of bourgeoisie created by the early abolition of zamindari system in East Pakistan[30]. This resulted in a factional conflict within the East Pakistani Muslim League which was itself an amalgam of regional political elites of pre-partition era, each with a different appeal and a different base of support. H.S. Suhrawardy, a strong supporter of a multilingual Bengali state, and A. K. Fazlul Haq, a champion of peasant movement, broke away from Khwaja Nazimuddin, who was closely associated with the nationalist Muslim League. Banking upon the support of the emerging vernacular elites, they mobilized the population based on the demand for East Pakistani autonomy and adoption of Bengali as an official language with equal status of Urdu and destroyed the League in the election of 1954. And it was from the ashes of these elections that the Awami League was born. With the adroit handling of West Pakistan by Suhrawardy and the excellent spade work done by Sheikh Mujibur Rahman and Maulana Abdul Hamid Bhasani in East Pakistan, where the insensitivity of the national political elites to its special problems and their insistence on adoption of Urdu as the sole official language of Pakistan because of their obsessive concern with the Islamic identity were thoroughly exposed, the Awami League emerged as a popular national political organisation, poised for certain victory in the prospective elections of 1959.[31] Had these elections been held and had the Awami League come to power, it would have become the first territorially based, issue-oriented aggregative national political party capable of symbolizing a purely Pakistani nationalism.[32] But the military coup of 1958 nullified these political developments. Ayub abrogated the Constitution of 1956 which was produced after years of protracted wrangling between the political elites of the two wings. Despite its defects it alone provided a common denominator between their divergent views and came to symbolize as an agreement based on a consensus-oriented Pakistani nationalism. The abolition of this Constitution and the postponement of the first general elections seemed, in retrospect, the main destroyers of the burgeoning Pakistani nationalism[33].

Ayub, too, tried in his own way to adopt integrative measures like the amalgation of the West wing, the establishment of Urdu and Bengali as two official languages, a strong central government controlled by civil military bureaucracy and rapid economic development through removal of regional imbalance. But his adoption of a political system based on parity between East and West and the election of representatives through a process of indirect election, called basic democracy and his proscription of political parties destroyed the vernacular elites' sense of participation in the political system. Increasingly they looked upon Ayub's rule as a West Pakistani dominated military-bureaucratic system out to exploit East Pakistan as a colony. And the point of no return came in 1971 during the time of Yahya Khan when Pakistan was dismembered and East Pakistan emerged as a full-fledged independent and sovereign state.

The impact of culture and history was clearly discernible in Pakistan's policy towards India. The crisis of identity in Pakistan had bred a growing sense of insecurity within the country, which found expression in the oft-repeated Pakistani propaganda that India was bent upon its dismemberment. As a scholar notes:[34]

> "So great was the feeling within Pakistan that it might not continue as a single state and so great was the reluctance to admit that the unique nature of their state demanded a unique constitutional arrangement between the two wings that the only escape left for the elite was to attribute all tendencies towards disintegration to persistent Indian machination in this regard."

The fact that relations with India were already strained provided the Pakistani leadership enough political grist to grind against India just to counter the growth of regional sentiments and to cover up the failure of their own measures which had precisely given rise to them. Secondly, its Islamic ideology had also shaped its policy towards the Muslim world. They are treated in greater details in pages to follow.

**Capabilities**

It is widely recognized that the analyst and the decision-maker share one analytical problem when they undertake to estimate and compare the human and non-human resources of a state.[35] The decision-maker is apt to engage in this intellectual task of evaluating the national power of foreign states in order to assess what it is likely to do and whether it has the capacity to support its policies and resist demands made by another. He also makes an appraisal of the relative power of his own state in order to keep it in tune with his own policies being fashioned to underwrite the foreign policy goals. In a similar vein, the analyst also assesses the national power so as to anticipate the choice of the policy-framer and to judge how far it diverges from the operational environment in which he functions. Throughout the course of world history, the perceptions of power have turned out to be "misleading and fleeting" to the statesman and scholars alike.[36] Every age has its own conception of power which cannot play the role of a single yardstick in world politics. Two major perspectives on power emerged out of the older normative "idealism" and the new fangled non-normative "realism" of 1930s which dominated the analysis of international politics in the pre-war period.[37] While space precludes a full-scale discussion of the evolution and growth of this burning concept, suffice it to say that the assumptions that underlay the school of thought that espoused "power as norm" crystallized in the view that power is a quantifiable mass and national power is a function of mobilizable and deployable military force of a state[38]. This tempted the analyst to compare the power of several states on the basis of their military establishments. This notion of power constitutes the central philosophy of the realist school. It found its able adherent in Hans J. Morgenthau, even though he opened the flood-gate of behavioral enquiry by defining power as a psychological relation.[39] The second perspective utilized the term "power" but in a truly non-normative sense of capability analysis.[40] He conceived power in terms of behavioural relationship and viewed the political relations of states as basically a problem of interaction between states. So, to cast the interaction of states in functional terms, he redefined the term "power" to denote relationship between states involving military conflict but used the term "influence" to connote a conflict of interest containing no trace of violence. Again to explain the totality of effect which a state's activity exerts in aggregate on the behaviour of other states, he fused the two terms into one semantic whole and conceptualized it as "Political Potential" that embraced both "military power" and "non-military influence".[41] Then he went on to trace empirically the ways in which the human and non-human factors set limits and provide opportunities to the "political potential" of states. This led to distinguish between the capability analysis and foreign policy analysis. He drew a sharp distinction between the relation of environmental factors to foreign policy decision on the one hand and to the operational results of the decision on the other. He concluded that environmental factors enter into both types of analysis but they become relevant to policy decision only to the extent that the decision-maker perceives them and takes them into account even if such factors are not perceived and accounted for in the formulation of policies?[42] A capability analyst is required to explain or predict the operational results of the decision. On the basis of enquiry of concrete cases, an analyst can assess the political potential of a given state. Still the problem persists. While he views that national power is a relational phenomenon and two dimensional embracing both possessed resources and interaction phenomena, nevertheless, he fails to conclude that national power can only be understood in terms of how the states relate to each other.[43] The resources which each state possesses are certainly relevant to the way in which they perceive each other but the outcome of the way they bring to bear power upon each other is determined by how they assess, accept or modify each other. The possessed dimension of power may not lead to desired outcome if those against whom it is directed perceive it otherwise. While possession of requisite resources enables one to move towards foreign policy goals, they must be appropriate to the situation involved. This naturally acquires a relational phenomena as the appropriateness to a given situation involves the resources and responses of other states. In such a situation, the analyst is forced to focus on both the resources and interaction dimensions for empirically assessing the capabilities of two or more states. This enables the state to engage not only in conflicting but also in cooperative issues facing it. It was James N. Rosenau who disaggregated the concept "power", dropped it altogether from his analytical vocabulary, reconceptualized "capabilities" which denote the resource and attribute dimensions while introducing a new term "control" to embrace the interaction phenomena of power.[44] In our treatment of the variable "capabilities", we have adopted this conceptualization. The ensuing analysis serves to show that the elements comprising the resource and attribute dimension of Pakistan affected its capabilities that has conditioned its foreign policy behaviour.

**Geography**

The most enduring factor influencing foreign policy decision of a nation is its geography which not only includes its strategic location to other land masses and waterways but the configuration of its land, its fertility and climate also. It naturally determines how far a nation can be self-sufficient and what is most essential for the realization of its foreign policy goals. It also influences the perceptions of its decision-makers of what they should do in order to fashion its political, economic and strategic links with the outside world. As a matter of fact, geopolitical thinking in the ordinary parlance of political speculation has an intellectual lineage that dates back to the hoary past of Kautilya and Aristotle. But as a more pervasive doctrine of modern times, it was propounded by the French philosopher Victor Cousin in the early nineteenth century.[45] As the century rolled on, it found its able adherents like Alfred Mahan, Halford Mackinder in the first half of the present century. Even statesmen also unequivocally shared this which can be gleaned from the remarks of French diplomat Jules Cambon way back in 1930. He wrote; "The geographical position of a nation...is the principal factor conditioning its foreign policy, the principal reason why it must have a foreign policy at all."[46]

It is plausible to argue that geopolitical thinking as a factor shaping foreign policy behaviour of a state has been downgraded with the advent of thermo-nuclear age which has witnessed impressive progress in the realm of cybernetics, rocketry, and chemical warfare. Yet it is equally fallacious to conclude that geography as an isolating factor has been altogether eliminated in the strategic thinking of the decision-makers of small or big states.[47] Certainly this factor is less salient than it was a half-century ago and industrial potential and technological progress have added new dimensions to the capabilities of States. Still it continues to function as independent and relational variable which is clearly evident from the works of present day scholars who have recognized a positive correlation between the environmental factors and the political phenomena and have made an analytical distinction between the relation of environmental factors to foreign policy decision on the one hand and to the operational results of the decision on the other. They have spawned new concepts, categories and theories to fruitfully analyse their impact[48]. In case of Pakistan, the purpose is to trace how geography has played the role of a relational variable of its capabilities which had conditioned its foreign policy behaviour during the period under analysis.

It is a well-known fact that the way Pakistan was born and composed of has few parallels in the history of modern times and this partly explained why geography weighed so enormously on its foreign policy thinking. Carved out of an organic British India in an orgy of communal holocaust on the basis of the "Two-Nation" theory, its two far-flung Muslim-dominated areas of East and West came to constitute the east and west wings of modern Pakistan separated by more than one thousand miles of sprawling Indian territory. The geographical features of the two wings differed so diversely that it could well be treated as two distinct geographical units for which it had earned the epitah ranging from "a double country" to "two separate land masses". Even some called it uncharitably, "a geographical monstrosity". As a matter of fact, there is an element of truth in each of these statements.

Geographically, West Pakistan consisted of three well-marked topographical divisions; the mountainous North and the North-West; the table-land of Baluchistan to the West of mountain wall and the plains of the Indus River basin. But, on the whole, West Pakistan had fertile land whether it be the dry hill sub-region of North-West that nestles the plain of Peshawar, Bannu and Dera Ismail Khan irrigated by canals emanating from Kabul and Swat or the plains of the Indus basin stretching from the foothills of North and North-West to the Arabian Sea on the South-West comprising the main bastion of agricultural productivity of the country, despite the arid plateau of Baluchistan and the mountainous range of the inhospitable Himalayas and the Hindukush. The climate was dry and hot. And the rainfall was scanty, a gambling in the monsoon. More than half of the area received less than ten inches of rainfall a year and the rest less than twenty inches. Agriculture, the mainstay of the economy, was mercifully dependent upon irrigation by canals drawn from the Indus and its tributaries. The three Western rivers—the Indus, Jhelum and Chenab flew into Pakistan from the present state of Jammu and Kashmir of the Indian union and eastern rivers Ravi, Beas and Sutlej, enter into Pakistan from India. The Radcliffe Line was so drawn that both the Madhopur Headwork on the Ravi river and the Ferozepur Headwork on the Sutlej river which controlled the entire irrigation system in the West Pakistan remained on the Indian side of border which put India in a position to interfere with the flow of irrigation water to Pakistan[49]. In contrast to this, the East Pakistan continued to be one of the largest deltaic regions of the world formed by two largest rivers of Asia the Ganges and the Brahmaputra known respectively in the lower reaches of East Pakistan as Padma and Jamuna. The land was a vast alluvial plain with tangled hills in east and north-east with foothills of the Himalayas spreading to north. The entire land mass was interspersed with numerous streams and rivulets which formed the net-work of its transport system. Its monsoon climate gave it an average rainfall of one hundred inches a year and nearly thirty to forty per cent of the land is inundated in flood. In the months following monsoon there used to be a heavy scarcity of water. However, there were few roads, few railways.

Boats were principal means of the transport. But it was a fertile region producing huge quantities of rice and jute.[50]

This geographical dualism presented Pakistan a two pronged problem-one for the country as a whole and the other between its two unequal regions, whose economic and strategic dimensions stood out most strikingly prominent as it served to shape its capabilities. On the economic plane, it has been well researched how it broke the organic growth of the economy fostered under the long period of British Raj with its concomitant specialization and symbiotic interdependence. The complementarity between the raw material and industry, between the product and the consumer was lost.[51] And the partition also left Pakistan with a narrow resource base in basic minerals, thus foreclosing her chances of becoming a modern industrial nation in near future. Besides, the policy adopted by successive governments for the intra-regional transfer of resources for bridging the gap did not bear fruit as the investment in the socio-economic overhead did not have a significant spread-over effect in the west wing leading to a heightened sense of deprivation on the part of the East Pakistan.[52]

On the strategic plane, it created two sets of frontier implying eight rather than four boundaries which served to compound its geo-military problems. Scholars argue that Pakistan with its divided territories was both a West Asian and South-East Asian country and this has led to different strategic interests[53]. This contention emanated from the fact that in the policy-making process there was a dominance of the West Pakistani elites whose conception of national interest was coterminous with their own vested interest. And to advance their point that the Muslim nations close to the West Pakistan were considered more important for security reasons than areas closer to the East Pakistan, they also claimed that Pakistan joined CENTO and SEATO to protect its western and eastern wings respectively. It is a truism that the people of the East Pakistan developed different perception of strategic interest being divorced from the mainstream of national life for the lack of communication, but empirical facts pointed to the view that this never influenced the core group of the strategic decision-makers even if the majority of them constituted the West Pakistan elites[54]. This was precisely for a variety of reasons. In the first place, elites, however, dominant they may be in the decision-making structure, cannot conceive the foreign policy of a nation in any other term than the national interest designed to preserve or modify existing international environment for the promotion of the good of the country, even if one can challenge their conception of national interest to be good or bad. As objective conditions undergo change, the policy-makers are forced to make appraisal of the policy. This had also happened in case of Pakistan. The geopolitical realities of Pakistan dictated a policy of non-alignment, which was the main guide post of its foreign policy in the early phase of its carrier. But it abandoned this stance for many compelling reasons and chose to become an advanced out-post of the Western-orchestrated moves to contain the rising wave of communism in the world and turned to be "the most allied ally" of the United States in Asia. But soon it read the writings on the communist wall, when Nikita S. Khrushchev declared: "From the lofty rostrum of the Soviet Union we warn once again those countries which make their territory available for the take off of planes with anti-Soviet intentions—do not play with fire, gentlemen."[55] This led to an agonizing reappraisal on the part of Pakistan as to whether their alliance with distant Americans had really benefitted them sufficiently to risk elimination at the hand of the next-door nuclear Super Power. Henceforward, they down-played their ideological affinity with the West and stressed more on their geographical proximity to the Soviet Union and China.[56]

That Pakistan took the Soviet threat seriously was born out by the fact that following the U-2 incident, it informed the United States that the use of Pakistan's airfield in future, even by unarmed American aircraft would have to be more firmly controlled by Pakistan. And the American aircraft would be able to use its airfield only after firm assurances had been given as to where they would go after they left Pakistan[57]. While one may ascribe the changes in Pakistan's foreign policy in the early sixties to numerous variables, still one found a permanent streak of geopolitical consideration that lent decisive weight. An authoritative exposition of this policy of bilateralism is contained in Mohammad Ayub Khan's autobiography where he noted:[58]

> "Take the geographical location first. Here is East Pakistan surrounded on three sides by India and the only approach is from the sea which is not difficult for an enemy to control. West Pakistan is wedged in between three enormous powers with the Soviet Union at the top, the people's Republic of China in the northeast and India in the south and east. I know of no other small country which has the somewhat dubious distinction of having three such mighty neighbours. Now, this location is a source of weakness in physical

terms but it could be converted into a source of strength if we could establish normal and mutually acceptable relations with the countries hemming us in".

Secondly, Pakistan has tried to ensure its security marginally by cultivating friendship equally with both the West Asia and the South-east Asia. This was borne out by the fact that it reached amicable border agreements with Iran with whom it had around 590 miles long frontier and with Burma which claimed more than 100 miles of its territory. Given common historical legacy of Burma and Pakistan, since both of them were part of British India, they had nursed a common fear of being absorbed forcibly within India. It was largely in view of these geopolitical realities, Pakistan looked upon Burma as a de facto ally in the common cause of defence against India, which was deemed as potentially aggressive[59]. It was geography and strategic considerations that have deepened their relations. The case was a little different in case of Iran where the past intruded the present. The very mention of the name of Iran raised before the Pakistani eye the great and immortal images of people like Al Beruni, Firdausi and others. Their shared faith and culture coupled with their ancient ties and traditions had led to a perceptual convergence of their strategic environment. Russian Bear was their real betenoire. The traditional Russian temptation of the Levant for oil resources of the West Asia and for access to the warm water-ports of the Indian ocean brought both Iran and Pakistan together which saw its culmination in the formation of the Central Treaty Organisation. Ayub echoing the Russian fear remarked: "As a student of war and strategy, I can see quite clearly the inexorable push of the North in the direction of the warm waters of the Indian Ocean".[60] Besides, Russian dominance in the affairs of Afghanistan is a matter of historical record. Even if Pakistan had given up its self-image as the legalities of the British side in the Great Game of Central Asian politics, still the rumblings of Russian fear lurked in the outer periphery of Afghanistan where a small strip of territory divided Pakistan from Russia. At one point, the Wakhan Tongue, as it was called, was only eight miles wide and it was possible to look across from Pakistan to the U.S.S.R. Pakistan controlled the northwest mountain passes through which a physical invasion of the Indian subcontinent was a historical fact. It was through these passes that the British in the nineteenth century, feared an invasion of the sub-continent by the Russians who were extending their empire in Central Asia[61]. Given the unhappy relationship between Pakistan and Afghanistan, Russian support to the latter on the "so-called Pakhtoonistan issue" (which involved major territorial claims on ethnic consideration advanced by Afganistan repudiating the Durand Line, the historic frontier between Afghanistan and British India, as a product of British imperialism), reinforced Pakistan's sense of insecurity. Here geography became Pakistan's unmitigating sorrow which she could neither hide nor lay bare. Similarly, Pakistan never joined SEATO to protect its east wing. There was clear evidence to suggest that from the very beginning, Pakistan never thought of any threat from China.[62] Zulfikar Ali Bhutto once remarked:[63] Given geography and power realities, the military threat to us, if there is one, would come more from the Soviet Union than from China". In fact, in the geopolitics of today, neither Pakistan nor China could afford to lose the other's goodwill. Pakistanis were fully conscious that China was the only big power which supported it on the crucial issue of Kashmir and would likely to continue to uphold them in future confrontation with India. China, too, could hardly disregard the fact that Pakistan was not only a highly strategic neighbour but currently also the largest country in the world friendly to her.[64] And the very fact that Pakistan concluded a border treaty with China amicably at the height of the Sino-Indian border clash and China unequivocally supported it in the Indo-Pakistan War of 1965 and 1971 confirmed the above contentions.

Thirdly, given the Indo-Pakistan hostilities over the last twenty-five years, the major threat to the territorial personality of Pakistan was undoubtedly India. The geographical diversity has compounded Pakistan's strategic dilemma because the common border of its East and West wings with India ran for more than 4000 miles, but this had not broken the unified strategic thinking of its decision-makers as their policies had been dominated by considerations of security and independence from its neighbour, India[65]. If the dominant view expressed by military planners from time to time that the West Pakistan must be made the first bulwork of defence against a military threat to Pakistan, the reasons were obvious. Pakistan within 25 years of existence had gone on war with India thrice. And wars had been fought in the Sind-Rajasthan-Punjab border. To its north lies the ceasefire line which was a fragile line, a line of uneasy separation between Indian-held Kashmir and Pakistani-held Azad Kashmir since 1949. It was being observed by a token presence of the United Nations Peace-keeping Force. The very fact that India crossed this international boundary line and did not invade East Pakistan at all underscored the strategic importance which West Pakistan possessed compared to its east wing, leaving aside the political considerations that might have influenced India. The major propelling reason seemed to be that India, in possession of Kashmir could make Pakistan strategically vulnerable. Birwood has highlighted this point:[65]

> "It was Radcliffe's award to India of the Gurdaspur and Batalla tehsils, with Muslim majority, which rendered possible the maintenance of an Indian force at Jammu based on Pathankot as railhead end which enabled India to consolidate her defences southwards all the way from Uri to the Pakistan border."

Further, Pakistan was narrow from the north to the south. The overall pattern of its border with India was generally flat. Its major cities of the West were fairly close to India. Every area in the West was literally a part of the frontier zone. It was an area where the tanks could roll easily well, whether it be the desert of Rajasthan, or plains of Punjab. Even its seaport, Karachi in the western flank, was vulnerable and could be blockaded very easily. This largely explained why Western wing had claimed the core component of defence planning and also underlay their disappointment. As a milatary strategist viewed:[67]

> "Ideally a country is safe when it has a very large area but a very small frontier to defend; on the other hand, a country that has a small area but, must defend its entire frontier is very precariously placed. Pakistan happens to be in that difficult position. Although we have a large surface area we must defend our entire frontier, 1100 miles on the east... an equal number of miles on the west... And we have a coastline of almost 500 miles to defend, then in the north we have a not very friendly neighbour (USSR)."

So the empirical facts cited above pointed to an irresistable conclusion that in the conception of security of the country as a whole, the planners did not betray a dichotomic view of Pakistan's geopolitical compulsions. Its decision to open the "Silk Route" linking Sinkia'ng with Gilgit to the Chinese, whose military significance is well known, further confirmed this. It is very often argued that Pakistan's geography dictated for a co-operative relations with India which could have strengthened her economically, militarily and politically to play a dominant role in the world politics, but the history of their independent existence had sadly ignored the timely advice of Sir Zafrullah Khan who once remarked:[68]

> "Their very situation, their economy, the considerations of their defence and security demand that they ought to stand in friendly, cooperative relationship with each other".

## Size

Scholars have tended to view the size of the nation as one of its major attributes conditioning the psychological and operational environment of its strategic decision-makers in particular and the people in general. As size comprises both human and non-human resources or lack of them, it serves to underlie how the decision-makers view the place of their nation in the overall scheme of world affairs. It is argued that people of a small nation tend to cultivate subconsciously a low-profile of their world image, while the people of a bigger state deem it as their pre-ordained destiny to be the prime-mover of world politics. But history of nations past and present very often refutes such a contention of its universal validity. It bears ample testimony that while small nations have swayed world politics to cataclysmic changes, bigger ones have failed miserably to make even a marginal mark. While so many variables can be teased out for this, the general hypothesis, that the correlation between size and resources is a high one[69], holds good. Now, the purpose of our enquiry is to test this hypothesis on the basis of empirical facts culled out from Pakistan's foreign policy within the framework of its treatment as a relational variable of its capabilities.

Pakistan commenced the innings of its career as an independent state with a glorious vision of its future. Comprising a total area of 364,737 square miles[70] with a population of 80,000,000, it was perched on the bridgehead between Asia and Europe for which it was deemed as one of the bigger nations of the world in terms of its population and geo-political significance. As a matter of fact, Pakistan was the largest Muslim state and the fifth largest country in the world. It was naturally expected that destiny had thrust upon it a potential role in the exciting political development of the Asian and the world affairs. Quaid-i-Azam Mohammad Ali Jinnah's statement addressed to the people on the first anniversary of its independence undoubtedly underscored the primacy of Pakistan when he remarked:[71] "Nature has given you everything; you have got unlimited resources. The foundations of your state have been laid and it is, now for you to build..." While one may conclude that this statement was a political gimmick couched in the rhetoric of an exhortation to the people to imbibe a sense of primacy of their nationhood in the world but it certainly never constituted the major component of the operational environment of its founding father who gave shape and content to its statehood in the initial years of its existence. It simply caught the essence of euphoric spirit animating every Pakistani on the morrow of its independence. But an attempt at throwing light on various aspects of its foreign policy would reveal unmistakably how size has conditioned the psychological and operational environment of its decision-makers, which partly explained why they failed to play a decisive role in the Asian developments and the world affairs, no matter what political rhetorics they indulged in for inducing an illusion of grandeur among the masses that bigness of its size made apparently vivid.

However, it will be more germane to our point of analysis to undertake a synoptic survey of its size as defined by the present day theorists to include both human and non-human resources. In the first place, coming to the non-human resource dimension, one finds Pakistan's resource base was too narrowly constricted to enable it to underwrite an ambitious foreign policy that the bigness of size entitled her. Being basically and predominantly an agrarian economy with a constantly rising population, any hope for raising the living standard of its people lay in rapid industrialization that would ultimately lead to an enhancement of its capabilities. As agriculture and industry are symbiotic what is needed for catching up with advanced industrialised nations is, an adequate natural resource of power and basic minerals. While technological progress has minimised the importance of natural resources, still the growth of advanced technology itself presupposes a certain level of industrialisation which is itself impossible to be achieved without a reasonable degree of resource potential. The present economic and military power enjoyed by the two superpowers can be explained partly in terms of their vast re source base. Undoubtedly, resources make the differential between two states with the same level of technological progress. A close perusal of statistics reveals that Pakistan lacked basic ingredients of power, coal, petroleum, hydro-electricity and natural gas and also minerals, iron ores, chromite and magnanese.[72] The coal reserves estimated between 160,000,000 to 200,000,000 tons were concentrated in the west and they were of high sulphur and ash content, and difficult of exploitation for its remoteness. Although its production doubled reaching a million tons a year, still it fell short of requirements which necessitated import of high grade coals. Similarly, the position was frustrating with regard to petroleum whose drilling and access were difficult in the remote western deserts and eastern jungles. Only a fifth of a country's needs were produced from the five small fields of Punjab. The big refineries of Karachi relied on supply from Gulf States. Though this problem was partly obviated by the discovery of natural gas in Sui of Bugh Hills near Karachi, yet the reserves could hardly last for four hundred years at the present rate of consumption. With regard to power, position looked up when complete dependence on thermal plants was supplanted by development of hydro-electricity and construction of National Water Grid. Still it was the west Pakistan with an installed capacity of 500,000 k.w. in 1963 which was the principal supplier. But it could not ensure the self-sufficiency for the country as a whole. Nature was not bounteous in endowing Pakistan with its rare gifts of minerals too. The position with regard to the deposits of iron ores was equally frustrating. Remoteness remained an insuperable problem for exploitation. The only known deposits of high grade iron ores lay in Chitral and North-west Baluchistan. Again antimony, chromite and manganese were a dream, a mere scratch on the surface. However, it can be concluded that the position of the country as a whole offered little scope for indigenous bases for progressive industrialization that could have taken the country out of the morass in which it found itself on the eve of its partition.

Coming to the human resources dimension, one found that Pakistan was the fifth largest country in the world in terms of population. As argued earlier, what makes differential between a big and small state is not only its non-human resources but also its human population. While traditional theorists have tended to distinguish between the qualitative and quantitative components of human factors, present day scholars emphasise the attribute of skill of the population as a salient factor in shaping the capabilities of states.[73] But the skill is determined by the quality of education imparted to the people by the Government which in turn depends to a large extent upon the educational policy followed by it.

It is well-known, long period of colonial rule had sapped the self-sufficient economy of undivided India and turned it as the producer of agricultural and mineral raw materials for the metropolitan capitals. The educational system introduced by the Britishers perpetuated their political and economic structure in India which failed to answer the problems of hunger, disease, illiteracy, poverty and unemployment that stared the Pakistanis after partition. It became imperative on their part to seek solution to these crying problems in the languages of science and technology, so that in a brief span of time they could enhance its capabilities to "catch up" with the rest of the world. Jinnah understood this and made a fervent plea in the first All Pakistan Educational Conference held in Karachi on 27 November 1947, where he said:[74]

> "...The importance of education and the right type of education cannot be overemphasized. Under foreign rule for over a century in the very nature of things, I regret sufficient attention has not been paid to the education of our people, and if we are to make any real,

> speedy, and substantial progress, we must earnestly tackle this question and bring our educational policy and programme on the lines suited to the genius of our people... having regard to the modern conditions and vast developments that have taken place all over the world... There is immediate and urgent need for training our people in the scientific, and technical education in order to build up our future economic life..."

In consonance with his wishes, the successive Governments of Pakistan in the last twenty five years, have committed themselves with single-minded devotion to solving country's pressing problems for enhancing its capabilities through the application of science and technology. But educational policies persued in the first three Five Year Plans continued to reflect the elitist bias and a selective approach to the expansion of various level of education. In the First Five Year Plan (1955-60) over 56 per cent of the education budget was earmarked for secondary and higher education. Technical education claimed barely 9 per cent of the budget. The main rationale behind this policy for favouring higher education was to provide highly qualified people for the bureaucracy which showed that planners have not freed themselves from the psychological grip of the colonial era. However, things underwent a drastic change with the coming into power of Ayub Khan. He appointed in 1958 a high-level Commission on National Education. It came up with two basic sets of recommendations:[75] One relating to the concept of education as an investment in national growth or as an economic investment... and other dealing with national integration. To underwrite its first objective it clearly highlighted the need for science and engineering study. It was the most neglected sector of the national education system. While favouring its massive expansion, it called for "...tapping the as yet unknown and unexploited wealth in our soil, our water and the products of our land and by discovering and developing processes for utilising those materials and resources to the full". Accordingly, in the Second Five Year Plan (1960-65), the trend was reversed. There were substantial increases for primary and technical education. As a result, 36 per cent of the educational budget was devoted to higher and secondary education. Underscoring the goals of his educational reform, Ayub observed:[77]

> "The plan provides for more and better primary schools, sufficient to educate three out of five of our children by 1965. It proposes to increase the number of students in secondary schools by a quarter and to expand the scale of University education. There is a special emphasis on technical education for, in this age of science and technology, we can make no progress if we do not develop technical

skills of a high order. Education is an investment in human resources and on it, more than any other single factor, depends the social and economic development of the nation".

**Table 1**

**Percentages of Allocated Funds Spent on Some Important Subsectors of Education[78]**

| *Subsector* | *First* | *Second* | *Third* |
|---|---|---|---|
| Primary | 18.0 | 14. 7 | 13.6 |
| Secondary | 26. 7 | 16. 9 | 20.8 |
| Teacher Training | 6. 6 | 4. 7 | 3.5 |
| Technical | 8.8 | 15. 6 | 26.0 |
| College | 13. 1 | 10. 6 | 8.2 |
| University | 15. 0 | 12. 6 | 11.7 |
| Other | 11. 8 | 24. 9 | 16.2 |
| Total | 100.0 | 100.0 | 100.0 |

Technical education took a big stride when 25 to 30 new polytechnique schools were established. Encouraged by the success of the Second Plan, the government adopted an ambitious educational development strategy aimed at broadening the base of scientific and technical education. In the Third Plan, massive annual enrolments were envisaged for polytechnique schools, engineering colleges, and universities. The plan favoured the opening of two new engineering colleges, two general universities, ten new colleges exclusively for science education. Most of the measures were implemented. Further progress was achieved during Yahya Khan. In March 1970, he announced a New Education Policy. It called for the reorientation of educational programme in the light of the economic needs of the society, particularly by shifting the emphasis to scientific, technical and vocational education.

One found that between 1960-71, there were 38,000 Bachelors of Science, over 12,500 Masters of Sciences in various branches of the discipline. During the same period, over 1,000,000 students completed 12 years of schooling with science as their major interest. By 1970, 11,000 students enrolled in various polytechnics, while the number of students in the industrial and vocational schools exceeded by 7,000. By the end of Ayub era, the educational system has taken long strides in Pakistan.

But with regard to its second objective of promoting national integration, the commission emphasized on learning the national language at the primary stage, holding a daily assembly to sing the national anthem, periodically hoisting the national flag, and giving inspirational talk on patriotism.[80] For secondary school, emphasis was put on the national culture and Islamic values[81]. Some concrete steps were taken to fulfil this

**Table 2**

**Output of Educated Persons, 1960-61 and 1970-71**[79]

| Year | Matriculation (000) | | Intermediate (000) | | Degrees All Subjects | | M.B.B.S. | | Masters All Subjects | | LLB |
|---|---|---|---|---|---|---|---|---|---|---|---|
| | Total | Female | Total | Female | Total | Female | Total | Female | Total | Female | Total |
| 1960-61 | 55.4 | 6.7 | 14.6 | 2.5 | 9,156 | 1,500 | 559 | 131 | 1,305 | 228 | 487 |
| 1961-62 | 50.9 | 7.6 | 15. 1 | 3.0 | 9,713 | 1,811 | 532 | 140 | 1,930 | 417 | 85 |
| 1962-63 | 72.5 | 11.5 | 27.1 | 4.9 | 12,494 | 2,085 | 607 | 194 | 2,437 | 576 | 880 |
| 1963-64 | 69.7 | 10.9 | 24.8 | 4.3 | 13,628 | 2,352 | 638 | 179 | 2,976 | 708 | 1,039 |
| 1964-65 | 72. 1 | 11.5 | 30.3 | 6.0 | 16,250 | 3,278 | 625 | 164 | 3,931 | 940 | 1,134 |
| 1965-66 | 83.5 | 14.1 | 31.3 | 5.7 | 20,259 | 3,826 | 736 | 190 | 4,631 | 1,062 | 1,358 |
| 1966-67 | 98.0 | 18.1 | 39.8 | 7.0 | 20.426 | 4,425 | 440 | 120 | 6,009 | 1,638 | 1,204 |
| 1967-68 | 103.5 | 19.4 | 49.4 | 10.2 | 23,404 | 4,917 | 608 | 118 | 5,976 | 1,525 | 839 |
| 1968-69 | 114.8 | 25.3 | 51.6 | 10.8 | 23,922 | 5,629 | 752 | 190 | 6,334 | 1,707 | 1,080 |
| 1969-70 | 136. 1 | 29.0 | 62.5 | 12.5 | 37,539 | 8,094 | 1,002 | 261 | 8,493 | 1,863 | 1,661 |
| 1970-71 | 139.9 | 31.2 | 59.2 | 13.3 | 35,185 | 9,526 | 942 | 211 | 7,493 | 1,863 | 1,661 |

goal. New history books were written which upgraded Emperor Aurangzeb, the symbol of Islamic orthodoxy and downgraded Emperer Akbar who projected a synthesis of Hinduism and Islam. The Muslim past of the West Pakistan was emphasized and its historical roots were linked with the pre-Hindu civilization of Mohenjodaro ignoring the Hindu interregnum. East Pakistan was shown as the modern successor to Buddhist religion converted Islam in 13th century. Muslim monuments like Taj Mahal, Red Fort and the Jama Masjid, though based in India, were presented as belonging to Pakistan in several geography books.

The foregoing analysis shows that the educational policies pursued by the successive Governments, particularly during Ayub Khan's tenure, have served to lay the foundation of a manpower resource equipped with scientific knowledge and technological know.how to usher in progressive industrialization to enhance the capabilities of the country. But, as a matter of fact, Pakistan had still to go[82] a long way to become a major power. The educational policies were yet to make a major dent on the problems of health, shelter, poverty and unemployment which continued to bedevil the Pakistani society and retard its progress. Besides, instead of promoting national integration it simply served to further embitter Pakistan's relation with India as a second generation of children grew up with distorted image of India.

This must have impressed upon the policy-makers the problems and possibilities of their state to function in a broader operational environment of the world in which both human and non-human resources set definite limits to the formulation and prosecution of foreign policy goals. Functioning in the context of the South Asia subordinate system, this problem was compounded because India became the major component of its operational environment. Given the unhappy relation between them and inability of Pakistan to get reconciled to the status of a small state in the subcontinent in which India was the larger neighbour, the operational environment of its successive decision-makers converged on the psychological environment of its founding fathers in broadly two ways; as their struggling present, enlivened by the fears wrapped in the mantle of the bitter past, projected the hopes of a rosy future. This partly explained its continuing predicament.

In the first place, the past of Pakistan was its freedom movement leading to partition from the undivided British India in an orgy of communal holocaust, an event not too distant in time to be pushed into the oblivion. For, its memory was too sordid, too bitter and hang, on enormously on the psyche of its people and policy-makers of the first generation to be effaced away with the passage of time. The event marked "a complete emotional upset of all the people in India and Pakistan." Beyond this, it should be noted that the Muslim League started its movement on the major plank of demand for parity of status between 25 per cent Muslim minority and the rest of India during British Raj. It ultimately reached its apogee with the demand for Pakistan on the basis of 'Two Nation' theory as the relative status of the two communities could not be ironed out by any rational solution. But it is a matter of historicity that the Muslim League was not lukewarm to the idea of two communities coexisting in a loose confederation as proposed by the Cabinet Mission plan. But when freedom was unhered in with the partition of the subcontinent into two sovereign states instead of a formal endorsement of the concept of two nations in Indian state, the problem of parity of status took on increasingly the garb of a status conflict between two independent states which was hardly distinguishable from the old rivalry of the Indian National Congress and the Muslim League. Jinnah had never agreed to any constitutional formula which would have denoted a lesser status for the Muslim League[84]. "India contained two nations: one sovereign nation is the equal of any other sovereign nation." This was the article of faith of its founder and he did not compromise with it after Pakistan acquired international personality in 1947. Even today, as Selig S. Harrison wrote:[85]

> "...Pakistan searches restlessly and endlessly for a degree of recognition and respect out of all proportion to its size. It huffs and puffs and still finds to its understandable despair that India is bigger. Each provocation from Pakistan, each gesture of self-assertion and definance serves to strengthen the demand in India to put Pakistan in its place."

Secondly, the present of Pakistan was one of ominous forebodings and inhospitable receptions. Distrust, the main basis of old rivalry continued to haunt the two states in all its virulence even after many years of their independent statehood. Dr. Prasad was writing in 1946 accurate when he observed:[86]

> "It is difficult to forecast what shapes this conflict may take in future... Distrust which is the basis of the proposal is bound to grow and any hope, that after separation things will settle down and the

independent states will soon become friendly, will have been build on sand..."

Years have passed by. One still found the nembers of passion not cooled down. Pakistan feared that it might be again reabsorbed in a Greater India. Many responsible Indian leaders, even after the partition, toyed with the idea of a re-union. This can be understood from their statements. Maulana Abul Kalam Azad had written that Sardar Patel was convinced that the new state of Pakistan was not viable, and could not last. It would collapse within a short time. He also expressed the full hope and confidence that sooner or later we would again be reunited in common allegiance to our country. Similarly, Mrs. Vijay Laxmi Pandit, in course of a statement in America, declared that her people agreed to partition only as a means of getting rid of the British[88]. Even Acharya Kripalani, the then President of the Indian National Congress, frankly stated: "Neither the Congress nor the nation has given up its claim of a United India." Besides, in the perspective of Pakistanis, India was an expansionist power entertaining imperial ambition. They recalled the statements of Indian political leaders to belabour their point that India envisaged for itself a leadership role in Asia. In the formative years they were panicked by the thesis of "manifest destiny" advanced by K. M. Panikkar, a trusted advisor of Nehru in foreign affairs. They also alleged India of "Brown Imperialism" in Kashmir. To prove their contention they characterized the merger of Goa with India as imperialistic. Similarly, Indian initiative in matters of Asian Cooperation was motivated by the Indian desire to establish itself as the prospective leader of Asia. In later years Pakistani Press and officials reacted bitterly when Johnson on his visit to the Southeast Asia and the South Asia in May 1961 made a statement that he had, on request from President Kennedy, urged Nehru to extend his leadership to other areas of the Southeast Asia[90]. Despite refutation by the United States official, Pakistan was hardly satisfied. The above facts indicated the depth of Pakistan's suspicion of India.

It may be argued that these statements were mere wishful thinkings of the Indian political leaders, as subsequent history had proved that India had not destroyed the territorial integrity of Pakistan, but coming as did from the persons belonging to the highest echelon of Indian policy-makers, it was natural that it queered the pitch for the normalization of relationship between the two states when subsequent actions of the Indian

Government regarding the evacuee property, denial of Ganga waters, refusal of holding a plebiscite in Kashmir lent credence to their statements. It all got enmeshed in conditioning the psychological environment of its early decision-makers. This was unmistakably reflected in the complaint lodged by 'Pakistan with the Security Council in 1948.[91] The Government of Pakistan alleged that "India has never wholeheartedly accepted the partition scheme and has, since June 1947, been making persistent attempts to undo it and that the objective of those in power in India was to "paralyse Pakistan at the very start".[92] So Selig. S. Harrison is right when he observed:[93]

> "Most Hindus would be satisfied with an acquiescent Pakistan within an Indian sphere of influence, some hope for a confederation and a vocal few would welcome an excuse to annul partition by force. Only a hardy band of westernised intellectuals and Congress moderates think in terms of a settlement with Pakistan taking into account Pakistan's own internal compulsions, India appears emotionally incapable of assuming the benign posture which might be expected of her as the overwhelmingly large of the two neighbours."

In view of these above facts, it is really difficult to disagree with what Keith Callard had observed:[94]

> "It follows that the issues of prestige had played a predominant part in Pakistan's relation with India. Many political leaders and most of the articulate section of the population have reacted with emotional intensity to any suggestion of Indian superiority in any field. This was probably the inevitable consequences of the year before Partition."

Coupled with the implacable hostility between the two states, were the differing attitudes of the world's leading powers to both the states in the initial years. While India was looked upon as the land of Gandhi and Nehru destined to play a seminal role in the affairs of mankind, Pakistan was a sad mistake whose future was a haunting question mark on the surface of the globe[95]. While India was a land with ancient tradition and cultural hertiage . Pakistan was a queerest state whose map could not be drawn.[96] While Harry S. Truman had some strange things to say in strong language concerning India and Nehru, his notions concerning Pakistan were exceedingly foggy.[97] Perhaps the last nail that was driven to its coffin was when Afghanistan, a Muslim country and being the only nation voted against its entry into the United Nations in 1948. This engendered a growing concern in Pakistan to resolve all outstanding disputes with its neighbours, particularly with India which was in part a reflection of the government's main objective to ensure a territorial personality of the State. Once the disputes were settled and border demarcated, the nation-state of Pakistan would emerge in full glare of its territorial integrity which would not be subject to challenge. Added to this was what Callard observed:[98]

> "The inevitable first objective of foreign policy had to show the world that Pakistan was a reality and was capable of maintaining its independence."

So the censorious perceptions of each other rooted in their historical experience was honed by the present realities of their operational world. This provided a frame of reference for interpreting each other's behaviour.[99] The interpretations so derived very often confirmed and sustained these images. This cycle has generated a deep mutual distrust in each other and in Pakistan's case an acute perception of threat to its national survival. This explained Pakistan's agonizing quest for military parity with India.

**Military Establishments**

What gave the factors of geography and size of a State its actual importance was its military preparedness and the dependence of the national power upon it is too obvious to need much elaboration. But in case of Pakistan, its deserves a special note, because it started its military establishment almost from a scratch. Describing the state of total disarray of the armed forces on the eve of its independence, Mohammad Ayub Khan ruefully remarked:[100]

> "When... Partition came, our man from units in India began to trickle back into Pakistan in small groups. In some cases they were unarmed and in others they had to fight their way out. So we had to start our army with bits and pieces like a gigantic jig-saw puzzle with some of the bits missing.
>
> ... Our army was badly equipped and terribly disorganised... We had no properly organised units, no equipments, and hardly any ammunition. The position was so bad that for the first few years we could only allow five rounds of practice ammunitions to each man a year. Our plight was indeed desperate."

The British Government decided on 1 July 1947 that Independent India and Pakistan would acquire operational control of the armed forces by 15 August, but administrative control was to continue under the supreme command, until the respective Governments were in a position to control and maintain their separate armed forces. Along with the establishment of the supreme command under the aegis of Field Marshal Auchinleck, a Joint Defence Council was set up, which was entrusted with task of making a fair and equitable distribution of the material assets of the British Indian Army between India and Pakistan. On the basis of an agreement on 24 September 1947, the Council agreed for the following figures of Units between India and Pakistan.

**Table 3**

**Division of Military Assets Between India and Pakistan.** [101]

| *Arms/Services* | *Pakistan* | *India* |
|---|---|---|
| Armoured Corps Regiments | 6 | 14 |
| Artillery Regiments (All types) | 8 | 40 |
| Engineering Groups | 1 | 2 |
| | [major proportion] | [and a part] |
| Infantry Regiments | 8 | 15 |
| | | (Including 6 Gorkha Regiments) |
| Pioneer Companies | 2 | 10 |
| Garrison Companies | 8 | 15 |
| Army Service Corps: | | |
| Supply Units | 23 | 40 |
| Transport (M.T.) | 24 | 53 |
| Transport (A.T.) | 3 | 4 |
| Ordinance Field Units | 4 | 9 |
| Ordinance Static Units | 11 | 32 |
| Workshop Companies E.M.E. | 13 | 20 |
| Medical Units: | | |
| Field | 9 | 18 |
| Specialised | 5 | 14 |
| Remount and Veterinary Units | 28 | 29 |

While officially it was agreed that ordinance shares were to be divided in a ratio of 36 to Pakistan to 64 to India, deliberate changes by India seriously affected Pakistan's position. The following figure shows the differential in regard to what Pakistan was promised and what it actually received.

**Table 4**

**The Differential of Assets Promised and Actually Received**[102]

| *Description* | *Pakistan's share* | *Receipt* |
|---|---|---|
| Ordinance Stores | 160,000 tons | 23, 225 tons |
| Vehicles-soft | 1,461 | 74 |
| Vehicles-armoured (including 118 Sherman and 46 Stuart tanks) | 249 | Nil |
| Ammunition of all types (including explosives) | 40,000<br>60,000 | nil |
| Engineering stores (including machinery) | 172,667 tons | 1,128 tons |

If the Council failed to discharge its function smoothly, it was precisely because allegedly India did not cooperate. As Birdwood later wrote:[103]

"It was Pakistan's bitter complaint that though the Defence Council might allocate stores and supplies to her Army, in fact orders were never translated into action. Pakistan claims that it has received less than justice in the division of military material. For this reason Pakistan viewed the decision to close down the supreme command in November with dismay. They had not received their fair share, and with the abolition of a central independent authority they saw no prospect ever doing so. Nor was the dissolution in accordance with the view of the supreme commander. We are forced to the conclusion that at this stage a certain lack of cooperation on the part of India was gradually undermining the effective functioning of the machinery".

However, Pakistan has moved beyond this, its military establishment grew apace over the years. Though, Pakistan has adopted voluntary military service, the earliest available data indicate that out of the total populace of 94,000,000, its total armed forces has reached the mark of 182,700 of which the army alone claimed 160,000, while navy accounted for 7,700 and the air force 15,000. Of the army, light divisions were organized on a triangular basis and equipped with Patton tanks. There were 25,000 lightly armed militia and about 30,000 Azad Kashmir troops. Of the navy, one finds that there were seven escorts and six mine sweepers. And of the air force there were one squadron consisting of seven B-57 Canberra bombers and one squadron of twelve F-104 fighters. By 1965, before the beginning of Indo-Pakistani war, the strength of the armed forces had gone up and was in the region of 168,000 to 42,080,000, of which army accounted for 160,000 to 180,000, consisting of six infantry divisions out of which one division was earmarked for the East Pakistan. It had also one air defence brigade. The armed forces included about ten regiments with M-47/48 Patton and M-4 Sherman medium tanks, and three regiments with M-24 Chaffee light tanks. These probably formed one armoured division of the two brigades, and a separate armoured brigade. Regarding paramilitary forces, one finds that there were around 70,000 out of which Frontier Corps (of tribesmen) accounted for 25,000, West Pakistan Rangers 10,000, East Pakistan Rifles 10,000 and Azad Kashmir troops 25,000. Coming to the Navy, one finds while its number had not gone up, its acquisition of weapon had changed. By 1965, it consisted of one light cruiser, five destroyers, two Ased fighters, one submarine, eight mine sweepers, four motor launches, and eight other ships, compared to one cruiser, eight destroyers, one frigate, and eleven other-ships in 1962-63. Besides, there was a coastal guard of 1,500 men. Coming to the airforce, one finds it strength had gone up to 20,000 and was in possession of 200 aircrafts. It consisted of two B-57B Canberra squadrons, four F-86F Sabre squadrons, one F-104A star fighter squadrons. Besides, RT-33A planes were used for reconnaissance purposes. And the transport force included 4C-103B Hercules, ten Bristol Mark 21 and Mark 31 tactical fighters and some T-6, T-33 and T.37 B jet trainers. By 1969, the position of the armed forces had undergone drastic changes with regard to both number and acquisition of weapons and formation of the command structure. However, one of the arresting features of this enhanced strength was the rapid increase in the number of paramilitary forces. Its total strength within a span of 15 years reached 200,000 which included frontier troops, armed tribal levies, and local defence units. Pakistan's defence expenditure also sheds enough light on the appreciable progress its defence establishment had registered over the years in terms of men and materials.

**Table 5**

**Defence Expenditure in Pakistan's Economy**[104]

| *Year* | *Defence Expenditure (in US $ million)* | *Defence Expenditure* | | |
|---|---|---|---|---|
| | | *Per Capital U.S. $* | *Of the total Governmental expenditure* | *% of G.N.P.* |
| 1947-48 | 32.4 | - | 50 | - |
| 1950 | 136.8 | - | 51 | - |
| 1961 | 234.2 | - | 58.7 | 3.1 |
| 1963 | 255 (289) | - | 18 | 3.2 |
| 1966 | 601.1 | - | 63.5 | 5.3 |
| 1967 | 468 | - | - | 3.6 |
| 1969 | 545.0 | 4 | 55.6 | 3.4 |
| 1970 | 626.0 | 5 | 53.4 | 5.3 |
| 1971 | 719.0 | 14 | 55.7 | 6.9 |

Behind this phenomenal increase of Pakistan's military capabilities lies American contribution. The Mutual Defense Assistance Agreement of 19 May 1954 and the secret *aide memoire* of 21 October 1954, marked the change in the nature of United States aid to Pakistan from 1954 onwards. These two agreements form both the formal and substantive basis of the Military Assistance Program (MAP) [105]. United States military commitments to Pakistan were further strengthened and substantiated by the latter's membership of the South-East-Asia Treaty Organisation (SEATO) in 1954 and the Baghdad Pact (CENTO) in 1955 and by the subsequent Agreement of Cooperation between the governments of the United States and Pakistan of 5 March 1959[106].

Prior to the military defence agreement with the United States, Pakistan, like India, purchased military equipment in the United States under the Reimbursable Military Assistance Program amounting to $26.5 million. Pakistan's purchases included three hundred and fifty two medium tanks, seventy five 90mm carriages (M36) and various types of ammunition (up to 90mm in size). It had secured these purchase with cash advances and letters of credit[107].

Under the terms of the Mutual Defence Assistance Agreement of 19 May 1954, the United States agreed to furnish military grant assistance to its new ally in South Asia. A survey mission headed by Brigadier General Harry F. Myers visited Pakistan to decide on its most urgent needs. Documents suggest that on the recommendations of General Myers the United States agreed to meet the following deficiencies in Pakistan:

- four infantry divisions and one and a half armoured division
- twelve vessels including destroyers and mine–sweepers.
- six squadrons of aircraft (three fighter–bombers, one interceptor day fighters, one light bomber and one transport) [108].

Provision had also been made for meeting the increased budgetary costs involved in the consumables and construction. This included costs of up to forty thousand additional troops needed to man the new equipment and cantonments, to improve airfields and Karachi harbour, and to provide ancillary equipment. The first United States shipment of military hardware under the new program arrived in Karachi in November 1954.

Pakistan's decision to sign a Mutual Defence Assistance Agreement with the United States was regarded by the Washington policy-makers as evidence of its increased participation in a common front against communism, the United States Government further believed that it was an important move in bringing about Pakistan's complete cooperation in the event of a general war. According to the Mutual Defence Assistance Agreement, the United States was to supply military equipment and training facilities for Pakistan's armed forces in exchange for Pakistan's full contribution permitted by its manpower, resources, facilities and general economic conditions to the development and maintenance of its own defensive strength and the defensive strength of the Free World[109].

Consequently, in view of 'Pakistan's attitude and key position among the countries of South Asia with respect to military collaboration with the West, Washington policy-makers tried to give special consideration to Pakistan in providing military assistance, including grants. Table 6 shows the approved United States strategic objectives for Pakistan[110].

**Table 6**

**United States Strategic Force Objective for Pakistan**

| *Unit* | *Strategic* | *MAP supported* |
|---|---|---|
| Infantry divisions | 4 | 4 |
| Armoured divisions | 1 ½ | 1 ½ |
| Vessels | 23 | 16 |
| Air squadrons | 11 | 9 |

In providing military aid to Pakistan, the United States was determined to resist any Pakistani effort to persuade the American government to increase the military aid program other than as mutually agreed upon. State Department officials also tried to encourage the effective use of military resources by Pakistan to the end that necessary force goals could be met with a progressive declining reliance on United States aid. Besides, the United States made efforts to avoid becoming committed to assuming any fixed share of Pakistani military maintenance policies in the post–buildup-period.

Neither the United States nor Pakistan has released any precise figures on military assistance received. However, sources and estimated costs of the military program in Pakistan (as indicated in National Security Council Reports which recently have been declassified) suggest that between 1955 to 1960, the United States made available to Pakistan under the Mutual Assistance Program $400 to $475 million[111]. According to the Draper Committee Report, Pakistan between 1955 to 1959, received $447.4 million as military assistance from the United States. Aside from the United States military assistance, recent declassified materials reveals that during the Fiscal Year 1950–58, Pakistan purchased from the United States under the Mutual Security Military Sales Program $427.4 million of military materials for the non-MAP support forces[112]. United States Government documents further confirm that the grant made available to Pakistan under MAP for the period FY 1950–58 was $352 million.

**Table 7**

**United States Grant to Pakistan under MAP, 1950-1958**

| *Items* | *US $ million* |
|---|---|
| Aircraft, spares and related equipment (included 120 F-86F aircraft and 16 T-33s | 41 |
| Ships harbour craft and spares (included 6 landing craft medium. 6 landing craft vehicles / personnel. 6 coastal mines weepers, and modernization, or replacement of 6 destroyers) | 36 |
| Tanks, other vehicles, weapons and artillery (included 72 medium tanks, over 3700½ ton cargo trailers, about 4200, 2½ ton trucks and over 3200 4½ ton trucks). | 98 |
| Ammunition (included war reserves and training) | 39 |
| Electronic and Communication equipment | 27 |
| Other Material (included base organization and ship equipment, training aids and equipment, medical supplies etc.). | 39 |
| Construction (included 2 army camps, 3 military airfields, a marine railway and wharves, ammunition storage facilities. The local currency costs of the construction program were being met from PL 480 sales and are not included here.) | 65 |
| Training services. | 7 |

The grant included major items belonging to the three branches of the Pakistan military force. Pakistan thus became heavily dependent on United States military technologies. Training services included the special training of several hundred Pakistani military officers in the United States. The cost of training was usually met by the United States Government under the mutual Defense Assistance Agreement. Documents confirm that Pakistani jet pilots had been trained in the United States long before the conclusion of the defence alliance between Pakistan and the United States [113].

The extent of military assistance to Pakistan has officially been kept secret. In the past, in the official United States statistics, the amount of military assistance to each country had, with the exception of Pakistan, been shown individually. Military assistance to Pakistan, however, was reported under Near East and South Asia Regions. The totals for this region as a whole and the recipient countries were shared but the actual amount to Pakistan and Saudi Arabia was regarded as classified information, quoted only under "Near East and South Asia Distribution". However, it is not difficult to make out that the United States was solely responsible for enhancing the military establishment of Pakistan, uptil 1965, when China entered the field in a big way.

**Table 8**

**Military assistance to classified countries of the Near East and South Asia Region, 1946-60 and 1962-69 (U.S. $ millions)[114]**

| *Year* | *Near East and South Asia Distribution* | *Countries sharing the amount.* |
|---|---|---|
| 1946 - 60 | 574.000 | Pakistan, Saudi Arabia |
| 1962 | 55.380 | Pakistan, Saudi Arabia |
| 1963 | 52.100 | -do- |
| 1964 | 94.900 | Pakistan, India, Nepal |
| 1965 | 87.781 | -do- |
| 1966 | 11.908 | -do- |
| 1967 | - | - |
| 1968 | - | - |
| 1969 | 0.171 | Pakistan ($. 088)<br>India ($. 053)<br>Nepal ($. 083) |
| **Total** | **875.740** | |

The table clearly reveals that out of $ 875.740 million of the United States military assistance given to Saudi Arabia, Pakistan, India and Nepal, $ 681.480 or 77.8 per cent, classified under "Near East and South Asia distribution", was given to Saudi Arabia and Pakistan covering the period 1947-60, 1962 and 1963. After 1963, when United States started military assistance to India, the amount given to Saudi Arabia was reported separately and was not included in the regional distribution. No figures were available for Pakistan for the years 1967 and 1968 but it can be inferred that the United States did not terminate assistance to Pakistan, after 1965 Indo-Pakistan war. The amount of military assistance given to Saudi Arabia, which was shown separately, indicates that the amount was comparatively small until late 1960s.[115] The major portion of the Near East and South

Asia Distribution during the years 1950 to 1960 has been given to Pakistan. This was confirmed by the official admission of the United States that "over 90 per cent of the military aid to the above-mentioned area was given to Pakistan, Iran, Greece and Turkey".[116]

Selig S. Harrison worked out the amount of military assistance to the tune of $ 522 millions by late 1959.[117]

To prove this, it is equally appropriate to make a "weapons analysis". The table below will show the weapons available to Pakistan between 1947-1965 and the country of their origin.[118]

**Table 9**

**Weapons Available to Pakistan: Source of Supply, 1947-65**

| *Weapon* | *Number* | *Source* |
|---|---|---|
| 9mm Sten Submachine gun | - | U.K. |
| . 303 Bren lightmachine gun | - | U.K. |
| 7.68mm Madsen machine gun | - | Denmark/Germany |
| .50 Cal. Browning machine gun | - | U.S. |
| 83 mm rocket launcher | - | - |
| 60 mm mortar | - | - |
| 81 mm mortar | - | - |
| 125 mm artillery | | U.S. |
| 150 mm artillery | | U.S. |
| 17 mm artillery | 900 | U.S. |
| 20 mm Oerlikon canon mounted on weapons carrier | - | - |
| 90 mm antiaircraft weapon | - | U.S. |
| 155 mm self-propelled guns | - | U.S. |
| M-4 Sherman tank | Probably about 200 | U.S. |
| M-24 Chaffee light tank | About 50 | U.S. |
| M-41 Bulldog light tank | About 50 | U.S. |
| M-47 and M-48 Patton tank | About 400 | U.S. |
| M-33 jet trainer | At least 6 | U.S. |
| M-37 jet trainer | At least 22 | U.S. |
| Martin B-57 bomber (Canberra) | 30 | U.S. |
| Canberra bomber | 50 | U. K. |
| F-86 Saberjet | 100 | U.S. |
| F-104 Starfighter | 50 | U.S. |
| Light Cruiser | 1 | U.K. |
| Destroyer | 8 | U. K. |
| Frigate | 3 | U. K. |
| Coastal minesweeper | 8 | U.S. |
| Patrol Craft | 4 | U. K. |
| Submarine | 1 | U.S. |

It is now crystal clear that during the period under review, the United States was primarily responsible for building up the military establishment of Pakistan and enhancing its fighting abilities, though the share of United Kingdom was also significant. However, since 1965 Pakistan had been receiving supplies from China. In fact, China proved to be the principal supplier of military aid to Pakistan in the years following 1965.[119]

The foregoing analysis based upon simple numerical data can enable an analyst to make some judgements about the fighting ability of the Pakistani army. But it should be brone in mind that the military capabilities themselves are very complex and variable phenomena.[120] While it is not possible to account for all the variables bearing upon its capabilities, one may trace certain built-in structural and functional constraints conditioning its operational efficiency that would make the analysis more meaningful.

Coming to the structural problems, in the first place, it can be said that Pakistan was a large country, possessed substantial pool of educated manpower, but it was basically a peasant society and its industrial sector was poorly developed to allow it to manufacture anything except infantry weapons. It is equally questionable whether the defence burden on the economy of a largely peasant-based society impeded or enhanced its growth, and to that extent self-defeating or self-promoting. Many Pakistanis favoured industry for manufacturing indigenous arms which chimed well with their drive for industrialization. As a matter of fact, the debate was on about the fundamental relationship between defence spending and economic development for over a long time, but it is crucial with regard to Pakistan which carried one of the highest relative burdens of defence spending. Some Pakistani generals pointed out that more defence expenditure on infrastructure and defence production had stimulated Pakistan's economy during 1950's when defence spending, foreign assistance and Pakistan's economy showed positive growth. But unfortunately no scholar was able to trace out the correlation.

Secondly, it can be said that the relationship between the army and the society is complex in case of all South Asian States, particularly Pakistan. This relationship affected their military ability, the way they perceived themselves and their society. It is a well-known fact that Pakistan was a peasant society poised on the threshold of an imperceptible transformation and drew its manpower overwhelmingly from this. For this reason, it had retained the 19th century office of J.C.O. (Junior Commissioned Officer) in the military command structure but it is very often forgotten that there was a positive correlation between the military structure, weapon system and the society since the J.C.O. were progressively rendered useless when called upon to handle most modern and sophisticated weapons.[121] To this extent, it has affected the operational efficiency of its military. Besides, as a necessary corollary of this unique relationship, was the fact of their representativeness of the Pakistani society. It can be well argued that the dominant representation of a particular region served to exclude others permanently from the military service of the nation which meant total deprivation from all the benefits and privileges that were associated with such a central institution. The idea of martial races did not actually reflect the regional, religious and ethnic differences in the country. East and West Pakistan achieved independence as a united state but without a shared perception of the nature of the role and structure of the military. As a matter of fact, the Pakistani armed forces comprising exclusively West Pakistanis (dominated by Punjabis and Pathans) tried to engraft a military ethos based upon the assumptions and beliefs animating the dominant martial races of the West Punjab and the North West Frontier Province.[122]

**Table 10**

**Military elites in Pakistan July 1955[123] (No. of Officers)**

| *Service* | *East* | *West* | *Pakistan Total* |
|---|---|---|---|
| Army | 14 | 894 | 904 |
| Navy | 7 | 593 | 600 |
| Air Force | 60 | 640 | 700 |
| | **81 (3.67 per cent)** | **2,127 (96.55 per cent)** | **2,204** |

This resulted in a strong distaste for the quality of Bengali officers who were non-martial and consequently a strong resistance for the subsequent increase in their representation. The Bengalis were barely 5 per cent in military officer crops. As army gradually got embroiled in politics of the country this feeling got accentuated as army over the years developed a strange relation with its eastern wing which held a sordid place in the military image of Pakistani politics.

An unhappy off-shoot of this was the view that the military was a special expression of the idea of Pakistan. Hence, it was their sacred duty for reforming Pakistani society when it fell below the point of excellence set by them. This was the consequence of their constant employment over the years in aid to the civil authority. The military used the "graphic metaphor" of "political vacuum" and "moral responsibility" to intervene in Pakistani politics to rationalize their institutionalization in power by terming them as the guardian of society. From Ayub onwards, they have sought to explain away their interventions on the ground of incompetence of the politicians, lest it would jeopardize the very existence of the military as a central institution in Pakistani national life. This had certainly eroded their professional competence which became glaringly visible in 1971 war. Cohen had rightly observed: [124]

> "...the Pakistan military are concerned that incompetent civilian leadership might hurt the quality and sometimes the very existence of the military as an organization and thus threaten what it believes to be the only real line of defence against India, and one of the main forces holding the state together....politicians come and go... but the military is permanent; it damages the long-term survival of the state by weakening the army's capacity to step in and set things right. Setting things right, of course, is the preferred model of intervention and the generals would like to see their involvement in politics as a glorified aid to the civil operation."

Thirdly, another structural problem that set limits to the operational efficiency of the Pakistani military was its plurastic organization. The officer corps was as divided as the broader society. It, in equal measure, reflected a sharp schism between "the insiders" and "the outsiders" of the Pakistani society. The armed forces were not drawn exclusively from the landed aristocracy of Punjab and N.W.F.P. While more than 12 per cent of the officers were outsiders belonging to the liberal centres of Muslim thought of Allahabad, Delhi and Lucknow, a majority of them were sons of professionals. This had certainly accentuated the problem of polarization, breaking its monolithic structure.

Lastly, the most serious structural problem for the army emanated from the way Pakistan was composed after partition. As we have argued earlier, topography intruded all the military planning of Pakistan and compounded its strategic dilemma which was something unique in case of Pakistan.

Coming to the functional constraints, it is well-known that Pakistan's complete dependence upon outside sources for supply of weapons positively affected its efficiency. Pakistan relied heavily on the United States for all major and minor equipments during 1950's. While the United States was quite liberal in equipping the Pakistani army with most sophisticated weapons, it was also selective in supporting its army. Its assistance were denied to the army in the Azad Kashmir and the East Pakistan. Such arrangements were consistent with the over-all United States policy in the South Asia,[125] whose major planks included safeguarding oil supplies from the Gulf to the industrialized world, and it can be effectively realized if sophisticated war technology is deployed in this region. The Azad Kashmir and The East Pakistan were obviously not strategic places for such purposes. Furthermore, as Kashmir was a bone of contention between India and Pakistan, it was not in the interest of the United States to alienate India by assisting Pakistani troops in Kashmir. True, Pakistan started massive programme of indigenous production of defence equipment with the Chinese and the French help after the termination of military assistance by the United States in 1965, yet it was still dependent on it for a number of weapons.[126] It did produce practically all of its light infantry weapons (the excellent G-3 rifle and a machine gun built under licence from West Germany), most ammunition, shells, explosives and mortars. What stood out most striking in this context that added to its perennial woe was the fact that Pakistan had no longer reliable friends who could be termed as regular supplier of key weapons whether for cash or for credit or as a grant. While states like France and Germany were ready to sell, they required cash which meant Pakistan had to relay upon others that would oblige this. It is a matter of record that the United States followed a restrictive policy of arms transfer |to the South Asian region since 1967. The Soviet Union has provided it with a few T-55 tanks but has tagged for their assistance on the solution of Kashmir disputes. Besides, as an author notes:[127]

> "...The Soviet arms deal with Pakistan is a commercial transaction. Unless Pakistan is able to expand its export to the Soviet Union to an appreciable extent... without at the same time allowing 'Soviet exports to Pakistan to increase, it would not be possible for Pakistan to achieve a sufficiently favourable balance of payments position to be able to pay (in commodities or in cash) for more than a limited supply of arms from the Soviet Union. That the Soviet will allow such a one-way expansion in exports, is to say the least, an impossibility".

It had procured weapons from all sources which included China, Great Britain, Italy and North Korea. While their supply was irregular and erratic, it had equally created problems of co-ordination. This was more pronounced in case of air crafts which had affected the operational efficiency of the air force. Lastly, another insoluble problem Pakistan faced in acquisition of weapons was that of servicing. A lot of money was required to be spent for repairs, for spare parts and the replenishments. In some cases, it has got to be done in the country of their origin. But finance stared in its face. Beyond this, supervened the political considerations of not alienating India by supplying weapons would be used against it.

**Economic Development**

The level of economic development operates in two broadways as independent variable influencing the capabilities of a state to frame its foreign policy goals and move towards their realization. In the first place, an economically developed state can easily devote a major chunk of its gross national product to undertake ambitious foreign policy ventures. But a developing state is bound to maintain a low profile in the realm of world politics. It is precisely because its domestic concerns are more overriding. As it is poised on the threshold of modernization and development, it must foster inter societal cohesion, insulate the political system from internal threat emanating from the "revolutions of rising expectation" of the masses and ensure its external security through the maintenance of an adequate military establishment. So, its basic objective remains to enhance the gross national product through rapid economic growth that will answer these bewildering problems. As a result, its energies and meagre resources get absorbed in the initial task of nation building.

Secondly, the level of economic development poses differing problems for the respective economies which contain very significant implications for their foreign policy behaviour. A developed economy has a well-chosen philosophy of growth within an avowed political system. The development strategy underlying it is a tried and tested one which has borne fruits over the years. True, sometimes it calls for new links to be fostered for importing different kinds of commodities, sustaining different kinds of monetary relations with the trading partners and procuring diverse varieties of knowledge from abroad. In contrast to this, a developing state in its initial years of its life gropes for an ideal political system that is suited to the genius of its people and reflects its traditional values. So, its quest for choosing a philosophy of economic growth that reflects its political ideology becomes an agonizing one. Once it embraces a particular philosophy of growth, it is called upon to formulate development strategy that is conceived in the broader context of the socio-economic milieu of the society. So, the formulation does not present the case of a freely floating variable to be manipulated as the economic forces dictate. In matter of reality, it grows out of the interactive influences of diverse groups of economic actors and very often reflects the hopes and fears of its ruling elites. Hence, it carries wider implication for the foreign policy behaviour of a state.

In the present analysis, the main thrust of my argument is cast in terms of two hypotheses. First, Pakistan being a developing country, chose diverse philosophy of economic development and adopted different development strategies growing out of the interactive influences of a congeries of economic actors which did not contribute significantly to its capabilities. Second, the philosophy of growth and the development strategy underlying it had high foreign aid component for its successful realization for which Pakistan was compelled to depend upon the power bloc which was in a position to render large scale economic aid during the period under review.

It should be noted that Pakistan at the time of partition bore all the characteristic features of an underdeveloped economy. Its mainstay was agriculture which contributed 60 per cent of its gross national product. The agricultural structure was preeminently feudal. The 5 per cent of its rural households controlled 70 per cent of all agricultural lands. This top 5 per cent included all those with more than 20 per cent of land. Large landlord families held more than 500 acres of land in West Pakistan. But land ownership was more dispersed in the East. There was hardly an owner who had more than 40 acres of land. But as ownership changed, very frequently because of abject poverty, there was acute fragmentation of land. Besides, agricultural output was always prone to the vagaries of flood and cyclone. Though economy was growing at the rate of 2.5 per cent, there was simultaneous increase of population at a rate of 2.4 per cent which left the per capita income static. Another index of its underdevelopment was the equation between the urban and rural population. While rural population accounted for 86.9 per cent of the total, urban sector formed barely 10.4 per cent. In urban areas, 16.2 per cent of the labour force was being absorbed in service while 7 per cent got employed in manufacturing. In rural areas, agricultural alone was providing jobs to 7.6 per cent.

Coming to industry, its position was equally frustrating. Under British Raj, initial phase of industrialization was concentrated around large ports and later expansion into hinterland occurred into areas full of natural resources. Besides, economy had grown up as an organic whole with a concomitant regional specialization. Jute would be grown in East Bengal and processed in Bengal and so also leather and cotton produced in East Punjab and manufactured in Bombay and Kanpur. But partition gave a jolt to this integrative economy of both the countries by snapping the links of complementarity between raw materials and industries and between the products and consumers[128]. The post-partition territories comprising Pakistan not only lacked many basic mineral resources so sorely needed for rapid industrialization, but also large scale industrial units were virtually non-existent. Of the total 14,677 industrial units, only 1414 or 9.6 per cent fell to Pakistan's lot. And manufacturing contributed barely 6 per cent of the Gross National Product. The tables below reflect all these grim facts.

**Table 11**

**Distribution of Land Ownership in East[129]**

| *Size of Holdings* | *Percentage of Owners* | *Percentage of Land owned* |
|---|---|---|
| 0.0. to 0.4 | 13 | 1 |
| 0.5 to 0.9 | 11 | 2 |
| 1.0 to 2.4 | 27 | 13 |
| 2.5 to 4.9 | 26 | 26 |
| 5.0 to 7.4 | 12 | 19 |
| 7.5 to 12.4 | 7 | 19 |
| 12.5 to 24.9 | 3 | 14 |
| 25.0 to 39.9 | 0 | 3 |
| 40.0 or above | - | 2 |

**Table 12**

**Distribution of Land Ownership in West Pakistan[130]**

| *Size of Holdings* | *Percentage of Owners* | *Percentage of land owned* |
|---|---|---|
| 5 or less | 64.5 | 15.0 |
| 5 to 25 | 28.5 | 31.7 |
| 25 to 100 | 5.7 | 22.4 |
| 100 to 500 | 1.1 | 15.9 |
| 500 or above | 0.1 | 15 |

**Table 13**

**Occupational Distribution of Labour Force in 1951[131]**

| *Economic Divisions* | *East Pakistan* | *West Pakistan* |
|---|---|---|
| Agriculture, Pasture and Forestry | 82.6 | 66 |
| Fishing | 1.5 | 0.2 |
| Industry - Manufacturing | 6.6 | 11.5 |
| Mining and Quarrying | - | 0.1 |
| Construction and Transport Trade and Commerce | 3.9 | 6.8 |
| Public Administration Public Services & Arts | 2.0 | 3.5 |
| Domestic and other services | 1.5 | 4.9 |
| Others | 0.8 | 7.7 |

**Table 14**
**Structure of Gross National Product in 1949-50 at Constant Factor Cost of 1959-60** [132]

| | Major Heads | Percentage of Share of G.N.P. | |
|---|---|---|---|
| 1. | Agriculture | | 59.9 |
| | a. Major Crops | 34.0 | |
| | b. Minor Crops | 10.0 | |
| | c. Live stock | 12.0 | |
| | d. Fishing | 3.5 | |
| | e. Forestry | 0.3 | |
| 2. | Mining and Quarrying | | 01 |
| 3. | Manufacturing | | 5.8 |
| | a. Large - scale | 1.4 | |
| | b. Small - scale | 4.4 | |
| 4. | Constructions | | 1.0 |
| 5. | Electricity, Gas, Water and Sanitary Services | | 0.1 |
| 6. | Transport, Storage and Communications | | 5.1 |
| 7. | Wholesale Trade, Retail Trade | | 11.7 |
| 8. | Banking and Insurance | | 0.3 |
| 9. | Ownership of Dwellings | | 5.7 |
| 10. | Public Administration and Defence | | 4.3 |
| 11. | Services | | 6.0 |
| | | | **100.00** |

Beyond all this, lies another crucial fact which was no sadly missing in Pakistani life at its birth. A country desirous of industrialization needs an economically viable community of industrialists who could spearhead the programme with their own resources or with the active help of the Government. Unfortunately it lacked both, the men with ample resources or a government which could mop up domestic savings. With few exceptions, the industrial families came from North India at the time of partition and their meager wealth was initially developed from commercial tradings. These families were caste-like communities like Bhoras, Khojas Ismails and Memons who also lacked experiences of modern industrial management. They did not inherit the tradition of industrial culture. They were basically merchants and traders. Considering all these it is difficult to disagree with the assessment of the United Nations based study which ranked Pakistan as the fifty seven nation in terms of the per capita income of its population in 1950 which was barely Rs. 312[133].

Despite all these constraints, Pakistan enjoyed some initial advantages. It inherited the vast agricultural granary of India located in East Punjab and Sind with a fine and well-developed irrigation system that gave it a surplus of food grain production. This area was also known for the major share of production of commercial crops like jute and cotton, which offered a unique opportunity for starting processing and consumer goods industries to cater to the domestic market where a void was created by the absence of industrial products from India after partition. So, these were the objective conditions in which Pakistan policy-framers formulated their economic policy for the country.

The first Industrial Policy Statement issued by the Government of Pakistan on 2 April 1948 categorically committed it to the philosophy of capitalistic mode of production. While state ownership was confined to three major areas of manufacturing, it expressed the keen desire of the government to associate individual initiative and private enterprise at every stage of industrialization[134]. In pursuance with this philosophy of economic growth, the government formulated a development strategy which rested on the doctrine of functional inequality. Its major premises admirably reflected the realities of Pakistani society in 1948. Pakistan was predominantly an agricultural feudal economy with no capitalist class to spearhead the process of industrialization and the people were poor, there was no savings. So a capitalist class had to be created and nurtured. The initial stage of capitalist development required a high degree of inequality. This was due to the necessity of channeling resources to those class which was assumed to have high propensity for savings[135]. These high savings would be later converted into investment which would raise the productivity of the economy. This development model necessarily implied in Pakistani context, first, providing all out incentives to the North India migrant traders to channel their merchant capital into industrial sector and heavy tariff protection to the infant domestic industries for ensuring high prices for locally produced consumer goods; secondly, the cost of industrial enterprises were reduced by artificially low import prices of capital goods as well as price ceilings on urban wage goods. Consequently, profit margins became high and encouraged the growth of industrial capital. And there was a diversion of resources from agricultural to industrialists in an effort to raise their incomes and consequently their savings[135]. So initial growth in income inequalities to reach higher levels of savings and investments for creating a greater national cake to be shared by the masses was accepted as an article of faith among the policy planners.

To underwrite this strategy of development, the planners clearly conceived the expansion in the economy to occur only by expanding the consumer goods industries and also by promoting the export of agricultural goods like jute and cotton for importing machinery for the capital intensive industries as there was absence of capital goods in the country. At the same time to save scarce foreign exchange, special emphasis was placed on import substituting industries. Two fortuitous international events propelled Pakistan's economy in the desired direction. First, it took advantage of British devaluation of pound in 1949 when it refused to go along with this. The gain was immediate in the sense that the overvalued exchange rate of Pakistani rupee had a favourable impact on the industrial sector as it drastically reduced the cost of imported capital machinery. Secondly, the outbreak of the Korean War in 1950 sent the prices of raw materials like jute and cotton skyrocketing. Pakistani traders earned huge foreign exchange surpluses from the export of these commodities to import capital machinery for renovating old units and starting fresh ones. Besides, the Government's deliberate adoption of import tariffs and the new fiscal policy that exempted the profits of new enterprises in certain approved areas gave a total monopoly of the domestic market to the emerging industrialists. Now the Government channelised the entire merchant capital into the industrial sector.

With the termination of the Korean War, the boom in export ended. There was an abrupt decline in the foreign exchange earnings. Compounding this crisis, was the failure of the industrialists to redeem the hope of the Government as they wasted the valuable foreign exchange for importing luxurious consumer goods. To mitigate this unforeseen situation, the Government reverted to a policy of controlled development within the overall framework of capitalist mode of production[136]. As a result, every dimension of industrial developmental process came to be controlled and determined by the bureaucracy : location and size of the industry, the licensing system, foreign exchange requirements, sanctions for new units and the expansions of the old. Besides, the Government resorted to heavy restrictions on import of consumer goods and low tariffs for capital goods. And this new dispensation became very conducive for the trading class to produce goods domestically while importing capital machinery for this purpose from the accumulated foreign exchange surpluses. The Government also set up institution like Pakistan Industrial Development

Corporation which raised capital and developed many projects to the stage of operation and finally handed them over to the private sectors. It also set up the Pakistan Planning Commission in 1954 which became the effective mechanism for co-ordinating the economic decisions. It drafted a series of five year plans which laid out allocation of resources for the development of private and public sector. The First Five Year Plan allocated 57 per cent of the total industrial development to the private sector, and the foreign aid component of the total expenditure accounted for 30 per cent in the First Five Year Plan, reflected in table 15, 16 and 17.

**Table 15**

**Private Sector Share in Industrial Investments [137] 1955-70**

| *Period* | *Public* | *Private* | *Total* | |
|---|---|---|---|---|
| (1) | (2) | (3) | (4) | (3) as per cent (4) |
| First Plan (1955-60) | 1300 | 1750 | 3050 | 57 per cent |
| Second Plan (1960-65) | 1470 | 3430 | 4900 | 70 per cent |
| Third Plan (1965-70) | 9160 | 9050 | 18,210 | 64 per cent |

**Table 16**

**Foreign Aid and Domestic Investment[138]**

| *Year* | *Foreign Assistance (Rs. in million)* | *Domestic Investment (Rs. in million)* | *Foreign Aid (as percentage of investment)* |
|---|---|---|---|
| 1964-65 | 3,163 | 8,066 | 39 |
| 1965-66 | 2,778 | 7,078 | 39 |
| 1966-67 | 3,242 | 8,517 | 38 |
| 1967-68 | 3,441 | 7,535 | 35 |
| 1964-65 | | | |
| 1967-68 | 12,624 | 31,196 | 38 |

**Table 17**
**Commitments of External Assistance (U.S.$. Million)[139]**

| | | Grants | | Loans repayable in foreign exchange | |
|---|---|---|---|---|---|
| *Period* | *Total Assistance* | *Amount* | *Per cent share* | *Amount* | *Per cent share* |
| Pre-1st Plan | 337 | 216 | 64 | 101 | 30 |
| First Plan | 1,073 | 578 | 54 | 221 | 21 |
| Second Plan | 2,757 | 1,105 | 40 | 1,559 | 57 |
| Third Plan | 2,746 | 704 | 26 | 2,042 | 74 |
| Five Years (1970-75) | 3,944 | 375 | 9 | 3,569 | 91 |
| 1975-76 | 958 | 102 | 11 | 856 | 89 |
| 1976-77 | 1,115 | 187 | 17 | 928 | 83 |
| 1977-78 | 979 | 151 | 15 | 828 | 85 |

Despite periodic policy changes, the per capita income in West Pakistan which registered 6.8 per cent in 1954 came down to a record low 0.3 per cent in 1958 and there was a steady decline in the per capita rural income during the decade reaching its lowest of Rs.195/- in 1958 as flaws and contradictions inherent in the development strategy surfaced by late fifties. The planners had blissfully forgotten that the major plank of their policy rested on successful growth in agricultural sector which was sadly neglected. The successive governments from 1948 to 1958 have failed to take initiatives for restructuring the land holding system, because of the fear of dominance of the big landed interests in the political structure. It seems in retrospect, the planners had underestimated the extent to which the success of their development strategy for rapid industrialization depended upon an equally rapid growth of the agricultural sector. Interestingly, the responsibility for its development rested with poorly endowed resources of the provincial government. Besides, this downward spiral was the product of the persistent policy of the Central Government to maintain prices of agricultural goods at a low level in order to provide cheap raw materials for the protected industries and cheap food for the emerging urban middle class. The farmers had to pay heavy high prices for the consumer goods produced by the industrial sector. The overvalued exchange rate became the mechanism of the Central Government to transfer resources from the agricultural sector to industry. As time wore on, agricultural sector became stagnant and the stagnation of income in this major commodity sector of the economy brought about a contraction of the domestic market for the commodity of the manufacturing sector. As a result, by mid fifties, the first phase of industrial capital was coming to a grinding halt, because the market for substituting the previously imported consumer goods by domestic products had been exhausted. Besides, the stagnant agriculture led to food deficit and a substantial amount of foreign exchange was absorbed by the import of food stuff, which limited the amount available for the import of capital goods. Beyond all this, nearly two-thirds of the Central Government revenues were earmarked for the defense expenditure which was twice of the total developmental expenditure. There was absolutely no scope for agricultural development.

As a measure of nation building the development strategy failed. The transfer of foreign exchange earnings earned by the jute exporters of East Pakistan to the industrialists of Punjab and Karachi became a symbol of Bengali exploitation. It simply fuelled the Bengali separatist movement for regional autonomy as years rolled by. Besides, the creation of the industrial class envisaged by the planners comprised mainly the Mahajjir trading class of Karachi which became also the financial capital of the country. It is these Mahajjirs who took advantage of the Korean boom and numerous fiscal and monetary concessions given by the Government for rapid industrialization because of their initial domination of the Central bureaucracy, close proximity to the power centre and their overriding market power. All licences and sanctions went to Karachi and Punjab which became the hub of industrial and commercial activities of Pakistan. By 1959, these migrants controlled over half of the industrial assets of the country and 70 per cent of the workers in Karachi industrial sector were refugees not local Sindhis. The emerging industrial elites of Pakistan were the Mahajjirs of Karachi and the landlords of Punjab. The latter's domination over the political structure ensured that mild land reforms for redistribution of assets were not introduced. This ethnic composition of elites only bred political tensions at different levels. Within bureaucracy which was totally dominated by the Mahajjirs, a contest started between them and the sons of the soil of West Pakistan to ease out the Mahajjirs from the position of authority and power and to ensure the entry of Punjabis. This was a synchronous process which occurred with the evolution of the bureaucratic-military complex at the Centre after the death of Liaqat Ali and reached its culmination in 1958. Now the domination of the Punjabis in Pakistani political life became a fiat accompli. At the broader societal level, the supremacy of the Mahajjirs and Punjabi elites entailed a denial of power to the majority ethnic group, the Bengalis and to the combined ethnic groups of the Sindhis, the Beluchis and the Pathans of West Pakistan.

When Ayub assumed power in 1958, Pakistani society was more divided than it was at the time of partition and the development strategy contributed in no small measure to this unhappy phenomenon. But Ayub could not tear himself away from the thinkings of the earlier planners. He was bent upon equally in creating a Punjabi Industrial Class that would compete with the Mahajjirs in spearheading national economic development, disregarding the larger issues of distributional equity. However, he made certain policy changes in tune with the prevailing trends in the national and international economy. Liberal flow of foreign economical aid emboldened Ayub to launch the Second Five Year Plan (1960-65). Accordingly, he liberalized the economy by replacing the excessive bureaucratic control with a market-oriented approach. The Government progressively dismantled all administrative restrictions and controls and liberalized import and export trade. A list of items were placed on free list to be freely imported. The Government also introduced the novel scheme called the Bonus Voucher Scheme in 1959 under which the exporters of certain raw materials and manufactured goods received import permits equivalent to 10-40 per cent of the value of the exported goods. As these were subject to transfer, the holders by selling their import permits received additional profits equal to 30-40 per cent of the value of their exports. This scheme gave a boost to exports and the exporters got an additional net transfer of resources from the rest of economy. As a result, without resorting to devaluation, the Government protected effectively the interests of the emerging industrial class without at the same time hurting the traders. Besides 70 per cent of the total industrial investment in the Second Five Year Plan went to the private sector which was greatly pampered by the Government. And until 1965, when in the wake of Indo-Pak War, the Aid-Pakistan Consortium and the United States put embargo on aid, foreign aid accounted for 50 per cent of the total expenditure of the Second Five Year Plan. With the resumption of American commodity aid programme, foreign economic aid became a critical component of total expenditure and the temporary withdrawal of earlier policy of liberalization was again revived at the behest of the United States.

Ayub's policy got a further impetus with the revolution in agricultural production. The adoption of high yielding varieties of seeds and fertilizers with efficient and economical water management measures resulted in a dramatic revival of agricultural sector. It was accompanied by increased mechanization process which led to the emergence of a new class of enterprising big farmers in Punjab who became the major beneficiaries of this phase of "Green Revolution" in Pakistan. The rural elites also remained unaffected by Ayub's cosmetic changes in the landholding system. In 1959, the land reforms had fixed the land ceiling on private ownership of land of 500 acres irrigated and 1000 acres unirrigated with exemptions for the orchards. Besides, it was fixed on in terms of individual rather than family holdings. As a result, hardly enough land was made available and 35 per cent of the excess land surrendered by the landlords were actually claimed by the Government for redistribution. So the policy of the Government made a mockery of the distributional justice in the country side.

Surveying old Pakistan economic scene on the threshold of the seventies, one is no doubt impressed by the striking growth rate maintained throughout the sixties as reflected in the Table below.

**Table 18**

**Average Annual Growth Rate of Key Sectors, 1960–70 ( per cent)[140]**

| *Growth rate* | *1959-60 to 1964-65* | *1964-65 to 1969-70* |
|---|---|---|
| Per capita income | 3.5 | 3.7 |
| Agriculture | 3.7 | 6.3 |
| Large scale manufacturing | 16.9 | 9.9 |

GNP grew annually at around 5.5 per cent through both the second and the third plan periods. Per capita GNP growth was nearly 3 per cent throughout the sixties. The growth in the manufacturing sector was particularly phenomenal during 1960-65, registering 17 per cent. But underlying this, too many stark facts emerge which make sixties more remarkable for failure than for achievement. Regional disparity in per capita income widened from 30 per cent in 1958 to 45per cent in 1965 to 61 per cent at the time of Ayub's fall[141]. The developmental obsession with the West wing was reinforced by the developmental institutions like World Bank, as it selected those projects which promised the highest rate of return and they invariably tended to be in West Pakistan. Secondly, the Third Five Year Plan reflected on the "considerable transfer of incomes from agriculture to the industrial sector during fifties... the rural areas were transferring savings to the fast modernizing urban industrial capitalist sector". And no more than 15-37 per cent of the amount transferred from the agricultural sector was turned into investment and the remaining 85-63 per cent dissipated in higher consumption by the urban capitalist elites, of which only twenty-two families owned between them 66 per cent of the industry, 97per cent of insurance and 80 per cent of the banking. Certainly, it was not a coincidence that the major beneficiaries became the Mahajjirs and Punjab Industrial elites. As a matter of fact it was not a product of conscious design but the outcome was inherent in the very structure of chosen development strategy which was marred by the fundamental flaws in the choice of objective. Sections of this elite formulated and executed Government policy. Resources at the command of the state were allocated to groups within this elite. This was done consciously by the Ayub Government like his predecessors on the ground that a concentration of income in the hands of elites would lead to higher savings and investment and consequently higher growth. But the concentration of economic power in the hands of bureaucrats playing hand in glove with the industrialists and rich landlords did not permit the gains on economic growth to percolate down the lowest strata of the society. This economic elitism with which Ayub regime was associated generated class polarization in Pakistani Society: the extremely wealthy urban group of Mahajjirs and Punjabis, the big landlords and large farmers of West Pakistan, the harbingers of "Green Revolution" and the more amorphous group consisted of middle class such as civil servants and high military officials as well as urban white-collar workers. In contrast to this small microscopic minority, the vast majority considered themselves as dispensable in the Government's strategy of economic growth, as ideas of equitable distribution were luxuries which only developed countries can afford. Pakistan, a developing country can "shelve to the distant future any aspiration for reducing inequalities".[142] The deficiencies of the development strategy was acknowledged in the Fourth Five Year Plan :... income distribution has become fairly skewed in the process of economic development. Real wages declined by about a third during the 1960's...."

It is a truism, Pakistan achieved a growth rate in early 1960's which was quite outstanding in view of the meagre resources and capital endowments at partition. This propelled many economists to acclaim it as a model of development for the emerging Third World countries. But it was little realized that this "shining model of free enterprise" was rendered possible solely for the infusion of foreign aid and growth rate would decline once foreign aid ceases. Table 16: reflects the amount of foreign aid received by Pakistan from 1964 to 1968. As claimed by Edward Mason, the increased flow of foreign aid per capita from Rs.10.8 in 1960 to

Rs.25.8 in 1965 was solely responsible for the phenomenal success story of the Pakistani economy in the first half of the sixties, while the "Green Revolution" contributed to it in the second half. It should also be borne in mind that the proportion of grants in total external assistance ranged from 64 per cent at the time of partition to 26 per cent at the end of third plan. Similarly, the proportion of loans repayable in foreign exchange ranged from 30 per cent to 74 per cent by 1970. Table 17 makes this clear. So, it can be concluded that the level of economic development because of its chosen strategy did not contribute significantly to the enhancement of its capabilities during the period 1947 to 1971. There was evidence on two counts. Pakistan's economy could not sustain the strain of the Indo-Pakistan War of 1965 as time passed on its debt, service ratio assumed a frightening proportion. Economists usually assume that a 20 per cent debt service ratio to export earnings is an alarming proportion. Justifying the aid Ayub remarked : "No country has ever been able to develop or attain what the economists call "take-off" stage without outside assistance. The industrialization of Britain came through assets. They then helped develop America So we have to rely on outside assistance. There is no need of being ashamed of it. It is a hard fact of life.[143]

**Table 19**

**Pakistan Debt Service Ratio, 1960-70[144]**

| *Period* | *Debt Service* | *Export Earnings* | *Debt Service Ratio for Export Earnings* |
|---|---|---|---|
| 1960-65 | 219 | 2,298 | 9.5 |
| 1965-70 | 612 | 3,155 | 19.5 |

With regard to our second hypothesis, the analysis proceeds as follows. It adopted the philosophy of free enterprise and formulated a development strategy that had high economic content for which it was compelled to bank upon external aid. Both were truly the handiwork of Jinnah and undoubtedly concessions to the domestic constituencies of merchant class who gave him their moral and material support during the Pakistan movement and convinced him that political progress must go hand in hand with the commercial and industrial progress. But to accept that they were alone responsible for it, is to fly in face of facts. Because overwhelming evidences now give insight that its leaders realized the value of American economic aid for the future development of their country even on the morrow of its independence and accordingly chosen the philosophy of growth and formulated its developmental strategy that would not queer the pitch.[145]

As mentioned earlier, Jinnah made the Industrial Policy Statement on 2 April 1948. It laid down the essential thesis of the philosophy of growth that was subsequently reinforced by his address on 27 April 1948 which emphasised on the development of the private sector. In the meanwhile, much has happened behind murky scene of politics. Record shows that barely two months after partition, he turned to the United States as "a regular source of finance" for industrial development and expansion of its military forces. On September 1947, Ghulam Mohammad, the finance minister in his Cabinet, approached American Charged' Affairs Charles W. Lewis in Karachi and impressed upon him the need for the development of its economy.[146] Again, in early 1947, his special emissary Mir Laik Ali met Winthrop W. Aldrich, Chairman of the Board of Directors of Chase National Bank and apprised him of the wish of the Government of Pakistan that "the Bank should represent it in connection with commercial matters...might have to do with the future development of the economy of Pakistan". Again on 17 October 1947 along with M.A.H. Ispahani, the Pakistan envoy to the United States, he handed over the memorandum to Aldrich which made it clear that the Government of Pakistan wished to designate the United States as its principal economic and military patron. The memorandum read.[147]

> "Primarily defence and secondly economic development are the two vitally essential features of Pakistan's life and for both of these she has to look firstly to U.S.A. and then to Great Britian for assistance... It has been broadly assessed that to enable Pakistan to hold a proper place in the comity of nations and to attain a reasonably independent position and to allow her to make a fair contribution to the stability of world peace, the Government of Pakistan would need a loan of approximately two billion dollar from the U.S.A. Government spreading over a period of about 5 years ."

After the death of Jinnah, Liaquat Ali Khan carried ^forward his unfinished mission. He manoeuvred successfully an invitation to visit the United States. He abandoned his projected trip to the Soviet Union. Commenting on this, the noted Pakistani scholar K. Sarwar Hasan observed:[148]

> "But, the statesman that he was, Mr. Liaquat Ali Khan was not a doctrinaire politician. He was a realist, whose aim was to raise the living standards of the poverty-striken masses of his people. This could only be done through large-scale economic development, for which there was neither capital nor plant nor technical skill in Pakstan.

These could only come from the West. So that he was actually dependent upon the West for the vital economic needs of the country. There was great enthusiasm in Pakistan for Mr. Liaquat Ali Khan's projected visit to Russia. He had to postpone—in effect to abandon—it and instead go to the United States, only on account of priorities that have been mentioned above".

During his brief sojourn in the United States, Liaquat Ali very forcefully and persuasively presented Pakistani case. He said:[149]

"I would like to say that except a few specified industries, we have thrown open the entire field of investment to private enterprise and we assure the great pioneers of this and other advanced countries of the warmest welcome and of the greatest goodwill on our part and we hope we shall have their goodwill and cooperation in return."

Liaquat did not live long to see the fruition of his dream. But within a brief span of time, he did substantial spade-work and the Americans gradually veered round to look at Pakistan through their own perspectives, though they felt their way gingerly for a tie. Explanation for this faltering step may lie elsewhere. But the fact remained that with Ghulam Mohammad, Ayub Khan and Iskander Mirza in firm saddle of power controlling the destiny of the country, the long process was gradually smoothened because they were the moving spirits behind Liaquat for an American tie-up. And finally, a break-through was achieved with the conclusion of the famous Mutual Defence Assistance Pact on 19 May 1954 which saw a massive inflow of American economic and military aid. Until 1954, of the total economic assistance disbursed by the United States, Pakistan got barely 0.2 per cent. But in the post-MDAP period, American economic aid shot up to an astronomic figure. It rose to 1.3 per cent in 1955, 2.9 per cent in 1958, 5.1 per cent in 1961 and 7.9 per cent in 1964.

**Table 20**

**Major U.S. Government Foreign Assistance to Pakistan[150] (in million dollar)**

| *Year* | *Total U.S. Aid* | *Aid to Pakistan* | *Percentage of Total* |
|---|---|---|---|
| Upto Dec. 1953 | 47,835 | 99 | .2 |
| Fy 1954 | 5,181 | 12 | .2 |
| Fy 1955 | 4,856 | 67 | 1.3 |
| Fy 1958 | 4,926 | 145 | 2.9 |
| Fy 1961 | 4,248 | 218 | 5.1 |
| Fy 1963 | 5,148 | 380 | 7.3 |
| Fy 1964 | 4,715 | 377 | 7.9 |

As a result, one finds that foreign aid which made a marginal contribution to its Gross National Product till 1955 increased substantially over the years. It rose to 5 per cent of the Gross National Product in 1959-60 and to 6.3 per cent in 1964-65.

**Table 21**

**Contribution of Foreign Assistance to Pakistan Economy[151] (million Rupees: 1959-60 prices)**

| *Major Heads* | *1949-50* | *1954-55* | *1954-60* | *1964-65* |
|---|---|---|---|---|
| Gross Investment | 1,120 | 2,200 | 3,430 | 6,4390 |
| Gross Domestic Savings | 1, 120 | 1,900 | 1,850 | 3,830 |
| Foreign Assistance | | 300 | 1,580 | 2,560 |
| Foreign Assistance as a percentage of | | | | |
| (a) Gross National Product | - | 1.1 | 5.0 | 6.3 |
| (b) Total Investment | - | 13.6 | 46.1 | 40.0 |

In the period ending on 31 December 1960, Pakistan got aid to the tune of $ 1,728.95 million allocated to it by different countries, the United Nations and its specialized agencies. America alone gave $ 1,528.83 million which amounted to 88.2 per cent of the total aid it received from others. It utilised $ 1,213.46 million, i.e., 87.7 per cent of the American aid. The socialist countries contributed nothing. So Pakistan's First Five Year Plan was entirely financed by the United States. In 1960 Aid-Pakistan Consortium was organised which comprised nine countries plus the World Bank and its soft-kitty International Development Agency. It coincided with Pakistan's launching of the Second Five Year Plan. Japan and Western European Countries participated in a big way. Although the United States share decreased to 46.4 per cent of the total economic aid received from consortium countries and others, but in terms of absolute amount of aid in dollars there was no fall. Rather there was a steady rise reaching from a paltry $ 62.5 million in 1955 to $ 213.9 million in 1964. Besides, as World Bank and IDA participated in aid programme, the United States being the major contributor to these agencies, indirectly aided Pakistan. During 1960-

65, the World Bank and IDA pledged to Pakistan an aid of $369.4 million. Although during this phase, the socialist countries of Soviet Union, China, Yugoslavia, Czechoslovakia, Poland started foreign aid to Pakistan, it was modest[152]. Countries like Switzerland and Denmark also gave Rs. 20 million aid to it. This was comparably small. So Pakistan's Second Five Year Plan was entirely financed by Consortium in which the United States was the dominant partner both individually and as a major collective subscriber to the World Bank and IDA.[153]

After the I ndo-Pakistan War of 1965, aid did not decline. It managed to get more aid in absolute terms and under hardened conditions. There were clearly three periods [in Pakistan's history of foreign aid: (1) 1950-55 when Pakistan got outright grants; (2) 1950-60 when Pakistan was 'granted increased loans but reduced grants; and (3) 1960-65 when it received large loans with high interest rates coupled with harsh conditions.[154] This could be gleaned from the table below. There was a sudden change in grants and loans composition from the First to the Second Plan and then grants declined sharply.

**Table 22**

**Foreign Assistance to Pakistan 1950-70[155] (in million U.S. dollar)**

| *Period* | *Total Assistance* | *Grants* | *Grants as a percentage of total assistance* |
|---|---|---|---|
| Pre-First Plan (1950-55) | 337 | 216 | 64 |
| First Plan (1955-60) | 1,073 | 578 | 54 |
| Second Plan (1960-65) | 2,757 | 1,105 | 40 |
| Third Plan (1968-70) | 2,747 | 704 | 26 |

Now coming to the foreign policy behaviour of Pakistan during the period 1950-70, Pakistan gave unstinted support to the United States on all major international issues during the period 1950-61. The Americans had it almost in their "hip pocket". As the United States's aid as flowing like champagne whose major components were grants, it really became the most "allied ally" of the Americans. So one can safely establish a correlation between the foreign aid (which was necessitated by the level of economic development) and the foreign policy behaviour of Pakistan.

But during the period following the Summer of 1961 till the advent of Yahya Khan, one found streaks of autonomous and independent foreign policy postures. This is the period when Pakistan made a clear shift in its foreign policy towards the Communist world, particularly China. Our review of foreign aid shows that though grants declined, aid from the United States increased in absolute terms of dollars throughout. Pakistan like the yester years was vociferously claiming itself as the land of free enterprise and persuasively presenting its case for more economic aid from the Consortium and particularly from the United States for its Second Five Year Plan.[156]

Now a most pertinent point arises as to why Pakistan turned to the Communist World. Was it that it wanted more aid from them? A superficial analysis can readily agree with this bland fact because there were many straws in the wind. Pakistan, during this period, 'bitterly assailed the United States for assisting neutrals like India, and neglecting the allies. The statement of Pakistani leaders inflamed the domestic opinion which pressed it for opting out of the alliance and strike an Independent path in foreign policy so that it could garner the benefits from both the world, like India. Besides, the period also saw more stringent conditions of American aid and Pakistan made fervent plea for restructuring the world trade policies as the prices of primary commodities were going down in comparison with the prices of manufactured goods of the industrialized world in which it became the worst sufferer[157].

But an analysis of foreign aid that Pakistan received from the socialist world, particularly from the Soviet Union and China will lead to the conclusion that aid was never so substantial as to warrant a major shift in its foreign policy. In the first place, it should be borne in mind that only in March 1961 Pakistan signed an aid agreement with the Soviet Union which carried a $ 30 million loan for oil exploration and China, too, gave a credit of $ 60 million only in 1964. Considering the huge domestic investment during the period 1960-70, their aid was just a drop in the ocean, because the combined aid from both the Communist giants totalled only $ 645 million. Secondly, another crucial point must be noted in this connection. The aid was meant for investment in public sector. Given Pakistan's philosophy of growth and developmental strategy underlying it, it could hardly afford to alter its character. Pakistan's overwhelming commitment to the capitalist style of growth remained and its dependence on the United States and the Western world had so much structural linkage that it could not undergo so sudden a change. It could have been possible had the Communist world particularly the Soviet Union and China fuelled the Pakistani economy with all the investment resources it needed. In that event, Pakistan would have jettisoned the old philosophy of growth in favour of planed socialist economy or at least for a concept of mixed economy. Interestingly enough, major chunk of Chinese aid came only in 1970. Record shows that Pakistan continued to adhere to the old strategy of growth without slightest tinkering, let alone total overhauling, when Ayub hinted in 1962 that Pakistan might be compelled to look for protection elsewhere if her allies continued to disappoint her. *The Dawn* commented editorially:[158]

> "If we decide to take the plunge, we must be prepared to go to the full length in other direction... Interestingly, the capitalist pattern of so-called free economy which we have imported-along with American dollars—will have to be scrapped, and we must take the path of socialsm.....If Pakistan "looks for protection" to the other side, the alignment with that side will have to be of the closest nature".

These empirical facts point to the irresistable conclusion that Pakistan's development strategy, which sought to underwrite capitalist pattern of development in which foreign aid played a dominant role, was not the potent variable influencing its major shift in foreign policy behaviour during the period 1960-70. What variable or variables became more dominant that impelled the policy shift, we have to look for explanation elsewhere.

**Table 23**

**Pakistan–Foreign Economic Aid 1960-70[159] (U.S. $ million)**

| *Period* | *U.S.S.R.* | *China* |
|---|---|---|
| 1961 | 30 | 0 |
| 1962 | 0 | 0 |
| 1963 | 0 | 0 |
| 1964 | 39 | 60 |
| 1965 | 50 | 0 |
| 1966 | 112 | 0 |
| 1967 | 0 | 7 |
| 1968 | 67 | 42 |
| 1969 | 28 | 0 |
| 1970 | 10 | 200 |

## References

1. James N. Rosenau, ed., *International Politics and Foreign Policy* (New York, 1969), p. 171.

2. James N. Rosenau, "The Study of Foreign Policy", in James N. Rosenau and other, eds., *The World Politics: An Inroduction* (New York, 1976), pp. 13-36
3. Stanley A. Kochanek, *Interest Groups and Development: Business and Politics in Pakistan* (New Delhi, 1983).
4. Anil Seal, *The Emergence of Indian Nationalism* (Cambridge, 1976) pp. 298-340.
5. Honna Papanek, "Pakistan's New Industrialists and Businessmen: Focus on New Memons" in Milton Singer, ed., *Entrepreneurship and Modernisation of Occupational Cultures in South Asia* (Durham, 1973), pp. 61-106.
6. Seal, n. 4, pp. 300-3.
7. Paul Brass, *Language, Religion and Politics in North India* (New York, 1974), pp. 119-81.
8. For details see, Ishtiq Husain Qureshi, *Ulema in Politics* (Karachi, 1972).
9. Seal, n. 4, pp. 315-38.
10. Shahid Javed Burki, *Social Groups and Development: A Case Study of Pakistan* (Cambridge, Harvard, 1971), pp.7-17.
11. Jamil-ud-Din Ahmad, ed., *Historic Documents of the Muslim League Freedom Movement* (Lahore, 1970), p. 43.
12. K.K. Aziz, ed., *The Indian Khilafat Movement, 1915-33: A Documentary Record* (Karachi, 1972), pp.70-71.
13. Khalid Bin Sayeed, Pakistan, *The Formative Phase 1857-1948* (London, 1968), p.75.
14. Michael Brecher, *Nehru: A Political Biography* (Bombay, 1959), p. 129.
15. Hector Belitho, *Jinnah, Creator of Pakistan* (Karachi, 1966), p. 111.
16. *Ibid.*, p. 113.
17. Percival Griffiths, *The British Impact on India* (London, 1952), p. 340.
18. M. M. Qureshi, *Jinnah and the Making of a Nation* (Karachi, 1969) , p. 54.
19. Ahmad, n. 11, p. 204. Letter dated 9th March, 1937.
20. Belitho, n. 15, p. 114.
21. *Ibid.*, p.115.
22. CM. Naim, ed., *Iqbal, Jinnah and Pakistan: The Vision and Reality* (Syracuse, 1979), Appendix-I, pp. 191-207.
23. Manzooruddin Ahmed, "Iqbal and Jinnah on the 'Two-Nations' Theory" in C.M. Naim, ed., n. 22, p. 64.
24. Ahmad, n.11, p. 381.
25. Pakistan Resolution of the Lahore Session of the All-India Muslim League, 22-24 March, 1940; see Sir Maurice Gawyer and A. Appadorai, *Speeches and Documents on the Indian Constitution, 1921-47* (Bombay, 1957), Vol.11, p. 443.

26. Mohammad Ali Jinnah's speech in the Constituent Assembly of Pakistan on 11 August 1947, see *Quaid-i-Azam Mohammad Ali Jinnah, Speeches as Governor-General of Pakistan, 1947-48* (Karachi, n.d.), pp.8-9.
27. Sisir Gupta, "Pakistan's Domestic Crisis and Foreign Policy", South Asia Studies (Jaipur), Vol.7, no. l, January 1972, pp.114-26.
28. Ibid., p. 117.
29. Saleem M.M. Qureshi, "Pakistani Nationalism Reconsidered", *Pacific Affairs* (Vancouver, B.C.), Vol. 45, no. 4, Winter 1972-73, pp. 556-72.
30. For a detailed study of the political elites in West and East Pakistan, see Talukder Maniruzzaman, "Group Interests in Pakistan Politics 1947-58," *Pacific Affairs*, Vol. 39, no. 1-2, Spring-Summer, 1966-67, pp. 83-97.
31. M. Rashiduzzaman, "The Awami League in the Political Development of Pakistan", *Asian Survey* (Berkeley, Calif.), Vol.10, no.7, July 1970, pp.
32. Qureshi, n.29, p.564.
33. *Ibid.*, p. 565.
34. Gupta, n. 27, p. 118.
35. Rosenau, n. 1, p. 171.
36. Stanley Hoffman, "Notes on the Elusiveness of Modern Power", *International Journal* (Toronto, ont.), Vol.30, no.25, Spring 1975, pp. 183-205.
37. James N. Rosenau and others, eds., The Analysis of International Politics (New York, 1972), p. 4.
38. Harold and Margaret Sprout, *Foundation of International Politics* (New York, 1972), p. 137.
39. Charles A. Macleeland, "On the Fourth Wave: Past and Future in the Study of International Politics" in James N. Rosenau and others (eds.), *The Analysis of International Politics* (New York, 1972), pp. 15-37.
40. For the details see, Harold and Margaret Sprout, Foundations of National Power (Princeton, 1945).
41. Sprouts, n.38, p. 158.
42. Harold and Margaret Sprout, "Environmental factors in the study of International Politics", *Journal of Conflict Resolution* (New Haven), Vol. 1, no.4, December 1957, pp- 309-28.
43. James N. Rosenau, *The Study of Global Interdependence: Essays on the Transnationalisation of World Affairs* (New York, 1980), p. 36.
44. James N. Rosenau, *The Scientific Study of Foreign Policy* (New York, 1971), pp. 197-237.
45. J. Bandyopadhyaya, *The Making of India's Foreign Policy* (Calcutta, 1980), p.29.

46. J. Cambon, "The Permanent Bases of French Foreign Policy", *Foreign Affairs* (New York), Vol. 8, no. 2, January 1930, p. 174.
47. Hans J. Morgenthau, *Politics Among Nations: The Struggle for Power and Peace* (Calcutta, 1976), revd. edn., p. 112.
48. Sprouts, n.42, pp. 309-28.
49. Chaudhuri Muhammad Ali, *The Emergence of Pakistan* (London, 1967), p. 319; Ayub also once remarked: "Just look at the location of the three rivers on which the life of the whole of West Pakistan, of some 45 million people depends. As our population increases, every drop of that water has got to be disbanded, stored and utilised", see Rais Ahmad Jafri, *Ayub: Soldier and Statesman* (Lahore, 1966), p.156.
50. O.H.K. Spate and A.T.A. Learmonth, *India and Pakistan, Land, People and Economy* (Bombay, 1972), pp. 14-120.
51. C. N. Vakil, *Economic Consequences of Divided India: A Study of the Economy of India and Pakistan* (Bombay, 1950), pp. 247-50.
52. Rounaq Jahan, *Pakistan: Failure in National Integration* (Dacca, 1972), p. 10.
53. Khalid Bin Sayeed, *Southeast Asian Pakistan Foreign Policy, Pacific Affairs* (Vancouver, B.C.) Vol. 41, no. 2, Summer 1968, pp. 230-45.
54. *Ibid.*, pp. 230-45.
55. United States, Senate, Khrushev's warning, 85 Cong, 2 sess., Committee on Foreign Relations, Hearings, *Events Incident to the Summit Conference* (Washington D.C. 1960), *Appendix one.*
56. S.M. Burke, *Mainsprings of Indian and Pakistani Foreign Policies* (Minneapolis, 1974), p. 179.
57. *Dawn* (Karachi), 15, May 1960.
58. Mohammad Ayub Khan *Friends Not Masters: A Political Autobiography* (London, 1967), p. 177.
59. Razvi, Mujtaba, *The Frontiers of Pakistan: A Study in Frontier Problems in Pakistan's Foreign Policy* (Karachi, 1971), p. 194.
60. Mohammad Ayub Khan, "Pakistan Perspective", *Foreign Affairs* (New York), Vol. 38, no. 1, July 1960, p. 556.
61. K. Sarwar Hasan, *Pakistan and the United Nations* (New York, 1960), p.52.
62. Sayeed, n. 53, p. 233.
63. *The Washington Post*, 10 March 1963.
64. S.M- Burke, Pakistan's Foreign Policy: Historical Analysis (London, 1973), p.364.
65. Hasan, n. 61, p. 50.
66. Lord Birdwood, *India and Pakistan: A Continent Decides* (New York, 1954), p. 236.

67. Stephen P. Cohen, *The Pakistan Army* (New Delhi, 1984), pp. 141-42.
68. Sir Zafrullah Khan, *Pakistan Foreign Relations* (Karachi, 1951), p. 8.
69. Ayub, n. 60, p. 547.
70. For data on the nature of this correlation, see R.J. Rummel, "Some Findings on Nations and Their Behaviour", *World Politics* (Princeton), Vol. 21, no.1, January 1969, pp. 226-41; Maurice A. East, "Size and Foreign Policy Behaviour: A Test of Two Models", *World Politics* (Princeton), Vol. 25, no. 4, July 1973, pp. 556-76.
71. *Quaid-i-Azam Speaks* (Karachi, n. d.), p. 250.
72. O.H.K. Spate and A.T.E. Learmonth, *India and Pakistan: A General and Regional Geography* (1967), p.304.
73. Rosenau, n. 2, pp. 15-36.
74. Jinnah, n. 26, p. 36.
75. *Report of the Commission on National Education, Government of Pakistan,* (Karachi, Jan-Aug- 1959), p. 9.
76. *Ibid.*, p. 63.
77. *Speeches and Statements Mohammad Ayub Khan* (Karachi, n. d. ), Part-2, p. 83.
78. *Government of Pakistan, Finance Division, Pakistan Economic Survey, 1976-77* (Islamabad, 1977), p. 198.
79. *Government of Pakistan, Finance Division, Pakistan Economic Survey, 1978-79* (Islamabad, 1979), Table 13.2, p. 199.
80. Report, n. 75, pp. 177-78.
81. *Ibid.*, p.117.
82. Cohen, n. 67, p. 13.
83. Sisir Gupta, "Indo-Pakistan Relations" *International Studies* (New Delhi) Vol.5, no. 1-2, July-Oct 1963, pp.174-79.
84. Keith Callard, *Pakistan: A Political Study* (London, 1957), p. 304.
85. Selig S. Harrison, "Troubled India and Her Neighbours", *Foreign Affairs* (New York), Vol. 43, no.2, January 1965, pp. 313-30.
86. Rajendra Prasad, *India Divided* (Bombay, 1947), p.337.
87. Maulana Abul Kalam Azad, *India Wins Freedom: An Autobniographical Narrative* (New York, 1960), p. 242. See also Selig S. Harrison, who wrote: "Ironically, though, it was Patel in the end who clinched the creation of Pakistan Congress Councils that the new State would never be viable. It would be good radiance to get at least some of the Muslims off his hand, if only, temporarily and would teach them a lesson. At best, they would ultimately have to come back on Hindu-dictated terms; at worst, India could enforce its dominion over its weaker neighbour". p. 85. pp. 313-30.

88. *Dwan* (Karachi), 22 August 1951.
89. Quoted by Ayub, n. 58, p.115; see also Indian National Congress, *Congress Bulletin* (New Delhi), 10 July 1947.
90. *New York Times*, 25 May 1961, also see "Pakistan: President Ayub and President Kennedy", *The Round Table* (London), Vol. 50, no. 247, September 1961, pp. 407-19.
91. United Nations, Security Council, *Official Records* (S.C.O.R.), Supplementary for November 1948, pp. 72-73.
92. While these above facts are historically authentic they do not represent the official position of the Government of India whose official spokesman was Prime Minister Mr. Nehru. To set at rest all these doubts he once declared in a public meeting: "Partition is a fait accompli and India is aware that it cannot reverse history". He added, "we have accepted the creation of Pakistan with full consideration and will never think of undoing it." *The Hindu* (Madras), 2 February 1957. On another occasion, Mr. Nehru (replying to Gen Ayub Khan's charges that India was trying to isolate Pakistan), attributed it to Pakistan's belief that India had not reconciled to partition and it wanted to keep Pakistan weak etc "Any thing more unrealistic and devoid of fact, I cannot imagine..." India, Rajya Sabha, *Debates*, 15 December 1958, cols. 2257-58.
93. Harrison, n. 85, p. 319.
94. Callard, n. 84, p. 304.
95. Burke, n. 64, p. 116.
96. Edgar Snow, Quoted by S.M. Burke, in Burke, n. 64, p.116.
97. M.S. Venkataramani, *The American Role in Pakistan* (New Delhi, 1982), p. 5.
98. Callard, n. 84, p. 303.
99. Stephen P. Cohen, "Image and Perception in India-Pakistan Relations" in M.S. Rajan and Sivaji Ganguly, eds. , *Great Power Relation World Order and the Third World* (New Delhi, 1981), pp. 281-90.
100. Ayub, n. 58, pp. 20-21.
101. Fazal Muqueem Khan, *The Story of the Pakistan Army* (Karachi, 1963), p. 29.
102. *Ibid.*, p. 40.
103. Birdwood, n. 66, pp. 84-85.
104. For details see, The International Institute of Strategic Studies, The Military Balance, 1965-1970 / 80 (London, 1966-68). Bilal Hashmi has quoted this figure but omitted for the year 1963, see, Bilal Hashmi, "Dragon Seed: Military in the State", Hassan Gardezi and Jamil Rashid, eds., Pakistan:

The Roots of Dictatorship, The Political Economy of a Praetorian State (Delhi, 1983), pp. 148-79.

105. Defense Comments, Financial Appendix and NSC 5909/1.U.S. Policy Toward South Asia (India, Pakistan, Afghanistan, Ceylon and Nepal), quoted by Sultana Afroz, The Cold War and United States Military Aid to Pakistan 1947-1960: A reassessment' in South Asia, Vol. XVII, no.1 (1994), pp.57-72.
106. Defense Comments; Financial Appendix to NSC 5909/1.
107. United States Policy Toward South Asia; Financial Appendix to NSC 5909/ 1.
108. Financial Appendix to NSC 5909/1.
109. 'Pakistan Mutual Defense Assistance', 19 May 1954, U.S. Treaties and other International Agreements (Department of State, Washington, U.S. Government Printing Office, 1955), pp. 852-57.
110. Financial Appendix to NSC 5909/1.
111. Amon A. Jordan Jr., Foreign Aid and Defense of Southeast Asia; and Harrison, 'Cost of a Mistake', The New Republic (24 August 1959), p. 23.
112. Defense Comments, Financial Appendix to NSC 5909/1.
113. Sultana Afroz, The Cold War and United States Military Aid to Pakistan 1947-1960: A Reassessment in South Asia, Vol. XVII, no.1 (1994), pp. 57-72.
114. Hamza Alvi and Amir Khusro, "Pakistan: The Burden of U.S. Aid", in Robert Rhodes, ed., Imperialism and under development (New York, 1970). See also, United States President's Report to the Congress, Fiscal Years 1962, 1963-1969 (Washington D.C.)
115. Saudi Arabia's figures for the U.S. military assistance for which data are available as follows: 1964 ($ 1.3 million); 1965 ($ 1.474 million); 1966 ($ .799 million); 1967 ($ 1.04 million); 1968 ($ .906 million); and 1969 ($ 757 million); for details, see United States President's Reports to the Congress, Military Assistance Programme for the fiscal years 1965 to 1969.
116. Amos A. Jordan, Jr., *Foreign Aid and Defence of South Asia* (New York, 1962), p. 209.
117. Selig S. Harrison, "India, Pakistan and The United States: Case History of a Mistake", *The New Republic*, 141(6/7), 10 August 1959, pp. 10-17. His figure does not tally with the one provided by the Foreign Military Assistance Pacts.
118. United States Arms Control and Disarmament Agency, *The Control of Local Conflict: A Design Study on Arms Control and Limited War in Developing Areas, ACDA/WEC-98*, Vol.3, 1967, p. 329.

119. G.W. Choudhury, "Pakistan and the Communist World", *Pacific Community* (Tokyo), vol. 6, no. 1, October 1974, pp. 107-39.
120. Klaus Knorr, "Notes on the Analysis of National Capabilities in James N. Roseau and others, eds., *The Analysis of International Politics* (New York, 1972), p. 180.
121. Cohen, n. 67, p. 35.
122. It is pointed out by Khalid Bin Sayeed that the Pakistani army in the late 1960's was almost entirely recruited from four districts in the North Punjab, Rawalpindi, Cambellpore, Jhelum and Gujrat. While 60 per cent of the troops were Punjabis, 40 per cent were of Pathans, see John Adams and Sabita Iqbal, *Exports, Politics and Economic Development in Pakistan*, 1970-82 (Colorado 1983), p.71.
123. Jahan, n. 52, p. 25; *Dawn* (Karachi), 8 January 1965.
124. Cohen, n. 67, p. 119.
125. Olaf Caroe, *Wells of Power: The Oilfields of South Western Asia: A Regional and Global Study* (London, 1951), Introduction, pp. IX; XVIII.
126. They include new tanks, APCS, aircraft of all kinds, ''soft-skinned vehicles, artillery, electronics, radar and fire control systems, See Cohen, n. 67, p. 150.
127. Mohammed Ayoob, "Pakistan's Soviet Policy, 1950-68: A Balance Sheet" in M.S. Rajan, ed. *Studies in Politics: National and International* (New Delhi 1971), p. 245. It should be borne in mind that the Soviet Union does not agree to a one-way expansion in flow of trade as such increase would affect its balance of payment position, and force it to supply weapons to Pakistan in lieu of other exports. It carries on trade on a barter basis, thus securing its comfortable balance of payments position. This clearly rules out more than a symbolic supply of Soviet arms in exchange for Pakistani exports.
128. C.N. Vakil, *Economic Consequences of Divided India: A study of the Economy of India and Pakistan* (Bombay, 1950), pp. 245-50.
129. Government of Pakistan, Ministry of Food and Agriculture, Agricultural Census Organisation, Pakistan Census of Agriculture, East Pakistan (Karachi, 1959), Vol. 1, Table 3, p. 33.
130. West Pakistan, Land Reforms Commission Report, 1959, Appendix-One, Quoted in Rounaq Jahan, *Pakistan: Failure in National Integration* (Dacca, 1977), revd. edn., p.15.
131. B.M. Bhatia, Pakistan's Economic Development, 1948-78 (New Delhi, 1979), p. 40.
132. Government of Pakistan, Finance Division, Pakistan Economic Survey, 1965-68 (Rawalpindi, 1968), p. 4.

133. United Nations, Statistical Office, Department of Economic Affairs, National Per capita Income of Seventy Countries, Statistical Report Series, E. No. 1 (New York 1950), pp. 14-16.
134. Government of Pakistan, Planning Commission, Industrial Policy of the Government of Pakistan (Karachi, 1961), p. 5.
135. Keith, Griffin and Azizur Rahman, eds., *Growth and Inequality in Pakistan* (London, 1972), p. 25.
136. For details see, John Adams and Sabita Iqbal, *Exports, Politics and Economic Development in Pakistan*, 1970-82 (Colorado, 1983), pp. 117.
137. National Institute of Economic Research, Role of Private Sector in Pakistan's Development (Karachi, NIER, 1970), p. 22.
138. The Government of Pakistan, Minister of Finance, Planning Commission, Fourth Five Year Plan and Memorandum on Aid, Pakistan Consortium, 1968-69 (Islamabad, 1970).
139. Pakistan Economic Survey, 1981-82. Quoted by *Omar Noman in Pakistan: A Political and Economic History since 1947* (London, 1988), p. 92.
140. Pakistan Economic Survey, 1979-80.
141. Mahbub Ul Haq, The Strategy of Economic Planning (1967, London), p. 266.
142. Haq, *Ibid.*, p. 9. also quoted by Omar Noman, n. 139, p. 40.
143. Rais Ahmed Jafri, *Ayub Soldier and Statesman.*
144. The Government of Pakistan, Finance Division, Pakistan's Economic Survey, 1973 – 74 (Islamabad, 1974).
145. It won't be out of a place to mention here that one of the primary interests of the United States Government was to advocate the admission of Private American Capital into the South Asia. Considerable pressure was put on Nehru for modifying the terms of the Industrial Policy Resolution of 1948, during his visit to the United States. It is presumed that similarly, Pakistan might have been pressurized, see Jayantanuja Bandyopadhyaya, "The Role of External Powers in South Asian Affairs" *India Quarterly* (New Delhi), Vol. 30 No. 45. October-December, 1974, p. 278.
146. Venkataramani, n. 97 p. 16.
147. *Ibid.*, pp. 17-18.
148. K. Sarwar Hasan, "The Foreign Policy of Mr. Liaquat Ali Khan", *Pakistan Horizon* (Karachi), Vol. 4, no. 4, December 1951, pp. 184-93.
149. Liaquat Ali Khan, *Pakistan: The Heart of Asia* (Cambridge, 1950), pp. 31-34.
150. *Statistical Abstract of the United States* (Washington D.C), 1961, Table 1197, p. 873 and for 1965, Table 1232, p. 864.
151. *Government of Pakistan, Planning Division, Third Five Year Plan*, 1965 (Islamabad, 1966), p. 8.

152. See, table 23 p. 138.
153. For a brilliant analysis of foreign aid, see Mohammed Ayoob, "U.S. Economic Assistance to Pakistan 1954-65: A Case Study in the Politics of Foreign Aid", *India Quarterly* (New Delhi), Vol. 23, no. 2, April-June 1967, pp. 127-44.
154. Jamil Rashid, "Pakistan in the Debt Trap" in Hassan Gardezi and Jamil Rashid, eds., *Pakistan: The Roots of Dictatorship* (London, 1983), pp. 173-91.
155. *The Government of Pakistan, Finance Division, Pakistan Economic Survey,* 1978-79 (Islamabad, 1979), p. 146.
156. Bhutto, "Bases of Pakistan's Second Five Year Plan" in Hamid Jalal and Khalid Hassan, eds., Reshaping Foreign Policy (Karachi, n.d.), p. 117-27
157. *Ibid.*, pp. 104-12.
158. *Dawn,* 14, May 1962.
159. United States, Department of State, Bureau of Intelligence and Research. *Annual Reports on Communist aid to the Less Developed Countries.* (Title Varies) RSB-173, 14 November, 1962; RSB-43, 18 June 1964; RSB-65, 4 August 1965; RSB-50, 17 June 1966; RSB-80, 21 July 1967; RSE-120, 14 August, 1968; RSE-65, 5 September 1969; RECS-5, 9 July 1970; RECS-15, 22 September 1971 (Washington D.C., 1972).

# 4
# Systemic Sources

Foreign policy does not occur in a vacuum. Nor does it arise exclusively out of the demands that originate within societies. The all encompassing international system of which societies are subsystems also serve as stimuli to behaviour. One cannot study the external behaviour of nation states independently of the larger international context in which it occurs and towards which it is precisely directed. The linkage between the international system and the various national subsystems has become so pervasive that it has almost become a given datum for any analyst, analysing the behaviour of a state, to proceed on the basis of some estimate of the relative potency of systemic variables.

But the problem that baffles an analyst is how to conceive the international phenomenon in such a way that would lend itself to a systematic comprehension of the impact of its major variables on the behaviour of a State. The earlier efforts of the traditionalists to define the "world" as "the family of nations" or "the international society" to conceptualize the organization of international relations with a precise empirical referent confounded rather that clarified a sound analysis of international politics. As a result, with the advent of behavioural revolution, this imprecise and value laden concept "World" was gettisoned. And this unhappy experience was sought to be obviated by the efforts of the behaviouralists who conceived the world as "system" and redefined it as the "International system". This betook clearly an expression of their desire to adopt a precise concept, "system", which had already proved its potentialities as an analytical tool of immense utility in the study of social and physical sciences. As is understood in normal parlance in these sciences, the concept, "system", is said to exist, in an environment and to be composed of parts which, through interaction, are in relation to each other. Consequently, a system has a structure and encompasses functions through which it is either sustained or changed. If international phenomenon can be conceived in this way, the analyst can fruitfully analyse the major variables of the field under three foci, because a systemic perspective enables him to focus upon the actions of nations as the components of the system; upon the structure and functioning of the system which emanate from the interactions of the nations and upon the environmental factors which condition both the actions of the states and the operation of the system[1].

However, the concept of the international system poses some methodological problems for analysis despite its tantalizing simplicity. In the first place, while states, .or individuals, or groups are considered to be international actors forming a congeries of global systems, for reasons of both substance and manageability, it is necessary to distinguish between the international system and the many National subsystems. The special problems of states of the South Asia can be analysed in systemic terms; it is also possible to place them in the broader context of the international system as they are being affected by it through their membership. So, it is legitimate to view the South Asia as a sub-system as it conforms to the functional requirements of the larger international system. As the latter bears no characteristic of a subsystem, it can truly be called the only one international system.

Secondly, the identification of the units or actors of the international system presents another problem. It is a truism that a variety of units ranging from individuals, like public officials or private citizens, to collectivities comprising groups, governments, states or supranational bodies are considered to be initiators of action that sustains the international system. But, to the analyst, his goal will determine whether he treats individuals or collectivities as international actors. If his purpose is to explain the stability and change in the international system, he must perforce focus on states as actors. But if he is concerned with the behaviour of a single state or with a particular pattern of interaction among several states, he must dwell upon the persons who are legitimate decision-makers for the state. But most analysts combine those two levels of analysis by posting the state as decision-makers model of actors who comprise the international system. This boils down to the fact that action in international system is usually attributed to states, but these states are recognised to be a group of Government officials who act as the strategic decision-makers.

Thirdly, another set of methodological problems that confront the analyst concerns the international environment and its nexus with the international system. While the environment of a system is viewed as consisting of everything that lie outside that system, it is not very helpful when such a conception is applied to a system that comprises all the states of the world. Logically, one can equate outer space with the environment of the international system. But, as a matter of fact, the analyst is mainly interested in the political phenomena. Other kinds of phenomena are also analysed which shed light on the political dimension of the behaviour of the international actors. So, it is legitimate to view the environment of the international system as comprising all those events and conditions, both human and non-human, which are non-political in nature and which affect the behaviour of states and the operation of the international system. But, as the analyst is primarily concerned with an international political system, it further poses the problem of making an analytical separation from all other overlapping and co-existing non-political systems.[2] This naturally begs the most crucial question as how to conceptualize the politics of international life in such a way that defines the international political system. As the international political relations involve relations between nations, there is a pervasive tendency among the analysts to assume that the boundaries of international political system are delineated by the interactions between the governments. Now a pertinent point arises which must be answered first as to what differentiates an international political act from all those acts that are non-political in nature.

Harold J. Sprout and Margaret Sprout sought to address this task when they defined the international political act in terms of a particular actor–the organized political community—rather than in terms of certain qualities of the act itself which made no conceptual room for accounting other international actors that have entered into the changed arena of the global politics[3]. Similarly, Harold Lasswell, Morton A. Kaplan, Robert A. Dahl, Talcott Parsons and Edward C Banfield attempted to define politics 'and the common thread running through all their conceptualisations stresses that any political situation is an interaction pattern in which some actors are either producing or attempting to produce behavioural modifications on the part of other actors.[4] As every social role requires that its occupant attempts to modify the behaviour of others certain ways, the formulation fails to identify criteria for differentiating those behavioural modifications that are attempted in situations with high political content from those that are induced in situations with a low content. In James N. Rosenau's view, the mark of difference between the two situations lies in "functional distance" that separates controller from the controllee on those issues that initiate and sustain interactions between them. So, according to him, the boundaries of the international political system are determined by the actions and resources that contribute to the initiation and maintenance of control relations between functionally distant international factors[5]. By differentiating international politics from other types of politics on the basis of much greater functional distance that separates its actors, his conceptualization of the international political system served to draw its much complicated boundary.

Lastly, the systemic perspective still presents another problem. There is a strong conviction that in the systems concept, a bias is built in favour of stability. As a matter of fact, a system analyst never assumes that the requisite functions will be performed always. He willy-nilly makes enough conceptual norm for accounting for instability that leads to the collapse of the system into its environment or to its transformation, so it is possible to view that any international system as located at any moment in time somewhere on a continuum that ranges from perfect stability to perfect instability and to treat the shifts in location that occurs through time as a systemic transformation.

**Great Power Structure**

If the international system is defined in this way, then the most important systemic variable is the pattern of relationship prevailing among Great Powers in any era of human history. As argued earlier, while a seamless web of structures are formed out of interactions of states, individuals, and non-governmental actors, what is most salient is the one that emerges out of the behaviour of Great Powers. But it varies over the spectrum of time depending upon the number of Great Powers involved and distribution of capabilities among them. As a result, the theorists have labelled the various pattern of relationships marking the different phases of international politics in terms of distinct systems. It has been contended by a theorist that when five or more states enjoy the Great Power status on the basis of relative capabilities, the international politics is termed as a balance of power system[6]. Similarly, when the Great Powers dominate the world and the lesser powers side with one or the other, with an ideological or emotional commitment that precludes the chances of their breaking away from their blocs, the resulting pattern is viewed as a tight bipolar system. Further, a new structure of relationship emerges when the hierarchy of the system disintegrates consequent upon lesser states moving to the Great Power status and shifting their intra-bloc loyalties, it is viewed as a loose bipolar system. But, it must be said without any fear of contradiction that, as "reality" of world politics differs in the perspective of the observer, any attempt to trace the exact dates and duration of such systems in the history of modern times, is bound to be arbitrary. Nevertheless, the theorists contend that the balance of power system prevailed during the nineteenth century and continued till the break of the Second World War. From 1945 to 1959, the world was truly characterized by tight bipolar system, and world became a loose bipolar system during 1960' s. But a new pattern reminiscent of the 19th century classical balance of power system emerged in 1970's.

It has been widely assumed by the theorists that prevailing structure of the international system implies a number of crucial inputs into the behaviour of a state, no matter what order of ranking it holds in the prevailing hiearchy of world politics. The rules governing the conduct of its foreign relations are derived from the dispensations reached by the Great Powers to cope with their international environment for shaping the major issues of any era. Even if, these rules may not be categorically specified, their salience in shaping decisions on the part of the policy framers of a state is simply overwhelming.

Robert L. Rothstein, who has written a book on the interactions between small powers and their systemic environments notes that small nations are dominated by the system in the sense that the opportunities they have are dependent on the kind of system that exists. They can rarely create their own opportunities[7]. His basic thesis is that the influence of the small states as well as their security primarily depends on the balance of power between the dominant powers of the system and the level of conflict among them. As Pakistan is a new state with marginal international influence on the eve of its creation, the ensuing analysis will serve to highlight the hypotheses: If systemic variable was potent in influencing the formulation and conduct of Pakistan's foreign policy, then its continuity and change are correlated, with systemic requirements and changes from time to time. To prove this, historical details will be subordinated to analytical perspective.

The Second World War came to a close in 1945. It shattered the old balance of power system prevailing in world politics. The configuration of power was yet to take a definite shape. But the fact remained, Germany, Japan and Italy lay prostrate, the first divided, and the first and second occupied. France and China, though victorious, were weak and exhausted.

The Western Hemisphere was firmly in the grip of the United States of America. Africa and the West Asia were politically controlled by its allies. The Southern Arc was still a part of the British empire while the sphere of influence of the Soviet Union was confined to Eastern Europe, North Korea and North Vietnam. The level of power remained essentially of the order of 1939-45, with the United States and the Soviet Union emerging as formidable powers and the British Empire was down and out. But, there was a notable exception in case of the United States which had acquired an embryonic nuclear capability. With regard to the stratification of power the gap between the two and other international actors was great but less frightening as it assumed a decade later. In systems term, there was only one universal actor, the United Nations, but no formal institutionalized structure of military organization existed either for the system as a whole or for any group of actors. But a number of functional organizations like International Labour Organisation, Food and Agricultural Organisation etc. operated with partial membership attached to it. The Third world was yet to emerge as the process of decolonisation in Asia, Africa and Latin America had just commenced.

The Great War bequeathed two problems which defied solution and hangs fire even today[8]. In the first place, the political vacuum created by the elimination of the hegemonies here-to-fore exercised by Germany and Japan over the vast areas of the Northern Hemisphere was to be filled up. Disagreement arose concerning not only of Central and Eastern Europe but also parts of the East Asia overrun by the Japanese and surprisingly too of the Indo-China. And the settlement of the Asian aspect of the problem came to involve not only the United States and the Soviet Union and the people of the affected areas but also the new Communist Government in China after the consumation of the Chinese Revolution. Secondly, as the original inventor and user of nuclear weapon, the United States bore the onus of how to integrate it into the structure of its national arsenal and to define its relationship with the traditional concept of the role of weaponry as a technique of diplomacy. In the coming decades, it faced dilemmas of decision on many related issues of its control, use and denial to other adversaries. For the present, the two problems became mutually interlinked and interacting. On the one hand, the political conflicts arising over the problem of filling up vacuums threatened hostilities with all the potentialities of escalating into global war while, on the other, the tendency persisted that the exclusive possession of the nuclear weapon would be decisive factor in the solution of these great issues of the day.

The twin problem could have been solved in the post-war years had the Western Powers led by its prima donna, the United States and the Soviet Union carried forward the Grand Alliance of War-time Cooperation. But all such hopes wilted away as the Grand Alliance petered out. President Harry S. Truman recalls in his memoirs that early in 1946, Russian activities in Iran threatened world peace[9]. Instead of leaving Iran on the appointed day, they attempted to instal a "revolutionary Government" in Azerbaijan and vacated only at the behest of the United States. Similarly, in July 1946, the Soviet Union made an open bid to control Turkey by proposing to the Turkish Government that the Dardenelles be placed under the Joint Turkish-Soviet Control. Turkey spurned the offer with the active backing of the United States. Came close on its heel, in early 1947, an attempt by the pro-Moscow Communist faction in Greece to overthrow the national Government. These Soviet designs unnerved the Western Powers. Further, Russian actions in Central and Eastern Europe also served to harden the Western attitudes. Although the Western Powers, after the conclusion of War, conceded the Soviet Union a dominant position in Europe and Far East, with an assumption that a stronger Russia would prevent the resurgence of a revanchist Germany and Japan, it was soon belied as Russian intention gradually revealed. The Soviet Union turned a political revisionist and tried to communize the whole of Eastern Europe. This was done by making the belt of states between Germany and the Soviet Union into a "Cordon Communiste" which could bloc the corridor through which the Germany army had passed in the past with least topographical resistance[10]. It had a frightful consequence. The extension of Russia's political and military power into the heart of Europe represented a major alteration in the world strategic and political balance which few foresaw in 1945[11].

The Western powers could not view these developments with equanimity. The United States was compelled to shade off its isolationist stance in continental affairs and returned to a more powerful anti-Communist alliance opposed to such Communist advance. The first American response to the Soviet challenge regarding Greece and Turkey came on 12 March 1947 in the form of an address by the President Truman to a Joint session of the Congress. On 22 May 1947, the President signed a Congressional bill committing the United States to support these two states against the Soviet designs, assuming for the first time total responsibility for the British undertakings in both the countries. This policy soon acquir. the appellation of "Truman Doctrine", though conceived in the narrow context of threat to the two states. It, in fact, heralded the process of direct containment of the Soviet influence by laying down the general principles of the United States to support free people who were resisting attempted subjugation by armed minorities or by outside pressures. Then came in July 1947, the famous address at Harvard by the Secretary of State, George C. Marshall in which he expounded his famous "Marshall Plan" for the speedy economic recovery of the devastated Europe. As it was meant for all, in July, the representatives of Sixteen States—all of non-Communist Europe except Spain plus Ireland and Turkey—met at Paris along with the Soviet Union, Poland and Czechoslovakia. But the Soviet Foreign Minister Vyacheslov Molotov with its allies left the conference in a huff. This action set the seal to the breach between the West and the Soviet bloc. The history of Europe for years ahead was settled within these two weeks[12]. It served only to usher in the Cold War whose coming was clearly fore-shadowed in the salutary warning of Sir Winston Leonard Spencer Churchill sounded at Fulton, Missori on 5 March 1946 in words that have become immortal: "From Stattin on the Baltic to Trieste in the Adriatic, an iron curtain has descended across the continent". Since then international relations have been characterized by extreme hostility .and psychological warfares between the two powers. As time wore on, this assumed the form of a relentless struggle between Communist and Western political ideas each embodied in powerful armed coalition of states that tended to cast its dark shadow over the world politics.

Coming to the various phases of the Cold War, it is clearly deciphered that neither side was directly pitted against the other during the period 1945-47. True, economically United States was stronger as its G.N.P. after the War, was thrice approximately to that of the Soviet Union. Similarly, in the military sphere, the United States had a clear advantage as its ground forces, after demobilization, came roughly to 670,000 men whereas the Soviet Union had 2.8 million and the latter did not possess a Navy or Air Force comparable to the former. Besides, the Soviet Union had no answer to the nuclear monopoly of the United States. And the combined strength of the Western Powers was overwhelmingly superior to that of the Soviet Union. But what prevented both sides for a policy of direct confrontation, the following explanations seem plausible. In the first place, both were operating without clear-cut policies backed by domestic support. Secondly, the nuclear monopoly of the United States and its vast economic power contained premonitions for the Soviet Union in the event of a prolonged conflict. Similarly, the Soviet advantage on the ground in the context of an European War and the considerable uncertainty as to the destructiveness of the new atomic weapons coupled with the actual ability of the United States to deliver them on the Soviet target to ensure its total elimination compelled the Americans not to contest Russian primacy in Central Europe for its possible push westward, while the Soviet Union remained pre-occupied with consolidating its war-time gains and only half-heartedly probed its newly established perimeters, lest the West exploit its weaknesses.[13]

However, as 1947 wore on, there emerged a form of political consensus within both societies. The defeat of Henry Wallace and the appearance of bipartisan support for an actively anti-Soviet policy ended the post-war uncertainty in the United States, while the imposition of Stalinist terror conjured up the spectre of capitalist encirclement that served to fuel an implacable ideological hostility towards its rival. So, the confrontation took definitely a recognizable shape during the period 1948-52, because by July 1947, the United States goal of fashioning a comprehensive strategy for countering Soviet power was expressed theoretically in the "policy of containment"[14] and the Soviet Union responded in equal measure by bringing all the East European States under its tight hegemonistic control. While United States continued to enjoy distinct advantage in economic power which grew to over $ 400 billion (in 1966 dollars) and enforced a vital political link with the Western Powers by the infusion of massive aid, the Soviet Union also crossed its pre-War G.N.P. reaching $ 150 billion mark (in 1966 dollars) and became ideologically aligned with the Communist Government in China after it came to power in 1949. But relatively, the military power of the United States worsened when the Soviet Union broke its, monopoly by the explosion of an atomic device in 1949.

The above foregoing served as the major strand of development in the international system against the background of which Pakistan acquired international personality as an independent nation on 14 August 1947 out of the undivided British India. So it's founding father was called upon to formulate its foreign policy in an era of confrontation. Enunciating the broad contours of his country's foreign policy, Mohammad Ali Jinnah observed in his broadcast to the people of the United States in February 1948:[15]

> "Our foreign policy is one of friendliness and goodwill towards all nations of the world. We do not cherish aggressive designs against

any country or nation. We believe in the principle of honesty and fair-play in national and international dealings and are prepared to make contribution to the promotion of peace and prosperity among all nations of the world. Pakistan will never be lacking in extending the material and moral support to the oppressed and suppressed peoples of the world and in upholding the principles of the United Nations Charter".

So Pakistan adopted an independent foreign policy. True, Jinnah did not live long to see his policy took deep root, but his trusted lieutenant Nawabzada Liaquat Ali Khan carried forward his unfulfilled task and unswervingly adhered to it till his assassination in 1951. In a forceful reiteration of Jinnah's policy, he observed:[16]

"Pakistan was neither tied to the apron-strings of the Anglo-American bloc, nor was it a camp follower of the Communist bloc. It steered clear of the intra-bloc rivalry and had an absolutely independent foreign policy. Pakistan had all along been uninfluenced by the intra-bloc struggle going on in the world and had supported the cause which it considered to be just. The records of the U.N. debates bear testimony to this fact- Sometimes we agreed with the Western bloc and sometimes with the Communist bloc as the situation and the matter under discussion demanded. Pakistan could pursue such an independent course because it was not under the obligation of any foreign power. So we have not been assisted by any country in the world and whatever we have achieved has been through our own resources. Therefore, the question of subservience in foreign policy does not arise".

Now to test the hypothesis enumerated earlier, it is to be proved how systemic variable influenced the formulation and conduct of Pakistan's foreign policy.

It is a well-known fact of history that the Soviet Union, because of its self-imposed isolation, its relative self-sufficiency and powerful ethnocentric tendencies, was basically ignorant about the non-Western world. From the beginning of the Soviet rule in Russia, the question of proper policy towards developing countries called for an urgent answer. Lenin, right from 1921, had opted for a cautious policy of support to the nationalist but non-Communist regimes. It served Russian interests by strengthening the nationalist regimes in Turkey, Iran, Afghanistan as buffers against a revival of British control or influence. But during Stalin's time, the dogma that the world is divided into two hostile "camps" was reinforced and it persisted during the initial post-war years when it was viewed that anyone not in the Socialist camp was a stooge of the Imperialists. By 1947, Soviet policy became increasingly militant being reflective of a vituperative attack directed against all non-Communist states and forces. Capitalism and Imperialism were believed to be characterized at the time by the aggravated internal contradictions and on the way out. On ideological ground, it was believed that only national liberation movement led by the commnist parties would lead to the emancipation of the people of the colonies. So they were encouraged.[17]

Came the partition of India. It was natural that the Soviet Union looked upon the independence of India and Pakistan as a convenient arrangement between the British Imperialist on the one hand and the bourgeoisie of the two countries for the exploitation of the masses of the sub-continent. Even the country's leaders were not spared.[18] Jinnah's appointment as the Governor-General of Pakistan was referred to by the Moscow Radio as a clever trick pulled off by the Muslim League.[19] To a communist observing the British officers in the Indian and Pakistan armed forces, the British business operating in both countries and their membership in the Commonwealth, it seemed obvious that both remained dependencies of their former colonies.[20]

It is usually contended that the Soviet Union's early indifference towards the South Asian States was a reflection of a lack of a calculated Asian policy in Moscow rather than any concentrated effort to foment revolutions in this part of the world. Competent analysts of the Stalin period viewed that the so-called Zhdanov line was not meant to be applied to in any calculated way in the South Asia. It was precisely because of two reasons.[21] In the first place, the behaviour of local Communists was no surest indicator of Soviet foreign policy, even if they owed allegiance to it and it was also likely that the nuances of policy were determined by them often in a manner unknown to the Soviet policy makers.

Secondly, Stalin's major preoccupation in the post-war period was to determine the Soviet policy in Europe where the conflict was raging and where he had a distinct possibility of advancing the Soviet interests. Asia was peripheral in terms of the Soviet power politics and he could do little to influence events in Asia except keeping himself absorbed in the developments in China.

However, the creation of a state so close to their border must have made an immediate impression on them. Pakistan inherited those parts of the undivided India which had been the traditional source of Soviet interest in the South Asia. They had a systematic understanding of the Southern approaches to their frontiers and generally of the areas that lie between those frontiers and the Arabian Sea. The significance of Karachi sea and airport, as a strategic base and the nerve-centre of communication could not have been lost upon them. As Toynbee pointed out: "Since the days of Tsar Ivan the Terrible (Imperabat A.D. 153384) Russia had been seeking an outlet to an ice-free open sea.... for Russia in the twentieth century, an outlet on the Indian Ocean was the sole still untried possibility".[22]

This was evident from the fact that when in April 1948, Pakistan proposed the exchange of diplomatic relations, the Soviet Union responded readily, even enthusiastically. And in 1949, even before formal diplomatic relations could be established, Prime Minister Liaquat Ali was invited to visit the Soviet Union.[23]

As a matter of fact, Liaquat did not go. Pakistan badly needed economic and military aid, neither of which the Soviet Union was in a position to render. So, Stalin's invitation did not cut much ice with him. Besides, he was not enamoured of the Soviet system. Nor could he contemplate with serenity the idea of an alliance with the Soviet Union, for they have to change their political and economic system, adopt Communism and identify themselves with it in matters of foreign policy goals. They were firmly convinced that Russian policy was one of expansionism designed to create trouble, even to promote revolution because Communism thrives on chaos. So, it was repugnant to Liaquat. Besides, Pakistanis were bitterly disappointed by the indifferent attitude of the Soviet Union in the Security Council towards the Kashmir question during those years.[24]

But still, from the Soviet side there was no dearth of gestures to improve relations with Pakistan particularly in economic and cultural spheres. Till 1952, Pakistan enjoyed a favourable balance of trade with the Russians. In September 1952, when it faced food shortage, the Soviet Union signed a barter deal for immediate supply of wheat in exchange for raw Jute and cotton.[25] In April 1952, the Soviet Union also offered machinery and agricultural implements and textiles to Pakistan and also invited an industrial delegation to visit their country. However, despite all these friendly gestures, criticism of the policy of Pakistani leaders continued unabated in Soviet press media. Way back in December 1949, when Pakistan hosted an International Islamic Economic Conference in Karachi in order to find a middle way between Communism and Capitalism for the Islamic bloc, the Soviet Press dubbed this Pan-Islamism as an effort by Pakistan to prepare the ground for a Moslem political and military bloc.[26] But, on the whole, it can be said that the Soviet propaganda offensive was coupled with a desire to maintain and improve relation with Pakistan. There was no demand from the Soviet side to toe its line in foreign policy. Similarly, Pakistan was not keen to go beyond the point of bilateral contact. A line of distinction was made, during this period, in Pakistan's policies between anti-Communism at home and an overtly anti-Soviet foreign policy abroad".[27]

Coming to the policy of the United States towards the subcontinent, one finds that when India and Pakistan emerged as independent states, it, unlike the Soviet Union, greeted the two new members of the Comity of Nations warmly.[28] Recognizing the new Dominion of Pakistan, Secretary Marshall wrote that Pakistan, with a population of seventy million persons, would be the largest Muslim country in the world and would occupy one of the most strategic areas of the world[29]. Marshall in his usual characteristic style had underscored two points of key importance:

(a) Pakistan would be the largest Muslim country in the world; and

(b) Pakistan would occupy "one of the most strategic areas in the world".

It meant that when one or both factors became important for American objectives, Pakistan would be courted by them. It exactly happened in the years to come.

In the initial post-war years, even Upto 1953, the United States was preoccupied, like the Soviet Union with more urgent problems facing Europe, and the Far East. The South Asia was never an area of high priority for Washington. And there was hardly any attempt on its part to evolve an autonomous approach to the region as a whole. The major thrust of its policy was to get along with the Russians. As the South Asia was relatively free from immediate tension, Washington's first phase of policy (1947-53) was confined to pious gesture of goodwill and small amount of economic assistance.[30] No major diplomatic, or military investment was contemplated. And its policy on Indo-Pakistani disputes like Kashmir was guided by mostly by the British advice, the subcontinent was still treated as the British "sphere of influence". However, trends in the South Asia were kept under active observation as the United States feared Kremlin may turn to direct involvement and exploitation of what Stalin once termed the great reserves of the revolution in the colonies and dependent territories.[31] This was clearly evident from the behind the scene exercises conducted by the policy planners. Both Marshall and Forrestal—the chief architects of the victory in the Second World War—were aware of the Soviet-German Accord of 1940 which affirmed that the area South of Batum and Baku in the general direction of the Persian Gulf was recognized as the centre of aspiration of the Soviets.[32] And a comprehensive report of the Joint Strategic Plans Committee on South and South-West Asia approved by the Joint Chiefs of Staff on 29 April 1947 (JCS 1769/1) was under study, which had stressed "the strategic importance of the area not only because of the great oil resources processing facilities, but also because it offers possibilities of direct contact with our ideological enemies".[33] Synchronizing with it, was the record of the Defence Secretary James Forrestal's diary which revealed his considered view about the Soviet threat to the oil-bearing areas of the West Asia, and the possibility of an impending Arab-Israeli conflict and its likely impact on other parts of the world where the United States interest was certain to be affected, such as Egypt, Pakistan and North Africa.[34]

But Pakistan, right from its birth, was keenly obsessed with the desire to foster relationship with the United States.[35] The record revealed that its leaders realized the value of American economic and military aid for its development, adopted accordingly a philosophy of growth based on the capitalist pattern of production and turned to it for a regular source for supply of capital on the morrow of its independence. If Liaquat cancelled his Russian trip and chose to go to the United States, the purpose was too well-known to need elaboration. Speaking in the United States, he remarked that in a world of conflicting ideologies, at least Pakistan did not suffer from such confusions and its people were free from disintegrating doubts and confusion. Analysing the reason why he went to U.S.A. and not to the Soviet Union, a study group of Pakistani Institute of International Affairs wrote:[36]

> "There are important divergences of outlook between Pakistan, with its Islamic background and the Soviet Union with its background of Marxism which is atheistic... Pakistan had noticed the subservience which was forced upon the allies of the Soviet Union... Furthermore, there was the question whether Russia could supply the aid, both material and technical, which Pakistan so urgently needed".

Despite ardent desire of Liaquat, the policy planners of the United States were lukewarm to any meaningful tie with Pakistan. India received greater attention till 1949, when Jawaharlal Nehru visited America, the United States government put pressure on him for joining a security arrangement in the East under its leadership. But no exact strategy was defined clearly nor did the United States Government proceed to involve Pakistan or the Southeast Asian States in such a security arrangement immediately. True, in the last years of Truman administration there was a high-level conference held at Nu Wara Eliya in Ceylon on 28 February 1951 presided over by George C. McGhee, where the entire gamut of the United States policy towards the region as well as each individual country was discussed. It was also agreed that the most effective military defence of the South Asia would require strong flanks and Turkey, Iran and Pakistan were of primary importance on the West and Indo-China on the East.[37] The Truman administration appeared to have toyed with the idea of basing the Western defence of the West Asia upon the control of the Indian subcontinent. And with the appointment of Henry A. Byroade as Assistant Secretary for the Near East and the South Asia talks with Pakistan for a limited arms agreement, which was very much rife in the air, got off the ground and agreement in principle was reached. But as the officials like Chester Bowles, George F. Kennan and Dean Acheson opposed the move, the Truman administration, which was on its last leg, preferred to hold off.

Considering these facts, it is now clear that there was no systemic compulsion weighing with Pakistan policy-makers to align itself with any power bloc. It must be borne in mind that two major variables—its capabilities and its relationship with India—which influenced its foreign policy in the initial years argued that it could have easily cast its lot with the Western Powers, particularly the United States. But as the United States did not consider it as a participant in its global strategic system, Pakistan remained far-off. When Ghulam Mohammad made strenuous effort for a regional security system in which Pakistan would be the nucleus, the Truman administration did not oblige and simply encouraged it to form a Consultative Organisation of Muslim States to review matters of mutual interest which was politically and strategically a less inflammable proposition for the United States poised for the national election.[38]

By mid-1951, there was a hopeful sign that Joseph Stalin was exploring a flexible policy and essentially the Soviet policy was marking time.[39] It was evidently clear in the Nineteenth Party Congress of October 1952, when Stalin's spokesmen abandoned the post-war dogma which divided the world into two hostile camps and pictured a tripartite division: the "imperialists", the Communist bloc of "peace and socialism", and a third group of developing and largely "uncommitted countries". The countries which were gaining their independence were termed as "national democracies". They were in a transitional phase between the earlier stage of "bourgeois nationalist revolution" and the distant goal of building socialism. It was argued that these "national democracies", by adopting various socialistic measures, would move steadily away from the thraldom of imperialism and take more and more of a socialist content until one day they found themselves in the advanced stage of building the "foundation of socialism".[40]

Stalin died on 5 March 1953. Sharp debates ensued over the entire gamut of basic domestic and foreign policy. His successors made an agonizing reappraisal of the world situation, decided to relax tension within the Soviet society and within the non-Communist world and also to take a fresh look at the Asian states. Despite opposition of the "anti-Party group" of Molotov, Malenkov and others, Nikita S. Khrushchev made drastic reorientation by working out a modus vivendi with Marshall Tito's dissident Communist regime, redressing "the overtly irritating aspect of relationship" established between Stalin and Mao Tse-tung in 1949. Further he signed the Austrian Peace Treaty that ended the occupation of her Eastern portion. Khrushchev flew from one state capital to other in Asia and Africa with lavish promises of economic, military and political assistance for the Third World. He also initiated a series of steps for the East-West detente eventuating in the summit meeting at Geneva in 1955. To cap it all, came the Twentieth Congress of the Communist Party of the Soviet Union in 1956, which set the tone for the process of destalinisation. The Soviet Union now proclaimed that there are many roads to Communism. In some countries Communist can come to power through parliamentary elections. In some they can share power with bourgeoisie nationalist parties.[41]

This new flexble strategy was codified at the International Conference of Communist Parties in 1957. All these betook the dawn of a new era based on a more realistic appreciation of the world situation and representing a significant process of adoption and adjustment.[42] Since Khrushchev laid down the thesis that the principle of peaceful coexistence would govern the relation between states with different social and political system which eschewed interference in the internal affairs of other states for the purpose of altering their system of government or mode of life.[43]

But by the end of 1957, the leaders of the Sino-Soviet bloc had reverted to a more militant policy in dealing with problems within the bloc and in their approach to the West and other countries allied to it. The shift might have been caused by several factors. The sudden release of pent-up forces within the Communist bloc culminating in the Hungarian revolt presented the Soviet

Union an insoluble problem threatening the monolithic Soviet bloc. Besides, Mao's "Hundred Flowers Campaign" led to an eruption of bitting criticism of regime which convinced its leaders that little gains would accrue from "soft line". Besides, the reassessment of the world balance of forces stimulated by Russian success in launching on Inter Continental Ballistic Missile and on earth satellite in late 1957 was also a factor for the shift.[44] Mao's speech on the 40th anniversary of the Bolshevik Revolution lent credence to this. He declared on 18 November 1957:[45]

> "There are two winds in the world, the east wind and the west wind. There is a saying in China: If the east wind does not prevail over the west wind, then the latter will prevail over the former. I think the east wind prevails over the west wind; that is the strength of socialism exceeds the strength of imperialism".

So the Soviet concept of detente changed. In the early 1950's it was primarily designed to shore up a threatened status quo; but in late 1950's it was meant to effect a change in it. The Soviet leaders sought to combine summit from a position of apparent strength with a recourse to open threat.[46] Soviet activity acquired for the first time a distinctly global range being honed by Khrushchev's so-called "national liberation struggle" Speech of January 1961. Its message was clear. Ideologically decisive change could be effected by "national liberation struggles" under the protective care of Soviet power. It became the Soviet version of Dulle's policy of "massive retaliation". But the Soviet Union over-estimated the revolutionary potential for radical global change. As a matter of fact, conditions were not ripe for a Soviet policy that was meant to be both revolutionary and global. Cuban confrontation which reflected the elan of the new spirit made it clear that the policy was based on an insufficient base of power. So the East-West detente, which was going on, received a setback. It egged on the United States to go for a massive strategic build-up in 1960's.

During this period (1952-61), the Soviet Union became increasingly keen to get a foothold in the countries of the West Asia and the South Asia to counteract the efforts of the United States which was getting entrenched in the region, establishing political, economic and military ties with many countries as British and French power receded. The Soviet Union had two assets to counter the American and British efforts. The Post-Stalin leaders recognized that tension existed between the Asian States and the West on the one hand and between themselves on the other. The Governments of India, Egypt, and Indonesia were opposed to the Western influence in the area. And their policy of "non-alignment" was not only genuine but could be capitalized. By supporting one side or the other in the intra-regional disputes, it would exacerbate the difficulties facing the West and gain some influence. Such a policy would mean abandoning for the time being any hope of gaining a foothold in the countries attacked but a partial position in the area was better than none at all.[47] Another scholar also observed:[48]

> "The Soviet policy began actively to woo the Government of India. The essence of that policy was to take advantage of the tensions between India and Pakistan... The Soviet Government appears to have perceived more clearly than the Britishers or Americans ever done that antipathy to Pakistan is the pivot of India's foreign policy".

So in the context of Indo-Pakistani subcontinent, the Soviet Union policy came to rest on two premises. First, it accorded respectability to the Indian policy of "non-alignment" which was dubbed by John Forster Dulles as "immoral and short-sighted". To underwrite it as a viable policy intended to achieve a desired foreign policy pay-off, it unflinchingly supported India on the issue of Kashmir dispute in the United Nations. It, thereby, underscored the point which was brought home to Pakistan that policy of alignment with the Western Powers, particularly United States, has not paid it enough dividend in terms of solution of Kashmir dispute in its favour. The Soviet 79th veto on the Four-Power Resoluton was a case in point which shelved the Kashmir issue for ever.[49] Secondly, it was in a position, because of the state of its economy by mid-1950's, to spare enough arms, equipments and machinery for the Asian States. So, it relied more on material aid to these countries than on conventional tools of propaganda and diplomacy. This policy was applied to India with a hope that it would reinforce the inclination and ability of India to stand up to the West. The Soviet Union also dangled this bait before the Pakistanis. While bitterly assailing its leadership for their avowed pro-Western policy, the Soviet Union was equally prepared to carry on aid and trade ties with it. Numerous overtures of aid and attractive terms of trade were ignored by Pakistan which had a favourable balance of trade with the Soviet Union.[50] A scholar has argued that as economic consideration was a subsidiary factor in its relation with the United States, it coolly turned down the Russian offer.[51] While not joining issue on this score whether political or economic considerations were more paramount, it can be pointed out on the basis of overwhelming evidence that the Russian aid had no attraction for it for the following reasons. The Soviet aid, during 1954-63, to non-Communist less developed countries was only one-eighth, of those of the United States, and the Soviet programme was even smaller in terms of actual aid expenditures. While more than 5 per cent of the Soviet economic assistance has been extended in the form of non-repayable aid; almost 60 per cent of U.S. aid to developing countries comprised free grants.[52] The following figure will make it clear. While India got $1011 million from the Soviet Union, Pakistan received a paltry sum of $44 million. When it is set against the amount Pakistan received from the United States, one can well express it in a latter day term as "peanuts".

**Table 24**

**Soviet Economic Credits and Grants Extended to Non-Communist Less Developed Countries, 1 January 1954 to 30 June 1964**

| *Area and the recipient country* | *Million in current U.S.$* |
|---|---|
| Asia | 1999 |
| Afghanistan | 500 |
| Burma | 14 |
| Cambodia | 21 |
| Ceylon | 30 |
| India | 1011 |
| Indonesia | 369 |
| Nepal | 10 |
| Pakistan | 44 |

Besides, Pakistan economic system which was based on capitalist mode of production, had developed certain structural linkage into which the Soviet aid, with its emphasis on public sector enterprises, could not be fitted unless there was a total change in the economic system. In that event, it would have entailed a massive outlay which could hardly be guaranteed by the Soviet Union.[54] To the Pakistanis, the United States with its phenomenal economic growth and political power represented the wave of the future with which an alliance was worthwhile. So, while the first premise helped the Soviet Union making Pakistan realise the value of its political support, the second one failed because of its in-built limitations.

Regarding the United States policy, it is found that with the ushering in of the Republican administration headed by Dwight E. Eisenhower in January 1953, a basic departure from its strategy of "containment" seemed to be in order. It decisively opted for an offensive policy of liberation designed to roll back the Soviet power from its newly acquired East European allies.[55] It progressively possessed a strategic capability for inflicting damage on the Soviet Union. The United States became committed to the Doctrine of Massive Retaliation and expansion of Strategic Air Command (SAC). Given the crusading mood of Washington, it lent credibility to the offensive character of its policy. It created a situation of high Soviet vulnerability to large-scale American nuclear attack.

But the international situation was turning distinctly less favourable to the United States. By 1960, it found itself in a minority on the China question and defensive on such issues as Cuba or Congo. Cuba became a source of considerable embarrassment. The Soviet Union, assertive and dynamic, was pitted against, "a fumbling and defensive" America. Kennedy highlighted the "missile gap" in his election campaign. And the American weakness was ruthlessly exposed by the abortive invasion of Cuba and its total helplessness when the Soviet Union took unilateral decision to partition Berlin.

Decisive change occurred in the institutional fabric of the United Nations system which, too eroded the American influence. From an initial membership of 50, the United Nations moved to 84 when 18 members joined in the "African Year" of 1960. The impact was immediate and far-reaching, in style and tone, foci of interest and distribution of influence.[56] The Latin American Group, which controlled 40 per cent of the votes of the General Assembly since its inception, was now reduced to 20 per cent of membership. Its position as a pre-eminent interest group was taken up by this newly emerging Afro-Asian Group, which had grown from a dozen votes in 1955 to almost 50 at the end of 1961. They rarely voted in unision. For long the direct Soviet-American confrontation which dominated the Assembly and resulted in "politically unreal but numerically decisive majorities", now got diverted to new and large constituencies with diverse interests. When the West needed their support, to deny this strategic advantage to its rival, they were courted. And the Soviet Union gained even more from this new configuration, as it escaped the near-permanent status of isolated minority in Assembly voting during early 1950's. So the Afro-Asian Group held a clear balance of strength in the assembly voting which contained a lot of implications for Great Power behaviour in global system.

With the advent of Kennedy administration, the defence expenditure went up in the United States. Both conventional and strategic forces were reinforced. The United States was, in fact, widening its strategic base. The asymmetry in power unnerved the Soviet Union and its attempt to introduce Medium Range Ballistic Missiles clandestinely into Cuba triggered off protest from the United States for which it backed down, thereby underscoring American pre-ponderance in strategic sphere. It was a great setback to the Soviet global ambition.

With regard to the Asian political scene, it is found that while the United States had clear-cut policy to counter the Soviet power in Western Europe, it faltered and fumbled for a policy with regard to the great Arch of countries stretching from Morocco to China. Its helplessness was clearly highlighted during the Korean War when its defence position in Japan was threatened by the entry of China in late 1950. During the Truman Administration it was agreed in principle that the immense geographical advantage that the Sino-Soviet bloc enjoyed should be counteracted by the establishment of a ring of bases around its perimeter. American strategists believed that the only way to deter the Soviet attack was to overwhelm it with vastly American air-atomic power targeted from bases in countries ringing the Sino-Soviet land mass.[57] During this period, the major task of American diplomacy became one of initiating measures for enlisting the support of the concerned countries for providing facilities sorely needed by the Pentagon. In the fag-end of the Truman administration, the Secretaries of State and Defence and the Director of Mutual Security submitted a report to the National Security Council, entitled "Re-examination of United States Programs for National Security which underscored the following points.[58]

In the first place, there was a clear need for the United States to make its interest in the Middle East and South Asian region more explicit and to assume increasing responsibility. This could be achieved through the creation of a Middle East Defence Organisation in which Egypt would be the nucleus. Secondly, it also predicted that in Pakistan there would be greater readiness to cooperate. Thirdly, this could be a feasible proposition provided the United States carry out programmes of military and economic aid to a number of Middle Eastern States in addition to Greece, Turkey and Iran. Fourthly, it made no secret of the fact that India was a key country in South Asia. It favoured for substantial economic aid to India to off-set any negative fall-out from any of its proposed military aid programme to Pakistan. So it seems that the United States was quite keen to retain India's goodwill, even if, Pakistan was cut out for a vital role in this exciting enterprise.

This report with its recommendations became, as a matter of fact, the accepted blue print of policy for the Eisenhower administration whose Secretary of State, John Forster Dulles, gave it an institutional shape not only for the containment of the Soviet power but also for ushering in Pakistan in the American alliance system.[59] In keeping with this policy profile, Dulles gave immediate attention to the West Asia and the South Asia on his assumption of office. He visited eleven States of the area commencing on 9 May 1953 with the ostensible purpose of getting acquainted with the prevailing political realities and of assessing the extent of possibility for the emergence of the contemplated concept of the Middle East Defence Organisation. On 22 May 1953, Dulles arrived in Karachi and was given a tumultous ovation. He held a prolonged discussion with Pakistani leadership and was deeply carried away by the spiritual faith and martial spirit of Pakistanis and the geopolitical potential of their country.[60] He was also highly impressed by their understanding of world problems and their tenacity to fight the menace of Godless communism. He also did not fail to decipher that there was a perceptual convergence of Pakistan and the United States approach to major issues of the era so clearly demonstrated earlier by Pakistan's helpful and cooperative stand on the Korean war in the United Nations and the signing of the Japanese Peace Treaty.

Dulles then visited Egypt which was "aflame with anti-British sentiment", as the British was stoutly opposing any revision of the base agreement demanded by the new regime of Naquib. Dulles was fully aware of the strategic significant of air base.[61] But it was difficult for him to isolate American position from that of the British Government for enlisting Naquib's support. Dulles then promised to bring about a solution to the issues at dispute between Egypt and Great Britain, but he was equally sure, that the Anglo-Egyptian crisis could not be solved" in a clear-cut way at the present time and there was not much chance of "bringing up Egypt in an economic and military way". It could not become the main bastion of Middle East Defence Organisation. Similarly, situation in Iran with Mossadeg at the helm of affairs was inhospitable for the American enterprise as it was locked up in a dispute with Great Britain over the nationalisation of Anglo-Iranian Oil Company.

Dulles, summing up his impression on the conclusion of his visit, told the National Security Council that the concept of a Middle East Organisation was not a feasible proposition.[63] The United States should, therefore, work out a different sort of arrangement. Presenting his arguments at the close-door meeting of the Committee on Foreign Relation, he concluded that Turkey was really a strong point in the contemplated scheme of Northern Tier, whose fear of Soviet menace was real and deep-seated and they were strong, prepared to fight, and allied with US in spirit. "At another end, here you have got Pakistan... which can be a very strong point..." Though Syria and Iraq were "firm friends with pretty good Governments", the Arab States would be unwilling to "go along with defence organisation packed with non-Arab countries." In the circumstances, Dulles favoured the idea of a network of bilateral arrangements. He hopefully anticipated that once a Turko-Pak tie was hammered out, then Iran and other Arab states to the South could be enticed to join in future, thus making the security system a reality.

However, two events forced the pace for the implementation of the Northern Tier system with Pakistan and Turkey as the two strong points. In the first place, the Soviet Union's explosion of a thermo-nuclear bomb on 10 August 1953 had a profound psychological grip on the Eisenhower administration. Though the Strategic Air Command was in fine shape to counter the Soviet threat, a quest was on for acquiring bases in countries perching on the periphery of the Sino-Soviet bloc. As Suez base was refused by Abdul Gamel Nasser, Pakistan loomed large as the only ray of hope in the strategic perspective of the United States planners. Secondly, Mossadeq was ousted in Iran and Shah returned to power with a demonstration largely engineered by the Central Intelligence Agency.[64] Shah became and remained, according to Henry A. Kissinger, "an unconditional ally..." So, there was now a better opportunity to achieve the United States objectives with regard to Iran. Iran, with its 1500 miles of common border with the Soviet Union could now more easily be persuaded to join the American alliance structure.

Now, the National Security Council clearly laid down in its "Basic National Security Policy", the task for the planners to cope with the emerging situation:[65]

> "The effective use of strategic air power against the USSR will require overseas bases on foreign territory for some years to come. Such bases will continue indefinitely to be an important additional element of U.S. strategic air capability and to be essential for the conduct of our military operations on the Eurasian continent in case of general war. And the availability of those bases and their use by the United States will depend, in most cases, on the consent and cooperation of the nations where they are located".

It also clearly envisaged the eventual emergence of regional security arrangements in the Far East and the Middle East under the sponsorship of the United States and favoured limited economic and miltary assistance as the price to purchase the consent and cooperation of the target countries.[66]

On 30 October 1953 Eisenhower approved this document which set the tone for subsequent American action for realising its foreign policy goals.

It must be borne in mind that October 1953 was the month of hectic consultation of the American leaders with their Pakistani counterparts. Mohammad Ayub Khan had already had extensive talks before Zafrullah Khan joined him in October. What exactly transpired from their long stay in the United States was not known, but it is fairly inferred that it served to crystallize the on-going debate whether the United States should give military aid in lieu of Pakistan's joining American alliance structure.[67] And whatever iota of doubt lingered in American mind about the bonafide of Pakistani intention and in Pakistani mind about American sincerity was certainly dispelled after Vice-President Richard M. Nixon's visit to Pakistan in December 1953.[68] In the National Security Council which met on 19 February 1954, Nixon made a strong plea for military aid to Pakistan and for the creation of a military crescent that should include Turkey, Iran, Pakistan, Indo-China, Formosa and Japan. Interestingly enough, the NSC tamely endorsed this view and recommended that the United States should give military assistance to Pakistan.[69] But it added one rider that its formal announcement and military implementation should follow the conclusion of a military accord between Pakistan and Turkey. It was clearly in pursuance of such a decision and in response to the American prodding that a momentous decision was taken by Turkey and Pakistan. A Joint Communique, simultaneously announced in their respective capitals on 19 February said that the Governments of the two countries have agreed to study methods of realising closer cooperation in political, economic and cultural spheres as well as strengthening peace and security. By such a manoeuvre the American planners believed that they could keep Jawaharlal Nehru at bay, as it was not simply an American programme to supply arms to Pakistan, but a Turko-Pak alliance to which Iraq and eventually Iran were likely to accede, and it would take the wind out of the sails of the pro-Indian lobby in the American Congress where military aid to Pakistan would appear no more an indefensible proposition.

Came the historic day of 25th February 1954. President announced that the United States intended to respond favourably to Pakistan's request. Close on its heel, on 19 May 1954, Foreign Minister Zafrullah Khan of Pakistan signed the Mutual Defence Assistance Agreement with the United States. Thus, the dice was finally cast.

While these dramatic developments were taking place in the South Asia, the defeat of the French at Dien Bien Phu and the subsequent conference on Indo-China at Geneva called for new policy response from the Eisenhower administration to ward off the looming communist danger. The National Security Council viewed that communist domination, with the progressive withdrawal of the French power, by whatever means, of all the South-East Asia would seriously jeopardize in short term as well as in long term the Security interests of the United States.[70] The situational location and the respective equation of the countries of the area was such that loss of one country, Vietnam, would lead to capitulation to Communism by other remaining States. If all of the South-East Asia fell to communism an alignment with Communism in India and the Middle-East would threaten the security and stability of Europe. Pressures would be generated that would make it difficult to keep Japan free of the lure of Communism. So the administration discarded its long-held view that regional defence organization should grow out of indigenous forces, and decided to set up an organisation by rallying as many nations possible as were willing to work with the interested Western Powers. It would not only countervail any Communist aggression but also provide the Western Powers with a locus standi in the area.

Pakistan seemed to be ideal choice as it bordered on the South East and the West Asia and could be linked to a network of other organizations which the United States hoped to set up in future. But the American planners initially did not think of Pakistan as a possible participant. Pakistan was equally lukewarm to the idea because it was loathe to antagonise China. Its rulers were more keen on the formation of the "Northern Tier" system, so also Americans before. But when American requirements and priorities changed and Pakistan's membership of the South East Asia Treaty Organization was deemed desirable, it found itself a member of the organisation, lest it would forfeit its claim on United States' political, military and economic support. On 9 September 1954, Zafrulla Khan signed the famous Southeast Asia Collective Defence Treaty, committing Pakistan, for realization of the Western strategic objectives in Asia.

While this was in progress, the faint outlines of a "Nothern Tier" system emerged in the horizon of the Asia. America stood on the sidelines and encouraged Great Britain to take the lead precisely because of the imperatives of the prevailing realities. Any move by the former to entice Iraq in the alliance would have met with stiff opposition from the members of the Arab League, particularly Egypt, its arch rival. As Britain's agreement with Iran, which enabled it to operate two air bases and station troops, was to expire in 1957, it was believed that the best way to ensure Britain's continued presence in Iraq would be through its induction in the "Northern Tier" system. So the United States encouraged Britain to bear the mantle of Western leadership.[71] As regards Iran, another potential participant, the United States was aware of its treaty obligation to the Soviet Union which entitled it to send its troops to northern Iran if external forces entered. The National Security Council cautioned, in view of the fluid political situation obtaining on the eve of Shah's return to power, that the United States should move warily so as to avoid any policy directly provocative to the Soviet Union.[72] So Pakistan took the initiative with the blessings of Britain and the United States.[73] On 24 February 1955, the Turco-Iraqi Pact was signed as a first step towards the formation of the regional security system. Five days later Anthony Eden announced the British decision to join the Pact "to forge a new association with Iraq which would bring our relations into line with those which already exists with Turkey and other partners in NATO". Pakistan joined in September followed by Iran in October. The Pact came to be known in history as the Baghdad Pact. In 1959, Pakistan signed a bilateral agreement with the United States which was designed to further reinforce the defensive purposes of the Central Treaty Organisation as it was renamed subsequently with the withdrawal of Iraq.[74]

The foregoing facts go to validate our hypothesis that the continuity and change in Pakistan's foreign policy can be partly explained in terms of the systemic forces. It became evidently clear that Pakistan's long quest, which started even before its inception for a military alliance with the United States in the hope of enlisting its diplomatic support against India and of procuring economic and military aid for enhancing its capabilities, succeeded only when the global strategic forces underwent drastic configuration that threatened the security interests of the Western Powers, particularly the United States. It was only then that the United States enlisted Pakistan to serve its strategic interests by sucking it into its alliance structure. With the advent of 1957, America's strategic dilemma became more acute and need for Pakistan became more insistent, as a result relation deepened. So its alignment with the United States was partly a product of systemic compulsions.

In the early 1960's, the trends and developments whose outlines were faintly emerging in the late 1950's crystallized and altered the prevailing configuration of power.[75] The system changed into a truly loose bipolar one. In the first place, the intra-bloc rift took a cognizable shape during the early 1960's. The assertion of independence by France within the Western bloc gradually strained its unity. The French disaffection with the Western alliance structure began with the United States stand on the Anglo-French assault in the Suez Crisis in 1956 and the combined Anglo-American rejection of De Gaulle's proposed triumvirate of the West in 1958. It, however, reached its apogee with the French withdrawal from the integrated military command of NATO, and its rejection of British application for the membership of the European Economic Community. Though it restrained from opting out of the bloc, its attitude became defiant with the passing of years. It achieved a burgeoining and protected missile complex, a delivery system of manned bombers and a few Hydrogen bombs. It refused participation in all formal international conferences on arms control and agreements on nuclear weapons. It staked unmistakably its claim to a Super Power status and criticised everything Anglo-American. Similar was the case with China. Though it started with rift with the Soviet Union which surfaced clearly at the Twenty-Second Congress of the Communist Party of the Soviet Union in 1961 and became implacable after the Sino-Indian War and the Cuban missile crisis of 1962, it really affected every facet of international life. As a scholar observed:[76]

> "No analysis of relationship between Washington and Moscow, of the problem of nuclear proliferation, of the orientation of the Indian nationalism, of the thrust of the revolutionary movements in the Third World would be complete without taking into account the impact of the increasingly bitter dispute between the one-time seemingly close allies."

While not going into the details of the cause of 'the dispute, it can be said that the dialogue between the two Communist giants concerning territory, ideology and foreign policy set in motion a pattern of "dynamic escalation" in which the dispute slided down remorselessly, first into conflict and finally into an irreconcilable rift. As a result, unlike France, it opted out of the Soviet bloc, and challenged the Soviet Union for the leadership of the Communist bloc. Within a brief span of 30 months, it moved from a primitive atomic device to an hydrogen bomb, and staked its claim for a Super Power status. Besides, the events of Polish October and the Hungarian revolt which heralded a new phase of the intra-bloc autonomy reached its culmination in the Czechoslovakia uprising. Though, the hegemony of the Soviet Union remained unchallenged in East European security matters, its control over internal party issues, economic planning and foreign policy was now curtailed by national pressures within the Bloc.

Though this basic structural change was foreshadowed by the behaviour of China and France in the late 1950's, it was consumated by their persistent dissent in 1960's. By the mid-1960's both constituted two autonomous units of decision-making far removed from their Bloc affiliations. During this period, their policies revealed interesting parallelism. Each opposed the Soviet and American global condomonium which would freeze the status quo in Asia and Europe. Both went on increasing the stockpile of nuclear weapons, partly as a symbol of Great Power status, and partly to achieve greater autonomy in international politics. Each encouraged the other's assertion of indepencence from its Bloc leader. Each penetrated the new States of Asia, Africa and Latin America offering alternatives of aid and assistance to their dependence upon both the Super Powers.[77]

Secondly, there was a major change in the geographic location and technique of conflict between the two Super Powers. The Third World took definitely a recognizable shape as the process of decolonisation reached its final consummation in 1960's in Asia, Africa and Latin America. It was caught up more intensely in the vortex of Super Power globalism and actively courted and patronised by them. But during 1960's, some of the leaders of the Third World died and some were ousted. Particularly, the removal of Ben Bella, Nkrumah, Soekarno from the world political scene hurt the Soviet globalism which had already suffered its reversal in the Cuban Missile Crisis and the Sino-Indian War of 1962. It sapped the Soviet confidence already eroded by the Sino-Soviet rift. The period saw the rise of the American globalism based on strategic superiority.[78] But the most redeeming feature of the situation was that while ideological differences persisted, they were devoid of the emotional intensity of earlier years. Both recoiled from the prospect of a nuclear war. The new technocratic leadership of the Soviet Union remained deeply committed to Communism but not at the risk of a thermonuclear war. There was also a noticeable shift in the tone and tenor of the functioning of American diplomacy. Under Kennedy era, the need for a modus operandi with the Soviets received top priority. The centrifugal tendencies in both blocs coupled with the "balance of terror" compelled a renewed dialogue between them that commenced with the Khruschev-Kennedy Summit of 1961. The Moscow Test Ban Treaty of 1963 and the Washington-Moscow "Hot-Line" reflected their growing stake in stabilizing the spiralling arms race that would remove threat to the Central Power balance. President Lyndon B. Johnson went a step further when he altered the previous western priorities in Europe by making the East-West detente the basis for an European settlement that would eventually lead to the solution of the most sensitive Germany problem.[79]

With the onset of the Vietnam War, situation underwent radical change. It sapped the American economy despite its increased G.N.P. of $762 billion. It also eroded the post-war domestic consensus concerning foreign policy.[80] The ruling elites were deeply divided. As a result, the American global engagement became devoid of domestic support. In contrast to it, the Soviet economy got a quantum jump with G.N.P. reaching $ 372 billion in 1967. Defence spending touched $55 billion in 1968, thereby effectively outstripping the U.S. defence spending outside the Vietnam war effort. Thus by 1968, the Soviet Union was well on the way to eroding the margin of superiority. Both sides had a capability to destroy each other as a viable society but neither possessed a decisive first-strike capability. But initiative passed into the Soviet side. This changed relationship imposed on both sides a greater obligation to observe restraints in any unilateral use of force in international crisis.

This affected the Third World adversely in two ways. In the first place, to quote a scholar:[82]

> "The very stability of the global power balance and the determination of the Great Powers to avoid a confrontation makes them prone to seek lower levels of conflict and less dangerous ways of conducting their rivalries, which, in effect, means a concerted attempt to confine their conflicts to problems that impinge on them less directly and to localise them in such areas as are far removed from the areas where their vital interests are involved. To fight out their battles in the Third World is one way of ensuring that their own worlds are not touched by their conflicts and they retain a greater measure of option to escalate and de-escalate these conflicts according to the needs of their relaionship".

Secondly, it increases the dangers of local clashes and conflicts among the states of the Third World. To quote the same authour:[83]

> "To the extent that the Central power balance has become immune from the contagious effects of Third World conflicts, to the extent that the stability of Great Power relations can be maintained in spite of local and regional disturbances, such conflicts and such disturbances have become permissible... Indeed, the 1967 agreement at Glassboro is of great relevance in this context, as indication of what the Great Power can and cannot do."

So the major strand of the Super Powers' role in the Indian subcontinent particularly in Pakistan has to be viewed in the wider spectrum of their diplomacy in the Third World during this period.

Coming to the United States policy towards the South Asia, one finds that its broader conceptual framework was laid down by the Kennedy administration and was followed by his successor Lyndon B. Johnson. Its main planks were as follows.[84] In the first place, though the American strategic base was widened, there was concerted but simultaneous effort to reach accommodation with the Soviet Union. As a result, China replaced the Soviet Union as the principal enemy of the Capitalist System and progressively the policy of containment of Communism became synonymous with containment of China. Secondly, the non-aligned states were cultivated with greater understanding and sympathy. It was widely believed that their economic development and stable political order would enable them to eradicate their social evil and eliminate their economic inertia. In their effort to achieve these socio-economic goals with the ultimate objective of combating communism, Americans found in them an admirable congruence of interests. So Kennedy enunciated a "new alliance of progress" in lieu of military alliances for the developing countries, and pledged considerable economic aid to them.[85] Thirdly, there was corresponding decline in the value of "allies", because the development of ICBM and Polaris submarine had reduced the strategic importance of military bases and other facilities around the periphery of the Soviet Union and after the Sino-Soviet rift, China became the common enemy of both the Super Powers.[86]

In keeping with this, President Kennedy wanted to reorient the policy towards the Indian subcontinent. As a Senator, he once said: "We (want) India to be a free and thriving leader of a free and thriving Asia.[87] He strongly believed that India and China were engaged in a struggle for the economic and political leadership of the East.[88] So in their global policy of containment of China, India was expected to play a major role. But this did not blur his vision as to the strategic importance of Pakistan and the reason why Pakistan should be accorded a higher priority in the over-all global strategy of the United States. Though he was opposed to military aid and political support to Pakistan, he always favoured economic aid. But on coming to power, he revised his stand as the United States had a network of alliances with it, buttressed by the numerous commitments and assurances.[89] So, he made almost super human efforts to court Ayub and Nehru at the same time. He made it clear that the United States would continue military aid to both Pakistan and India only if the security of the subcontinent was directly threatened and in the event of the latter, Pakistan would be consulted in advance. At the same time, he made it crystal clear that he would not withhold the economic aid to India, even if, it refused to agree to a settlement of Kashmir. As it was an emotive issue he thought it would adversely affect the Indo-U.S. relations. This political equation remained basically unaltered despite the visit of both Ayub and Nehru to the United States.

The Sino-Indian War of 1962 radically altered the equation. The United States at long last got the opportunity to fulfil its long cherished wish that India should stand up against China and immediately initiated a programme of military assistance on an unprecedented scale. Pakistan bitterly complained as it was expected to be consulted in advance. However, to pacify its ruffled feelings, the Western Powers strove for a settlement of Kashmir dispute. Under concerted pressure, Nehru made renewed efforts to solve the problem. But when Sino-Pakistan border agreement was signed on 2 March 1963, Nehru told the Indian Parliament that it was meant to prejudice the joint talk on Kashmir[90] and again declared in the Lok Sabha on 13 August that the concessions offered to Pakistan must be treated as withdrawn.[91] However, Kennedy in a personal letter to Ayub assured him of American assistance in the event of an Indian attack on Pakistan.[92] He even confirmed in a press conference on 22 November that American aid was meant for the purpose of defeating Chinese aggression.[93] Though Ayub remained dissatisfied, the United States' policy makers were firmly convinced that any concession to Ayub on this score would amount to allowing him a near-veto power. By informing him in adequate advance of time of its plan, the United States has fulfilled its part of commitment.

This was too much for Pakistan to stomach. When it joined the alliance, "non-alignment was suspect in American eyes.... Over the years it came to assume a mantle of respectability...."[94] Perhaps nothing could be more a quirk of destiny for Ayub than the fact that it was he who as the C-in-C of the Pakistani armed forces, negotiated the military agreement, but now, forced by the turn of events, presided over its erosion as the President of the country. Making an agonizing reappraisal of the situation in the subcontinent after 1962 war, he came to a gradual but painful conclusion that the new trends in the American foreign policy were not a product of cosmetic changes in its policy towards the subcontinent but certainly reflective of broader changes in the international system. "Ever since the Soviet Union and the United States have come closer to accepting the gospel of coexistence, the need for their wooing of the smaller countries for support has receded. Aid was used as an instrument of the cold war, but in view of the new situation, ...he doubted very much whether it will remain aid at all..."[95] He also further reasoned that the war of 1962 coincided with the surfacing of the Sino-Soviet dispute. "Both these events led to a closer association between India and Western countries on the one side and India and the Soviet Union on the other." "Both the Super Powers started competing with each other in supplying arms to India; one to prepare it to face China and the other to maintain the balance in Asia." The net result was Pakistan stood in the dock, defenceless for none of its fault; the solution of Kashmir dispute went by the Western powers' default because the United States thought that in the existing circumstances a direct U.S. role in the talks would not be productive; and there is an unprecedented accretion of military capabilities of India as a result of massive onrush of Western weapons which Pakistan failed to stop. Ruefully reflecting on his shared anguish and fear with his nation over the relationship which was nurtured and built up with a lavish care of hard work in the fifties, he noted in his autobiography how it had ceased to command respect in the sixties:[96]

> "The United States' thinkers and planners developed an anxiety to build up certain countries in Asia as bulworks against China. They selected Japan and India for this purpose. Building upon India meant providing her with vast quantities of military hardware which naturally created a sense of apprehension among her small neighbours. Since Pakistan was regarded by India as her enemy number one, Pakistan was first to be affected by the change in American policy."

It also struck him that India might even turn its newly acquired might against Pakistan when a suitable opportunity occurred, particularly at a time when the Western countries were so preoccupied with their problems that they could not undertake any military commitment in the subcontinent or find it risky to do so for the fear of provoking a world conflagration. The feeling also persisted with him that in the event of India attacking Pakistan, it was most unlikely that the United States would honour its commitment to come to its aid.

Pakistan certainly had reached the dead end, particularly Ayub felt ditched and cornered. For long, he was toying the idea of reorienting the country's foreign policy but odds were heavily against him as his country was an integral part of an interlocking Western alliance structure from which it was difficult to wriggle out for striking out an independent path in foreign policy, let alone, making terms with the communists. But he was shrewd enough to realise that the changed international system, even if bristled with many problems, had equally opened up new vistas of opportunities which must be cashed in so as to turn them into diplomatic advantages. In the first place, the ongoing process of detente between the Super Powers would make it easier for Pakistan to go for normalization of relationship with the Soviet Union without encountering American opposition. Secondly, the convergence of policy of the Super Powers with regard to China, with the twin objective of preventing it from attaining a status of equality with them and containing its influence in Asia by bolstering up India militarily and casting it in the role of a rival leader in Asia, would certainly force China to come to term with its neighbour Pakistan. So it was pregnant with strategic significance which would be invaluable for Pakistan, it comes out of the American embrace and refuses to compose its irreconcilable hostility with India. Now, Ayub, at long last, reformulated his foreign policy which he fashionably termed as the policy of "bilateral equations". Its main thesis as laid down by him were as follows: In the first place, geography was the sorrow of Pakistan, for East Pakistan was surrounded on three sides by India and the only approach was from the sea and "West Pakistan was wedged in between three enormous powers with the Soviet Union at the top, the people's Republic of China in the Northeast and India in the South and East.[97] Ever since its birth, India had continued its implacable hostility, which precluded any possibility for establishing normal neighbourly relation in any conceivable future. Similarly, the Soviet Union and China were highly critical of its membership of the Western alliance structure. The former resenting its membership of CENTO and the latter of SEATO. But, it was possible to normalise relationship with them if doubts and misgivings on this score were removed. Secondly, history had placed Pakistan in the pathway of the conflicting interests of all major powers. Its location gave Pakistan strategic importance both in the South-East Asia and in the West Asia. So the developments of the post-war international politics in Asia in general and in the South Asia in particular could not be viewed in isolation divorced from the politics of Super Powers in the world. It is a truism, that the Super Powers have evolved over the years distinct policies for a particular region which were inextricably interwoven with the framework of their global policy. Besides, they have global strategy and global instruments of power to underwrite that strategy. The South Asia was one of such regions in their global diplomacy.[98] Lastly, the fact of life imposed another insuperable constraint on Pakistan which it could not transcend. Being a backward and developing country facing a hostile neighbour with rapidly developing capabilities, Pakistan had to bank upon the Western Powers, particularly the United States for enhancing its capabilities to countervail India's power for which it must perforce maintain good relation with those who were in a position to help it both militarily and economically.

Ayub was shrewd enough to judge that the foreign policy conceived in an era of cold war could hardly answer the problems thrown up by the emerging multipolar international system. So he endeavoured "to set up bilateral equation with each one of them (the United States, the Soviet Union and China) with a clear understanding that the nature and complexion of the equation should be such as to promote Pakistan's mutual interest, without adversely affecting the legitimate interest of third parties.[99] He was also acutely conscious of the fact that any bilateral equation could not be established in isolation; other equations would influence its level. In the end, each equation would be determined by the limits of tolerance of the third party. So each equation would have to be acceptable, to third party with whom it might be able to establish bilateral relations of mutual benefit. Ayub knew that difficulties and complications would rise as it was difficult to determine clearly the limits of tolerance within which bilateral equations could be fostered. It would be like just walking on a triangular tightrope. In fact, this policy wore the guise of a quadrilateral tightrope walking,[100] because, Indian variable is quite salient in Pakistan's foreign policy which necessarily postulated that in addition to the mutual equations which Pakistan maintained with the three major powers, the equations that each of these powers have built up with India has got to be taken into account in shaping Pakistan's foreign policy. In sum, it boiled down to the fact that while geographical compulsion weighed with him for reorienting his foreign policy, it served more as a rhetorical justification for the policy change than the political constraint which emanated from the multi-polar international system. He himself lent support to this line of reasoning when he stated:[101]

> "... clearly the whole pattern of our relations with others required fundamental rethinking. Some of the essential elements in our geographical situation had not been recognised, nor was there a clear concept of the nature of the political compulsions to which we would be subjected. I think it was the force of events which compelled us to undertake this exercise".

Ayub's revised policy choice was reflected in its new policy towards China and as expected, the United States took strong exception to it.[102] It triggered off extensively critical reactions from the Pakistan ruling elites. The Pakistan Foreign Minister, Zulfikar Ali Bhutto emphatically declared:[103] "We will undergo miseries but will not barter away our sovereignty which we have achieved after valient struggle and sacrifice." He went on to say that Pakistan was not going to accept dictation from any power and that no inducement motivated by economic assistance or military aid could allure Pakistan into subjecting itself to alien domination. Similarly, Ayub added in a bitter reparte to President Johnson: "My reaction to all these was as simple as that of any patriotic Pakistani who values his nation's honour and security more than anything else."[104] Finally, the rupture came when the Indo-Pakistan war broke out in September 1965 and the State Department issued a statement declaring the United States neutrality on the conflict and its policy to run in conformity with the action of the United Nations.[105] Economic aid was halted. On top of it, came the American embargo on military supplies to the subcontinent. Finally, the special relationship was formally broken when Pakistan intimated its decision to the United States to close down its strategic communication centre at Bedbar.

In the mid-1960's, the American attitude and involvement in the subcontinental affairs underwent radical change.[106] The Indian image was badly sullied by the October War of 1962. It finally gave up its long-cherished hope of building up India as a counterpoise to China in the Asian affairs. Similarly, Pakistan's credibility as an ally was called into doubt. And the rationale of the military aid as an effective instrumentality for the promotion of its foreign policy goals was also utterly disproved. The sordid spectacle of the two nations fighting with each other with the American arms confirmed the widespread doubt that the American supply of arms had only contributed to the spiralling local arms race instead of strengthening the security of the non-Communist world. After the Indo-Pakistan war of 1965, the United States kept its hands off and encouraged the Soviet Union to mediate in the subcontinental dispute. As the Sino-Soviet rivalry continued for gaining increasing influence in the area the United States chose the role of a passive spectator looking for an opportunistic crumb to fall from their conflicts as it remained pervasively preoccupied with cultivating the Soviet goodwill for winning the Vietnam War. As a scholar wrote:[107]

> In the mid-1960's, the United States was trying to convey the Soviet Union that if it played the game in other areas of the world (particularly Vietnam) a special position for it in South Asia would be the reward it could expect from its limited adversaries in the West. Tashkent was in all probability a manifestation of this phenomenon... Subsequently the United States seemed to have worked out a model that the Soviet Union and China should be engaged in a relationship of conflict in the subcontinent because of their relative influence over India and Pakistan. Washington could permit China to be as influential in Pakistan as the Soviet Union is in India, and then derive some advantage from the consequent conflict between the two Great Asian Powers over the future of subcontinent."

Now coming to the Soviet Union's policy towards Pakistan, it should be borne in mind that though the U-2 incident marked an all-time low in the level of relationship, there was deliberate efforts by both sides to isolate this incident which was fairly evident from the fact that continued negotiation concerning Soviet technical aid to Pakistan for exploration of mineral and oil resources was underway even in those crisis-ridden days.[108] Barely three months after this incident, on 9 August 1960, Pakistan announced that it had accepted an offer from the Soviet Union to help prospect its mineral resources, especially oil. Negotiation to this effect started in Karachi on 10 September 1960 and were carried on in Moscow by Pakistan's Minister for Natural Resources, Z.A. Bhutto. The oil pact was signed in March 1961.[109]

By the end of 1962, the "new trends" in Pakistan's foreign policy which reflected its growing compulsions of improving relations with the Soviet Union and China was clearly discernible to the unerring eyes of the Kremlin leaders. Numerous factors dictated a reorientation of the Soviet policy towards the subcontinent, particularly towards Pakistan. In the first place, consequent upon the Sino-Indian war, Russian anxiety sharply increased, that India might be lured away to the Western camp as Nehru's foreign policy came under blistering attack from the Rightists in India, some of whom pressed for an alliance with the West.[110] Contrarily, the more Pakistanis grew disenchanted with the United States, the more acceptable its foreign policy became in the Russian eyes. Secondly, given the Sino-Soviet rift and their acute rivalry in the non-aligned world especially in Asia, the Soviet Union did not relish the idea of a Sino-Pakistani axis emerging in international politics of the South Asia. India's debacle brought home the truth that it was no match to China militarily. Unless she composed her differences with Pakistan, it cannot stand up to China. So, it acted as a mediator between the two countries with the twin objectives of preventing Sino-Pakistan entente and ushering in a rapprochement for weakening Chinese influence in the South Asia.

To underwrite its new policy, a series of dialogues began between the two sides. The first step in breaking the barrier was achieved with the signing of a cultural agreement on 11 June 1964.[111] But the most tangible expression of its desire for a new relationship was its spectacular support extended to Pakistan when Kashmir question was debated in the Security Council on 3 February and 13 May 1964. There was a perceptible shift from its earlier position when its delegates called for a peaceful settlement of the dispute by the two interested parties.[112] Then came the removal of N.S. Khrushchev from the Soviet political scene in October 1964, which Pakistan heartily hailed. It was primarily because Khrushchev was hated for his unabashed pro-Indian policy, especially on the question of Kashmir. It was felt by Pakistani ruling elites that the removal of Khrushchev from power would introduce new elements in the Soviet-Pakistan relations. It was unlikely that Kosygin would strictly adhere to Khrushchev's policy.

However, the efforts culminated in Ayub's visit to the Soviet Union in April 1965 (at the invitation of Khrushchev but it materialised after his fall). It greatly helped both sides to be intimately familiar with each other's points of view on various issues affecting the relationship, Ayub himself wrote:[113]

> "It was not until 1965 that Pakistan was able to establish direct contact with the USSR. For eighteen years we knew little about each other at the human level. Inevitably, both sides acted under preconceived notions and suffered from a sense of distance."

He met Kosygin for the first time on 3 April 1965 on a cold and gloomy afternoon. He was greeted by a delegation looking stolid and sullen. Ayub, after the usual exchange of pleasantries, straightaway dwelt on the relation of the Soviet Union with India and the manner in which it affected Pakistan. He also raked up the issues of differences between India and Pakistan and put the onus of responsibility on both the United States and the Soviet Union for massive supply of arms to India. But, Kosygin very shrewdly traced the cause as a product of legacy of imperialism and blamed the Imperialist powers for perpetuating tension in the subcontinent. He ably contended that this was due to supply of arms either by the United States or by the Soviet Union. Though Ayub contested his view by bringing home the fact, that India was an expansionist power and not content with its present sphere of influence it failed to carry conviction with the Russian leader like Brezhnev who dismissed it by terming India as "a non-aligned" state which irked Ayub. Kosygin then turned to Pakistan's membership of SEATO and CENTO which as he put it, the "U.S. rules the roost".[114] But Ayub very deftly put across his views before the Russians:[115]

> "The Soviet Union had legitimate cause to complain about" the Pacts; but, they had to appreciate our position. India's avowed policy was to isolate us and we had to seek friends somewhere. We had not joined the Pacts to encourage aggression in any direction; our sole concern was our security... I then explained that our presence in the Pacts was serving as a moderate influence and in any case, the Pacts were not hurting the USSR."

To this Kosygin replied, "They may not be hurting us, but they give us no pleasure either".[116] However, the Soviet leaders appreciated Pakistani predicament with sympathy. Kosygin observed that they had been able to do considerable positive work in less than two hours than what others had done in eighteen years. Ayub noted that "there was general recognition on both sides that the meeting might prove a turning point in the relationship. And they recognised Pakistan's sincerity and came to have a better appreciation of its position."[117] The Kashmir question, which constituted for Pakistan the touchstone for testing the attitude of a Super Power like the Soviet Union, was never directly referred to in the joint communique, but it was couched in sufficiently vague terms for which Pakistan read different meaning into it.[118] However, the major spin-off of the visit was a reversal of the Soviet stand on Indo-Pak disputes. This was clearly reflected during the visit of India's Premier, Lal Bahadur Shastri to the Soviet Union in May 1965. In the Indo-Soviet joint communque issued on 19 May 1965, there was no mention of Kashmir or the Rann of Kutch, where both countries were fighting each other. It not only showed greater understanding of its "respected southern neighbour" but the Tass in a statement circulated on 8 May, urged both Pakistan and India to settle disputes by bilateral talks through peaceful means.[119] Commenting on the new Soviet behaviour. *The Economist*, wrote:

> "In short, the Russians made it plain that they had no intention of getting involved in India's problem with its neighbours... Though their public exchanges (Shastri's and Kosygin's) were remarkably cordial, Russians reservations were plain enough between the lines. Mr. Kosygin was clearly thinking of Pakistan when he said that peace-loving countries and people need not take any development in Russian-Indian ties as directed against them... The impression left was that the Russians would aim to keep both Pakistan and India looking equally, to Moscow as a friend."[120]

The same non-partisan attitude marked Soviet stand in the Indo-Pak war of September 1965. Immediately, on outbreak of the hostilities, Kosygin appealed to both Ayub and Lal Bahadur for immediate cessation of military operations. *Pravda* openly declared: [121] There is no doubt that the conflict in Kashmir cannot benefit either of the parties who are direct participants in the disputes". Interestingly enough, while the Soviet Union did not intend to blame either side for starting the conflict, its basic stand in respect of Kashmir's accession to India was unchanged. Both in the *Pravda* statement on Kashmir of 21 August 1965 and in the speech of the Soviet delegate in the Security Council on 4 September 1965, Kashmir was referred to as the "Indian State of Jammu and Kashmir."[122] It showed that even if the Soviet attitude towards Pakistan had mellowed over the years, its basic stand on Kashmir remained as before. After the cessation of the war, Kosygin played a major role for preserving peace in the subcontinent by inviting Ayub Khan and Lal Bahadur Shastri to come to a common table in its own soil–Taskent and succeeded in making both subscribe to a joint Declaration. As a Pakistani study commented:[123]

> "An important element in the bilateral meeting was the role of the Soviet Government. Mr. Kosygin sought to avoid all interference in their (India's and Pakistan's) affairs but at the same time he strove for the success of the conference. He played his part not as the

representative of the world revolutionary movement but as a classical peace-maker in a classical situation of diplomatic mediation... Mr. Kosygin conducted himself at Taskent in the role of an intermediary with most scrupulous impartiality".

It was a master-stroke of Soviet diplomacy that served to enhance its prestige in the Afro-Asian world where it was vying for influence with China. The Soviet diplomacy long excluded by the Britishers, staged a comeback and became firmly entrenched as a major power in the politics of South Asia.

Another major objective of Ayub to improve relation with the Soviet Union related to countervailing India's power–superiority in the subcontinent. The western arms aid to India had tilted adversely the military balance in its favour. Besides, Soviet arms aid to India was making the situation still worse, for whatever compulsion India had for coming to a settlement, completely evaporated. So he most persuasively made out cases against Soviet arms aid and presented the Russian two plausible alternatives. Either they must stop it or they must supply Pakistan with arms on an equal footing with India. Speaking at an official banquet in the Kremlin during his trip to the Soviet Union in September-October 1967, he declared:[124] "The indiscriminate increase in armaments and the growing military imbalance in the subcontinent is... a danger to peace". But he failed to bring the Kremlin leaders to his point of view. The Soviet Union frankly demanded the closer of Bedbar base as a price for the Soviet supply of arms.[125] Brezhnev made it pointedly clear that as long as it allowed its territory to be used for espionage by the United States communication centre there would be no change in their policy. Faced with an obdurate Russian attitude, he gave in. He served a notice on the United States on 7 April 1968 that the lease of the base would not be renewed beyond the expiry of 1 July 1968. This certainly removed a major irritant in Soviet-Pakistan relationship. Numerous variables dictated such a course of action by Ayub. In the first place, the upheavals in China during the Cultural Revolution made him nervous and he kept his fingers crossed as to its final outcome and its bearing on the Sino-Pakistan relation. So, he looked to the Russians for protection in any eventuality. Secondly, he was panicked over continued supply of Soviet arms to India on a massive scale. Pakistan took strong exception to it but was helpless when early in 1968 the Soviet Union decided to supply a hundred Su-7 fighter bombers to India. Pakistan Foreign Minister, Sharifuddin Pirzada made no secret of it when he declared: "This will further widen the military imbalance between India and Pakistan and thereby contribute to the threatening arms race between them to the detriment of their economic development". Thirdly, India was not adversely affected by the American embargo. Within two weeks of Ayub's decision, Kosygin visited Pakistan in April 1968. Ayub succeeded in extracting several commitments from Kosygin on the question of economic assistance, but their talks ran into difficulties on the question of Russian arms aid to India and the United States' use of the Peshawar base.[127] However, the talk was "a good augury for the development of future relations between the two countries but it underscored the divergency of outlook of both countries on the sensitive issues like the supply of arms to India and the Soviet stand on Kashmir.[128] But, on the whole, it paved the way for the lifting of the Russian embargo on the sale of arms to Pakistan which was announced at the end of a visit to the Soviet Union by a Pakistani military delegation headed by the Commander-in-Chief, General Yahya Khan, in 1968.[129] Though the supply was resumed, it was never satisfactory nor regular. Ayub resigned in March 1969.

On the basis of the foregoing facts, it can be reasonably concluded that Pakistan, during the period, 1960-69, ceased to be a Western satellite. It attempted to maintain a balance of cordiality between the Super Powers. While expressing gratitude to the United States for the economic aid that has been given to Pakistan, it indicated a deep awareness of the American global interests, and did not venture at all to antagonise the Soviet Union. Ayub convinced the Russians that Pakistan joined the Western alliance system only to ensure its security. He emphatically denied this as a product of a policy of expediency. As he wrote:[130]

> "If their global policy is served by our understanding of their problems and not by our not acting against them, well and good. But, if the demand goes beyond that and requires us to do something that is against the interests of another power, then we will have to decline because that would be going against the interests of Pakistan".

*The Time* Magazine's comment is appropriate when it observed that the year 1960 might come to be known as the year when neutralism in Pakistan's foreign policy became respectable.[131]

On the basis of foregoing analysis, it is possible on the part of scholars to attribute numerous variables influencing Pakistan's policy of "bilateral equations". Pakistan's disenchantment with the Western Powers, particularly the United States, began much earlier than 1960, though honed by the October War. Similarly, Pakistan's desire to improve ties with the Soviet Union was equally reciprocated by the Soviet Union, though there was no love lost between them. If one looks for explanation as to why Pakistan failed to reorient its foreign policy, then it is the systemic variable which provides the answer. Pakistan which was a member of the United States orchestrated Western alliance could not just simply ignore its treaty obligations in an era of Cold War. As systemic changes occurred, when growing East-West detente spelt greater understanding between the two Super Powers and the Soviet Union flaunted the olive branch of Peaceful Co-existence between the two different systems and the values of allies dwindled for them, then it became opportunistic and easy for Pakistan to strike out independent posture in its foreign policy behaviour. It got further opportunity as the Sino-Soviet rift deepened and each vied for influence in Afro-Asian world, particularly in the South Asia. Further, as Sino-Pakistani axis was taking shape in the wake of Sino-Indian conflict, it compelled the Soviet Union to come to terms with Pakistan which also found a congenial international milieu to refashion its foreign policy.

In the period following 1969, Khrushchev's successors were animated with a belief that the world was moving away from a quiescent state into a dynamic phase conducive to revolutionary upheavals. So they pursued a selective strategy of concentration on the Eurasian Continent. Its main planks were: First, the isolation of China in the East and the flirtation with Japan; the consolidation of their position in the South Asia and presence in the West Asia and Mediterranean.[132] To underwrite this strategy, they relied more on diplomacy and military presence, exploited nationalism and reoriented their foreign economic aid to a few select countries. This strategy synchronized with the reappraisal of American foreign policy initiated by Richard Nixon after the assumption of Office of Presidency in 1969. It rested on two major premises. In the first place, the United States was pursuing a policy of detente with the Soviet Union in a radically different situation in which the latter had erased the long-held strategic superiority of the former. So, its success depends on a balanced relationship with China that would shore up its bargaining position for striking a strategic deal with the Soviet Union. Secondly, the growing Sino-Soviet cleavage opened up a new vista for the United States to pursue a triangular pattern of global politics. Although it was enunciated as a systematic policy option only in 1972, its bare outlines were faintly visible much before. A scholar aptly observed:[133]

> "The very success of the Soviet Union in emerging as an equal of the United States and in preparing the ground for a meaningful

partnership has at last temporarily made the United States averse to the simple idea of Soviet-American cooperation. It had at one stage fondly hoped to create such a partnership on the basis of the accepted superiority of American power but it is not yet prepared to carry the logic of Soviet-American parity to its full length. It is not impossible that once the parity of power, between the two is recognized to be the best available situation, the United States... will revert back to the old ideas. But at the moment, Washington appears quite keen to come to terms with a triangular world balance..."

So, the main thrust of Nixon's foreign policy was the reinstatement of the Soviet Union as necessarily the main rival of the United States and the reduction of America's engagement against China around the periphery of the People's Republic. During 1969 and 1970, this reduction of the American presence in Asia began under the so-called "Guam Doctrine". By the beginning of 1971, the United States and China were both ready to undertake its complement—the improvement of the Sino-American relations as a means of shoring up the position of both against their common rival-the Soviet Union. In response, the Soviet Union (faced with an implacable Chinese hostility) was deeply concerned about the fast crystallizing Washington-Peking ties and made strenous effort to balance its negative fallout through its own initiative vis-a-vis Washington designed to convey the greater desirability of an American-Soviet accommodation. But at the same time, it went ahead with some programmes of acquiring a first strike capability and roughly matched the United States, by mid-1970's, in strategic sector. The result was that both powers were, by early 1970's, checking each other and their power in some cases overlapped (as in Mediterranean). This promoted heightened pressures on them to develop more stable rules of behaviour.

With the assumption of office of Presidency by Richard M. Nixon in 1969, one finds a noticeable shift in the attitude of the United States towards Pakistan.[134] It was made adequately evident in Aid-Pakistan Consortium meeting held in Paris in May 1969. Subsequent visit of Nixon also spoke volumes of his sincerity for strengthening the loose tie of friendship with Pakistan. He made it unequivocally clear that now as President, with somewhat more power and influence, he was going to work hard for the cause he had espoused throughout his political career.[135] As a token of magnanimous gesture, he reversed the earlier policy when, on 8 October 1970, it was announced in Washington that as "an exception to the general policy", the United States had decided to sell Pakistan military equipments to replace the equipments previously supplied. It was also to include sophisticated fighter planes.[136]

Similarly, the Soviet Union continued, without any let-up, its efforts to bring about a rapprochement between India and Pakistan with the twin objective of enabling India to stand upto China and weaning away Pakistan from the Western and the Chinese embrace. In pursuance of this goal, the Soviet Union stepped up its trade and aid to Pakistan. It also agreed to supply military equipments. President Yahya Khan also visited the Soviet Union twice. But the most interesting development was Pakistan's rejection of Kosygin's plan for a Regional Economic Grouping and Brezhnev's plan for an Asian Security System.[137] It was contended by scholars that the policy framers of Pakistan were aware of the fact that Russian initiative for cultivating friendship with countries on the periphery of China could not be isolated from the Sino-Soviet conflict which became acute after 1969. And the Soviets were working towards some economic and military groupings with the objective of curtailing the Chinese influence and power in Asia, particularly, in the subcontinent. So, Pakistani leadership realised its grave implications, for it would jeopardize its relation with China on whom they have relied heavily for any potential threat from India.[138]

While not denying the underlying reasons, it becomes difficult to reconcile the rejection of the plans as being directed against the Chinese with Yahya's decision to oblige the Russians by closing down the Bedbar Intelligence Centre, only in too recent past. The analyst must look beyond. Perhaps, the variable which became dominant to influence Yahya to take such a drastic decision was the systemic changes, of which he was perceptive enough to judge, as in the ongoing process of the Sino-American rapproachement, he was directly involved. This is ably borne out by a scholar who was his foreign policy adviser:[139]

> "Nixon, during his 22 hours visit to Pakistan in 1969, had an exelusive dialogue with Yahya for about two hours, and requested him to find from the Chinese the reaction to his new China policy. Yahya... did this job most conscientiously and with utmost secrecy; messages from Peking were delivered directly by the Chinese Ambassador in Pakistan to Yahya who sent them straight to the White House, to Dr. Henry Kissinger and finally to President Nixon... The usual diplomatic channel was avoided. When Yahya visited Washington in October and Peking in November 1970, his main subject of discussion with Nixon and Chou-en-lai was Sino-American relations".

This is also corroborated by Henry A. Kissinger, who observed:[140] "But Pakistan was our sole channel to China; once it was sealed off it would take months to make alternative arrangements. We had every reason to maintain Pakistan's goodwill".

In the face of these glaring facts, it is plausible to affirm that Yahya Khan, the channel of communication between the United States and China, understood how the considerations of great power relations would secure for him the American support for spurning all the Soviet proposals. His visit to the Soviet Union, it appears in retrospect, were mere smokescreen for carrying out clandestine missions for the American master.

Similar was the case during the Bangladesh crisis when Pakistan's response was shaped by equally systemic influence. Although the internal dynamics of Pakistan sparked off the crisis, India's subsequent involvement engaged the subcontinent in a wider pattern of conflict in which major powers got involved because the crisis threatened the very existence of Pakistan. The growing prospect of a new equilibrium of world forces with ominous implications for the South Asia, which was very much implicit in the Sino-U.S. detente, unnerved the Soviet Union. As it betook the ushering in of a new triangular balance in the South Asia, it was feared that the Soviet Union would be pushed into the corner. It meant that it would be left with one-third of the total influence in Pakistan and India marking a total reversal of its South Asian diplomacy which it was vigorously pursuing since the days of Tashkent. All its endeavours and ambitions to bring about a rapprochement between India and Pakistan in order to enlist former's support in its dispute with China and to open the overland route to India via Pakistan and Afghanistan to deepen her influence in the region and to reach Arabian sea were frustrated. Equally, the United States found its stakes were being jeopardized. It viewed that the strategy adopted by the Soviet Union was to humiliate China, undo its China initiative and to prove the futility of reliance either on China or the United States as an ally. If the Soviet power succeeded too easily, the United States concluded that it might be tempted to adopt comparable tactics in other volatile areas of the world, especially making it difficult for the much awaited West Asia settlement.

At the same time the United States was equally keen to consummate the Moscow Summit. War in the subcontinent should be avoided not least because of the damage it might do to Soviet-American relations on the eve of the "era of negotiation" which it was hoped that President Nixon's visit to Moscow in 1972 would consolidate. So the Americans were concerned to preserve China trip. As Kissinger said:[141] "Without China trip, we would not have a Moscow trip". As both the Chinese and the Americans were gingerly feeling their way towards a new relationship based on the hope that it would usher in a new equilibrium of global forces, their perception converged in an identity of interests in Indian subcontinent. Neither felt confident that the unresolved problems in other areas of world would not throw spanners into their policy of detente. So they were perforce to discover and sustain an area of agreement. The subcontinent remained an area where they would continue to supplement each other's power to limit Soviet influence and Indian power. [142] Kissinger made this point very clear. [143]

> "The festering crisis naturally came up in my conversation in Peking; Chou En-lai's perspective could not have been different from the conventional wisdom in Washington. Chou insisted that China would not be indifferent if India attacked Pakistan. He even asked me to convey this expression of Chinese support to Yahya a gesture intended for Washington".

So when the stakes of Great Powers seemed threatened with the eruption of crisis, they got willy-nilly involved.

## References

1. James N. Rosenau, *International Politics and Foreign Policy* (New York, 1969), p. 71.
2. James N. Rosenau, *The Scientific Study of Foreign Policy* (New York, 1971), p. 201.
3. Harold and Margaret Sprout, *Foundation of International Politics* (Princeton, 1962), p.75.
4. See Robert A. Dahl, "The Concept of Power", *Behavioural Science* (New Haven), Vol. no. 2, July 1957, pp. 201-15; Edward C. Banfield, *Political Influence* (New York, -1961), p.4; Talcott Parsons, "Voting and the Equilibrium of the American Political system" in Eugene Burdick and Arthur J. Brodbeck, eds, *American Voting Behaviour* (Glencoe, 1959), pp. 80-120.
5. Rosenau, n. 2, pp. 197-237.
6. These distinctions were first developed in Morton A. Kaplan, *System and Process in International Politics* (New York, 1957).
7. For detail, see Robert L. Rothstein, *Alliances and Small Powers* (New York, 1968).

8. George F. Kennan, "After the Cold War", *Foreign Affairs* (New York), Vol. 51, no.1, October 1972, pp. 211-27.
9. Harry S. Truman, *Memoirs*, Vol. II: *Years of Trial and Hope* (New York, 1956), pp. 93-107.
10. F.S. Northedge and M.J. Grieve, *A Hundred Years of International Relations* (London, 1971), p. 254.
11. George F. Kennan, "Peaceful Coexistence: A Western View'. *Foreign Affairs* (New York), Vol. 38, no. 2, January 1960, pp. 172-90.
12. Herbert Luethy, *France Against Herself* (New York, 1955), p. 353.
13. Zbigniew K. Brzezinski, "How the Cold War was Played", *Foreign Affairs*, Vol.51, no. 1, October 1972, pp. 181-211.
14. This policy received its most persuasive treatment in George F. Kennan's article in *Foreign Affairs* of July 1947 entitled: "The Source of Soviet Conduct". The essence of the policy was the conviction that Soviet pressure against the institutions of the Western world was something that could be contained by adroit and vigilant application of counterforce at a series of constantly shifting, geographical and political points corresponding to the shifts and manoeuvres of Soviet policy. If the United States was successful in this, it would force upon Kremlin a far degree of moderation and circumspection that she had to observe in recent years and in this way promote tendencies which must find their outlet in either break-up or the gradual mellowing of Soviet power". *Foreign Affairs*, Vol. 25, no. 4, July 1947, pp. 566-82.
15. M. A. H. Ispahani, *Qaid-i-Azam Jinnah As I Knew Him* (Karachi, 1967), rev. edn., p. 266.
16. *Dawn* (Karachi), 19 March 1951.
17. Jayantanuja Bandyopadhaya, "The Role of External Powers in South Asian Affairs", *India Quarterly* (New Delhi), Vol. 30, no.4, October-December 1974, pp. 276-95.
18. A.M. Dyakov, "Partitioned India", *New Times* (Moscow), no.3, 1948.
19. *Glasgow Herald*, 15 July 1947.
20. William J. Barnds, *India, Pakistan and the Great Powers* (London, 1972), p. 111.
21. Sisir Gupta, "Bases of Friendship", *Seminar* (New Delhi), Vol. 73, September 1965, pp. 28-31.
22. Arnold J. Toynbee, *A Study of History* (London, 1954), Vol. 8, p. 691.
23. *New York Times*, 9 June 1949.
24. K. Sarwar Hasan, *Pakistan and the United Nations* (New York, 1960), p. 54.
25. *Dawn* (Karachi), 27 September 1952.

26. *The Hindu* (Madras), 1 January 1950.
27. Aswini K. Ray, *Domestic Compulsions and Foreign Policy: Pakistan in Indo-Soviet Relations, 1947-58* (New Delhi, 1975), p. 23.
28. President Truman's message to India and Pakistan on 15 August 1947 in *A Decade of Foreign Policy (1950)*, by U.S. Senate and State Department (Washington, D.C., 1950) pp. 782-83.
29. Memorandum to the President (Harry S. Truman), by the Secretary of State (Marshall), 17 July 1947, *Papers of Harry S. Truman*, Truman Library, Independence, Missourie.
30. G.W. Choudhury, "U.S. Policy Towards the Sub continent", *Pacific Community* (Tokyo), Vol. 5, no. I, October 1973, pp. 97-113.
31. Quoted in Raymond A. Hare, NEA: South Asia, to Loy W. Henderson, Chairman, SANACC Sub-Committee for NEA, "Need for SANACC Appraisal of Possible United States Military Interests in South Asian Regions", 19 May 1948. *Records of the Military Advisor to the Office of Near Eastern and African Affairs*, Record group 59, National Archives (Washination, D.C.).
32. *Nazi-Soviet Documents: 1939-41* (Washington D.C., 1948), pp. 251-257.
33. JCS 1769/1, 27 April 1947, "United States Assistance to other Countries from the Point of National Security", *Foreign Relations of the United States 1947* (Washington, 1972), Vol. 1, pp. 738-50.
34. *The Forrestal Dairies* (New York, 1951), p. 440.
35. See my Chapter two.
36. Quoted by S.M. Burke, *Pakistan's Foreign Policy: An Historical Analysis* (London, 1973), p. 100.
37. M.S. Venkataramani, *The American Role in Pakistan* (New Delhi, 1982), p. 148.
38. Avra M. Warren, "Pakistan in the World Today", *Department of State Bulletin* (Washington, D.C., 1952), no. 26, 30 June 1952, pp. 1011-12.
39. Richard P. Stebbins, *The United States in World Affairs*, 1952 (New York, 1953), p. 43.
40. Philip E. Mosley, "The Soviet Policy in the Developing Countries", *Foreign Affairs*, Vol.43, no.I, October 1964, pp. 67-98.
41. Philip E. Mosley, "The Kremlin and the Third World", *Foreign Affairs*, Vol. 46, no. 7, October 1967, pp. 64-77.
42. Arthur Stein, "India's Relation with the U.S.S.R., 1953-63", *Orbis* (Philadelphia, Pa.), Vol. 8, no. 2, Summer 1964, pp.361-73.
43. Nikita S. Khrushchev, "On Peaceful Coexistence", *Foreign Affairs*, Vol. 38, no.I, October 1959, pp. 1-18.

44. A. Doak Barnett, *Communist China and Asia: Challenge to American Policy* (New York, 1960), p. 107.
45. Mao Tse-tung's Speech on 18 November 1957,in Moscow, in Mao Tse-tung on "Imperialists and Reactionaries", *Current Background* (Hongkong), no. 534, 12 November 1958.
46. Brzezinski, n. 13, p. 190.
47. Barnds, n. 20, p.115.
48. G.F. Hudson, "The Soviet Policy in Asia". *Soviet Survey*, June-July 1957, quoted in G.W. Choudhury, "Pakistan and the Communist World", *Pacific Community* (Tokyo), Vol. 6, no. l, October 1974, pp. 107-139.
49. United Nations, *Security Council official Records* (SSOR), yr.12, mtg770, 18 February 1957, pp. 38-39.
50. For details, Ray, n. 27 p. 4.
51. *Ibid.*, p. 54.
52. Milton Kovner, "Soviet Aid Strategy in Developing Countries", *Orbis* (Philadelphia, pa.) Vol. 8, no. 3, Fall 1964, pp. 624-40.
53. United States, Congress, Joint Economic Committee, *Annual Economic Indicators for the USSR* (Washington, D.C., 1964), p. 115.
54. Moscow asserted that the rendering of aid to newly independent states did not mean that it had money to spare. It warned that it could no longer remain indifferent to the objectives on which its aid funds were being spent. See *Pravada*, 3 May 1961, p.6. Attacking the ulterior motive of Soviet Foreign aid policy, the Chinese said, "They have gone so far as to cancel aid, withdraw exports and, tear up contracts as a means of applying pressure on it", *Peking Review*, (Peking), 26 June 1964, p. 10.
55. Brzezinski, n.13, p. 187.
56. Michael Brecher, *The Israeli Foreign Policy System: Setting, Images, Process* (London, 1972), p. 29.
57. Venkataramani, n. 37, p. 214.
58. "A Report to the NSC by the Secretaries of State and Defence and the Director of Mutual Security on Reexamination of United States Programme for National Security", 19 January 1953, *Collection of National Security Council Documents*, Modern Military Records Branch, National Archives (Washington, D.C.).
59. In fairness to Dulles, it must be noted that he only carried to its logical conclusion the policies with regard to Pakistan and the Soviet Union that had been conceived by national security planners of the Truman Administration. As a matter of fact, the American officials, for long, had been toying with the idea of basing the Western defence of West Asia upon

the control of Indian subcontinent. And they derived their impulse from the views of Sir Olaf Cqroe set forth in his book, "The Wells of Power. The Oilfields of South Western Asia-A Regional and Global Study", who, as Foreign Secretary of the British India, was intimately familiar with the strategic dimension of the security problem of the Indian subcontinent. See Selig S. Harrison, *India, Pakistan and the United States, Part-I, Case History of a Mistake, New Republic* (Washington, D.C.), 141 (67), 10 August 1959, pp. 10-17.

60. Press Release 313, 12 June 1953, *Department of State Bulletin* (Washington, D.C., 1953), 28 (22 June 1953), pp.890-91.
61. Testimony in executive session, 3 June 1953. US Senate, 83 Cong., 1 sess., Executive Sessions of the Senate Foreign Relations Committee (Historical Series, Washington D.C., 1977), Vol. 438-39, pp. 441-43.
62. *Ibid.*, p.441.
63. *Ibid.*, pp. 454-55.
64. Mohammed Raza Shah Pehlavi, *Mission for my Country* (London, 1961), pp. 82-110.
65. "Statement of Policy by the National Security Policy", 30 October 1953, *Collection of National Security Council Documents*, Modern Military Records Branch, National Archives (Washington, D.C.).
66. *Ibid.*
67. Noor A. Husain, "Pakistan-US Security Relations: Arms Sale, Bases, Nuclear Issues". *Strategic Studies* (Islamabad), Vol.8, no.3, Spring 1985, pp.17-33.
68. During Vice-President Nixon's visit in December 1953, Ayub briefed him that the Soviet Union would use India as a cat's paw for establishing a presence in the South Asia. And concluding his visit, Nixon declared on Radio Pakistan: "A strong independent Pakistan is an asset to the Free World" *New York Times*, 9, 10, 14 December 1953.
69. NSC 5409, "The United States Policy Toward South Asia", 19 February 194, *Collection of National Security Council Documents*, Modern Military Records Branch, National Archives (Washington, D.C.).
70. "Statement of Policy by the National Security Council on United States objectives and courses of Action with Respect to South Asia, 16 January 1954, U.S. Vietnam Relations, 1945-67: Study prepared by the Department of Defence, Vols. 12 (Washington, D.C., 1971), Vol. 9, pp. 217-18.
71. NSC 175, "A Report to the National Security Council by the NSC Planning Board on United States Policy Towards Iran", 21 December 1953, Collection of National Security Council Documents, n. 58.
72. *Ibid.*

73. *The Times* (London), 22 February 1955.
74. Mohammad Ayub Khan, "The Pakistan-American Alliance: Stressess and Strains", *Foreign Affairs*, Vol. 42, no.1, January 1964, pp. 195-210.
75. Brecher, n. 56, p. 27.
76. Zbigniew K, Brzezinski, *The Soviet Bloc, Unity and Conflict* (Massachusetts, rev. edn., 1971), p. 397.
77. Brecher, n.56, p.34.
78. Brzezinski, n.31, p. 194.
79. *Ibid.*, p. 194.
80. See for detail, Ole R. Holsti and James N. Rosenau, *American Leadership in World Affairs: Vietnam and the Breakdown of Consensus* (Boston, 1984).
81. Brzezinski, n. 13, p. 196.
82. Sisir Gupta, "Great Power Relations, World Order and the Third World", *Foreign Affairs Report* (New Delhi), Vol.27, nos.7-8, July-August 1978, p. 134.
83. *Ibid.*, p. 135.
84. Barnds, n. 20, p. 166.
85. Chaudhury, n. 30, p. 102.
86. *Ibid.*
87. John F. Kennedy, *The Strategy of Peace* (London, 1960), pp. 142-47.
88. *Ibid.*, p. 142.
89. Assurances were also given by Kennedy and Johnson which were contained in Kennedy's letter to President Ayub Khan on 6 January 1962, an aide-memoire presented by the U.S. Ambassador on 5 November 1962 and an oral pledge by Johnson to Ayub on 15 December 1965. See Henry A. Kissinger *The White House Years* (New Delhi, 1979).
90. Jawaharlal Nehru, *Speeches* (New Delhi: Ministry of Information and Broadcasting, Government of India), Vol. IV, p. 307.
91. *Asian Recorder* (New Delhi), Vol. 19, 10 September 1963, p.5403.
92. Chaudhury, n.30, p. 105.
93. *United States Department of State Bulletin* (Washington, D.C., 1962), 10 December 1962.
94. Mohammad Ayub Khan, *Friends Not Masters: A Political Autobiography* (London 1967), p. 132.
95. *Ibid.*, p. 183.
96. *Ibid.*, p. 129.
97. *Ibid.*, p. 117.
98. V.P. Dutt, "Symposium on the Role of Major Powers in the South Asia", in S.P. Varma and K.P. Misra, eds., *Foreign Policies in South Asia*, (Bombay, 1969), p. 327.

99. Ayub, n. 96, p. 118.
100. Mohammed Ayoob, "Pakistan's Soviet Policy, 1950-68: A Balance Sheet", M.S. Rajan (ed.), *Studies in Politics National and International* (Delhi, 1971), pp. 231-50.
101. Ayub, n. 94, p. 116.
102. For details of many coercive economic and political measures, see Mohammed Ayoob, "U.S. Economic Assistance to Pakistan, 1954-65: A Case Study in the Politics of Foreign Aid", *India Quarterly* (New Delhi), Vol. 23, no.2, April-June 1967, pp.127-45. See for elaboration my Second Chapter.
103. *Dawn*, 14 July 1965.
104. *Dawn*, 21 August 1965.
105. *Pakistan Horizon* (Karachi), Vol.18, no.4, 4th quarter, 1965.
106. Barnds, n. 20, p. 22.
107. Sisir Gupta, "Sino-U.S. Detente and India", *India Quarterly* (New Delhi), Vol.26, no.3, July-September 1971, pp. 179-84.
108. Ayoob, n. 100, pp. 231-50.
109. The United States showed deep concern about it, but Ayub went ahead; see, n.96, p. 118.
110. S. M. Burke, *Mainsprings of Indian and Pakistani Foreign Policies* (Minneapolis, 1974), p.180.
111. G.W. Chaudhury, "Pakistan and the Communist World", *Pacific Community* (Tokyo), Vol. 6, no.l, October 1974, pp.106-37.
112. United Nations, Security Council, *Official Records*, 1091st meeting, 14 February 1965. Lal Bahadur Sastri, India's Premier, observing the changing trend in Russian policy remarked: "We are aware that they were changing their policy and that there was nothing we could do about it." See Selig S. Harrison, "America, India and Pakistan", *Harper's Magazine* (New York), July 1966.
113. Ayub, n. 94, p. 168.
114. Ayub, n. 94, p. 171.
115. *Ibid.*
116. *Ibid.*
117. *Ibid.*, p. 173.
118. "Pakistan-Soviet Joint Communique", *Pakistan Horizon,* (Karachi), Vol.18, no.2, April-May 1965, p. 187.
119. *Asian Recorder* (New Delhi), Vol. 21, 26-27 May 1965, p. 6464.
120. *The Economist* (London), 22-28 May 1965, p. 897.
121. *Current Digest of the Soviet Press* (Ann Arbor, Mich.), Vol.17, no. 34. 15 September 1965, p. 15.

122. Staff Study, "Pakistan and the World–Quarterly Survey", *Pakistan Horizon*, Vol.19, 1st Quarter 1966, pp. 5-6.
123. *United Nations*, *Security Council*, *Official Records*, Yr. 20, mtg.1237, 4 September 1965, p. 35.
124. *Keesing's Contemporary Archives* (Bristol), Vol. 16 (1967-68), p. 22345.
125. "Chaudhury, n. 113, p. 113.
126. *Pakistan Times* (Lahore), 11 February 1968.
127. *The Statesman* (New Delhi), 11 February 1968.
128. *Ibid.*
129. *New York Times*, 10 July 1968.
130. Ayub, n. 94, p. 119.
131. *Dawn*, 24 October 1960.
132. Brzezinski, n. 13, p. 198.
133. Sisir Gupta, "Triangular Power Balance" *Seminar* (New Delhi), no. 133, September 1973, pp. 21-29.
134. For a discussion of these themes, see "Nixon's Philosophy of Foreign Policy", *The Round Table* (London), no.248, October 1972, pp.403-10.
135. *New York Times*, 2 August 1969.
136. *New York Times*, 11 October 1970.
137. *Dawn*, 11 July 1969.
138. Kosygin's plan was first announced during his visit to Afghanistan in early 1968. It called for a regional economic grouping comprising Afghanistan, India, Iran, Pakistan and the Soviet Union. Similarly, Brezhnev set forth his concept of "Collective Security for Asia" in an address at the International Meeting of the Communist and Workers Parties in Moscow on 7 June 1969; see speech by L.I. Brezhnev, General Secretary of the Central Committee of Communist Party of the Soviet Union at the International Meeting of Communist and Workers' Parties in Moscow, 7 June 1969, *International Affairs* (Moscow), Vol. 15, no.7, July 1969, p. 21.
139. Chaudhury, n. 30, p. 107.
140. Henry A. Kissinger, *The White House Years* (New Delhi, 1979), p. 853.
141. Kissinger, n. 142, p. 886.

# 5

# Regional Sub-Systemic Sources

Until a few years ago, the level of analysis in international politics was mostly the nation-state. The traditional scholars adopted this approach. It gained rapid acceptance as there was relative abundance of data on the state actor. This focus, micro-analysis, was widely used because "as things stand today...there can be no serious doubt about the paramount position of the nation-state or about the superiority of its influence and power".[1] Similarly, there was another perspective which equally vied for acceptance. This focus, macro-analysis, can roughly claim its recognition from late 1940's. One of its early proponents remarked way back in 1944:[2]

> "...We will never reach (a well-ordered world) by ignoring the differences between the elephants and squirrels of international politics."

This focus saw equally the burgeoning of analysis with marked emphasis on Soviet-American relations in post-Second World War years. Its primary thesis rests on the fact that the Super Powers are the only members of the system. Hence, they determine all or most of the actions of the small powers.

With the advent of the behavioural revolution these two perspectives continued but in different forms. There was an ever-growing tendency to treat the nation-state as the national system and the world as international system. And theorists have spawned various theories how both function. They are, as a result, divided into two broad categories. One group is interested in discerning regularities in the behaviour of actors, the common goals that are sought, in the means and processes through which the goal-seeking behaviour is sustained and in the sources of goals and means selected. They are known as foreign policy analysts or theorists. The other group is mainly concerned with the patterns that recur in the interactions of states, in the balances and imbalances that develop under varying circumstances and in the formation of coalitions and other factors that precipitate changes in international system. They are concerned with the study of international politics.[3]

But there are a few scholars who study the interaction among states in a particular region rather action alone, i.e., the foreign policy of one state.[4] While they make the analysis within the "systems perspective," for them the unit of analysis is not the national political system but the subordinate state system. In their view the concept—system—is said to exist in an environment and to be composed of parts, which through interaction, are in relation to each other. Consequently, a system has a structure and encompasses functions through which it is sustained or changed. In their views, if regional international politics phenomena can be conceived in this way, the analyst can focus upon the actions of the states as components of the subordinate system, upon the structure and functioning of the system which emanate from the interaction of the nations and upon the environmental factors that condition both the actions of the states and operations of the system. That it has a basic pattern of relationship, Michael Brecher made clear:[5]

> "But there is an array of inter-state problems, conflicts, and relationships among actors outside the blocs that have nothing or little to do with the bloc system, in America, Africa, Asia and even in Europe; and these are ignored or distorted, by a model that identifies the bipolar bloc system with the totality of inter-state politics".

While there is enough element of truth in this statement, we have recognised this problem in our model as not a problem of levels of analysis but a case of level of aggregation within the broader international system of which it is a regional subsystem. Regarding the problem of conceptualizing the regional international politics for delineating the boundary of the subordinate state system, Rosenau's conceptualization of international politics mentioned earlier is helpful. In the ensuing analysis, an attempt is made to uncover the impact of regional systemic variable on Pakistan's foreign policy behaviour since 1947.

**(A) The Subordinate System of the South Asia**

**(i) India**

A most enduring fact of post-war international politics in the South Asian subsystem is the implacable hostility between India and Pakistan since their gaining independence from the British Raj in August 1947. It is usually assumed by scholars that the bases of this hostility are wider.[6] Diverse variables have interacted over the years to condition the psychological and operational environment of the strategic decision-makers of both countries. It has become so basic to their respective domestic and foreign politics that it might continue notwithstanding the settlement of existing disputes.[7] So scholars viewed that this had served to make both the countries factors in each other's foreign policy behaviour, and in case -of Pakistan, India was more pervasively a dominant factor. This is clearly borne out in the analysis of a Pakistani author who observed:[8] "The ruling passion in Pakistan's foreign policy, a passion which has influenced its behaviour towards all other countries, has always been the fear of India". This has engendered, on the part of Pakistan, an agonizing quest for security and independence from India.

In real terms, this quest has boiled down to a search for enhancing power to countervail India's power eminence in the subcontinent. So naturally its efforts to underwrite security and independence became bidimensional because power, as defined by present day theorists, embraces both resource and interaction dimensions. In his book, *Pakistan: The Heart of Asia*, its first Prime Minister Liaquat Ali Khan succinctly summed up the main objectives of Pakistan's foreign policy.[9] Coming to the first dimension, he said the goal was to build up a well-trained, and well-equipped army in order to preserve territorial integrity and internal security and to achieve rapid economic development through adequate foreign aid. Dwelling on the second, he said, the goal was to enhance international prestige and obtain strong international support on Kashmir and other major disputes with India. Underlying these was the over-arching policy of meeting the "India Complex" in South Asia; to contain the influence of India in Asia and to achieve an equality of status with India in the international field.This goal in Pakistani foreign policy was also highlighted by a foreign scholar who observed:[10]

> "Pakistan is an example of a nation having among her neighbours one other nation larger and more powerful than herself with which her relations have been constantly unfriendly. India, therefore, the most important constant and controlling factor in Pakistan's foreign policy...Therefore, the main problem of Pakistan's foreign policy has been: Where to turn for support in her dispute with her neighbour and for some redress of power-disparity between that neighbour and herself."

We have explored elsewhere,[11] how Pakistan's drive for security and independence from India has led to a never-ending quest for augmenting the resource dimension of its capabilities that partly explained its foreign policy behaviour. In the ensuing analysis, an attempt is made to reveal how far this very drive has led to a search for procuring political and diplomatic support of the Great Powers to shore up the capabilities for redressing the disparity of power in the subcontinent with the ultimate objective of resolving the Kashmir issue in its terms.

Since the establishment of Pakistan, its foreign policy has been mostly concerned with India. And it is conflict with India which has largely determined its approach to almost every single international problem.[12] For reasons already stated, Pakistan looked upon India as the enemy number one and a hegemonistic power. Ayub Khan observed:[13]

> "India regards herself as a big power in Asia. Her eventual aim has been and still is, to have her spheres of influence in Southeast Asia. The Indian leaders have often stated that their true border extends from the Hindu Kush mountains to the Mekong River, that is to say, wherever the influence of Hinduism existed in the past...
>
> There are other reasons why we apprehend India may launch an aggressive venture against Pakistan. It is well known to the students of the subcontinent's history that the Hindus of India were against the creation of a separate homeland for Muslims in the form of Pakistan, and after opposing it tooth and nail for years, gave in because they could not otherwise get rid of the British. Thereafter, while consolidating and building up their own strength, the Indians have let no opportunity pass for weakening and neutralising Pakistan. The present Indian leadership makes no secret of the fact that it regards Pakistan as India's enemy number one."

Hence, it was natural on its part to assume India to be its adversary. And there was no gain-saying in the fact that right from its birth it cast itself, in its role in international sphere, in the image of "brave little Belgium" of Asia for evoking sympathy and support of the world for its stand on major issues directly or indirectly affecting India. True to its antagonistic perception, it minced no words in assailing India's much-cherished policy of non-alignment as a policy of blackmail to get aid from both the Communist and the Western Powers. It also decried Nehru's policy of Panchsheel and advanced its thesis of "Seven Pillars of Peace", in Bandung, which sought to approve military pacts and alliances. In the initial years, it pretended to be anti-Communist with lots of theological and ideological justifications underlying the schism between the world of Communism and Islam.[14] While examples will multiply to illustrate Pakistan's policy of persistent hostility and India-baiting, the initial bonus accrued to it was clear. Pakistan ingratiated itself into the favour of those whom it wanted most - the Americans. By 1960's, the line of divergence in Pakistani and Indian perception of the world system and the question of order and change in the world were clearly drawn when the former subscribed to the ideas of "confrontation" as formulated by Soekarno in opposition to Nehru's idea of "international cooperation" as constituting two opposite ideological poles for the developing world.[15]

Now, if one agreed that Pakistan's foreign policy was concerned with India, as a necessary corollary, one must say that it was Kashmir with which it was primarily interested, for Indian control of Kashmir stood as a denial of the 'Two-Nation' theory which was the basis of Pakistan and its continuing raison d' etre. And the clash over Kashmir was symbolic not only of the validity of the 'Two-Nation' theory, but also of the conflict of the two independent nations. So, the main objective of Pakistan's foreign policy in post-independent era was to acquire the territory of Kashmir and the success or failure of its foreign policy came to be bound up with the resolution of this crucial dispute. Besides, as the Kashmir question became the principal factor in shaping Pakistani attitude towards foreign policy questions, it tended to judge over the years many issues in world affairs by the litmus test of how far they contributed to support of Pakistan on this burning question.[16] As a necessary corollary, Pakistani ruling elites applied the same yardstick to measure whether a country or individual were friendly or hostile towards Pakistan. This was borne out clearly in the editorial comment of the *Dawn* which observed:[17]

> "While those who have been on the side of the truth and justice in Kashmir have forged a new and deeper comradeship with the people of Pakistan, those that stand on the fense in this vital issue, may no longer be counted as our friends, however prepossessing their exterior or valuable and traceable their professions. On this criteria of value, we must continue to appraise our international relations."

The first Great Power to whom Pakistan looked for support and sustenance in the post-independent era was Great Britain. Its decision-makers entertained the hope that the Muslim League's preferential relationship with the British Government in the pre-Raj would be transferred to it after 1947 that would actively back Pakistan in its dispute with India. As an Indian scholar wrote:[18]

> "Just as in the Congress-League conflict before freedom it was the Muslim League's expectation that the supremacy of British authority in the subcontinent world lead to the settlement of issues in their

favour, so in the post-freedom phase it was expected that the influence and power of Britain could still be invoked on her side by Pakistan. Such expectations were obviously based on an exaggerated assumption of Britain's capacity to play a major role in the subcontinent and the British Government itself had no pretensions of being able to play the role of the arbitar in Indo-Pakistan problems."

But Pakistan's calculation went awry. Strangely enough, British decision to retain India within the Commonwealth, at the cost of modifying the very philosophy underlying its Constitution, made it awake of its day-dream and finally convinced it that India would always carry greater weight in the Commonwealth. So Pakistan also rebuffed Britain, when, consequent upon the British decision to devalue pound in September, it refused to follow suit unlike India which reduced the per value of rupee correspondingly. If the Pak-British relationship did not slide for worse, though soured for a moment, one has to look for explanation elsewhere. Pakistan's decision not to severe relationship with the Commonwealth was itself a reflection of fact that it still retained the hope in this ideal international forum to manoeuvre support of its members for its stand on Kashmir. On numerous occasions the heads of Commonwealth countries have unofficially debated the issue and made appeals to both India and Pakistan to settle it peacefully.[19] With the passage of time, Pakistan's experience had bordered on frustration. Kashmir still remained a standing challenge to the Commonwealth conception as an association of equal and peaceful nations. This was expressed by Sir Zafrullah Khan when he ruefully remarked:[20]

> "If that challenge is met, if that trial is successfully withstood, the stock of the Commonwealth as a peaceful association of equal and sovereign nations will rise for ever. But unfortunately that should not be so, the future of Commonwealth is not worth an hour's purchase."

The real reason seemed to be that Britain was still a powerful member of the United Nations in which Pakistan has reposed an unbounded faith for the solution of Kashmir dispute. And given the system of big-power-veto in the Security Council which was a cynical expression of real-politik of world diplomacy, it would be a height of naivety to alienate Britain which with its veto-power could considerably sway the world body's decision in its favour. However, this did not blur the Pakistani vision that in the post-War years Britain was a crumbling world power and could only play second fiddle to the United States in world politics. Hence, the desire of the Pakistanis to court the Americans while at the same time keeping their trump-card with their old imperial master through which the United States mediated its policy in South Asia in the 1950's.[21] It was in this backdrop that Pakistan began to grope for new allies. Its romantic vision of a United Muslim World prompted it to make a fresh bid to bring all the Muslim nations of the world on the common platform of Islamic religion to weave a powerful political entity under its leadership. But it was a dismal failure for which it was compelled to look for alternative policies.

Under this shadow of frustration, Pakistan made numerous overtures to the United States for an alliance. As argued elsewhere, the alliance was consummated at a time when the United States had a positive motivation of enlisting Pakistan in its global strategy of containing the expansive world communism and was deeply sore with India for its differing outlook on world communist movement. Pakistan took advantage of this by flaunting its anti-Communist pretensions and fear of India. But the fact remained that Pakistan's real motivation emanated more from the aggressive India than from aggressive communism. Mere dislike of India and the hope of augmenting its capabilities through Western economic and military aid made it pretend to be anti-Communist which was certainly made of thinnest material of opportunism and political expediency. It was clearly revealed first at Manila Conference, as argued earlier,[22] and in subsequent periods. Now a question crops up as to why it was so desperate to shore up its capabilities vis-a-vis India and for what purpose. And why it gave up its much-proclaimed policy of non-alignment of earlier years to seek alliance with the United States, and to join its alliance system. Part of the explanation for this perhaps lies in the fact that its early decision-makers were clearly disillusioned with the United Nations in the way it handled the Kashmir issue. If one agreed with Liaquat Ali Khan that acquisition of the territory of Kashmir was the permanent component of Pakistan's foreign policy, then it was imperative for it to ally with a Super Power whose unflinching support in the Security Council could make substantial difference to the solution of the issue in Pakistan's favour. Britain's unequivocal endorsement of Pakistani position on the issue was inconceivable for the simple reason that it could not afford to ignore India. And Pakistan, realising that the Indo-American relations had been sufficiently strained, gave that alliance a bitter anti-Indian flavour.

Now as anticipated, Pakistani decision-makers after 1954 received increasing diplomatic support from Western Powers orchestrated mainly by the United States inside the United Nations when Kashmir issue used to be deliberated in the Security Council. The most significant Four-Power resolution in favour of Pakistan was introduced by the Western powers in 1957.[23] For a time it looked as if Pakistanis would carry the day in the Security Council. Prime Minister Suhrawardy paid glowing tribute to the Western Powers for their role in the Council deliberations. He particularly singled out the United Kingdom for the signal service rendered to Pakistan. *The Dawn* commented:[24]

> "The new resolution... does not fulfil the expectations aroused by the firm action which that body had taken to deal with the Anglo-French-Israeli aggression against Egypt... However, the new resolution does mark an advance from the statement which Bharat desired... The resolution not only "notes" Pakistan's proposals for a UNEF for Kashmir but expressly states the "belief" of the Security Council that the proposal deserves consideration."

Though Soviet veto nipped all their hopes in the bud and in the words of Noel-Baker the greatest and gravest single issue in international affairs remained unsettled, the story did not end there. The United States went on supporting Pakistan in the years to come. When the issue was subsequently raised in 21 June 1962,[26] the United States supported the Irish Resolution much to the disappointment of India. As before, the Soviet Union (and Romania) killed it by its veto. However, the Foreign Minister of Pakistan expressed his gratitude to the Western Powers who supported the Irish Resolution.[27] The Indo-Soviet axis succeeded through power politics and pressure tactics in persuading neutral countries to withhold support on such an important question. In India, Prime Minister Nehru bitterly complained that the Western powers were almost invariably against India on matters that created passionate feelings in the country (like Goa and Kashmir).[28]

The Kashmir issue which seemed for a time to have been put in cold storage again got a fresh lease of life following Chinese aggression of India on 20 October 1962. When a high-power delegation of Western Powers led by Duncan Sandys, the Secretary of State for Commonwealth Relations of United Kingdom and Averell Harriman, United States Assistant Secretary of State for Far Eastern Affairs, visited India in response to its appeal for military assistance, Nehru agreed under concerted pressure from them to make renewed efforts to settle the dispute bilaterally. The new situation in the subcontinent in the wake of Chinese invasion, certainly increased the West's capacity to influence thinking in New Delhi and paved the ground for fresh negotiation. But unfortunately, seven rounds of talks between the two countries proved infructuous and the issue again reverted to the Security Council. The Security Council took up the matter for a full-scale debate on 10 February 1964.[29] It prolonged it for a long period. No tangible solutions could be found. But it was clear while the Western Powers supported Pakistani stand to the hilt by categorically endorsing the proposition of the Ivory Coast representative, a different view was expressed by the delegates of Czechoslovakia and the Soviet Union.[30] And things changed radically with rapid political developments in the valley with the release of Seikh Abdullah and subsequent passing away of Nehru on 27 May 1964.

We have argued elsewhere[31] how Pakistan was utterly disillusioned with the Western Powers for which Ayub Khan looked increasingly towards the Communist bloc particularly the Soviet Union, and especially China after 1962. It can be surmised with a reasonable degree of confidence that failure of Western diplomacy with regard to Kashmir was partly responsible for this. It was a painful realisation on the part of Pakistan that unless it came to term with the Soviet Union and neutralises its continuing opposition, there would be no substantial change in the situation. As stated in our foregoing pages.[32] Pakistan steadily worked to blunt Russian antipathy for which Russia travelled from a position of complete endorsement of India's stand on Kashmir in 1955 to one of neutrality in the late 1960's. Similarly, Pakistan, through its persistent effort of cultivating friendly relations with China was fully successful in persuading it to veer round to its point of view on Kashmir.

**(ii) China**

It is aptly remarked that the Sino-Pakistani relation is one of the enigmas of contemporary international relations, as an avowedly Marxist-Leninist State has made terms with a 'praetorian state' based on the most conservative forces of religion, feudalism and capitalism. While scholars have isolated diverse interactive variables to explain this phenomenon, it is assumed in the forthcoming analysis that the regional sub-systemic variable was a potent one influencing Pakistan's foreign policy behaviour during that period. This was precisely for two reasons. In the first place, Pakistan's policy was largely developed, as claimed by its policy-makers, in response to its security needs. And consideration of its security was largely influenced by India from whom the main threat to its basic survival as a nation-state has been perceived to be emanating. Secondly, China and Pakistan, as claimed by a scholar, have discovered in the Indian subcontinent an area of agreement where the two countries had a clear perception of their interests and a coincidence of their basic objectives regarding India which was their common enemy.[33] So, they have consistently followed a cooperative policy to supplement each other's effort to contain the Indian power. The ensuing analysis purports to test this assumption to prove as to what extent China shaped Pakistan's international behaviour during 1949-1971. Though arbitrary, the entire spectrum of the Sino-Pakistani relations is divided into three broad phases to trace the impact of China on Pakistan's foreign policy.

**1949-53**

China was in the throes of a civil war when Pakistan was born. The Kuomintang regime under Generalssimo Chiangkaishek was fast crumbling and the Communist party led by Mao Tse-tung was riding the crest of victory. The situation, though fluid, continued to absorb the attention of world leaders. The Pakistani leadership watched the movement of events with great expectation and concern. The expectation was understandable, for a great and ancient nation which shared the common destiny of long foreign domination, was struggling to be reborn, thus adding a chink in the armoury of the Western Colonial Powers. Similarly, the concern was self-explanatory. In the history of Chinese civilization, the rise of a strong and Unified Central Government had always proved to be expansive and revisionist, and with the Communist ideological underpinning it might lead to the disruption of the existing State-system in Asia particularly in the South Asia where states were not only wedded to different political systems but shared traditionally disputed frontiers. With regard to frontier questions, the attitude of the Communist had been similar to that of their predecessors. It was natural that the Pakistani leadership nurtured in the tradition of British parliamentary system, could not view with equanimity the prospect of China going red but at the same time the alternative before them was still worse. They were equally luke-warm in their support to Chiangkaishek regime for historical reasons. As is well-known, Chiang opposed Muslim League's demand for a separate home land for Muslims during the League's struggle for Pakistan. So, they preferred to view the unfolding drama with a philosophic unconcern which was very characteristically reflected in the statement of a Pakistani author:[34]

> "Who eventually wins or loses the Civil War (in China) will have a great effect on the future of the whole of Asia. If Nationalists win, China will remain a democracy as we have known it in England and

the United States. If the Communists win, the Soviet bloc will become the greatest force in the world. Whatever happens, the fate of China will leave its permanent marks on the South and South East Asia. We cannot but watch the situation with the keenest interest."

However, with the end of Civil strife and ushering in of the Communist victory, the Peoples' Republic of China was established on 1 October 1949. As a matter of fact, the Pakistani leadership showed remarkable statesmanship by according recognition to the new government on 4 January 1950 within a few days of India's decision to do so and became the first Muslim country and the second member of the Commonwealth to grant recognition. Hailing the Chinese revolution as the opening of a new chapter in the chequered history of Asia, its leadership viewed:[35]

> "Its profound significance for the rest of Asia arises from the fact that it is an indigenous revolution, bred essentially in an Asian environment. Whatever be the sources of its emotional inspiration, it does not owe its birth and fruition to foreign influence".

The press communique embodying the act of recognition said that the Government of Pakistan "trust that friendly and cordial relations between China and Pakistan will be cemented in all spheres to their mutual advantages."[36] But the Pakistani gesture of goodwill was not duly reciprocated by the Chinese. It was because the Chinese had no autonomous policy towards Pakistan. Their policy towards the South Asia, during this phase (1949-53), was in tune with their general pattern of policy towards Asia as a whole. Besides, Mao categorically stated in 1949, even before the formal installation of the Communist Government in China, of Peking's determination to "lean to one side in the worldwide conflict." The corner-stone of their policy was the alignment with the Soviet Union. The Chinese were convinced that in the fluid state of post-War Asia, revolution was bound to sweep the entire continent under the impetus of the Communist victory in China. They argued for a militantly revolutionary policy for which they showed open contempt and positive hostility towards the Asian leaders calling them as "the hirelings of imperialism". Because Mao himself stated in 1949, "The world was divided into two camps; no third road existed."[37] So, Pakistan was no exception to this general policy.

In sharp contrast to this, Pakistan worked steadily to blunt Chinese hostility for a good neighbourly relationship rejecting the prevailing Western view that the Chinese government was not legitimate and could not be expected to carry out obligations attached to the membership of the United Nations. It, without slightest reservation, supported the Indian

Resolution of September 1950 seeking to replace the delegation of the Nationalist China with that of the People's Republic. Speaking in the General Assembly, its Foreign Minister, Muhammad Zafrullah Khan, underscored these points when he observed:[38]

> "China is not applying for admission to the United Nations. It is a Member State, a permanent member of the Security Council, one of the Big Five... It is entitled as of right to be represented in the United Nations like every other member State until it is expelled in accordance with the provisions of the Charter."

The sole question, Sir Zafrullah, asked as to who was entitled to represent China?[39]

> "...The delegation from which the delegation present here purports to draw its authority, has for months ceased to exercise jurisdiction over any portion of the Chinese Mainland... The truth of the matter is that the General Assembly is unwilling to concede the existence of a fact, not because the fact has not been established but because the majority regard it as unpleasant".

Later in the year, Pakistan and China established diplomatic missions between the two countries. In the meanwhile, the conflict in Korea broke out. Prime Minister Liaquat Ali Khan was on a state visit to the United States. In a statement issued in Boston on 27 June 1950, he declared his government's support to the Security Council resolution of 25 June and 26 June and for any measure that the Council should decide to take to help South Korea against aggression from the north. He said that as loyal member of the United Nations, it was Pakistan's duty to adopt that attitude. But interestingly enough, Pakistan did not contribute its military forces to the Korean War effort on the plea that it was insufficient for its own defence requirement. Besides, while it voted in favour of General Assembly resolution branding North Korea as aggressor in the war, it abstained on the resolution branding Communist China as an aggressor in Korea and as well as on the resolution imposing embargo on export of certain items of goods to Communist China.[40] These two incidents showed how sensitive was Pakistan in earlier years on issues that affected the susceptibility of China. Sarwar Hasan rightly remarked:[41]

> "This independent approach to Cold War issues paved the way for mutual friendship between Pakistan and China. The foundations of

that friendship were so firmly laid that later developments in Pakistan's foreign policy did not destroy it."

From this brief track record, it was evident that Pakistan followed an independent policy towards China which undoubtedly justified Liaquat's statement that Pakistan started, on its career without any narrow and special commitments and without any prejudice in the international sphere. It should be borne in mind that it was a very trying period in Pakistani national life. Moreover, during this period, it was frantically trying for a relationship with the United States, the arch enemy of China. It was natural that it should have followed a policy more appealing to the Americans. But as revealed elsewhere,[42] there was no systemic compulsion on Pakistan either to follow the United States lead in world affairs, or the line of Soviet foreign policy. Pakistan was free to strike out an independent path in its foreign policy behaviour. But as pointed out in the foregoing pages, there was equally no demand from the Chinese to adopt pliant policies to sooth their sentiment. If one were to explain why Pakistan behaved towards China as it did, we are left to explain this behaviour only in term of regional systemic variable which seemed potent from 1949-53 for the following reasons. First, Pakistan had a rare fortune of having Sir Zafrullah Khan as its Foreign Minister. Zafrullah had served wartime China as the British Agent General and had an intimate perception of the Communist mind. He must have played a key role in fashioning the policy towards China as was evident from his fiery espousal of the Chinese cause throughout his eventful career. As an astute politician and diplomat of distinction, he must have understood that China, in the long history, had always been expansionist and revisionist whenever it had come under, a unified and strong central government. With a Communist ideological dogma, it was bound to prove more disruptive of existing state system in Asia. Besides, being a vast country with boundless resources, though underdeveloped, it was bound to loom large in the Asian politics. Its borders with India and Pakistan were unsettled, being a left-over of the British imperialism. Sooner or later Communist China would lay claim to regain its old frontiers which included all of the Himalayan regions, along with Nepal, Bhutan and parts of northern India. This would certainly bring it into direct collision with Pakistan, and India. So conflict with India was an inevitability. To add to this, India was a formidable barrier to Chinese ambition to play the role of Asian leadership. Time was not far-off when both would vie with each other to attract other Asian States to follow their competitive model of economic growth and political system. A scholar observed:[43]

> "The real issue is whether India and China, representing two vastly differing ideological and political systems, can coexist in peace on the basis of equality and respect for each other's vital interests. It raises the fundamental question of the present and future role of India and China in Asia and indeed in the world."

Pakistani leadership acted with the prescience of statesmanship to make China a possible counterpoise to India in its ambition to dominate Asia, particularly the South Asia. Their initial decision to grant recognition to Mao's government was certainly reflective of these considerations. That it came within a few days of India's decision to do so was certainly impelled by the consideration of denying India any diplomatic mileage in terms of Chinese goodwill. Similarly, subsequent espousal of Chinese cause by Pakistanis showed that India could not be looked upon by the Chinese as the only votary of their cause when they were in a state of isolation in the international community. Lastly, while it would ingratiate Pakistanis into the Russian favour, Americans too would take note of Pakistani ability to come to terms with communists out of sheer necessity of survival in face of India's enmity.

On the basis of the foregoing fact, it can be said that Pakistan's policy towards China evolved as a result of regional compulsions that confronted the policy-makers in terms of security dilemma posed by India. Nowhere there was evidence to suggest that there was any explicit or implicit effort by China to shape Pakistan's foreign policy behaviour. The Chinese policy of "peaceful coexistence" made significant advances following the signing of the Korean truce in June 1953 and the conclusion of the Geneva Agreement in April 1954, and reached its high water-mark in the signing of the Indo-China Treaty on 24 April 1954. This was in consonance with the policy of the Soviet Union. Enunciating the policy, the Soviet Premier Nikita S.Khrushchev observed:[44]

> "The principle of peaceful coexistence signifies a renunciation of interference in the internal affairs of other countries with the object of altering their system of government or mode of life or for any other motives. The doctrine of peaceful coexistence also presupposes that political and economic relations between countries are to be based upon complete equality of the parties concerned, and on mutual benefit."

The new Chinese line sought to mobilise Asian sympathies against western-sponsored military alliances, to create a benign image of Communist China and reduce the fear of communists. This policy of sweet reasonableness found adequate expression in the historic Bandung Conference, held in April 1955, where Chou En-lai made a lasting impression on the Asian leaders, broadened China's contact with the Afro-Asians and learned much about them. The Conference really marked the transition of China from the status of a purely Asian power to that of an Afro-Asian power.[45] These were the years when Asian statesmen, including Chou En-lai, were visiting each other frequently and constantly reiterating their solemn dedication to world peace and cooperation. It particularly heralded a new era of abiding friendship for China and India and the slogan "Hindi Chin Bhai Bhai" rented the air in Peking and New Delhi.

But this phase of Bandung spirit lasted for a very brief period. Towards the end of 1957 China faced heavy odds. The rivalry between the Soviet and the Chinese Communist regime which was latent from the beginning came to surface after Stalin's death and assumed serious proportion threatening the bloc unity. It was in part differing reactions to the events of Polish and Hungarian uprisings that caused the Chinese-Soviet relations to become sour.[46] While the Russians found it necessary to absorb the shock and lesson of Hungary, it became intolerable for the Chinese whose revolution was in a different stage and who had different political needs. The Soviet Union under Nikita S. Khrushchev clearly objected to the concept of "way of Mao Tse-tung" with its overtone of Chinese leadership in Asia.[47] The relationship reached its nadir in the wake of the Sino-Indian border trouble when, consequent upon Chinese absorption of Tibet in 1959, the Soviet Union refused for the first time to support a Communist State involved in a quarrel with a bourgeoisie government and adopted neutrality.[48]

China gradually felt beleaqured in Asia. Its problem became formidable with each passing year. While its aspiration to bear the mantle of leadership of the international proletarian movement was frustrated by the Soviet Union, its hope of emerging the main spokesman for Asia was equally challenged by the Soviet Union, the United States and India. The Soviet policy of using India as a pawn to counter the Chinese inroads in the South Asia and isolating it in Asia progressed well. Similarly, China found itself pitted against the United States as the leader of the hostile bloc and against India as the pioneer of an alternative system in Asia and its ambition not to play second fiddle to India in Asian affairs. And after 1960, the United States cast India increasingly in the role of a counterpoise to China. So it seemed probable that China's disappointment on external front might have contributed partly to tougher policy abroad.

Coming to Pakistan's foreign policy during the period (1954-57), one found that it underwent dramatic changes following its decision to align with the United States. In quick succession, it joined one military alliance after another and became the major centre-piece of American policy of containment of communism, particularly the Chinese power. But at the same time, record showed that Pakistan had most cordial and intimate relationship with the Chinese. While a facile interpretation attributed this to a master-stroke of diplomacy, serious analyst contended that deeper forces were working underneath. Some scholars argued that this could be possible because Pakistan's pro-western policy was tolerated by the Chinese who were at the crest of the new policy offensive of "peaceful coexistence" at the behest of the Soviet Union, and there was no divergence of policy of the bloc towards the Afro-Asian countries. Further, it was argued, the Chinese maintained that in contemporary international relations all serious contradictions resulted from the conduct of the Western imperialist powers.[49] Relations of Asians with one another were not marked by "mutually antagonistic contradictions". And any contradictions that might seem to exist in their relations were of a non-antagonistic nature and were amenable to peaceful solution. To prove their contention, scholars have cited the case of the Southeast Asia Treaty Organization and the Chinese attitude to it. It is on record that China minced no words to describe it as an aggressive military alliance directed against the people of China and of various Asian countries.[50] But surprisingly enough, it did not even send a formal note of protest to Pakistan against its joining the Pact. Its disapproval of Pakistan's participation was certainly one of marked moderation, while it bitterly assailed the United States. Peking remarked that in establishing SEATO the United States was certainly not aiming at self-defence but at undermining peace in Indo-China and perpetuating tension in the Far East. It came to a definite conclusion that since the creation of SEATO, the United States had been building up its military presence and bases in Pakistan, Thailand and Philippines, interfering in their domestic affairs, and fastening them to the American War chariot. In sharp contrast to this, the main points of criticism of Pakistan, as reported by *New China News Agency*,[51] were that the acceptance of American military aid and the concomitant obligation would make the country an American satellite and isolate it from the Afro-Asian countries.[52]

These facts certainly explained China's attitude towards other Asian countries like Thailand and Philippines but not towards Pakistan. The fact of the matter was that China understood, as record revealed, Pakistan's compulsion for entering into the Western bandwagon, in which regional systemic variable played a dominant role and this partly explain why China behaved so indulgently towards it. To prove this, scholars said[53] that at the Manila Conference which set up SEATO, Pakistan's Foreign Minister Zafrullah Khan opposed the applicability of the Treaty to Communist aggression alone and insisted to bring within its ambit all aggressions including the conflict between India and Pakistan.[54] In the chess-board of international politics, certain words carry implications for the policy-makers of countries for which they are intended. Chou En-lai too knew how to make moves that required no reciprocity. This was clarified further when Pakistani Prime Minister Mohammad Ali Bogra met the Chinese Premier Chou En-lai in the Bandung Conference and assured him that SEATO was a defensive alliance as far as Pakistan was concerned and that Pakistan had entered in to the pact to defend itself from aggression by India and not because of any hostility towards China. Chou En-lai declared at a meeting of the Political Committee of the Bandung Conference of Bogra's assurance to him that though[55] Pakistan was a party to a military treaty it was not directed against China. Pakistan had no fear that China would permit aggression against it. Bogra further assured him that if the United States launched a global war, Pakistan would not be involved. This led to a mutuality of understanding which was further strengthened when Karachi received a private message from Peking just after the conclusion of the Bandung Conference which read as follows.[56]

> "The Chinese People's Government assured the Government of Pakistan that there was no conceivable clash of interests between the two countries which could imperil their friendly relations; but that this position did not apply to Indo-Chinese relations, in which a definite conflict of interest could be expected in the near future".

Similarly, the Chinese attitude to the most contentious Indo-Pakistan issue—the Kashmir problem—was also a rare piece of shrewd diplomacy. They were well aware of the fact that attitude to Kashmir was "the touch-stone by which friendship and animosity were tested by Pakistan.[57] So, in the hey-day of "Hindi Chin Bhai Bhai", Peking scrupulously refrained from committing itself to any stand that might even remotely be considered as betraying an anti-Pakistan disposition and endorsing the Indian claim that Kashmir formed an integral part of the Indian Union. Its main arguments were as follows: Kashmir problem was the creation of nefarious Western design. It should be amicably settled between India and Pakistan. No tangible gains could be achieved if it was taken to the United Nations which was an instrument of the United States. It accepted the right of the people of Jammu & Kashmir alone to determine their own fate and future. The position remained as usual despite the visit of the Prime Minister H.S. Suhrawardy to China and the return visit of Chou En-lai to Pakistan in December 1956. It was clear on the basis of foregoing facts that while India took Chinese friendship a little too literally and seriously, China showed a particular awareness of the future conflict with India. Chou Enlai had a sense of history. And history suggests that it is usually advantageous to align oneself with the weaker of two antagonistic partners, because this acted as a restraint on the stronger. It was an established fact that India and Pakistan were two antagonistic partners. So, Chinese support to Pakistan was a foregone conclusion despite all its loud protestations of friendship for India. An eminent sinologist has accurately viewed that right from the commencement of the Chinese regime, they had clearly perceived the enormous advantage of exploiting Indo-Pakistani hostility to serve their national interest.[59]

China's sympathetic understanding of Pakistani predicament was demonstrated on another occasion also. During Prime Minister H.S. Suhrawardy's state visit to the United States in the summer of 1957, he bitterly assailed the Chinese policy as one of aggressive expansionism threatening peace and freedom in Asia. Surprisingly, the Chinese played it cool and took it in their stride. Though they were irritated by his remarks, as expected, The *Peoples Daily* remarked that Suhrawardy should want to say pleasant things about the Americans in order to get more aid.[60] In view of these facts, it is plausible to agree with a scholar that both Pakistan and China had a clear perception of the convergence of their interests and coincidence of their objectives regarding India. So it can be concluded that Pakistan's policy towards China during the period from 1954 to 1957, was partly shaped by the regional systemic variable which was dominant during this period. If a flourishing relation developed between China and Pakistan, it was this benign attitude of the former which predominantly shaped it.

However, during the period from 1957 to 1959 the Sino-Pakistani relations showed a significant deviation from the general run of the policies followed by the respective governments. Scholars agreed that it entered rough weather towards the fag-end of Suhrawardy's Prime Ministership.

The down-hill trend which commenced roughly from 1957 onwards continued through the first two years of Ayub Khan's Presidency. But they differed as to the factors responsible for such a sudden cooling off of an otherwise warm relationship which again bounced back in 1960. Some scholars contended that it was Ayub Khan's accession to power which gave a severe blow to an already worsening relationship, for the Chinese were aware of his prominent role in the conclusion of the Mutual Defence Assistance Agreement with the United States in 1954.[62] And subsequently, Chinese suspicion was confirmed when Ayub took two important decisions that had considerable bearing on Chinese interest: first, his offer of a joint-defence plan to India to protect the subcontinent from the invasion from North,[63] and, second, his signing of a bilateral defence agreement with the United States in 1959. These two actions of Ayub soured Pakistan's relations with China.

The question is why Ayub was impelled to adopt policies towards China which were an exception to the general pattern of relationship prevailing between the two states. Interestingly enough, when Ayub came to power he categorically stated that a nation has no eternal enemy or friend but eternal national interest. He also declared to pursue a policy that Pakistan's interests and geography dictated. The Martial Law Proclamation lent credence to his sincere desire when it condemned efforts at creating "bad blood and misunderstanding between US and countries like the U.S.S.R.... and the People's Republic of China[64]. Coming to the specific policy of China, one finds that there was no action of China directed towards Pakistan. This was corroborated by the fact that China, "unlike Soviet Union," did not send any protest note on the bilateral defence agreement which was being negotiated in 1959 between Pakistan and the United States."[65] This showed that China adopted an over-indulgent attitude towards Pakistan. Then why the cooling off process ensued. Probably the explanation for this lies in Chinese behaviour in general.

The Chinese policy underwent drastic changes following 1957 in line with the changed policy of the Communist bloc. Split was yet to occur. By the end of 1957 the leaders of the Sino-Soviet bloc had reverted to a more militant posture in dealing with problems within the bloc and in their approach to the United States and its allies.[66] Mao, addressing the Communist parties on the occasion of the 40th anniversary of the Bolshevik Revolution, emphasized stongly the East-West struggle.[67] This policy of "hard-line manifested no where more clearly than in the Indian Subcontinent when China forcibly occupied Tibet and extinguished their much cherished freedom. This lesson must have gone home with Ayub whose fear of international communism got further reinforced. It certainly unnerved him and heightened his concern regarding communist threat to the subcontinent for which he made his famous offer of a Joint-defence plan to India. It is contended to be more of a ploy to extract some diplomatic gains in a Indo-Pak settlement on Kashmir.[68] But it can be stated that any Pakistani policy-maker in place of Ayub would have behaved in the same way, given the general attitude of China, even though evidence suggested that China was not hostile to Pakistan and treated it differently from the rest of the allies of the United States. Given the fact of Indo-Pakistan hostility as a constant factor, the regional systemic compulsion was heavy with Pakistani policy-makers who had no go except to work for seeking a modus vivendi with its foe, India.

This line of interpretation drew its plausibility and strength from the fact that Pakistani behaviour changed abruptly once China recoiled from its aggressive policy and adopted more conciliatory postures in its foreign policy goals. After 1959, the key-stone of China's new South Asia policy was Pakistan and Peking continued to give strong political support and increasing amounts of economic aid. Realising that growing tension on the Sino-Indian border was bound ultimately to lead to a military confrontation, China now turned to Pakistan to stave off any trouble from that quarter. As its relationship with the Soviet Union was fast deteriorating, it was keen to lure away Pakistan which was equally looking for a protector. Proverbially, enemy of one's enemy is a friend. So befriending China preeminently suited Pakistan. Now, Pakistan turned seriously towards mending its fences with China and repairing any damage that might have been done to Sino-Pakistani relations by the joint-defence offer to India. It was deeply concerned not to allow the emergence of a situation on the border between Pakistan's Azad Kashmir and China's Sinkiang Province equivalent to that existed on the Sino-Indian border. The Pakistan foreign minister, Zulfikar Ali Bhutto clearly expressed the anxiety of his Government:

> "Surely as a Government it is our responsibility to see that such a situation (as one that existed on the Sino-Indian border), God forbid, is not repeated for our people in which we are unnecessarily involved in a misunderstanding with a neighbour and a Great Power. Surely, we would not like to see the tantrums and all the crisis that have been repeated as a result of misunderstanding over the boundary between the People's Republic of China and India."[71]

The first opportunity presented itself to Pakistan to repair its ruptured relations with China in 1960. During a Sino-Indian border talk, China flatly refused to concede the Indian demand that the border west of Karakoram Pass between China's Sinkiang Province and Azad Kashmir under Pakistan control should be included. This was a signal for Pakistan which it was intelligent enough to take up. On 28 March 1961, Pakistani Government sent a formal diplomatic note proposing boundary agreement with the Chinese Government. Talks formally started between the two governments on the demarcation of border between them on 12 October 1962.

With the outbreak of Sino-Indian border war on 21 October 1962 and the subsequent Western military aid to India brought about a radical change in the subcontinent and the attitude of both countries towards each other became unusually friendly for reasons already cited. China, after the conclusion of the war, became almost desperate to reach border settlements with all the peripheral countries like Burma, Nepal, Mongolia. Border talks started with Pakistan in all earnestness. On 2 March 1963 a provisional border agreement was signed between the two Governments.[73] While diverse motives on both sides might have contributed to the signing of the agreement, it was generally agreed that Pakistanis succumbed to the Chinese offer out of a genuine fear that an undemarcated border with China was pregnant with future problems. It admirably answered the needs of both countries. Pakistan got most favourable terms as it was concluded in the midst of a raging Sino-Indian border trouble. The Chinese, "since they had been branded in the West as an aggressor in their border dispute with India", were interested in changing their tarnished profile and presenting themselves as a reasonable and friendly power.[73] What is more salutary in terms of political fall-out was that it served to embarrass India, countered its allegation against China as an aggressive power and fortified their military and diplomatic position with respect to India. Then, close on its heel, came another move to further cement the Sino-Pak relationship in which Chinese influence was clearly discernible. Pakistan took the most momentous decision to enter into an air transit agreement in the face of stiff opposition from the United States which termed it as "an unfortunate breach of free world solidarity"[74]. It remained undaunted when the United States cancelled a loan pledged to Pakistan to build a new airport at Dacca. By now, China changed Pakistan's foreign policy behaviour. In the words of a Pakistani author, "its foreign policy began to move to the pleasure of Peking and to the annoyance and displeasure of the Johnson administration in Washington and to worries in New Delhi and uneasiness in Moscow."[75]

This was clearly reflected in Pakistan's voting of the United States on the issue of China's representation and its gradual process of disengagement from SEATO. In 1961 Pakistan abstained from voting in favour of the United States resolution. In 1963 it supported a joint Albanian-Cambodian resolution calling for the seating of China in the United Nations. That Pakistani policy behaviour changed under the stimulus of Peking's diplomacy was also reflected in Pakistan's reservations in the SEATO Communique of 1965 and 1966, particularly with regard to the United States policy in Vietnam. Chen Yi, the Chinese Foreign Minister, remarked in 1967:[76]

> "Recently in disregard from countries like Pakistan, the U.S. imperialism took advantage of a SEATO ministerial meeting and raised the clamour that 'Communist aggression' constituted a 'major threat' in Southeast Asia."

Then came the Indo-Pakistan war of 1965 in which China played its part. While it is difficult precisely to trace the role of Chinese in the causation of the war, record revealed that they had a decisive say in the prosecution and conclusion of the war. With regard to its causation, available evidence suggested as follows: During a meeting in 1965, Chou En-lai, was said to have made a remark to Ayub that a just settlement of the Kashmir dispute would not materialize unless Pakistanis were willing to make sacrifices. When Chen Yi stopped at Karachi airport on 4 September (two days before the actual occurrence of war) he was told by Pakistanis that they were now ready to make such sacrifices.[77] While Pakistani diplomats denied this to be treated even remotely as incitement to go to war against India, the fact of the matter was that only Ayub, Bhutto and a few Generals knew the actual plan. But with the onset of war, Chinese stand became quite clear. *The People's Daily* declared:[78]

> "In short, it was not Pakistan but India that first crossed the ceasefire in Kashmir. It was not Pakistan but India that first threw its airforce into action and bombed peaceful cities of the other side. It was not Pakistan but India that first crossed the international border...So India is in *every* case, the aggressor and Pakistan its victim."

This statement clearly showed that China by putting the onus of responsibility on India for starting the war gave a blanket support to Pakistan. Again by issuing a series of ultimatums, China gave the impression to the world that it was a war of attrition against a common enemy in which they might be involved. On 7 September 1965, it issued a statement condemning Indian aggression:[79]

"The Indian Government's armed attack on Pakistan is an act of naked aggression. It not only is a crude violation of all principles guiding international relations but also constitutes a grave threat to peace in this part of Asia. The Chinese Government sternly condemns India for its criminal aggression and expresses firm support for Pakistan in its just struggle against aggression and solemnly warns the Indian that it must bear the responsibility for all the consequences of its criminal and extended aggression."

Its protest note on 16 September was in the form of an ultimatum which demanded that the Indian Government dismantle all its military works for aggression on the Chinese side of the China-Sikkim boundary, or on the boundary within three days of the delivery of the present note or be ready to "bear full responsibility for all the grave consequences arising therefrom". On 19 September it extended the deadline by another three days. More important than this was the increased activity of the armed forces of China on the Sino-Indian border with a view to obliging India to keep a large contigent of its army stationed on its border with Tibet and thus taking some pressure off Pakistan. Commenting on this, a Pakistani author observed:[80]

"Indeed, one inevitably receives the impression that India's action vis-a-vis Pakistan were as much responsible for occasioning the protest as any injuries that China might herself have sustained at Indian hands. This linkage of Sino-Indian and Indo-Pakistan conflicts was evident in every note that the Chinese Government addressed to India during this period. The Chinese also found occasion to assert in these notes that, come what might, they would not be stopped from supporting Pakistan's fight against Indian aggression."

Similarly, it was China which was responsible for Pakistan's acceptance of ceasefire.[81] A Pakistani author revealed that Ayub, in the midst of the crisis visited China and had an extended discussion with the Chinese leaders. He was quite anxious that before the acceptance of ceasefire was announced, the Chinese friends must be taken into full confidence, and their reaction must be given the fullest consideration. Ayub was candid enough to admit of "crude pressures" of the two Super Powers. But he took the most fateful decision of ceasefire only at the behest of the Chinese leaders. This illustrated beyond a shred of doubt how China shaped Pakistan's foreign policy decision during the r crucial period of Pakistani history.

Coming to Pakistani behaviour during the period from 1965 to 1971, it is explored elsewhere[82] that it was systemic rather than regional systemic variables which became very dominant for which Pakistan became the "Courier" of the United States and ultimately became a victim of the interventionary pressures of China and the United States in their search for a new triangular balance of power in the world.

**(B) West Asian Subordinate System**

Pakistan acquired independent statehood with a growing awareness of its belonging to a community that dwelled all over the globe right from Singapore in Asia to Morocco in Africa.[83] It was too, placed in an historical setting which related its pitiful present to a past which was pristine in its glory of which it gradually discovered and became legitimately proud. So, it was natural on the part of the Pakistani leadership to view the successful fruition of their freedom struggle as a clear manifestation of a renewed sense of Islamic belonging which became resurgent consequent upon the Second World War. Muslim unity was long shattered by the machination of the Western imperialist powers. And with their fast retreat from the peninsula of Asia and Africa, it was again rising like a phoenix from its ashes. So, in the aftermath of the independence, the Pakistani leadership made a fervent plea for reviving this world spirit, for which they increasingly stressed their natural and religious links, common culture and identity of economic interests between Pakistan and other Muslim countries.[84] Animated with this sublime faith, they hoped that the Muslim countries of the world would one day draw closer to it and might move towards a Pan-Islamic grouping of states. A.B. Rajput made this point amply clear when he remarked:[85] "Thus with the birth of Pakistan, the hope of Pan-Islamic unity and brotherhood brightened afresh amongst the Islamic states of Asia." It is a truism, that Pakistan's quest for a world Muslim unity was born out of its deep ideological conviction underlying the formation of its statehood and its subsequent reorganization. It was made abundantly clear in one of the directive principles of state policy under the new Constitution of Pakistan which provided: "The state shall endeavour to strengthen the bonds of unity among Muslim countries."[86]

As a matter of fact, the analysts isolate diverse variables that influenced its policy towards the Muslim world out of which two appear most dominant. In the first place, as Callard viewed, "...Pakistan could find no single country which could be counted as an unfailing friend and ally willing to lend aid and comfort in time of need. In this bleak situation

Islam appeared to Pakistan to offer the only bond of belonging in whose name she could appeal for other nations' support.[87] This line of argument is easily intelligible when one viewed it in the context of India's hostility right from its birth, against which Pakistan endeavoured to present a United Muslim world as a balancing counterpoise. A Pakistani author lent considerable support to this view behind Pakistan's fiery espousal of the Muslim cause when he observed:[88]

> "It is, however, not correct to say that the ideal of pan-Islamism has been an active force in Pakistani politics. The basic considerations in Pakistan's foreign policy have been fear of Indian aggression and the liberation of the Muslims of Kashmir."

Secondly, there was also an over-arching ambition to bear the mantle of leadership of the Muslim world for which they constantly referred to Pakistan as the biggest Muslim country and the natural leader of the fraternity of the Muslim world. "In the laboratory of Pakistan, we are experimenting with the principles and ideals of Islam and hope to put before the world a progressive code of life."[89] Though, the love of Pakistanis for Islam was genuine, they made no bones about their much-cherished wish to lead the world Muslims along a new path.

If the above two hypotheses are valid, the forthcoming analysis will serve to highlight the fact that Pakistan which initially treated the Muslim world as a single unity, received no input for the realisation of its objectives for which it was forced to treat the Muslim world at the level of individual countries with the acceptance of the concomitant compulsions of international diplomacy.

It is a matter of historical record that Pakistan, right from its inception, espoused the claim to independence of all Muslim countries which were once part of the colonial empires. It supported inside and outside the United Nations the right to self-determination of the Muslim populations of Palestine, Indonesia, Tunisia, Morocco, Algeria and Libya. As a Pakistani author wrote:[90]

> "With the exception of the Kashmir question, no issue that has come up before the United Nations has so stirred the people of Pakistan, or has called forth such exertions from its representatives as the question of Palestine."

The point that needs further clarification here is that there was no positive stimulus either in the form of pressure or persuasion from the Muslim world for Pakistan to advocate their cause. Rather, King Farooq of Egypt was reported to have ridiculed Pakistan's devotion to Islamic causes by saying to his courtiers, "Don't you know that Islam was born on 14 August 1947?"[91] Similarly, Indonesia, whose struggle for independence moved Zafrullah Khan to remark that Pakistan "felt like a bird one of whose wing was free but the other was still nailed to the ground", described Nehru as the "second father of the Republic of Indonesia."[92] Its poor opinion of the Pakistanis was also noted by a member of Pakistani Parliament on 23 March 1950.[93]

> "I have met many Indonesians, high and low, in Karachi, Calcutta, and Rangoon. Many of them still hold the mistaken notion, so ridiculously spread by Bharati propagandists, that the Muslims of this subcontinent have made no sacrifices for the freedom of their country and it is the Congress and the Hindus alone who fought against foreign domination."

Pakistan's effort to set up an institutionalized structure for promotion of world Islamic solidarity also met dismal failure for lack of any reverse flow of stimuli from the Muslim countries. True, Pakistan revived the old Motamar-e-Alam-e-Islami (Moslem World Conference) which held its first session at Mecca in 1926 and remained dormant since then. Under its auspices, the third session of the Motamar was held at Karachi in February 1949 with delegates from seven countries participating in its deliberations. Its fourth session was held subsequently in February 1951 at Karachi and the representatives swelled up to thirty-six countries. Delivering the inaugural address, Liaquat Ali affirmed, "To Pakistanis nothing was more dearer than the prospect of strengthening of the world-wide Muslim brotherhood." Though Motamar started functioning on a permanent basis at Karachi and proved most enduring of all, yet when, on return from London, Liaquat Ali wanted to convene an Islamic Conference at the governmental level, the Arab and non-Arab states did not show much enthusiasm, because, as reported in the *Dawn* in its issue of 30 May 1949, Pakistan wanted a treaty of formal alliances to be signed between the Muslim countries.

Their lack of interest was evident when Choudhury Khaliquzzaman, the President of the ruling Muslim League Party, went to the West Asian countries in September 1949 to explore the possibility of the formation of a peoples organisation representing all the Muslim countries of the world with a view to discussing common factors among themselves as also evolving, if necessary, a common policy which would benefit Islam and the Muslim world as a whole. Though, he started with the humble mission of working for an Islamic bloc to cement Muslim solidarity on a people to people basis, he exceeded his brief, visited London and discussed "Islamistan" with the responsible British officials for concluding a security pact with British blessing.[94]

However, it was an irony that this governmental effort at Pan-Islamic integration failed miserably to materialize. But, an International Islamic Economic Conference was held at Karachi on 25 November 1949, under the non-official auspices, in which twenty-one countries participated. The notable absentee was Indonesia. At the conference the Prime Minister of Pakistan said in his inaugural address:[95] "We all belong to the great brotherhood of Islam. Islam alone can solve some of the problems facing the world today". In his presidential address, Finance Minister Ghulam Muhammad echoed the same sentiment when he exhorted the Muslim countries to go beyond economic cooperation and become an organic whole in which each part strengthen the whole and the whole imparts life to each part and also develop a system of collective bargaining and collective system. He also underscored the necessity of an ideology to form the basis of World Muslim Unity. And Islam was such an ideology, as he remarked:[96]

> "We cannot put implicit faith in the Western democratic system nor can we subscribe to Communism, although there are some aspects of this vast and comprehensive experiment which we must appreciate... Islamic society has never been subject to the stresses and strains of class war and morbid hatred of the rich has never been one of its characteristics... Islam is the golden mean between these two extremes; it is a non-violent method of rectifying unsocial and detrimental inequalities."

Despite all the eloquent protestations of world Islamic brotherhood, the conference never fulfilled the expectation of its patrons for economic interaction among the Muslims as a prelude to a contemplated political integration. The Conference set up International Islamic Economic Organisation which convened its second session in Tehran. At its third session at Karachi in 1954, the Foreign Minister Zafrullah Khan rightly voiced his disappointment in his presidential address, when he said that it was a profound pity that the progress achieved did not match the high expectation and early euphoria and it gradually petered out after the first conference. But one crucial point thrown up by the whole process was that Pakistan's effort to assume the leadership of the Muslim countries, met a premature demise. The wider question, as *The Economist* commented,[97] behind the whole meeting was, "whether Pakistan will be able to assume the leadership of widely flung peoples who, however much they may have in common, have hitherto been more noted for their "agreement to disagree" than for any effective co-operation. Pakistan undoubtedly has ambition of this sort." The forced abandonment of the project of convening a Muslim Prime Ministers' Conference at Karachi on account of inhospitable reception of the idea by the invitees illustrates the above point. *The Economist* further observed that Pakistan's latest initiative in international politics has disillusioned them and there would be an end to the Pan-Islamic trend in Pakistan. A Pakistani writer analyzed a few years later that owing to lack of enthusiasm for it, the project had to be abandoned.[98] This period commenced with the death of Jinnah in September 1948 and ended in 1953 with the dismissal of Khwaja Nazimuddin as the Prime Minister. Pakistan now rediscovered the Muslim world where political realities were radically different from those envisioned by it. Each Muslim country had its distinctive history and political ethos. Except religion, the Arab and non-Arab Muslims had nothing in common. Mecca might be the past or present symbol of Muslim religious unity but certainly not the hub of political gravity. A Pakistani author underscored this split personality of the Muslim world when he wrote:[99]

> "The mythical Arab nationalism itself was torn by territorial loyalties, divergence of economic interests, and differences of political outlook. There was not one Arab nationalism but as many nationalisms as there were Arab states. Some of them were bitterly anti-west and others were well-disposed towards it, depending partly upon the character and composition of their governments and partly on their economic interests. The ill-equipped monarchies had to seek external support in the face of the challenge from powerful republics."

So, one found that after 1953, a trend was disernible in Pakistan's foreign policy that took account of the pluralistic character of the Muslim world and accordingly underwent radical reorientation as it received stimuli from different countries from time to time. Perhaps in this on-going process, two factors further served to leaven its policy towards each country with distinct individualistic flavour. In the first place, political transformation in West Asia consequent upon the Egyptian Revolution of 1952, had opened up new vistas of Arab nationalism and brought about a complete secularization of Arab politics. Pakistan was caught up in the web of contradictions which was revealed between the interests of these countries and the Western powers, symbolized by the Mossadegh's nationalisation of the Anglo-Iranian oil company.[100] Secondly, Pakistan's membership of the Commonwealth and its generally Pro-Western policies culminating in its alliance with the Western-sponsored pacts projected it in an entirely different role in the West Asian politics than the one advocated by its early decision-makers. Egypt under Nasser was not only the symbol of Pan-Arabianism but the main bastion of opposition to Western ambition. In the crescendo of this movement, Pakistan's policy was deemed to be an attempt to divide the Arab world and to throw a spanner to its unity of Nasser's conception for perpetuating the Western domination. Perhaps Nasser treated it as a challenge to his claim of leadership of the Muslim world with Egypt as the political nerve-centre of the Arab and not of the Muslim West Asia which Pakistan had tried to build but in vain. Certainly, "Pakistan fell in the estimation of the Arabs who are strongly opposed to alignment with the West." As a Pakistani author summed up.[101]

> "The Bagdad Pact undoubtedly divided the Arab world; Pakistan by its membership in that pact was held responsible for contributing to that division. By destroying Arab unity and by making the Arabs more suspicious of Western intentions, the Bagdad Pact increased instability in the region."

The net outcome of this development was a clear configuration of powers in the West Asia. While Egypt spearheaded opposition to the Western alliance structure, Turkey and Iran lent unqualified support. Accordingly Pakistan drifted with the prevailing current. It was clearly evident with the onset of the Anglo-French action in Suez, the countries which supported the Dulles plan included the Bagdad Pact States of Turkey, Iran and Pakistan and those who opposed it were Indonesia and India. Defending the Western action, Suhrawardy was said to have viewed it as an attempt on the part of these powers to see that the Suez canal remained free for international navigation. The invasion aimed at restricting the sovereignty of one country for the benefit of the world. He also admitted with characteristic frankness that the days of Pan-Islamism were over and Pakistanis should first safeguard the legitimate interests of their own Muslims.[102] On another occasion he also ran down Nasser. This was more or less a patterned behaviour, except for a brief interlude during April 1960, when Nasser visited Pakistan.

In sharp contrast to this, Turkey and Iran moved closer to Pakistan. At the initiative of Ayub Khan, a Regional Cooperation for Development with the headquarter at Teheran was set up in July 1964 which envisioned a joint collaborative programme of development in the spheres of industry, agriculture, mineral resources, communication, education, health and cultural exchanges. A number of "joint enterprises, i.e., industrial and manufacturing projects were run by two or all of the partners."[103] For this also, Ayub got more inspiration from the legislators who suggested for a confederation of the RCD countries.[104] It is clear beyond doubt that Pakistani gesture for utilizing religion as a force for alliance with Middle Eastern countries has never been reciprocated, for which dissatisfaction was expressed by the legislators regarding the response to "...emotions and sentiments which we display towards them at all times".[105]

Our enquiry into the impact of regional systemic source shows that India, China and the West Asian countries have deeply influenced its foreign policy behaviour. India remained its principal enemy from which threat is perceived by its successive policy-makers to emanate to its territorial integrity. As a necessary corollary, it was Kashmir with which it was primarily concerned, for the India control of Kashmir stood as a denial of the "Two-Nation" theory, the main basis of Pakistan and its continued *raison d'etre.* As a result, since its birth, the search for security and independence from India and the solution of the Kashmir dispute to its satisfaction had led to an agonising quest for augmenting its capabilities in terms of procuring military aid and diplomatic support from the Big Powers especially the United States. Kashmir became the litmus test for judging the cordiality or hostility of any country or an individual for Pakistan over the years. Its growing affinity and consequent disillusionment with the Western Powers particularly the United States stemed mainly from this issue, so also its declining faith in the efficiency of the United Nations. Its policy shift in early 1960's towards the Communist world was also dictated by this consideration. The issue still continued to be the main stumbling block for Indo-Pakistan rapprochement, even if the bases of hostility were wider than Kashmir.

With regard to China, our enquiry reveals that China's policy towards Pakistan in the years 1947-53 was in keeping with its general pattern of policy towards Asia as a whole. It was one of militantly revolutionary policy marked by open hostility and contempt towards Asian leaders branding them as the hire lings of imperialism. But Pakistanis responded with a measure of shrewd diplomacy: they recognised China; advocated its admission in to the United Nations and refused to brand it as the aggressor in the Korean war. It showed that Pakistan was *very* sensitive on issues hurting Chinese susceptibility. Perhaps this laid down the foundation for future cordiality. Interestingly enough, China on its part had never endorsed India's claim to Kashmir even in the hey-days of Sino-

Indian relationship, it played cool Pakistan's membership of the SEATO, because in the Bandung Conference, Mohammad Ali Bogra, Pakistan's Premier assured him that it was not directed against them as the real enemy of Pakistan was India.

In the aftermath of Indo-Chinese war of 1962, China courted Pakistan and the vice-versa. Both discovered in the Indian subcontinent an area of agreement as a clear perception of their interest resulted in the coincidence of their objective to contain India which was their common enemy. Henceforward, they followed a cooperative policy which led to the endorsement of Pakistan's view regarding Kashmir by China, and it eventuated in the Indo-Pakistani war of 1965 which was even terminated at the behest of the Chinese authorities. This was also repeated in 1971 war.

With regard to the West Asia, it is revealed that Pakistani leadership viewed the successful fruition of their freedom struggle as a manifestation of a renewed sense of Islamic belonging made resurgent in the aftermath of the Second World War, they made a fervent plea for reviving this world spirit. So, it stressed their natural and religious links, common culture, and identity of economic interests. With this objective, its hosted numerous international conferences to discuss problems of mutual security and economic interests for promoting world Islamic Solidarity. Underlying this, was its desire to acquire the mantle of leadership of the Muslim World, and to enlist their support in its disputes with India.

Pakistan's intentions were revealed and became suspect when it joined the Western alliance system orchestrated by the United States which was directed to divide the Arab world. Its stand on the Suez crisis was deplored by the Muslim countries. As it encountered increasing opposition, it gave up its pet idea of promoting economic integration as a prelude to political integration of the Muslim World. It progressively discovered its pluralistic character, and as there was no reverse flow of stimuli from them, it abandoned the idea of treating them as an organic entity and instead followed a policy at the level of individual countries with the acceptance of the concomitant compulsions of international diplomacy.

## References

1. Arnold Wolfers, "The Actors in International Politics" in William T.R. Fox, ed., *Theoretical Aspects of International Relations* (Notre Dome, 1959), p. 101.

2. William T.R. Fox, *The Super Powers–The United States, Britain and the Soviet Union: Their Responsibility for Peace* (New York, 1944), p. 3.
3. James N. Rosenau, ed., *International Politics and Foreign Policy* (New York, 1969), Introduction, p. XVIII.
4. Michael Brecher, "The Subordinate State System in Southern Asia" in James N. Rosenau, ed., *International Politics and Foreign Policy* (New York, 1969), pp. 153-74; Leonard Binder, "The Middle East as a Subordinate International System", *World Politics* (Princeton), Vol.10, no.3, April 1958, pp. 408-29; George Modelski, "International Relations and Area Studies: The Case of South-East Asia", *International Relations* (London), Vol.11, no.7, April 1961, pp. 143-55.
5. Brecher, n. 4, p. 156.
6. Sisir Gupta, "Indo-Pakistan Relations," *International Studies* (New Delhi), Vol. 5, no. 1-2, July-October 1963, pp. 174-79.
7. M.S. Rajan, "India and Pakistan as Factors for Each Other's Foreign Policy and Relations", in *International Studies*, Vol. 3, no. 4, April 1962, pp. 349-94.
8. Khalid Bin Sayeed, "Pakistan and China: The Scope and Limits of Convergent Policies", A.M. Halpern, ed., *Policies Towards China: Views from Six Continents* (New York, 1965), pp. 229-62.
9. Liaquat Ali Khan, Pakistan: *The Heart of Asia* (Cambridge, 1950), pp. 11-6; and Arif Hussain, *Pakistan: Its Ideology and Foreign Policy* (London, 1906), chapters 5-8.
10. William S. Metz, *Pakistan: Government and Politics* (New Haven, 1956), p. 171.
11. See my third Chapter.
12. Gupta, n.6, p. 228.
13. Mohammad Ayub Khan, "The Pakistan-American Alliance: Stresses and Strains", *Foreign Affairs* (New York), Vol. 42, no. 2, January 1964, pp. 199-206.
14. S.M. Burke, Main Springs of Indian and Pakistan' s Foreign Policies (Minneapolis, 1974), pp. 50-54.
15. Sisir Gupta, "Great Power Relations, World Order and the Third World", *Foreign Affairs Reports* (New Delhi) Vol. 27, no. 7-8, July-August, 1978, pp. 110-54.
16. Rajan, n. 7, p. 60.
17. *Dawn* (Karachi), 27 February 1957.
18. Sisir Gupta, *Kashmir: A Study in India and Pakistan Relations* (Bombay, 1966), p. 420.

19. K. Sarwar Hasan, *Pakistan and the United Nations* (New York, 1960), p.144.
20. Mushtaq Ahmad, *Pakistan's Foreign Policy* (Karachi, 1968), p. 99.
21. For details see, Olaf Caroe, *The Wells of Power: The Oil Fields of South Western Asia: A Regional and Global Study* (London, 1951).
22. M.A.H. Ispahani, "Pakistan and New Regional Arrangements", *Pakistan Horizon* (Karachi), Vol. 22, no.3, Third Quarter, 1969, pp. 199-207.
23. United Nations, Security Council, *Official Records, Yr*, 12, Supplementary for January through March 1957, mtg.764, Document S/3787, pp. 7-8.
24. *Dawn* (Karachi), 17 February 1957.
25. United Nations, Security Council, *Official Records*, yr.12, mtg-769 and 770, 17 and 18 February 1957, Documents S/3787, pp. 7-8 and 38-39.
26. United Nations, Security Council, *Official Records*, yr. 17, mtg.1013 and 1016, 21 and 22 June, 1962.
27. Pakistan, National Assembly, *Debates*, Vol.1, no. 2, 27 June 1962, pp. 389-91.
28. India, Rajya Sabha, *Debates*, 23 June 1962 (Foreign Affairs Record), Vol.8, p. 116.
29. United Nations, Security Council, *Official Records, yr.* 19, mtg, 1087 and 1090- 3 and 18 February 1964.
30. *Ibid*, yr.19, mtg. 1091, 10 February 1964.
31. See my fourth Chapter.
32. *Ibid.*
33. Mohammad Ayoob, "India as a Factor in Sino-Pakistani Relations", *International Studies* (New Delhi), Vol. 9, no. 1, January 1968, p. 279.
34. Ahmed Ali, "China Today", *Pakistan Horizon* (Karachi), Vol.1, no. 2, 2nd Quarter, April-June 1948, pp. 111-12.
35. Mushtaq Ahmad, "Pakistan's Policies in Southeast and East Asia", *Pakistan Horizon*, (Karachi), Vol. 4, no. 2, 2nd Quarter 1951, p. 88.
36. *Dawn* (Karachi), 5 January 1950.
37. Conard Brandt, Bengam in Schwartz and John K. Fairbank, *A Documentary Hi story of Chinese Communism* (Cambridge, 1952), pp. 449-61.
38. United Nations, *General Assembly, Official Records* (GAOR) Session 5, Plen, mtg 283, 25 September 1950, p. 97.
39. *Ibid.*, p. 97.
40. K. Sarwar Hasan, *Pakistan and the United Nations* (New York, 1960), p. 252.
41. A Staff Study, "Pakistan's Relations with the People's Republic of China", *Pakistan Horizon*, Vol. 14, no.3, 3rd quarter 1961, p. 217.

42. See my first Chapter.
43. 43 CN. Satyapalan, "The Sino-Indian Border Conflict", *Orbis* (Philadelphia, Pa), Vol.8, no. 2, Summer 1964, pp. 374-90.
44. Nikita S. Khrushchev, "On Peaceful Coexistence", *Foreign Affairs* (New York) Vol.38, no.l, October 1959, pp. 1-18.
45. Harold C Hinton, *Communist China in World Politics* (Boston, 1966), p. 30.
46. George F. Kennan, "Polycentrism and Western Policy", *Foreign Affairs*, Vol. 42, no. 2, January 1964, pp.171-83.
47. William J. Barnds, *India, Pakistan and the Great Powers* (London, 1972), p. 157.
48. K.P.S. Menon, *Changing Pattern of Diplomacy* (Bombay, 1977), p. 24.
49. Anwar Hussain Syed, *China and Pakistan: Diplomacy of an Entente Cordiale* (London, 1974), p. 60.
50. *The Statesman* (New Delhi), 5 September 1954.
51. *New China News Agency* (Beijing), 20 May 1954.
52. *Ibid.*, 12 January 1955.
53. Sayed, n.49, p.58.
54. *Dawn* (Karachi), 7 September 1954.
55. *New York Times*, 25 April 1955; see also Pakistan, National Assembly (second), *Debates*, vol.1, no.2, 27 June 1962, pp. 622-23.
56. L.F. Rushbrook Williams, *The State of Pakistan* (London, 1962), p. 120.
57. Werner Levi, "Pakistan, the Soviet Union, and China", *Pacific Affairs* (Vancouver, B.C.), Vol.35, no.2, Fall, 1962, pp. 211-22.
58. Henry A. Kissinger, *The White House Years* (New Delhi, 1979 p.178.
59. Vidya Prakash Dutt, *China and the World* (New York, 1966, pp. 230-31.
60. *The Peoples Daily* (Peking) 24 July 1957.
61. Ayoob, n. 32, p. 279.
62. Mohammed Ahmed, *My Chef* (Lahore, 1960), pp. 73-76.
63. Mohammad Ayub Khan, "Pakistan Perspective", *Foreign Affair* Vol. 38, no.1, July 1960, p. 556.
64. *Dawn* (Karachi), 8 October 1958.
65. *A Staff Study*, n. 41, p. 226.
66. A. Doak Barnett, *Communist China and Asia: Challenges to American Policy* (New York, 1960), pp. 106-7.
67. Mao Tse-tung Speech in Moscow on 18 November 1957 in Mao Tse-tung on "Imperialists and Reactionaries", *Current Background* (Hongkong), Vol. 534, 12 November, 1958.
68. Ayoob, n. 33, p. 281.
69. Barnett, n. 66, p. 316.

70. Sayeed, n. 8, p. 243.
71. *Dawn* (Karachi), 3 March 1963.
72. Nasim Ahmed, "China's Himalayan Frontiers: Pakistan's Attitude", *International Affairs* (Moscow), Vol. 7, no. 10, October 1962, p. 428.
73. Khalid Bin Sayeed, "Pakistan's Foreign Policy: An Analysis of Pakistan's Fears and Interests", *Asian Survey* (Berkeley, Calif), Vol. 4, no. 3, March 1964, pp. 746-756.
74. *Dawn* (Karachi), 7 July 1963.
75. G.W. Choudhury, "Pakistan and the Communist World", *Pacific Community* (Tokyo), Vol. 6, no. 1, October 1974, pp. 107-39.
76. Quoted in Choudhury, n. 75, p. 122.
77. Syed, n. 49, p. 117.
78. See the text of the statement in *Peking Review* (Peking), Vol. 8, 10 September 1965, pp. 12-13.
79. K. Sarwar Hasan, ed., *Documents on the Foreign Policy of Pakistan: China, India and Pakistan* (Karachi, 1967), pp. 361-62.
80. Syed , n. 49, p. 115.
81. Choudhury, n. 75, p. 123.
82. See my fourth chapter.
83. Wilfred Cantwell Smith, "Islam in the Modern World" in *Current History*, (Philadelphia, Pa.), Vol. 52, no. 190, June 1957, pp. 321-25.
84. G.W. Choudhury, "The Impact of Islam in Pakistan" in *Current History*, Vol. 52, no. 190, June 1951, pp. 339-44.
85. A.B. Rajput, *The Muslim* (Lahore, 1948), p. 204.
86. G.W. Choudhury, *Constitutional Development in Pakistan* (London, 1969), revd. edn. , p. 103.
87. Keith Callard, *Pakistan: A Political Study* (London, 1957), p. 314.
88. Choudhury, n. 84, p. 343.
89. Aslam Siddiqui, *Pakistan Seeks Security* (Lahore, 1960), p. 17.
90. Hasan, n. 19, p. 165.
91. *Dawn* (Karachi), 27 September 1956.
92. *The Statesman* (Calcutta), 6 December 1949.
93. *The Statesman* (Calcutta), 9 June 1950.
94. *Dawn* (Karachi), 15 November 1949.
95. *Dawn* (Karachi), 26 November 1949.
96. *Dawn*, 26 November 1949.
97. *The Economist* (London), 24 May 1952.
98. Hafeez-ur-Rahman Khan, "Pakistan's Relation with U.A.R," *Pakistan Horizon*, Vol. 13, no.3, 3rd Quarter 1960, p. 212.

99. Ahmad, n. 20, p. 69.
100. Sisir Gupta, "Islam As a Factor in Pakistani Foreign Policy," *India Quarterly*, Vol.18, no.3, July-September, 1962, pp. 230-53.
101. Hasan, n. 19, p. 76.
102. For details see my Sixth Chapter.
103. Mohammad Ayub Khan, *Friends Not Masters: A Political Autobiography* (London, 1967), pp. 156-7.
104. Pakistan (Second) *National Assembly, Debates*, Vol. 2-11, nos. 2-8, 21-29 November 1962, pp. 3-261.
105. Pakistan (Second) *National Assembly Debates*, Vol.1, no. 2, 27 June 1962, pp. 584-91.

# 6
# Governmental Sources

## Governmental Structure

It is usually assumed by the foreign policy theorists that the basic arrangements that organize the structure of authority among different agencies and personnel of the Government, constitute a potent variable influencing the foreign policy behaviour of a State.[1] The Governments, that came to prevail in the post-War international system, are termed either as highly centralized and authoritarian or as relatively decentralised and democratic. What is crucial about them is that the consequences of their diversified decision-making structures served to mould their foreign policy behaviour in different ways. This is underscored in two specific ways. In the first place, the degree to which the decision-makers of a state are accountable to its public has a significant bearing on the formulation and execution of a policy. It is because, in a relatively decentralised and democratic system, which is, by definition, an open system, legal rights are an operational reality, and political accountability is ensured through various instrumentalities like legislative over-sight, party-competition and national election. As the demands of the people are freely articulated and aggregated, they are naturally anticipated by and get transmitted to the policymakers who habitually receive a free-flow of information and advice from the officials about the prevailing state of world politics. As a result, there is less of discrepancy between their perception and reality. In contrast to this, in a highly centralized and authoritarian governmental structure which is, by definition, a closed system, political accountability is nearly marginal as political dissent is nil, there is no organised groups to articulate public demands and get them transmitted, political and civil rights are a living myth and the foreign policy was the most zealously-guarded preserve of a coterie of individuals. As a result, the decision-makers of this system are not sensitive to the fury and fluctuation of public reactions. Consequently, they tend to be isolated from their operational world; as their views of the world are dependent on the analysis and advice provided by officials who present them in a manner that their masters desire. The variable that is salient in this regard is that the decision-makers of this system can more easily reverse a course of foreign policy action than their counterparts in an open system, because the latter, in that event, enter a perilous political zone as the price of altered policy very often amounts to their political harakiri or fall from power.

Secondly, even among democratic governments, structures can contribute significantly to the content and quality of foreign policy decision-making as there is a difference between the Cabinet and Presidential System of Government. In the former system, the executive (i.e., Cabinet) is elected and removed by the legislature, whereas in the latter system, the executive is not a creature of the legislature, has separate electoral constituencies and is elected at different times. As a result, the executive and the legislative relations in this system are different and are likely to be more uncertain and strained than in the former system. For the foreign policy analyst, these differences are vital and affect the degree to which uncertainty marks the foreign policy behaviour of a State.

In the ensuing analysis, an attempt is made to explore how the governmental structure of Pakistan, which adopted a democratic system of the Westminster variety in the first decade of its independence and functioned as an open society, was replaced by a relatively decentralised system of Presidential Government of a novel variety under a monolithic dictatorship with tight political regimentation that bordered on almost a closed society in the second decade, influenced its foreign policy behaviour during the period 1947 to 1971. Analysis is focussed on how political accountability is ensured through legislative over-sight within the broader canvas of the executive and the legislative relationship that obtained in different systems which prevailed during the period, and it is preceded by a brief account of the working of various systems.

With the attainment of its statehood, Pakistan opted for a democratic polity and became a federal country comprising two provinces of West Pakistan and East Pakistan. It was precisely because its founding fathers were themselves nurtured in the great liberal tradition of British constitutionalism, and Parliamentary form of Government and had some participatory experiences in the working of federalism in the undivided India introduced by the Government of India Act, 1935, for which they retained provisions in the Section 8 of the Indian Independence Act, 1947 to make the 1935 Act as the 'interim working constitution' for their new Dominion till a new constitution was framed and came into operation. While its early effort to adopt a democratic polity and persevere with an open society was somewhat strained with the creation of a relatively decentralised governmental structure under the Ayub regime with its accent on political regimentation of a closed system, it continued as a federal country till its final break-up in 1971.

The first federal legislature of the new-born state of Pakistan was known as the First Constituent Assembly and was the result of transfer of power in August 1947.[2] It retained this nomenclature till 24 October 1954. The First Constituent Assembly under the provisions of the Indian Independence Act, 1947 was endowed with dual functions, to prepare a constitution for Pakistan and to act as the federal legislature for the country till a new constitution was framed and put into effective operation. It was empowered to exercise all the powers and functions previously discharged by the Central Legislature of the undivided India constituted under the provision of the 1935 Act. It was further empowered to amend or repeal any provision of both the 1935 Act and 1947 Act, in order to make them suitable for application in the emerging conditions of Pakistan.

With regard to its composition, one finds that originally it consisted of sixty-nine members but subsequently rose to seventy-nine.[3] J.N. Mandal, a member of the minority community from East Pakistan was elected unanimously as its temporary Chairman for the first session, and Quaid-i-Azam Mohammad Ali Jinnah was chosen its first President. The Muslim League ruled the roost in the Assembly with its initial strength of forty-nine in 1947 which swelled upto sixty-two in 1954. The Congress was the second largest party whose initial strength of sixteen declined to ten in 1953. As regards the territorial representation, a major chunk of members came from East Pakistan and Punjab contributed the second largest. And the composition of the House truly reflected the prevailing social structure of Pakistan which was being dominated by the emerging middle class and the old feudal class of East and West Pakistan to the complete exclusion of the peasantry, the labour and the industry which were yet to make their debut in national politics. The table below reveals the picture.

**Table 25**

**Profile of Representatives of the First Constituent Assembly[4]**

| | |
|---|---|
| Lawyers | 31 |
| Landlords | 27 |
| Business | 9 |
| Other Professionals (Excluding Law) | 12 |
| Total | 79 |

This Constituent Assembly which continued for a long span of seven years failed in its principal task of framing a constitution and was unceremoniously dissolved on 24 October 1954 by the then Governor-General of Pakistan, Ghulam Mohammad.[5]

After a lapse of eight months, election to the Second Constituent Assembly was held in the summer of 1955. It consisted of eighty members to be elected indirectly by provincial legislatures and the specially constituted electoral college for Karachi and Baluchistan. In its composition, it widely differed from its predecessor in many ways. Three major parties, the Muslim League with twenty-six seats, the United Front with sixteen seats and the Awami League with thirteen seats were represented in the Assembly which had also a plethora of independents numbering sixteen. It contained such prominent figures like Feroz Khan Noon, Abdur Rashid, Fazlur Rahman, Dr. Khan Saheb and Mian Iftikhar-ud-Din. The League, though the largest party in the House, had no absolute majority. And within a.short time, it lost its monolithic character. This Assembly was more reflective of the plurality of Pakistani society than previous ones as it contained not only landlords, the educated elites but also the poor peasantry and the working class who were semi-literates. This is evident from the table below. Besides, another remarkable feature was that the majority of the members were new entrants in politics, only fourteen old members returned. It was convened on 7 July 1955.

**Table 26**

**Profile of Representatives of the Second Constituent Assembly[6]**

| | *Pakistan* | *West Pakistan* | *East Pakistan* |
|---|---|---|---|
| Landlords | 28 | 28 | - |
| Lawyers | 23 | 3 | 20 |
| Professionals | 14 | 5 | 9 |
| Industry and Commerce | 7 | 4 | 3 |
| Others | 8 | - | 8 |
| | 80 | 40 | 40 |

One of the notable achievements of this Assembly was the framing of a constitution which was adopted on 29 February 1956 and came into operation on 23 March 1956. It was a singular success of Mohammad Ali Bogra who succeeded where others, more politically astute, had failed previously. It declared Pakistan to be an Islamic Republic where the Head of State, the President, must be a Muslim. As it provided for a Parliamentary System of government, the Head of State was to be elected indirectly and to function as a mere titular ruler, where real executive authority was vested in the Cabinet headed by the Prime Minister responsible to the national legislature. The Parliament of Pakistan consisted of the President, and one House, the National Assembly. Besides, it was a federal Constitution. The National Assembly was to consist of 310 members equally divided between East and West Pakistan.[7] This Second Constituent Assembly after the adoption of the Constitution was to be transformed in to the First National Assembly of Pakistan until election was held and a new House was set-up.

This Second Constituent Assembly, which started its innings under the premiership of Chaudhuri Mohammad Ali and subsequently rechristened as the First National Assembly, had a brief tenure of a two and a half year, when it came to an end before election was held for reconstitution of a new House. However, this period saw the rise to power of four governments and their unceremonial exist from power. Chaudhuri who forged a coalition Cabinet comprising the Muslim League and its few rumps styling themselves as the Republicans resigned on 8 September 1956. Again, a new Coalition comprising the Awami League of H. S. Suhrawardy and the Republicans of Dr. Khan Saheb took office on 12 September 1956 under the leadership of Suhrawardy.

It, too, fell on 11 October 1957 with the latter's resignation. Again, the Republicans forged an alliance with the Muslim League and formed the Government with I.I. Chundrigar as the Premier, which fell barely completing two months in office, on 16 December. Then, President Iskander Mirza called Feroz Khan Noon to head a coalition Cabinet comprising the Republicans, the Pakistan National Congress and the National Awami Party. The Awami League supported it but refused to join.[8] Commenting on the anatomy of party politics, Callard remarked:[9]

> "The general pattern of politics of Pakistan has been for individual leaders to attempt to establish their personal leadership while those who are left out of office or become disappointed with their share of power and prestige form together in a temporary alliance to dislodge

the ministry. Thus, no basis for a lasting consolidation of political groups has emerged or seems likely to emerge."

The changing configuration of the various party alignments in the House during this period is revealed in the table below.

**Table 27**

**Changes in Party Alignment in Central[10] Legislature (June 1955-December 1957)**

| *Party* | *June 1955* | *Dec 1956* | *Oct. 1957* | *Dec. 1957* |
|---|---|---|---|---|
| Muslim League | 26 | 11 | 12 | 15 |
| United Front | 16 | 15 | - | - |
| Awami League | 13 | 14 | 13 | 13 |
| Republican Party | - | 26 | 21 | 21 |
| Krishik Shramik Party | - | - | 7 | 6 |
| National Awami Party | - | - | 4 | 4 |
| Azad Pakistan Party | - | 1 | - | - |
| Ganatantri Dal | - | 1 | - | - |
| Nizam-i-Islam Party | - | - | 3 | 3 |
| People's Progressive Party | 2 | - | 1 | 1 |
| Pakistan National Congress | 4 | 5 | 4 | 4 |
| Schedule Caste Federation | 3 | 2 | 2 | 2 |
| Independents | 16 | 5 | 11 | 8 |
| Vacant Seats | - | -- | 2 | 3 |
| Total | 80 | 80 | 80 | 80 |

The First National Assembly was dissolved on the night of 7 October 1958 when the then President Iskander Mirza issued a proclamation abrogating the Constitution, dismissing the central and provincial Governments and declaring Martial Law througout Pakistan.

Following the imposition of Martial Law, political life in Pakistan underwent radical change. Its brief experiment in democracy and open society had a premature demise. Ayub ruled the country without a Constitution for almost four years. Pakistani society slided on the path of 'Praetorianism' and became truely a 'Garrison State'. But things looked up when Ayub appointed a Constitution Commission to redeem his pledge held out to the people to restore democracy. The Commission was headed by Justice Mohammad Shahabuddin, a former Chief Justice of Pakistan, a man known for integrity and probity. The Commission submitted its report to the President on May 1961 which was again reconsidered by a Drafting Committee comprising legal luminaries. The Constitution which finally emerged from this body was presented to the nation by the president on 1 March 1962.

The Constitution established a Presidential System of government. It also envisaged a Federation. But as a matter of fact, it introduced so many innovative provisions that it hardly retained the traditional trappings usually associated with a democratic polity and a Presidential form of government. Besides, as election was held in an atmosphere where all prominent political parties were proscribed and free political activities banned it made democracy a mockery. But Ayub justified this by asserting that his Constitution was "a blending of democracy with discipline". He clearly set forth his idea on government when he said that the technique and modus operandi for political participation by the people of an Asian country like Pakistan cannot be same as those in advanced Western countries where socio-economic realities were different.[11]

The Constitution of 1962 gave the country its Second National Assembly. It consisted of 150 members equally divided between its two wings. Six women (three each), were chosen from both wings by their respective Assemblies. Other members were indirectly elected by an electoral college consisting of 80,000 Basic Democrats. The new Assembly saw a reemergence of the old pattern of composition as the lawyers from East Pakistan and the feudal lords from West Pakistan dominated it. But one noticeable change was the representation of business and industrial class which gradually began to extend their sway in national politics. Even if, many of them were new entrants in the political arena, their combined strength of 136 out of 156 made them an important factor to be reckoned with. In contrast to this, the position of the peasantry and industrial workers was hopeless as they were hardly represented in the House. And the conspicuous absence of veteran parliamentarians of earlier years left them with no votaries for their cause. With regard to its working, a most innovative departure was made by an amendment to the Constitution which enabled its members to join the Presidential Cabinet. This, by implication, made the Head of State accountable to the legislature, and at the same time gave him, in turn, an effective instrument through the ministers to control the Assembly.

These innovative features served to bring the practices of the Parliamentary System through the backdoor. Though, the Assembly was elected on a non-party basis, the members of the Convention Muslim League identified them as the Treasury Bench, for many of them accepted ministerial berths in Ayub Government. As they had a majority strength of seventy-six, they ruled the roost in the House, while the Pakistan Peoples Group, the Progressive Group and the Pakistan Independent Group acted as a combined opposition with an effective strength of sixty. The Assembly functioned truely as a representative chamber of the people reflecting popular urges and aspiration for four years, when following Presidential election it was dissolved and fresh election to the Third National Assembly was duly held in March 1966.

In the Third National Assembly, the Pakistan Muslim League of Ayub got a steam-roller majority capturing 124 seats out of a total of 156. The Combined Opposition bagged barely fifteen seats, while the independents swamped the House with seventeen seats. One of the distinctive marks of its composition was the dominance of the businessmen and industrialists with the landlords and lawyers following closely.[12] This Assembly was slated to have a stormy career as political upheavals of the time got reflected in the House. Very soon, it was engulfed in a crisis when some of its members belonging to the opposition party of a particular political group resigned en masse. Finally, in February 1969, it was prorogued, thus bringing to an end a spell of seven years of continued legislative life in Pakistan.

It was followed by another bout of military rule in Pakistan, with the resignation of Ayub Khan in March 1969 and installation of General Yahya Khan as Chief Martial Law Administrator. But Yahya Khan promised early election which was duly held in December 1970 on the basis of Universal Adult Suffrage for the first time in Pakistan's history. The election was held under the procedure set by the Legal Framework Order issued by him in his dual capacity as the President and the Chief Martial Law Administrator of Pakistan on 30 March 1970. In pursuance of this, the Fourth National Assembly was to be composed of 300 members out of which, would be drawn 162 members from East Pakistan, 82 from Punjab, 27 from Sind, 25 from the North-West Frontier Province, and 4 from Baluchistan. In the election which was held on 25 December 1970, the Awami League of Sheikh Mujibur Rahman of East Pakistan swept all the seats (160) in East wing and the Peoples Party of Z. A. Bhutto won the majority of seats from West Pakistan (81). The National Assembly was to act as a Constitution-making body and then convert itself into federal legislature but it was still-born as it never assembled before the break-up of the country in 1971.

From this brief historical analysis, certain common characteristics can be discerned in Pakistan's legislatures even though they operated under different systems and constitutions.[13] In the first place, as pointed out in the foregoing, the legislatures during the period under review (except

1970 election) were not popularly elected and lacked representative character. Secondly, landlords, lawyers, industrialists and professionals dominated the legislatures to the complete exclusion of the working class. Thirdly, the stability of the national government was determined, to a large extent, by the configuration of power that prevailed at the regional level, and sometimes they owed their existence to the inspiration and support of the Head of State. Fourthly, unstable multi party coalition governments and stable one-party and one-man rule marked Pakistani legislative life. Fifthly, the dissolutions of federal legislatures in 1955, in 1958 and again in 1969 were prompted by the personal ambitions of the executive to perpetuate itself in power. Sixthly, the traditions of party responsibility, strict discipline of party system, legislative initiative and responsibility were sadly missing. Lastly, each Government considered foreign affairs to be its exclusive preserve and prerogative.

Now, let us assess the nature and extent of legislative over-sight in Pakistan's foreign affairs and its impact on the policies made. In Pakistan, legislative participation in foreign affairs, like all democratic political systems, had taken many forms. In the first place, this was ensured through the Foreign Policy Debates when wide-ranging discussion on foreign policy was held by the legislators in response to a debate sponsored by the Government. Secondly, during the presentation of the annual Budget, the members used to get ample opportunities to debate foreign policy by way of reference to the demand for grants of the Ministry of External Affairs. Thirdly, they participated in wide-ranging discussion of foreign policy to deal with an emergency situation having significant bearing on the national interest. Lastly, the most formidable weapon which they employed, for ensuring executive accountability was by making constant probes into different dimensions of foreign policy during the Question Hour.[14]

Regarding the nature of the legislative debate, it ranged from broad policy goals to specific details of the foreign policy. But, if one seeks to assess the legislative impact on policy, it will be more profitable to take up broad areas of foreign policy than dealing with action-specific and in terms of the content of the debates, the broad areas could be identified as, the fundamentals of its policy, and its relation with India, China, the Soviet Union, the United States and the Afro-Asian World, especially the Muslim countries. The ensuing analysis will keep this framework for highlighting the legislative impact on policy during the period from 1947 to 1971.

The First Constituent Assembly debated many important policy matters which included Pakistan's membership of United Nations,

Kashmir's legal position with regard to accession, China's recognition, Pakistan's policy towards the Muslim world, its stand on the Korean dispute, Liaquat Ali's proposed visit to Russia, its relation with India and its alliance with the United States. The record of the debate of these issues, when peered through the distance of time, made the following facts clear whose real import was hardly realised in the formative phase of the foreign policy. In the first place, the fundamentals of foreign policy as laid down by Jinnah had a broad national consensus which was testified by the fact that it continued despite his sudden demise and of his trusted friend Liaquat. Not a whimper of protest was heard inside or outside the legislature. Pakistan's helpful stand on the Korean issue and its endorsement by the legislature, which worked as a catalyst for smoothening the process for a long and lasting friendship with the United States, was a clear testimony of faith in the undying legacy of Jinnah's foreign policy.[15]

Though Liaquat's cancellation of trip to the Soviet Union brought the accusation from a few members of being playing into the hands of pro-American lobby whipping up communist phobia, the view was never representative of the wider segment of the legislature which was being dominated by the Muslim League for whom Jinnah's words were Biblical revelations. Secondly, legislative concern for relations with India emanated not only from Kashmir alone but from a host of problems that bedevilled the relation between the two countries. But Kashmir was the most emotive issue for Pakistanis. Underscoring its importance, Mustaq Ahmad Gurmani, the Minister for Kashmir Affairs declared:[16]

> "The problem of Kashmir is a national problem of Pakistan. It is the integral part of our concept of Pakistan... freedom of Kashmir is the basic issue and a national claim of Pakistan in which all communities and all sections of our population is united. We shall deem no sacrifice too great to with our bretheren in Kashmir the right of self-determination and freedom which we have won for ourselves".

It seemed that legislative mistrust of India was deep-seated right from the beginning as the Assembly comprised members who had many shared memories of the traumatic events marking the partition. They were worry of any governmental move for rapprochement with India. So the Liaquat-Nehru pact of 1950 was never hailed as heralding a new phase of Indo-Pakistani relationship. In retrospect, it seemed, Liaquat Ali was swimming against the prevailing tide. Lastly, government's policy for a united Muslim world received substantial stimulus from the legislators as they lent their unqualified support for a conference of the Muslim Prime

Ministers along-with the move for promoting cultural and economic contacts with independent Muslim countries.[17]

This broad national consensus that marked the post-independent foreign policy broke down during the tenure of the First National Assembly when Muslim League lost its ascendency in national politics and new configuration of power appeared in the shape of competing political parties with divergency of approach and outlook on foreign policy. This was reflected in the first major foreign policy debate initiated on 22 February 1957 by the Awami League Government of H.S. Suhrawardy which was assailed for his "unabashedly pro-Western" foreign policy, even though he was underwriting Jinnah's most pious dream. Making a spirited defence of his foreign policy, Suhrawardy reiterated in the assembly on 22 December 1956[18]:

> "The question is asked: why don't we (the Muslim Countries) get together rather than tied to a big power like U.K. or America? My answer to that is zero plus zero plus zero is after all equal to zero. We have, therefore, to go farther a field rather than get all the zeros together."

Many legislators contested this view as they were divided on the issue of alliance with the West. While Treasury members hailed the pacts, the opposition members condemned them outright. Dr. Khan Saheb forcefully made out a case in favour of the Western alliance, while Mian Iftikhar-ud-Din termed them as signs of servility and implored the Government to give up the partisan foreign policy which had not only alienated the Soviet Union and the Afro-Asian World but the Arabs also.[19] And with reference to the Suez Crisis. Pakistan was asked not to share the same negotiating table with Britain. The anti-British sentiment was so strong in the House that the Muslim League opposition party called upon the Government to quit the Commonwealth which has failed to deliver any tangible benefit to Pakistan.[20] Though the House approved Government's Policy by a vote of 42 to 2,[21] the Muslim League abstained from voting, thus registering its solidarity with the nation which had seen, in recent past, a spate of demonstrations all over Pakistan in support of Egypt and against the country joining the Bagdad Pact sponsored by Britain.[22]

Suhrawardy was a shrewd politician and had an instinctive will to survive the vicissitudes of politics. In a clever bid to assuage the ruffled public feeling which found its deep echo in the House, he pulled off many diplomatic tricks to ward off the threat to his authority. He immediately organised a meeting of the Muslim members of the Bagdad Pact at Tehran in which Britain was not invited to participate and made much of political capital out of it by selling it to the domestic public. This was one of cases which clearly demonstrated that in Pakistan which adopted parliamentary democracy, the Government was always keen to ensure its accountability, even though it had requisite parliamentary majority to carry through its foreign policy.

Another major policy statement made by Suhrawardy was Pakistan's new openings to China. Speaking of his endeavour to improve relations with China, Suhrawardy observed:[23]

> "My visit to China and the subsequent visit of the Prime Minister of China has consolidated the bonds of friendship which existed between Pakistan and China since 1951 when we established diplomatic relations with Peoples Republic of China. We have both agreed that the difference in our political system and even the divergence of views on many problems will not stand in our way to strengthen the ties of friendship between us."

Record showed that China was once mentioned perfunctorily way back in 1953 when the members accused it of violating Pakistan's borders in Hunza and of closing its diplomatic offices in Tibet.[24] But, this time the debate was full scale and assumed a lot of significance for various reasons. In the first place, Suhrawardy was cultivating friendship with China which was evident from his visit to China and the wild ovation given to the Chinese Premier, Chou En-lai in Pakistan. This was something incomprehensible and unexpected of a man known for his pro-Western policy. Secondly, as argued elsewhere, the Chinese themselves were not very enthusiastic to cultivate relationship that would force them to cross the threshold beyond a limit. Thirdly, as records revealed, an overwhelming number of members consider China as a positive threat and its potential value as counterpoise for any future conflict against India was never realised.[25] Then one is left to wonder why Suhrawardy was so keen to cultivate the Chinese at the risk of alienating the United States. One plausible explanation can be offered. Suhrawardy was heading a coalition Cabinet comprising his own party and the volatile, opportunistic Republicans. His own Awami Party was itself a divided house, for the leftist faction, represented by the charismatic peasant leader Maulana Abdul Hamid Khan Bhashani was highly critical of Suhrawardy's pro-American and pro-Western foreign policy. He earnestly desired to stave off any possible rift with Bhasani that would split his party and pull down his government. So, sheer political survival dictated him to pay at least lip service to the pro-Peking opposition which became day by day uncompromising. Ultimately, Bhashani formed a new party known as the National Awami Party on 25 July 1957 and withdrew his support from Suhrawardy's government which fell before long.[26] So the point it illustrates is that in a parliamentary democracy, a coalition government hardly survives if there is wide divergence of outlook and approach on foreign policy among the partners.

Interestingly enough, during the tenure of the Second National Assembly, debate on foreign policy became more lively and revealed a high degree of involvement of the legislators. It reflected in diverse ways the thinking of the Ayub Government and the opposition members on various dimensions of the country's foreign policy. The reasons are not far-off to seek. In the first place, Ayub's novel system of Presidential government had a built-in-mechanism for airing of the views of the legislators, despite the ban on political parties and their activities. Secondly, the life of the Assembly coincided with two momentous events whose bearings on the national interest were significant and provided the members political axe to grind against Ayub.

Of all the debates, during the tenure of this Assembly, the one initiated on 21 November 1962 to discuss the emergency situation resulting from the large-scale supply of arms to India by the Western Powers consequent upon the outbreak of the Sino-Indian border war, was crucial and generated much heat and passion among all. In the first place, it was agreed, by and large, that China had no desire to conquer India. The aim of its military operation was limited. Basically, it arose out of a border dispute and in no way reflected a clash of political ideology as made out by the Western Powers.[27] The disposition of India's military deployment was poised against Pakistan, and not against China. As the military disparity between India and Pakistan was in the ratio of 4 to 1, the augmentation of India's military strength by the supply of arms and ammunition by the Pakistani friends was going to 'tilt' the balance in India's favour that would aggravate the situation in the subcontinent and spelt doom for Pakistan. The legislators were convinced that India, for long, wore the mask of non-alignment which was now sheared through. Secondly, they unanimously assailed the Western Powers, denounced the Pacts and their disenchantment bordered on the belief that Pakistan had been taken for a cool ride. Allies were treated on the same footing as the non-aligned states. So, a greater degree of realism seemed to have dawned on the policy-makers who remained so long in the world of their make-beliefs. The legislators also refused to be taken in by the assurances held out by the Government and openly condemned the British-American deception.[28] True, in spite of the chorus of protest against the continuance of the relationship with the Western Powers and the apparent agreement of the executive, no real change was effected. But they achieved in the long run what they failed at the moment. Lastly, the legislators' pro-China sentiment was equally shared by the Executive which set the tone for the emerging Sino-Pakistani axis of late 1960's. Bogra in his inimitable diplomatic jargon underscored the prevailing pro-China sentiment of the government when he remarked:[29]

> "In international relations there can be no eternal friends nor can there be eternal enemies... as situation changes, enemies can become friends and friends can become enemies."

Obviously, he was referring to China as the prospective friend of Pakistan. Subsequently, Z.A. Bhutto, Pakistan's foreign minister, echoed the same view when, in a debate in the House, he made a startling disclosure that an attack on Pakistan by India would involve "the largest state in Asia".[30] Bhutto's remark which purported to refer to China was clearly indicative of the emerging trend in Pakistan's foreign policy in early 1960's, though there was no truth in the statement as he clarified it later on when he dismissed it as a "strong assumption".[31] Certainly, Ayub Government successfully cashed in the anti-western feeling of the House in order to muster up support for moving closer to Peking.

In the debate which started on 17 November and continued for a couple of days, Indo-Pakistani relations came into sharper focus. The members singled out Indonesia and China and profusely praised them for their whole-hearted support during the Indo-Pakistani war of 1965.[32] They minced no words to assail the United Nations which acted as an instrument of the Super Powers during the whole crisis.[33]

The United States also came up for sustained criticism for enforcing an embargo on arms sale to both the aggressor and the aggressed, and also for not making any distinction between an ally and a friend.[34] Besides, the Foreign Ministry was equally censured for its failure to counter India's anti-Pakistani propaganda that sullied the country's image abroad. One of the surprising highlights of this continuing debate was the display of pro-Soviet sentiment which was shared by a wider segment of the House who categorically vouchsafed for relationship with the Soviet Union as they felt, "there is no reason to fear the loss of American friendship if we become friendly with Russia."[35] It was a widely-held view that the Soviet Union was deeply committed to India because of the folly of the Pakistani leaders to align so deeply with the Americans.[36] In retrospect, it seemed that the legislative debate for relationship with the Soviet Union served as a dress-rehearsal for Ayub who was keen to hammer out a triangular relationship involving China, the Soviet Union and the United States after the U-2 incident.

With regard to its policy towards the Muslim world, especially the Arabs, the members presented a very bleak and grim picture of the failure of the policy of the Government. The debate brought forth a candid admission of its failure and a trace of realism seemed to have marked the remark of Bogra when he stated in the House:[37]

> "While we feel great attachment to all of them (Muslims) on account of our sharing a common religious ideology, a common culture, a common religious tradition, and a common historical background, we found that leaders in these countries pay more emphasis on political considerations rather (than) on religious affinity. "

There was an unmistakable consensus that the Government should shed off its illusion long harboured and follow a more dynamic policy based on recognition of the actual correlation of forces favouring friendship with Pakistan and supporting its stand on various regional and international issues. It was also suggested that a scheme of Regional Cooperation for Development should be formed.[38] But the nebulous idea of a United Muslim world was thoroughly pooh-poohed. Now, it can be asserted with a plausibility that these debates significantly influenced Ayub who mooted the idea of RCD and also very deftly reversed the earlier policy towards the Muslim World. This legislative support was vital, as the policy had an emotive content for Pakistanis which must be dealt with care and diplomatic finesse by any Government in power.

The Third National Assembly met at a time when the nation was caught up in the state of euphoria generated by its victory in the Indo-Pakistani war of 1965 and the Government was equally flaunting its crowning achievement both in the hustings and in the diplomatic table at Tashkent. So, it was natural that the debate on foreign policy, which was initiated on 14 March 1966, reflected the confident mood of the people and the Government. Begum Khudeja G.A. Khan's feelings animated the House, who, while paying her tribute to the Pakistanis in the previous occasion said:[39]

"The Pakistanis here emerged like a single personality to defend their motherland. They are anxious to welcome death like moths round the candle. They are not prepared to bend their knees before the enemy and pass their lives in slavery and humiliation."

As it discussed the Tashkent Agreement, the debate touched upon some important areas of Pakistan's foreign policy. In the first place, it showed that the legislators fear of India was genuine, and like all previous moves for rapprochement by the various governments, this time, too, voice was raised against the agreement terming it as another case of complete betrayal and sell-out of the national interest.[40] The past memories of India's withholding of Pakistani assets during partition years, supply of waters, forcible annexation of areas legitimately belonging to Pakistan, contrived diplomatic isolation from the Arabs, were reiterated to prove that India's hostility was implacable. Secondly, regarding the role of the Soviet Union in the agreement there was difference of opinion. While Bhutto made a spirited defense of the agreement terming it as a landmark in Pak-Soviet relationship because the Soviet Union recognized Kashmir, other members deemed it a major stroke of Soviet diplomacy and a complete sell-out of Pakistani interest.[41] Lastly, there was near unanimity of view that China's unequivocal support to Pakistan in 1965 war proved it beyond a shred of doubt that China was its only sheet-anchor of hope in an hour of crisis.[42] So, naturally, the stock of Chinese goodwill rose rapidly in the estimation of Pakistanis which put its case in a new perspective in the legislative debate. The previous reservations regarding the bonafides of the Chinese intention gave way to an enthusiastic endorsement of the Government's China Policy which certainly gave a moral booster to the Government to place it on a more sound and solid footing. In the hindsight of time, it seems plausible to conclude that this unflinching support of the legislators which was simply reflective of prevailing popular opinion played a significant part in the emerging Sino-Pak axis of late 1960's when the new configuration of the world forces resulting from the rapprochement between the United States and China crystallized it in the early 1970's.

Now coming to our enquiry into the governmental structure, it is found that Pakistan adopted a democratic system of the Westminster variety from 1947 to 1958 and functioned as an open society. But the parliamentary democracy had a sad demise in October 1958, when Mohammad Ayub Khan imposed Martial Law, ruled for four years without a Constitution. He completely depoliticised the political system by banning political activities and proscribing political parties. In 1962, he promulgated a new Constitution, established Presidential democracy with all the trappings of a Parliamentary system. In 1965, he himself contested for the office of presidency from a political party owing its origin to his inspiration. After his fall, in 1968, Pakistan again reverted to Martial Law administration under Yahya Khan who held a general election on the basis of universal adult suffrage in 1970 but it was still-born as civil war broke out leading to the break-up of the country.

It is evident from our study that various legislators of Pakistan have taken keen interests to debate foreign policy issues, though it was the preserve of the executive. The debate ranged from broad foreign policy goals to specific details.

The first Constituent Assembly (1947-54) debated many vital policy matters which included Pakistan's membership of the United Nations, Kashmir, China's recognition, Pakistan's policy towards the Arab world, its stand on Korea, Liaquat Ali's proposed visit to Russia and above all its relations with India. It showed that the fundamentals of the foreign policy laid down by Jinnah had a broad national consensus and the legislature gave unstinted support to the executive. It also continued during the tenure of Liaquat Ali Khan. The Second Constituent Assembly (1954-56) hardly debated any important foreign policy issue. It was rechristened as the First National Assembly of Pakistan when election to the new House took place under the first republican Constitution of 1956. During the term of Suhrawardy who became the Prime Minister on 12 September 1956, the first major foreign policy debate was initiated. The pent-up feelings of the legislators gave way in a blistering attack on every facets of Pakistan's pro-Western foreign policy. Though Suhrawardy made a spirited defence of the policy of the previous government, and the House approved it, his government fell subsequently when the pro-Chinese Maulana Bhasani withdrew support and formed a new political party. It revealed the lack of consensual basis in Pakistan's foreign policy.

During the tenure of the Second National Assembly, debates generated much heat and passion. This period coincided with the large-scale supply of Western arms to India in the wake of the Sino-Indian war of 1962. Indian policy of non-alignment was bitterly assailed. Pakistan's membership with the Western alliance system came under heavy fire and members argued for a more realistic policy. The pro-Chinese sentiment of the nation came to sharper focus. In the debate that started in the aftermath of the Indo-Pakistani war of 1965, members profusely praised China and condemned the role of the United Kingdom and the United States. And the relationship with the Soviet Union found a responsive chord. This certainly served Ayub's objective to underwrite his policy of bilateralism. On the whole, it can be said that legislative debate in Pakistan reflected the national consensus or its absence in different times.

## References

1. James N. Rosenau, "The Study of Foreign Policy", James N. Rosenau and others, eds., *The World Politics: An Introduction* (New York, 1976), p. 35.
2. In May 1946, the Cabinet Mission Plan conceived a single Constituent Assembly for undivided India. It was to be an indirectly elected body. In pursuance of this plan, election to the Constituent Assembly was held in July 1946 in which the Congress Party bagged 199 of 210 Hindu seats, whereas the Muslim League got nearly all Muslim seats except five (70 out of 78) and became the second largest party. But the Muslim League boycotted the first session of the Assembly when it was convened on 9 December 1946, as acute differences arose with the Congress Party over the implementation of the plan. This triggered off the movement for Pakistan which was finally conceded by the British Government. The Indian Independence Act, 1947 was passed which stipulated the bifurcation of the Constituent Assembly, one for Pakistan and another for India. The inaugural session of the new Constituent Assembly of Pakistan was held in Karachi-the new capital from 10 to 14 August, 1947. For details see, G.W. Choudhury, *The Constitutional Development in Pakistan* (London, 1959), pp. 6-22.
3. Four more seats were created for Bahawalpur, Khairpur, Baluchistan, and the North West Frontier Province, to be filled up by nomination by the rulers. And further addition of six members was made (to give representation to new population; five for Punjab, and one for Sind to be elected by their respective legislatures), by the Assembly when it passed the Constituent Assembly of Pakistan (Increase and Redistribution of Seats) Act, 1949.
4. Mushtaq Ahmad, *Government and Politics in Pakistan* (Karachi, 1963), p. 97.
5. Close on the heels of defeat of the Muslim League Party in the Provincial election of East Pakistan in April 1954 and the advent to power of the United Front Government and its subsequent dismissal created an unprecedented political crisis in Pakistan. As the Muslim League was rejected at the poll, the segment of its representatives from East Pakistan lost their legitimacy in the Assembly and Ghulam Mohammad took advantage of this

to declare a state of emergency throughout the country, dismissed the Assembly and ruled with a Coalition Cabinet of his own choice. For details, see, *Gazette of Pakistan (Extraordinary)*, 24 October 1954.

6. Ahmad, n.4, p.115.
7. The Provinces of Baluchistan, Sind and Punjab and the North-West Frontier Province had ceased to exist and the "One Unit" concept for West Pakistan had already been legalised with the enactment of the Establishment of West Pakistan Act, on 14 October 1955 by the Second Constituent Assembly. A bill to provide a Constitution of Pakistan, see the full text in the Gazettee of Pakistan, 8 January 1956. It is also reporduced in K.J. Newman, *Essays on the Constitution of Pakistan* (Dacca, 1956), pp. 1-114.
8. For details, see, K.K. Aziz, *Party Politics in Pakistan, 1947-58* (Islamabad, 1976).
9. Keith Callard, "The Political Stability in Pakistan", *Pacific Affairs* (Vancouver, B.C.), Vol.29, no.1, March 1956, pp. 5-21.
10. Figures in the first column is drawn from *Dawn* (Karachi), 22 and 23 June 1955, and other figures are culled from *Pakistan Information 1956-57*, Press Information Department, Government of Pakistan (Karachi, 1957).
11. Interestingly, article 19 of the Constitution of 1962 laid down that the Central Legislature shall consist of the President and one House to be known as the National Assembly of Pakistan, thus making the Head of State an integral part of the legislature which runs counter to the principles of Presidential System based on the concept of separation of power. Similarly, coming to the election of 150 members of the National Assembly, as laid down in the Constitution, each province will have an equal number of (not less than 40,000) territorial units known as Electoral Units. Persons, not less than 21 years of age, if not otherwise disqualified, shall be entitled to be enrolled on the electoral roll for an Electoral Unit. The persons enrolled on the electoral roll for an Electoral Unit shall from time to time elect from among themselves a person who is not less than 25 years of age to be known as Elector for that Electoral Unit. In this way, the Electors for all Electoral Units in both provinces shall together constitute the Electoral College of Pakistan and shall be known as the members of Electoral College. Strangely enough, not only they will choose 150 members of the Assembly, but also elect the President of the country; For details, see Choudhury, n. 2.
12. Hamid H. Kizilbash and Khawar Mumtaz, *Pakistan Foreign Policy and Legislature: A Preliminar.y Report* (Lahore, 1976), p.10.
13. For details, see Aziz, n. 8.

14. Kizilbash and Khawar Mumtaz, n.12, pp. 16-22.
15. During the debate on Korea,Iftikhar-ud-Din was the only member who opposed the resolution moved by Liaquat in the Assembly. He regretted that Pakistan was supporting the most hated ruler of South Korea Syngman Rhee, a stooge of the American imperialism. For details, see Abdullah Malik, *Selected Speeches and Statements, Mian Iftikhar-ud-Din* (Lahore, 1971), p.275. He also drew a parallel with Kashmir. In both the cases aggression should be deplored. See, Pakistan, *(First) Constituent Assembly (Legislature), Debates*, Vol.2, no.8, 11 October 1950, pp.480-508.
16. Pakistan, *First Constituent Assembly (Legislature Debates*, Vol.2, no.14, 5 October 1950, pp. 208-57.
17. Pakistan, *First Constituent Assembly (Legislature Debates*, Vol.2, no.2, 16 October 1951, pp. 11-13.
18. Pakistan, *(First) Constituent Assembly (Legislature) Debates*, Vol.1, no.13, 22 February 1957, pp. 912-28.
19. It can be recalled as early as 1952, Iftikhar-ud-Din expressed his fear about Pakistan's ruling clique's participation in Western orchestrated defence Pacts. His fears were denied by the then Government in power. A. K. Brohi, the Minister for Law, Parliamentary and Minority Affairs, dismissed it as mere "kite-flying" in some section of the Press. But later, events proved his prophesy. See, Pakistan, *(First) Constituent Assemblv (Legislature), Debates*, Vol.2, no.17, 7 November 1957, pp.1443-46.
20. Pakistan, *(First) Constituent Assembly (Legislature), Debates*, Vol.1, no.15, 25 February 1957, pp. 1057-1102.
21. *Dawn*, 18 December 1956, 19, 23, 26 February 1957.
22. M.S. Venkataramani, *The American Role in Pakistan 1947-58* (New Delhi, 1982), p. 377.
23. Pakistan, *(First) Constituent Assembly (Legislature), Debates*, Vol.1, no. 13, 22 February 1957, pp. 910-928.
24. On April 2, 1953, in response to a question by Nur Mohammad, the then Foreign Minister, Chaudhuri Zafrullah Khan said that the Government of China had withdrawn its recognition of Tibet and Sinkiang and, therefore, it was necessary to close down Pakistan's diplomatic offices. Pakistan, *(First) Constituent Assembly (Legislature), Debates*, Vol.1, no.3, 23 March, 1957, pp.
25. There are exceptions; one of them was Iftikhar-ud-Din, the first political leader of Pakistan who realised the importance of Pakistan's relations with the Socialist countries, particularly with the Soviet Union and China. Though the government of Pakistan had recognised the Peoples Republic, yet it did

not show any warmth of cordiality for many obvious imperatives. Iftikhar made significant contribution (non-official) to the growth of the Sino-Pak relations when he visited China in response to an invitation from the Chinese Government to attend the Asian Peace Conference in Peking and other functions; See Pakistan, *First National Assembly (Legislature), Debates,* Vol.1, no. 14, 23 February 1957, pp. 950-1047.

26. See for details, Aziz, n. 8.
27. Pakistan, *(Second) National Assembly (Legislative Debates,* Vol.2, no.2, 22 November 1962, pp.3-11.
28. *Ibid.*, p. 16.
29. *Debates*, n. 25, pp.3-11.
30. Pakistan, *(Second) National Assembly, Debates,* Vol.2, part-2, no. 17-63, 17 July 1963, p. 1666.
31. *Morning News* (Karachi), 9 October 1963.
32. Pakistan, *(Second) National Assembly, Debates,* Vol.3, no.4, 19 November 1965, pp. 197-265.
33. *Ibid.*
34. Pakistan, *(Second) National Assembly, Debates,* Vol.3, no.3, 19 November 1965, pp.76-102.
35. For details, see the statement of Syed A. Sultan (East Pakistan), *(Second) National Assembly, Debates,* Vol.1, no.2, 27 June 1962, pp.584-91.
36. For details see the Statement of Mohammad Abdul Huq, Pakistan, *(Second) National Assembly, Debates,* Vol.2, no.12, 4 December 1962, pp.353-96.
37. *Debates* , n. 35, pp.584-91.
38. Pakistan, *(Second) National Assembly, Debates* , Vol. 11, no.8, 29 November 1962, pp.216-61.
39. Pakistan, *(Second) National Assembly, Debates* , Vol. 3, no. 3, 18 November 1965, pp. 117-75.
40. Pakistan, *(Third) National Assembly, Debates,* Vol.1, no.6, 14 March 1966, pp.355-419.
41. *Ibid*; Aleem L. Razee discribed Tashkent as "our magnificent defeat", while Mukhlessuz Khan termed it as "our humiliating surrender".
42. For detail comments of Afazuddin Fakir and Rana Ghulam Sahirkhan, see Pakistan, *(Second) National Assembly, Debates,* Vol.3, no.3, 18 November 1965, pp. 117-75.

# 7
# Idiosyncratic Sources

## Personality Characteristics of the Key Decision-makers

It is contended by theorists that the more authority the policy maker has over a nation's foreign policy machinery, the fewer the people there are above him in the foreign policy bureaucracy to change his decision. As Glen H. Strassen notes: "Top-level executives are not under tight hierarchical constraint. They must be persuaded and bargained with rather than simply commanded... Therefore, preferences and belief-sets are likely to be important for top-level executive decision-makers."[1] Similarly, it is also assumed that less well defined the policy-maker's role, the more likely his personality traits are to influence foreign policy. Richard C Snyder and James A. Robinson conclude that roles are less likely to be well-defined the higher one goes up in an organisation; the role occupant has more responsibility for delimiting or expanding his functions.[2]

Based on this rationale that the personalities of heads of state and foreign ministers will probably have more impact on the foreign policy behaviour of their governments than lesser personalities of the occupants of most other governmental positions, Margaret G. Hermann has come to the conclusion that 50 per cent (7 out of 14) of the predicted relationships between leader personality and foreign policy were significant or approached significance (P. 10; rank order correlations of .44 or greater) using heads of state.[3] The percentage of such bivariate relationship for policymakers lower in the foreign policy organisation is expected to be much less than 50 per cent. Besides, she has also empirically proved that the personality traits of policy makers significantly influence foreign policy decisions only under certain conditions, depriving them of any autonomous functions or operations.

Keeping the above contention in view, the ensuing analysis will highlight how the personality characteristics of the strategic decision-makers of Pakistan during the period 1947-71 influenced its foreign policy behaviour. In this connection, certain clarifications are in order. In the first place, it should be borne in mind that the personality traits are diverse and the entire gamut of them are operative and influence one way or the other the policy decisions of a country. But we have posited in our model that the belief system and cognitive process are central to the process of decision-making. So, is it pertinent that we should first of all construct their belief systems and cognitive styles and show their impact on various policy decisions, which means they should be treated as independent variables. But in our model, we have also posited the decision-making as the level of analysis which necessitates that the cognitive process and belief systems of policy-makers should be treated as intervening variables. Further, as our purpose is to trace the impact of factors that shape the policy-making process on outputs, it becomes an analytical challenge to treat them both simultaneously as independent and intervening variables. To solve this tangled problem, we seek to analyse in the present chapter the specific conditions (in the form of a few empirically tested propositions) present in Pakistan during the period 1947-71 which must have provided enough stimuli to the policy-makers to bring their idiosyncratic traits to bear upon their policy decisions. In the next chapter, an attempt is made to construct their belief systems and cognitive process and their impact on policy preference.

Secondly, a host of policy-makers presided over the decision-making structure of Pakistan during 1947 to 1971. Notables among them were Mohammad Ali Jinnah, Liaquat Ali Khan, Sir Zafrullah Khan, Khawaja Nazimuddin, Ghulam Mohammad, Mohammad Ali Bogra, H.S. Suhrawardy, Chaudhury Mohammad Ali, Iskander Mirza, Mohammad Ayub Khan, Zulfikar Ali Bhutto, and General Yahya Khan. Though in varying degree many of them have influenced the foreign policy decisions, few of them have directly participated in the decision-making. In the first four years of independence from 1947 to 1951, Jinnah and Liaquat provided strong political leadership to Pakistan. Confronted by the near chaos in the country and war with India, Jinnah increasingly turned to the bureaucracy to help consolidate the new nation and in the process restored the old viceregal system of administration. But he kept the Frankenstein's monster at bay, dominated the decision-making structure and laid down the essential thesis of foreign policy. This was faithfully carried out by Liaquat who like

Jinnah, assumed the supreme leadership of the party and government and ensured the dominance of the political elites in the political system. But with his death the Muslim League fragmented and there was gradual ascendancy of the Pakistani bureaucracy as a dominant force in the political system. The advent to power of two civil servants Ghulam Mohammad and Iskander Mirza in 1951 legitimized the strong paternalistic tradition and heritage of the Civil Service to restore the viceregal system of administration and marked the eclipse of the political elites as the articulate interest groups in the decision-making. During the period 1951 to 1958, the decision-making was dominated by the "hierarch" comprising Ghulam, Mirza and Ayub who took to its logical conclusion the major plank of Jinnah's foreign policy-relationship with the United States—though in the process they jettisoned its main thesis of nonalignment. This paved the way for Ayub to intervene. Though he was offered to take over earlier he refused. As a Cabinet Minister in charge of the Defence department, he tasted power and his influence increased, and in 1958 he finally established martial law, completely depoliticizing the political system. The centre of power shifted from bureaucracy to the military-bureaucratic elites, and Pakistan was ruled by a stratum drawn exclusively from West Pakistan. Despite Ayub's introduction of guided or basic democracy and end of martial law, the decision-making became highly centralized in the hands of the military-bureaucratic elites under the overall control of Ayub. The formulation and administration of most important governmental decisions were controlled by bureaucracy with no direct and very little indirect participation by elected assemblies.[4] After the collapse of Ayub regime, Yahya Khan created an inner cabinet of generals who functioned independently of the main body as a whole and provided a kind of collective leadership. Though he retained defence and foreign affairs, key decisions were made by the inner cabinet comprising Lt General, S.G.M. Peerzada, Brigadier Rahim Khan, Brigadier Karim Khan, General Abdul Hamid Khan, and Major General Ghulam Umar. In June 1970, he set up a civilian Cabinet consisting of ten members drawn equally from the two provinces. By February 1971, it was dissolved and the civilian secretaries ruled with a Cabinet of sorts. Thus the civil bureaucracy gradually began to replace the military in key decision-making as Pakistan slided on the path of the Civil War. The military regimes of Ayub Khan and Yahya Khan concentrated decision-making power in the hands of a coterie of centralized elites from which Bengalis were largely excluded. These regimes were highly personalized political systems which functioned through cliques and factions within the small governmental elites, and political elites were debarred from the decision-making.

The foregoing facts set against the available historical records make one point clear. In the decision-making structure of Pakistan during the period from 1947 to 1971, two figures dominated: Mohammad Ali Jinnah and Mohammad Ayub Khan. While this may appear a little arbitrary, one's choice of the key decision-makers is limited in the absence of evidence to the contrary.

Now, for the purpose of delineating the conditions we will take up our first proposition which reads:[5]

(a) The more dramatic are the means of assuming power, the more likely the personality characteristics of the head of state are to affect foreign policy behaviour.

It is a truism that Jinnah who became the first Governor-General of independent Pakistan never assumed power as a result of revolution or any landslide victory in a national election which are usually considered dramatic means of assuming power. Nor did he adopt subsequently any democratic process for legitimizing his rule among the Pakistanis. But it should be recalled, the movement for a Muslim home land that ultimately culminated in the birth of Pakistan had all the dimensions of a revolution infused with drama and struggle and certainly held the promise of a new social and political order for the exploited Muslims of the Indian subsontinent. Perhaps in this sense it was revolutionary and epoch-making. Jinnah was its author and the architect, and with the creation of Pakistan, he went down in the annals of history as an event-making man. Standing at the forking points of history, he created a fork in the historical road. So, it won't be a travesty of truth to say that the office of Governor-General was literally bestowed upon him by the Pakistanis which was a crowning recognition of Jinnah's supreme sacrifice for the cause of Islamic solidarity and his untirring quest to bring the vision of Iqbal to a living reality. With Jinnah, Pakistan was an article of faith, the summum bonum of his existence. As he said to Lieutenant Ahsen, while stepping into the Government House at Karachi after the assumption of office:"... I never expected to see Pakistan in my life time. We have to be very grateful to God for what we have achieved. That his elevation to the highest office of the land was cheerfully endorsed by the masses and he needed no legitimization could be clearly evident from the way he was greeted on his first arrival from Delhi at Karachi airport on 7 September 1947. Belitho graphically described the touching scene:[8]

"The aircraft landed and Mr. Jinnah was the first to step out, followed by his sister. The people cried "Pakistan Zindabad:" Pakistan Zindabad:" They pressed forward, close, hot and frenzied so that they might be as near as possible to their deliverer."

This statement underscores a simple fact that Jinnah who was the darling of millions of Muslims during the freedom struggle, had become their deliverer in the new state of Pakistan.

Jinnah was a charismatic leader if charisma is defined as leader's capacity to elicit from a following devotion and awe towards himself as the source of authority. During the penultimate phase of Pakistani freedom struggle, Jinnah succeeded in bringing all differing shades of Muslim political opinion in the Indian subcontinent under a common platform of the All India Muslim League which presented a united front to the Indian National Congress and the British Government. The Muslims henceforth spoke with one voice. As head of the Pakistani movement, Jinnah represented that voice which reflected the entire spectrum of muslim interests in the subcontinent. And his voice rose above the welter of voices of many disparate political actors within the Muslim League itself. This naturally bred in Jinnah a disposition to establish a Unitarian pattern of leadership which brooked no compromise, no dissent and no subordination to any other authority above him. This in turn spawned a repertoire of beliefs and myths among the political followers which, with the consummation of victory, got engraved in the masses and informed his style of functioning in subsequent period. Attitude, and behaviour change slowly but imperceptivity and over a period of time. Jinnah did not live long, he conducted the affairs of the new state of Pakistan as he was accustomed to run those of the Muslim League during the pre-partition days. His subordinates rendered the same loyalty and devotion that were the manifestation of their beliefs and faiths nurtured in earlier years. So when he chose to become the Governor-General rather than Prime Minister, he thereby clearly established the viceregal system of Government which would invest him with a panoply of executive powers and reducing others as mere trappings of the system. Not a single eye-brow was raised, Liaquat Ali, who was chosen by him to be his Prime Minister, acquiesced in the set-up, fully aware of the fact that what he got was the husk rather than the grain of power. Further, by assuming the President of the Constituent Assembly which was the first Parliament of Pakistan, Jinnah became the fountain-head of all power in the political system. To cap it all, he too became President of the Muslim League—the ruling party—thereby ensured that his fiat was only one that must run across all the length and breath of the state of Pakistan. Though he lived for a very brief span of time after partition, the concentration and personalization of all authority and power showed that he alone was the source of legitimacy of the government as he had been of the Pakistan Movement. If the Pakistanis shallowed this without a whimper of dissent, it was precisely because they looked upon him as their only saviour, who has not only freed them from the thraldom of servitude in undivided India, but also held the beacon light for guiding the destiny of the nation precariously poised in the throes of crisis. With each passing day, crisis multiplied and looked menacingly insoluble. So, people increasingly looked to Jinnah for an answer which he alone could provide. It was natural that the masses affectionately called him Quaid-i-Azam or a Great Leader and shared all his beliefs, attitudes, values and desires. Mourning the death of the Quaid-i-Azam, Liaquat observed:[12]

> "There is no better way of showing our love for and reverence to our beloved Quaid-i-Azam than to keep before us always that ideal which he placed before us and to make Pakistan as great a State as he wanted to. The Quaid-i-Azam was the symbol of national strength and determination and inspired by it, whatever constructive work the Government or the people of Pakistan do, will be a memorial to our beloved leader."

This simply validates our second proposition:

(b) The more charismatic is the head of state, the more likely his personality characteristics are to affect foreign policy behaviour.

With the death of Jinnah, Khawaja Nazimuddin succeeded to the Office of the Governor-General. Interestingly enough, the office was offered to him by Liaquat Ali, an event which itself gave a foretaste of things to come. Liaquat's first act as Prime Minister, was to divest the Governor-General of the portfolio of States and Frontier Regions which was a clear indication that henceforth Liaquat was to rule the roost in Pakistani politics. And in cabinet meetings Nazimuddin ceased to preside, thereby paving the way for the working of parliamentary democracy of Westminster model which Jinnah had introduced but never relished. Now the centre of power veered round the office of the Prime Minister. Liaquat, with a clear majority in the National Assembly, established Prime Ministerial dictatorship in the country. As a noted Pakistani writer remarked:[13]

> "He presided over the cabinet meetings not as a chairman for discovering majority opinion but as a president who could, if

necessary, determine the outcome of discussions in the face of an unwilling majority. He took vital decisions, sometimes even without prior consultation with his colleagues, in the knowledge and confidence that they would be endorsed by the cabinet and approved by the Parliament."

His decision to dismiss the Mamdot Ministry in Punjab in January 1949, Pakistan's support to the United Nations stand in the Korean War and negotiations with the Indian Prime Minister in 1951 were cited as instances where he acted without taking the cabinet into confidence. Gradually, Liaquat became controversial in national politics, and alienated himself from many important regional political actors which reached its culmination in the years following his assumption of the office of President of the Muslim League. Though endowed with sterling qualities of a statesman and he could charm vast and illiterate masses by his gift of the gab, he had all the failings of a politician which gradually surfaced as time rolled on.

Though a powerful personality, Liaquat never waivered from the path chosen by his mentor at least in the arena of foreign policy. Jinnah was its architect, provided its architectural design. Liaquat became its builder. Speaking of their relationship, Begum Liaquat remarked:[14]

"They had known each other from 1928 at the Calcutta conference where Jinnah was so humiliated. You will remember how he was cried down as not being in any sense an accepted leader of the Muslims. Liaquat was one of those who stood by him: he had always admired Jinnah and believed in him much then as he did at the end."

Right from 1927, Liaquat served Jinnah with unquestionable fidelity. In the years that followed, "When Jinnah enjoyed omnipotence, Liaquat Ali Khan did not mind; indeed it was part of his nature that he enjoyed the subtle rewards of second place". Precisely in recognition of this, Jinnah chose Liaquat to be the first Prime Minister of independent Pakistan. Belitho remarked: Jinnah was to find in him the complement to his own talents: together they were to become inviolable because they formed one mind and the trust between them remained absolute to the end." This alone explained, why he chose to visit the United States instead of Stalin's Russia as he was fulfilling the mission left unfinished by his master. In face of these facts, it seems plausible to conclude that at least in major policy preference Liaquat's personality traits had no significant bearing.

With Liaquat disappearance from Pakistani political scene, the Punjabi bureaucratic elite came to dominate the decision-making process during the period 1951 to 1958. The triumvirate that ruled Pakistan was Ghulam Mohammad, Iskander Ali Mirza and Mohammad Ayub Khan. A civil servant by profession, Ghulam was the first Finance Minister of independent Pakistan. He was a man of domineering personality and vaulting ambition. This is amply testified in the way he dismissed Nazimuddin, the ailing and sickly Prime Minister after Liaquat, and the United Front Government in East Pakistan and subsequently the Constituent Assembly when the latter attempted to curtail his powers as the Governor-General of Pakistan. Though Ghulam established complete sway over the decision-making structure, he ruled through Mirza and Ayub who became defence secretary and defence minister respectively in his Cabinet of national talents. It seems plausible to assume that Ghulam's personality characteristics had little bearing on major policy preference as all the three had a shared perception and there was evidence to suggest that the group characteristics of the "hierarch" was more salient during Ghulam's period. As a scholar noted:[16]

> "The leading lights of the Ghulam Mohammad Group had one interesting attribute in common in so far as their perception of Pakistan's foreign relations are concerned. They were men who had grown grey in the service of the British and they favoured 'very close' relations with the West, especially the United States. They were men who, even while their Prime Minister was contemplating a visit to Moscow, had impressed on American officials, their desire to associate themselves with the United States in the long-range defence planning. They constituted a sort of "U.S. Lobby" at the every centre of Pakistani Government."

After Ghulam, another member of his Group Mirza became the President under the first Republican Constitution. He successfully carried forward the original policy through four prime ministers out of which Chaudhuri Mohammad Ali and H.S. Suhrawardy were able exponents backed by Ayub Khan who was the Commander-in-Chief of the Armed Forces. Though known for political chicanery and intrique Mirza was never a forceful personality nor endeared himself to masses. As a result, his foreign policy decisions never bore any imprint of his own. All his attention and energy were consumed by domestic problms. On the whole, Pakistan during the period 1952-58 had a surfeit of politicians who chose to tread the oft-beaten tracks in foreign policy rather than bringing in any innovative departure. Ayub most nicely summed up the position:[17]

> "Those who followed Liaquat in political office proved unequal to the task. They did not understand the problems facing the country

nor did they have the courage to try to solve them. One after another they made a mess of things by trying to work on an unworkable system of government and the country slipping very fast. The central government gradually lost its grip over the affairs of the state being beset by the constant pressure tactics of parliamentarians and the growing relative strength of the provincial governments, who were virtually holding it to ransom."

In such a state of affairs, it is futile to expect the impact of personality traits of any decision-maker on foreign policy decision as Ghulam and Mirza simply carried forward the policy preference conceived by Jinnah and fulfilled their dream by committing Pakistan irrevocably to the Western alliance system, especially the United States, through the instrumentality of Zafrullah Khan and Ayub. The third of the trio was Mohammad Ayub Khan. As head of the military establishment, he has consistently played behind-the-scene role in the policy making process right from the time of Ghulam Mohammad till he finally came to power in 1958 through a coup d'etat on 7 October 1958. In a sense, it was dramatic, even though there was no bloodshed and Iskander Mirza tamely surrendered power and there was no popular uprising in defence of the coup. "The language was clearly that of Latin America, not of Bolshevik Russia or Revolutionary France." It was a military operation and aimed at replacing existing civil authority by military. It sought to organise, in coalition with bureaucracy, a new government in support of modernisation and against political confusion.

It was deemed inevitable by the masses as it was the logical culmination of events prior to 1958. In the country there was "ruthless struggle for power, corruption, the shameful exploitation of... simple, honest, patriotic and industrious masses, the lack of decorum and prostitution of Islam for political ends."[19] And the ruthless adventurers and exploiters were "getting richer by their nefarious practices and the politicians were talking of "bloody revolution." Traitors were approaching foreign countries for support and government action was necessary as well against smugglers, black-marketeers and hoarders. As Ayub rode to power on the crest of utter disenchantment of people with the prevailing system of government and the breed of politicians running it, he was welcomed by all and sundry, because the alternative was "choaos and confusion". Now, under Ayub's new dispensation, power was monopolized by the civil-bureaucracy. As a perceptive scholar of Pakistani scene remarked:[20]

"Bureaucratics, which emphasised blind obedience, unconditional grants of authority and arbitrary decision-making, replaced an incipient form of politics that the very least could not stifle factional competitiveness, a broad range of choice and an unusual flow of information. The Pathan period by contrast with the Punjabi thus emphasised the bureaucrat's penchant for law and order, and the soldier's code of discipline and efficiency. Material development became an all consuming concern and political activities were sacrificed on the altar of stability and national growth."

This statement truly sums up the characteristic of the regime presided over by Ayub for long ten years. So, it was natural that his thoughts and beliefs must have influenced the foreign policy decisions as he strode the decision-making process like a big colossus with pliant subordinates, and the masses gave him landslide majority when he sought legitimacy for his regime by openly contesting to the office of Presidency in 1965.

Now coming to our second proposition, we find that Ayub was never a charismatic leader. Nor he ever tried to empoly devices for acquiring those qualities that would have clothed him with an apparel of charisma. A few reasons can be cited for this. In the first place, he neglected to enlist the support of the public and leaned too heavily on the conventional bureaucracy. He also persisted in widening the gulf that separated his government from the youth. Secondly, it was a great paradox that while his attention was focussed on the mechanics of social mobilisation, his policies were never effectively communicated to the masses. As a result, it only served to stimulate fragmentation and alienation.[21] Partly his personal habits complicated the task with all strata of society. As a scholar observed:[22]

"Ayub's powerful personality and dominating presence would inevitably have commanded some public attention irrespective of his chosen profession, but popularity was a gratification that increasingly eluded him. Authoritarian values, an undemocratic nature, and erect and suggestively aloof bearing, an oratory fluctuating from a dry prosaic to a contrived informality, and an absence of charisma made him a respected but not universally loved figure."

Lastly, though Ayub undertook many basic and innovative reforms embracing all sectors of national life, he never believed in whipping up a public euphoria. He shunned the idea of adopting any sensational and eye-catching measures and preferred to work quietly. As he noted in his book:[23]

"I was not looking for dramatic results. The enthusiasm of the people could have been easily maintained at a high pitch by adopting

> sensational and extreme measures. I think there was some expectation that the revolutionary regime would provide dramatic openings and sequences. I was prepared to face a certain amount of dissatisfaction among the people and a measure of pessimism within the army itself. I was determined to go about my work in a moderate and rational way..."

This clearly shows that he never believed in rhetorics and if, he resorted to image-building it was only after the outbreak of 1965 war in which the victory was doubtful and he wanted to restore the tarnished image of the army which had become by then the self-styled guardian of the nation.

Though lacked charisma, he enjoyed the obedience of his followers and secured their loyalty. Generals like Mohammad Musa, and Yahya Khan and bureaucrats like Akt'ar Husain, S. M. Yusuf, Fida Hasan, Altaf Gauhar, served him with all fidelity. The political figures like Malik Amir, Mohammad Khan, Abdul Monem Khan and Z.A. Bhutto also gave him many valuable advice and strengthened his rule. The intellectuals like Manzur Qadir , I.H. Qureshi, Z.A. Suleri played vital roles. These prominent personalities influenced Ayub's decisions. They advised him and often he acted with their advice but only in rare occasions and for brief periods did they ever, sway him.[24] He remained his own decision-maker to the last.

> The third proposition is: The more general interest the head of State has in foreign policy, the more likely his personality characteristics are to affect foreign policy behaviour.[25]

It is a matter of historical record that the Muslim League, which under the stewardship of Jinnah brought into being the new state of Pakistan, had never played any significant role in the broader issues of peace and war affecting the mankind during the inter-war years. Though it liberally supported the Muslim causes in the world and passed many resolutions to that effect, it never committed itself on such vital issues as Spain, China, Abyssinia, and Czechoslovakia, Communism and Fascism like the Indian National Congress.[26] The demand for Pakistan and its realisation was a brief period overwhelmed by the Second World War, and there was considerable uncertainty as to the final outcome.[27] The entire energy of the Muslim League leaders was absorbed in the internal politics of manoeuvring against the Congress leader and the British authority. Set to achieve an impossible goal in the face of heavy odds, Jinnah's only ambition was to weld together the disparate Muslim elements into a unified whole under the banner of the Muslim League. His appeal to religion and his support to the Muslim causes in the world was reflective of the unique social structure that the Indian Muslims have evolved at the time: the old aristocratic and conservative attitudes persisted in isolation from the new attitudes and trends which the western impact on India had created.[28] In a period of growing cynicism about religion, it projected Jinnah in a unique role; as one more interested to solve internal problems of the Muslims in the subcontinent than the common external problems faced by the Asian and African countries. Besides, as all the states, including India, adopted the broad anti-imperialist front advocating the cause of all the subject people in the world, Pakistan's growing emphasis on the Muslim causes gave the League leadership a nationalistic flavour. As a result, Jinnah never acquired the status of a political leader with an international repute, nor for that matter anyone in the higher echelon of the League. But this should not be misconstrued to give the impression that he had no intellectual understanding of the changing forces of world politics or the importance of pursuing an active and rational foreign policy for the new state of Pakistan.

This is clearly evident for the following reasons. In the first place, it is reflected in the way he structured his governmental organisation. Immediately on assumption of office, he created two separate Departments to deal with foreign affairs: The Ministry of Foreign Affairs and Commonwealth Relations and the Ministry of Kashmir Affairs and Frontier Regions. While the first one looked after the general aspect of foreign relations, the second one dealt specifically with Kashmir. Kashmir, being an emotive issue, needed his personal attention for decision. Secondly, he lost no time in chosing Sir Zafrullah Khan, a veteran diplomat, to plead the Palestine case in the United Nations. As Palestine was a burning issue with wider implications for Pakistan's relations with the Muslim world, his choice of Zafrullah was an ideal one as later events bore it out. And his subsequent decision to induct him to the Cabinet as the Foreign Minister assured the country of the services of man who, with his background of outstanding legal knowledge and long years of distinguished diplomatic career, became an unfailing champion of Pakistani cause in the world forums and perhaps more than anyone else put Pakistan on the world map. M. A. H. Ispahani wrote to Jinnah:[29]

> "I can briefly tell you that the Pakistan Delegation to the United Nations has acquitted itself more than well. Sir Zafrullah delivered one of the finest speeches heard in the United Nations on the Palestine question... Pakistan is right on the map .... He is one of our able men and an asset."

Besides, his choice of Chaudhuri Mohammad Ali to head the foreign ministry and M.A.H. Ispahani to represent Pakistan in the United States showed his keen interest and primacy he accorded to foreign policy as both were his closest confidants. Thirdly, he came out with a clear and categorical enunciation of the country's foreign policy whose essential thesis were laid down by him that dispelled many a foreboding entertained in many quarters of the world.[30] As he opted for policy of non-alignment with the contending power blocs, it showed that Jinnah had an acute perception of the operational world in which Pakistan would function in coming years. Lastly, his secret diplomatic move to court the Americans for military and economic aid also proved that he was not oblivious of the poor capabilities of a nascent state pitted against a powerful adversary.[31] This revealed that though internal task before Jinnah was staggering and absorbed his attention, he had a sustained interest in foreign policy and took all major decisions of the period. Jinnah was impelled by two dominant considerations. Pakistan must emerge as a full-fledged territorial personality before the glare of world public in order to refute the Indian charges that it would collapse before long. Secondly, the threat of Indian aggression would be countered to ensure its security and development. As regards Liaquat, he took many vital and bold decisions, put across the case of his country most effectively before the western world particularly the United States,[32] actively sponsored many Islamic conferences to foster solidarity with the Muslim world and made strenuous efforts to ensure peace with India. But he stuck to the original framework of policy laid down, by Jinnah and never made any significant departure. Intra-party squabbles and domestic problems consumed a major slice of his tenure which was also very brief. Despite his general interest, he could not make much impact and allowed Zafrullah to handle most of the foreign policy issues, who was constantly engaged in giving the benefit of his advice to the Prime Minister, so much so that in the realm of foreign policy, he came to symbolise Pakistan before the world audience. But with the advent to power of Ghulam Mohammad, the basic postulates of foreign policy were changed. The way he worked, as revealed by records, to commit Pakistan into the western alliance system showed that foreign policy was his most obsessive concern,[33] though the decisions were made by the "hierarch". As a result, as argued in the foregoing, there was dominance of group characteristics in the decision-making with Ayub having major voice, leaving little lee-way for the impact of the personality traits of Ghulam Mohammad on pol icy decisions.

Now, if one operationalises interest as the percentage of events in which the head of state participates relative to the bureaucracy, then Ayub's era, which was crowded with many significant events, certainly carried indelible impact of his personality traits as he participated directly in the formulation and execution of numerous policy decisions. His offer of joint defence of the subcontinent to India and conclusion of the Indus Water Treaty, his effort to develop amicable relations with Afghanistan, his decision to legalise Pakistan's borders with China, Burma and Iran to forestall any possible sources of conflict, his attempt to develop satisfactory relations with the Soviet Union without undermining Pakistan's commitment to the Western alliance system and above all his decision to declare war against India in 1965 were some of the crucial decisions in which he was directly involved.[34]

This was plausible for two specific reasons. In the first place, he received his initial stimulus when he was chosen as the Commander-in-Chief of Pakistani armed forces by the Prime Minister superseding many distinguished and senior generals which showed that he enjoyed complete trust of Liaquat Ali. And in subsequent infighting between politicians he maintained strict neutrality and only invoked his support in the favour of ruling authority. Though, for a brief period he was the Defence Minister he again left the office to head the armed forces. He was deeply committed to enhancing the professional skill of the armed forces and within a short time, Pakistani armed forces became an impressive fighting force in Asia. As a result, Ayub earned the complete trust of the politicians, the public and the soldiers. When Ghulam Mohammad came to power and intra-party fighting threatened his authority and with it the challenge of Bengali nationalism to the dominance of Punjabi elites, Ayub's support became the most crucial factor for the continuance of Ghulam Mohammad and Punjabis in power structure. This phase coincided with Pakistan's decision to join the American alliance system in which the military dimension of the relationship assumed major importance. With it, the stock of Ayub went up. As the closest confident of Ghulam Mohammad and his known penchant for the American military hardware, Ayub was pre-eminently suited for hammering out a deal which he did with too much of secrecy and diplomatic finesse. As Ayub came to be progressively accepted in the military circles of the United States, the Pakistani government gave him a free hand in negotiating intricate military issues. The whole process became one of reinforcing Ayub's indispensibility. As a result, he emerged as the strong man and the key decision-maker which gave him access to the in and out of the government though he was just an army chief. This stood him in good stead in later years when he came to power, for he brought to the office of Presidency a wealth of experience and knowledge about the military and foreign policy issues and many of his settled views and beliefs influenced his decisions. While this could be proved in may cases, at least in the Indus Water Treaty it was clearly evident. As he wrote in his autobiography:[35]

> "... I should like, to describe the confrontation I had with our own technical experts and administrators. I sensed that they did not fully realise the gravity of the situation, and were asking for the moon when we were in a position of weakness all along the line. They were also trying to dictate policy and were taking up extreme positions. Some thirty or forty of them were assembled in the Government House, Lahore, where I addressed them. I said: 'Gentlemen' this problem is of far-reaching consequences to us. Let me tell you that every factor is against Pakistan....
>
> The responsibility does not lie on any one of you let me tell you very plainly that the policy is going to be mine. I shall consult you whenever I am in doubt regarding technical details, but if any one of you interferes with the policy, I shall deal with him myself."

Secondly, Ayub like Jinnah, completely dominated the decision-making structure. Though his cabinet contained people with differing political convictions, his word was the final decision. Any difference with him meant the forfeiture of ministership, or voluntary resignation. And without any scruple Ayub could sack his trusted and talented colleagues. This certainly inspired awe and fear among the incumbents and "the political machinery became a conduit of his dictatorial psychology."[36] In one instance this was clear. In the fall of 1966, not a single member of Ayub's first presidential cabinet remained. They all departed for different reasons. Bhutto who represented the anti-U.S. faction in his cabinet first challenged the wisdom of President's Taskent decision and was sacked. And to balance it, Mohammad Shoab, the Finance Minister, known for his pro-Western sympathy was dropped. Ayub did this only because Pakistan's international posture threatened his control over the policy-making machinery.[37] These facts served to validate another important proposition:

> The more authority a head of state has over foreign policy, the more likely his personality characteristics are to affect foreign policy behaviour.

The last condition responsible for the impact of the personality traits of the decision-makers in Pakistan was the lack of a developed and scientifically structured foreign policy organisation. In any political system, whether democratic or authoritarian, the importance of a foreign policy organisation is too well-known, on account of the far-flung and highly complex nature of foreign policy in the modern world. Not only it serves as the instrument for carrying out the policy decision and administrative directive of the political executive whose prerogative is foreign policy, but also its role as the agency for assimilating, and evaluating data, shifting and sorting out of intelligence analysis for a recommended policy option has become vital and indispensable. It is now thoroughly probed that in a developed and highly differentiated foreign policy organisation, prior policy commitment, organisational memory, parochial interests, standard operating procedure, normal bureaucratic inertia, and conflict resolution by bargaining, all of which are deeply rooted in the complex bureaucratic organisation, serve to limit the impact on policy ouputs of the decision-maker's personality traits, private prejudices and other cognitive traits,[38] because individuals with varying individual characteristics behave similarly when placed in common situations.[39] Realising this, the developed and highly industrialised countries of world expend enormous money for maintaining a well structured and scientifically planned foreign policy organisation.

This was singularly lacking in Pakistan. The administrative system was in a state of disarray, virtually it collapsed at the time of partition. The most formidable problem it faced was an acute shortage of administrative talent which was experienced in the complexity of decision-making at the highest level of government. This was equally applicable to the sphere of foreign policy. Though two distinct departments were created on the eve of independence, there was a dearth of diplomatic personnel to man them properly and to represent effectively the country in the various chancelleries of the world. Out of a total strength of 157 Muslim and other officers belonging to Indian Civil Service and Indian Political Service who opted for Pakistan at the partition, only 6 preferred diplomatic assignments.[40] Besides, being a poor and backward country it could not afford the luxury of spending huge amount of money that was initially needed for a well-planned and comprehensive foreign policy organisation and establishing diplomatic legations in every part of the globe. Ispahani's correspondence with Jinnah gives enough revelation of the condition of the Pakistani government.[41]

"I need not tell you how necessary it is to have the minimum staff, composed of individuals who may be expected to function effectively as a team. We are receiving little cooperation from the Finance Ministry... We cannot work indefinitely without sanction being given to essential expenditure and you have no idea what we have to put up with sometimes."

This shows the abject poverty of a nascent government. The appointment of a few eminent personalities to run the diplomatic service like Malik Feroz Khan Noon, Sir Mohammad Zafrullah Khan, M.A.H. Ispahani and others, while for a time, improved Pakistan's diplomacy, it was certainly not a substitute for a cadre-based permanent diplomatic personnel. All that they did was to carry out faithfully the policy decisions of Jinnah, for they were his most trusted friends.

Though in 1949, regular recruitment started for selecting officers to run the diplomatic service and their number considerabley increased over the years, and the Foreign Office expanded, specifically during the Ayub era, it became more a flabby body. No attempt was made to restructure it on the basis of some rational and sound principles of administrative organisation. During the Ayub era, it simply became an appendage of the President's cabinet and failed in the task of policy-making. It came in for bitter criticism on numerous occasions during the parliamentary debates. The failures of the foreign office as evident in the legislative commentary consisted of such phenomena as behaviour of diplomats, insufficient concern for Pakistani abroad, or lack of attention to a visiting delegation of distinguished members of Parliament, weakness of the foreign publicity and sheer incompetence.[42] Most crucial debates were concerned with the organization and training of the foreign office and the diplomats. Starting with educational qualifications, the legislators have literally questioned every aspect of the organization of the foreign office and the diplomatic service, which included the criteria of appointments, provincial quotas, expenditures, organization of the decision-making structure and goodwill missions abroad for effectively projecting country's image. Legislative attempts to deal with the Ministry of Foreign Affairs through a Standing Committee have not been successful. Once during the tenure of the Constituent Assembly and again once recently, brief references could be found to legislative attempts to make such Committee function.[43] For all practical purposes, its incumbents like Manzur Qadir, Mohammad Ali Bogra, Zulfikar Ali Bhutto, S. Sharifuddin Pirzada, and Mian Monem Khan served as errand boys for the great master Mohammad Ayub Khan.

In our focus on personality characteristics of Pakistani decision-makers, we have chosen only Mohammad Ali Jinnah and Mohammad Ayub Khan out of a host of many, as these two figures provided strong leadership in Pakistan during the period 1947-71. In this connection, we have delineated the specific conditions (in the form of a few empirically tested propositions) present in Pakistan during 1947 to 1971 which have provided enough stimuli to these key decision-makers to bring their idiosyncratic traits to bear upon their policy decisions. In the first place, we have proved that though Jinnah never assumed political power in dramatic way, the movement for Pakistan of which he was the author and architect had all the dimensions of a revolution. But in case of Ayub Khan he assumed power in a dramatic way. Secondly, Jinnah was a charismatic leader while Ayub had never the appeal of a charisma, though he enjoyed the obedience of his followers and secured their loyalty. Thirdly, both Jinnah and Ayub had general interests in foreign policy. Lastly, both dominated the decision-making structures and held complete sway over the policy-making.

## References


1. Glen H. Strassen, "Individual Preference versus Role-Constraint' in Policy-Making: Senatorial Response to Secretaries Acheson and Dulles", *World Politics* (Princeton), Vol. 25, no. l, October 1972, pp.96-119.
2. Richard C. Snyder and James A. Robinson, *National and International Decision-Making* (New York, 1961), p. 158.
3. Margaret G. Hermann, "When Leader Personality will affect Foreign policy: Some Propositions" in James N. Rosenau, ed., *In search of Global Patterns* (New York, 1976), pp. 326-33.
4. A. Lee Fritschler, "Business Participation in Administration" in Gurthrie S. Birkhead, ed., *Administrative Problems in Pakistan* (Syracuse, 1966), pp. 63-64.
5. Hermann, n. 3, p. 328.
6. Sharif Al Mujahid, *Quaid-i-Azam Jinnah: Studies in Interpretation* (Karachi, 1981), p.362.
7. Hector Belitho, *Jinnah, Creator of Pakistan* (Karachi, 1954), p. 195.
8. *Ibid.*, p. 195.
9. Ann R. Willner and Dorothy Willner, "The Rise and Role of Charismatic Leaders", *in Annals of the American Academy of Political and Social Science* (Philadelphia, pa.) Vol. 358, no. 2, March 1965, pp. 77-88.
10. Saleem M.M. Qureshi, "Iqbal and Jinnah: Personalities, Perceptions and politics" in C.M. Naim, ed., *Iqbal, Jinnah and Pakistan: The Vision and the Reality* (Syracuse, 1979), pp. 11-41.

11. *Ibid.*, p. 35.
12. M. Rafique Afzal, ed., *Speeches and Statements of Quaid-i Millat Liaquat Ali Khan* (Lahore, 1967), p. 171.
13. Mushtaq Ahmad, *Government and Politics in Pakistan* (Karachi, 1963), p. 47.
14. Belitho, n. 7, p. 104.
15. *Ibid.*, p. 104.
16. M.S. Venkataramani, *The American Role in Pakistan* (New Delhi, 1982), p.191.
17. Mohammad Ayub Khan, *Friends Not Masters: A Political Autobiography* (London, 1967), p. 49.
18. Wayne Ayres Wilcox, "The Pakistan Coup d'Etat of 1958", *Pacific Affairs* (Vancouver, B.C.), Vol. 38, no.2, Summer 1965, pp. 142-63.
19. *New York Times*, 8 October 1958.
20. Lawrence Ziring, "The phases of Pakistan's Political History" in C.M. Naim, ed., *Iqbai, Jinnah and Pakistan: The Vision and the Reality* (Syacuse, 1979), pp. 145-77.
21. Lawrence Ziring, *The Ayub Khan Era: Politics in Pakistan 1958-69* (Syracuse, 1971), p.1.
22. W.M. Dobell, "Ayub Khan As President of Pakistan", *Pacific Affairs* (Vancouver, B.C.), Vol. 42, no. 3, Fall 1969, pp. 294-311.
23. Ayub, n. 17, p.79.
24. Ziring, n. 21, p. 2.
25. Fred I. Greenstein, *Personality and Politics* (Chicago, 1969), p. 54.
26. Jawaharlal Nehru, *Discovery of India* (Calcutta, 1946), p. 447.
27. Sisir Gupta, "Islam as a factor in Pakistani Foreign Relations", *India Quarterly* (New Delhi), Vol.18, no.3, July-September 1962, pp.230-53.
28. Nehru, n. 26, pp. 563-67.
29. Z. H. Zaidi, ed., *M.A. Jinnah-Ispahani Correspondence 1936-48* (Karachi, 1976), pp. 535-54.
30. *Quaid-e-Azam Speaks* (Karachi, n. d.), p. 93.
31. Venkataramani, n. 16, pp. 33-128.
32. Liaquat Ali Khan, *Pakistan: The Heart of Asia* (Karachi, 1976), pp. 4-10.
33. See my third Chapter.
34. Ziring, n. 21, p. 60.
35. Ayub, n.17, pp.11-12.
36. Robert C. Tucker, "The Dictator and Totalitarianism", *World Politics* (Princeton), Vol.17, no.1, October 1965, pp.55-83.

37. Ziring, n.21, p.4.
38. Uric Bronfenbrenner, "Personality and Participation: The Case of the Vanishing Variables", *Journal of Social Issues* (New York), Vol.16, no.1, 1960, pp. 54-63.
39. Greenstein, n. 25, p. 54.
40. Ralph Braibanti, "Public Bureaucracy and Judiciary in Pakistan" in Joseph La Palombara, ed., *Bureaucracy* and *Political Development* (Princeton, 1963), pp. 360-441.
41. Ispahani, n. 29, p. 557.
42. Pakistan *(Second) National Assembly, Debates*, Vol. 1, no.12, 27 June 1962, pp.584-91.
43. The Committee consisted of five members and was expected to advise on matters with which the Ministry of Foreign Affairs was concerned.

# Part-III

# Decision-Making

# 8
# Decision-Making

This chapter purports to deal with the decision-making in Pakistan's foreign policy. It may be recalled that, as posited in our model, the decision-making process passes through two distinct stages: policy preference leading to decision, and action or output. In the first place, the policy-makers perform broad intellectual task of policy-making and reach a particular policy preference. And the manner in which they accomplish this task determines the boundary of the decision to which their policy preference leads. The influence of the key decision-maker's cognitive styles and belief systems predominates on policy preference though it is also influenced by other variables, and this leads to the final decision which is equally prone to influences of other variables. Precisely for this reason, the policy preference or the option the policy-maker prefers is treated as dependent variable in place of the decision or the option he finally choses. Secondly, between the decision and action or output, the bureaucratic and organizational dynamics distort the decision that shape the resultant action.

Keeping this analytical subtlety in view, this chapter is divided into two sections. Section A will highlight the cognitive beliefs of the decision-makers and their impact on policy preference, while Section B will be confined to exploring the bureaucratic and organizational variables and how they operated between decision and action. As data on decision-making in Pakistan's foreign policy are scarce, we have proposed perforce to test only one significant event: Pakistan's decision to conclude the Mutual Defence Assistance Agreement with the United States in 19 May 1954. This naturally makes it imperative for us to explore the cognitive beliefs only of those decision-makers who spanned the period 1947-54. As revealed in earlier chapters, Pakistan during the period 1947-51 was dominated by the Hindustanis under the leadership of Mohammad Ali

Jinnah and during the period 1951-54, it was controlled by the "hierarch". Interesecting these two groups and forging a link between them was Mohammad Ayub Khan. Though he played a significant role, it was in his capacity as the Commander-in-Chief of the Pakistani armed forces. So his role during this period will be consigned to Section B, while Jinnah, the architect of the foreign policy, will be the focus of enquiry in the Section A.

**Section A: The Impact of the Cognitive Beliefs of the Decision-makers**

In the preceeding chapter, we have outlined various conditions in Pakistan during the period 1947-71 which are usually assumed to impart sufficient stimuli to its decision-makers to bring to bear their personality characteristics on the foreign policy decision of their country. As we have recognized in our model, that of all the personality traits, cognitive style and belief system are central to the decision-making and the ensuing analysis will adopt the 'Operational Code' approach of Alexander L. George to construct them.

In this connection, it won't be out of place to mention that George was the first scholar who recognized the problem of developing an approach for conceptualizing the cognitive process model for decision-making so that in concrete decision-making situation, the belief-system of identifiable international actors and their impact as intervening variables could be empirically assessed. He successfully developed an approach which sought to generalize a method introduced by Nathan Leites in his two books, published in 1950's, *The Operational Code of Politburo and A Study of Bolshevism,* whose analytical value was unknown to Leites. In the introduction to the latter book, Leites remarked that the Bolshevik doctrine is the doctrine of how to conduct the Bolshevik party and added:[1]

> "I do not propose to analyse Bolshevik doctrine as fully as possible but rather to take one aspect of it; what I call the Operational Code, that is the conception of political strategy."

This conception of 'political strategy' which he called 'Operational Code' (OC) carried far-reaching implications for the imaginative mind of George. He rejected the term 'Operational Code' as signifying a conception of political strategy and gave a new meaning to it by redefining its function as one of providing the political actor with 'diagnostic propensities' and 'choice propensities'. He made this clear in the following words:[2]

> "The issues and questions around which the Bolshevik constructed a belief system about politics: They are stated here in general terms to emphasise the fact that they constitute fundamental issues about

which all political actors must formulate a set of beliefs and premises. The 'answers' other political actors give to these questions will probably differ from those the Bolsheviks gave. But an explicit statement of questions and issues should at least facilitate efforts to find out how different elites and political actors approach the problem of action". George then formulated ten questions, of which the first five concerned philosophical issues while the rest are more specifically oriented towards instrumental or policy questions, having to do with goals and means relationships:[3]

(a) Philosophical issues

(1) What is the essential nature of political life? Is the political universe one of harmony or conflict? What is the fundamental character of one's political opponents?

(2) What are the prospects for the eventual realisation of one' s fundamental political values and aspirations?

(3) Is the political future predictable? In what sense and to what extent?

(4) How much control one can have over historical development? What is one's role in moving and shaping history in the desired direction?

(5) What is the role of change in human affairs and in historical development?

(b) Instrumental or Policy issues

(1) What is the best approach for selecting goals or objectives for political action?

(2) How are goals of action pursued most effectively?

(3) How are the risks of political actions calculated and controlled, and accepted?

(4) What is the best timing of action to advance one's interest?

(5) What is the utility and the role of different means for advancing one's interests?

George characterized these beliefs as "Cognitive beliefs" and OC approach is often described as constituting the cognitive approaches to politics. Now, if one adds up the constituent components of George's definition, it amounts to this: an Operational Code consists of answers to these ten questions. These answers represent cognitive beliefs. They have certain functions in relating an actor's thought and action in decision-making process; by serving as a prism or a filter, they influence the actor's perception of political reality and provide him with 'diagnostic propensities' and 'choice propensities'. The beliefs provide norms and standards that influence the actor's choice of strategy and tactics as well as his restructuring and weighing of alternative choice of action. But it should be borne in mind that the relation between beliefs and these propensities and the actual decision-making is just probabilistic. To analyse the decision-making, other determining variables besides the actor's Operational Code have to be taken into account. It would not be out of place to mention here that although, George's reconceptualization of the Operational Code has been subject to criticism and a scholar has suggested an alternative set of Operational Code for more adequate and fruitful empirical analysis of decisional phenomena, it has spurred on an impressive array of case studies over the years pioneered first by Ole R. Holsti, Michael J. Shapiro and G. Mathew Bonham. In recent years, Robert Axelrod and others have refined cognitive maps as analytically more reliable. But Holsti still holds it as valid.[5] Though, controversy was on regarding the units of analysis, whether the individual leader or collective group of decision-makers should be at the starting point of analysis for belief systems and cognitive processes, and continues unabated even to-day, Holsti subscribes to the individual as the unit of analysis.

Coming to data problem, it still baffles the analyst. Whether written sources or interviews are used to reconstruct the perceptions of political leaders, the fundamental issue of validity has to be faced. Does the actor express what he perceives and does he perceive what he expresses? There is no easy solution to this problem which parallels with credibility problem facing actors involved in political interaction. The analyst runs the double risk of either overlooking significant nuances of a message (under-representation) or finding hidden meanings where there is none (over-interpretation). Whereas quantitative content analysis is more prone to under-interpretation, the temptation of over-interpretation looms large in non-quantitative, contextual analysis. However, we have adopted the latter method of analysis based on written sources.

## Cognitive Beliefs of Mohammad Ali Jinnah

It is not easy to construct the congitive beliefs of any decision-maker of a state in the vast stretches of time, specially of one who is no more. Had he been alive, personal interview would have yielded some data to supplement other sources. In his absence, one is perforce left to do this job relying on his speeches, policy pronouncements, personal writings and communications which together constitute the written sources. In case of Mohammad Ali Jinnah who is dead long since, a student seeking to isolate his cognitive beliefs, encounters problem even with regard to the written sources. In the first place, unlike Jawaharlal Nehru who spoke eloquently on foreign policy issue, Jinnah spoke very little; so was the case with the Muslim League unlike the Indian national Congress. His speeches and statements would reveal his pervasive pre-occupation with domestic and national issues and they, by and large, pertained to political matters. Basically they were either reactions to political developments or intended to arouse reactions in political adversaries. He wrote precious little beyond correspondence. However, they provided some clues to his concerns, feelings, thinkings and attitudes. Secondly, Jinnah, as the key decison-maker of independent Pakistan, though left an indelible impression on the policy-making process for reasons already cited, lived barely for thirteen months which was by any standard too short a period on the part of any political leader to evolve a different set of cognitive beliefs other than the one previously formed over long years of one's political apprenticeship. This was precisely the case with Jinnah whose cognitive beliefs were structured during his years of political life in undivided India prior to 1947. So any attempt at constructing them must be based on extrapolating his personality traits from earlier years as he had no expertise in foreign affairs to call on, no previous experience to suggest alternatives or plans of action when he came to preside over the decision-making structure in Pakistan after 1947. It is very natural and legitimate to assume that his innate problem-solving dispositions and his strong beliefs about the effects of certain strategy acquired and applied in political situations of earlier years must have intruded his formulation of foreign policy decisions after 1947. Lastly, as the cognitive beliefs constitute a sum total of answers to the five philosophical questions (belief system) and five instrument questions (cognitive process), it is not possible to answer them separately. They should be treated as an integrated whole as both the belief system and cognitive process of an individual are in an interactive relationship and together constitute the profile of cognitive beliefs.

The political career of Mohammad Ali Jinnah spanned almost half a century, from 1906 when he first participated in the Indian National Congress to the time of his death as the Governor-General of Pakistan in 1948. Before he started his political innings in undivided India the most impressionable period of his youth was spent in England where he came under the benign influence of Lord Morley whose liberalism enthralled him. He had the rare opportunity of watching the lively debates in the

British House of Commons over Gladstone's famous Irish Home Rule Bill, the growing ascendancy of the Labour Party in the political life of the country and the election of the first Indian, Dadabhai Naroji - the Grand Old Man of India - to the House of Commons from the Central Finsbury Constituency. Those were the most scintillating experiences for a budding youth trained in Anglo-Saxon tradition of law and jurisprudence with a penchant for British liberal values. Back home in 1896, Jinnah served Naroji as his private Secretary for long fourteen years.

Those early influences fired and caught the imagination of Jinnah and shaped his approach to political problems in the beginning of this century. While his innate love for Morley and the British liberalism made him a liberal democrat and a thorough- bred constitutionalist, his profound regard for Naroji made him a nationalist par excellence. His legal background and his assimilation of English liberal outlook on the role of religion in the state and politics helped him to perceive the world to rest upon the pillars of legal order, justice, fair play and equity where religion was purely a matter of individual conscience, nothing to do with the business of the state and the politics. He never condemned Islam or Hinduism or Christianity. Nor, he ever preached or philosophized how people should order their life in the society. His approach to life was essentially one of eclecticism and free play of its genius. It was with these settled attitudes to religion and politics, Jinnah made his debut in Indian political movement in 1906. It was natural that he received his political apprenticeship under the shadow of great veteran nationalists of those years who subscribed to British liberal tradition and endeavoured to bring about India's self-Government through the evolutionary path of constitutionalism and legalism. As a result, Gopal Krishna Gokhale became his model, W.C. Banerjee his leader and Dadabhai Naroji his political mentor. He imbibed from them the spirit of highest dedication and sacrifice for the nationalist cause. As a result, he came to develop a deep revulsion against demagogy and deprecated the idea that a leader should pander to the fury and fluctuation of the credulous masses. And within a short time, these sterling qualities earned him recognition when in 1909 he was elected by the Muslims of Bombay to represent them in the Imperial Legislative Council, and became the most 'waxing personality' in the Indian National Congress.[10]

True to his political and religious philosophy, he called himself an Indian rather than a Muslim. He was concerned with the regeneration of Indian people as a whole rather than that of Muslim Community alone. He worked for the cause of Indian independence in which he felt that the Muslims were equal partners.[11] He never conceived of Muslim freedom in isolation, even in his wildest dream. But at the same time, he was not oblivious of the plight and predicament of the Muslim community.[12] As they formed the substantial segment of the population, their interests could not be ignored in India's historic march to political independence. As he once remarked:[13]

> "I am an Indian first and a Muslim afterwards. But at the same time I agree that no Indian can ever serve his country if he neglects the interests of the Muslims."

This political scenario in the initial years (1906-20) served to shape his cognitive beliefs in the following way. In the first place, descending upon the Indian political scene at the young age of thirty, pulsating with liberal ideas and romantic vision of a free and United India, Jinnah found the political life one of struggle and sacrifice but full of promise. Perhaps, it appeared to him that he was cut out for an eventful role in the exciting drama of India's freedom struggle. Bred in liberal adition and tutored by the great nationalists of the time, he found that his fundamental political values were broadly shared and espoused by the Indian National Congress and there was a glowing prospect of its eventual realisation if he continued to give his unswerving loyalty to the organisation and work under its banner. So the political universe for him was one of harmony and peace. Weaved with it was his feeling that he along with his liberal political mentors could change the course of India's h: :torical development in their preferred direction. He was animated with the sublime hope that his twin goals of achieving India's freedom and Muslim's legitimate claim to sharing a slice of political power could be realised through the path of gradualism, legalism and constitutionalism for which he like other moderates, appealed to Britishers, to their magnanimity, their sense of justice and fairplay. So for the realisation of this objective of political action, he adopted an approach which was at once sober, rational, constructive and cautious. In an age, when political terrorism was becoming a fashionable proposition, he definitely eschewed it as he was convinced that the goals of political action could not be effectively pursued.[14] This found its eloquent reflection in the Lucknow Pact of 1916.

But with the advent of Gandhiji in 1920, the nature and character of Indian freedom movement underwent revolutionary change. Jinnah disagreed with Gandhi's avowed method of political action. His call for Civil Disobedience Movement which injected agitational politics into

Indian freedom movement unnerved Jinnah who perceived them to be destructive of an orderly world he wanted to promote. As the Congress was firmly committed to Gandhiji's leadership, he decided to severe his long years of association with the Congress. His letter to Gandhiji in 1920 in response to the latter's invitation to join him in the Civil Disobedience Movement amply bore this out:[15]

> "I thank you for your kind suggestion offering me 'to take my share in the new life that has opened up before the country'. If by 'new life' you mean your methods and programme, I am afraid I cannot accept them; for I am fully convinced that it must lead to disaster... Your methods have already caused split and division in almost every institution that you have approached hitherto, and in the public life of the country.... All this means complete disorganisation and chaos. What the consequences of this may be, I shudder to contemplate..."

The great divide with Gandhiji epitomized a conflict not of two great personalities over the issue of assuming leadership of the movement but of their fundamental political values and the method necessary for their eventual realization. It was an ideological schism whose gulf widened over the years as the unfolding events further threatened to erode all that Jinnah held dear in his political life. On Khilafat movement in which Muslim India was stirred to the marrow by this highly religious and emotional issue, Jinnah did not take any stand and this proved to be the proverbial last straw for him as mass frenzy was aroused to an unknown depth in the name of religion. A cold-blooded logician, he believed in reason and argument rather than in sheer agitation and propaganda; not in hypnotizing the masses but in convincing them through sheer strength of logic. He deprecated the idea that the masses should embrace an ideal blindly without consciously subscribing to it and launch a programme without making any calculation of its consequences.[16] In the Calcutta Conference of the Muslim League in 1920 which was called to endorse Gandhiji's non-cooperation to redeem Khilafat cause, he remarked:[17]

> "It is now for you to consider whether or not you approve of its principle and approving of its principle whether or not you approve of its details. The operation of this scheme will strike at the individual in each of you and, therefore, it rests with you alone to measure your strength and to weigh the pros and cons of the question before you arrive at a decision."

This passage reflected one of the outstanding attributes of his cognitive beliefs. Before deciding any political action, Jinnah used to calculate the risks involved, and he used to commend it to his followers with the suggestion that they must assess its pros and cons before accepting it for implementation. In the process he never imposed it from the above. For Jinnah, goals of political action could be pursued most effectively if the means were justified. He was a great stickler for means. He warned Gandhiji in the Nagpur Congress:[18] "You are making a declaration and committing the Indian National Congress to a programme which you will not be able to carry out." The only safe course for the Indians according to him, was constitutional agitation rather than civil resistance whose course was uncharted and no where in the world does a mob respond so quickly or so savagely to a firebrand's call for action, as in India.

Increasingly, for Jinnah the political universe after 1920 became one of unremitting gloom in which the prospect of realisation of his political objectives receded gradually like the morning star. The Calcutta Conference convinced Jinnah of the real intention and character of the Congress party under the leadership of Gandhiji and made untenable the erroneous claim of the Muslim League to represent the Muslims of India. Jinnah withdrew from the League, and stayed in England till 1934 when he came to India and again returned. Finally he left England for good in October 1935. Those were his years of political wilderness, but they were also moments of self-introspection. He vividly watched the political developments in India and being circumspect and cautious he did not intend to jump into the fray and burn his fingers again unless the Muslims of India wanted him to be their leader. As Belitho wrote:[19]

> "But he listened to Liaquat and in the end he said, you go back and survey the scene; test the feelings of all parts of the country. I trust your judgment. If you say 'come back', I will give up my life here and return."

While still in England he was elected by the Muslims of Bombay as an independent member to the Central Legislature without his consent. This proved his strength and popularity among the Muslim League. But till then, he had not recanted his earlier philosophy and prepared to work to bring about complete cooperation and amity between Hindus and Muslims. But the provincial election of 1937, the poor performance of the League, the attitude of the Congress ministries in the provinces, the treatment meted out to the members of the League, Iqbal's call for a Muslim state, the mass contact programme of the Congress to wipe out the League, the gradual dominance of the rightist forces in politics[20] and the outbreak of war, served to alter profoundly the psychological environment of Jinnah who lived so long in the world of his make-belief. The political universe or arena gradually changed to one of bitter conflict and racial disharmony. And political-life appeared to be one of unending struggle; of man against man, of man against his environment and it was a struggle on moral and ideological plane. He came to view Gandhiji along many dimensions; no longer a secular nationalist, but an avowedly religious person deeply influenced by the ancient Hindu scriptures, mythology and lore.[21] Not only his (Gandhi's) imageries came from them, he also invoked them to justify and substantiate his arguments.[22] He deliberately used the Vedic term *Swaraj* to denote the Dominion status, he also equated it with "*Ram Rajya*", the traditional Hindu 'golden age' in order to tap deftly the hidden feelings of emotions at the mass level. And all this Gandhi did with a view to associating them with the Congress Party to energize it for the freedom struggle. Jinnah knew that Gandhiji believed in Hindu-Muslim Unity. As Gandhiji once remarked in 1924: "I agree with Jinnah 'that Hindu-Muslim Unity means Swaraj". But whereas, Jinnah, because of his legalism, and constitutionalism, wanted it to be incorporated formally in a pact with adequate safegurads for the minorities, Gandhiji instead, wanted to enshrine it in mutual trust, without any formal enactment of law for regulating their relationship in the society. But the credibility of Gandhiji gradually eroded in his eyes after 1937 when he came to view Gandhiji as a shrewd political strategist bent upon out manouvering him in the game of sub-continental politics. As a result, the political arena appeared to him as one of status conflict, where he, as the supreme leader of Muslim masses, was locked up in a political battle with Gandhiji, the undisputed leader of the Indian National Congress. To determine this status would atuomatically resolve the problem of parity of twenty-five per cent Muslims with the rest of Indian population. Besides, it called for a new strategy of political action, for, in the present state of things, Gandhiji symbolizing the Indian National Congress, was the main stumbling block to the realization of the fundamental political values of Jinnah, the President of the Muslim League. And to challenge Gandhiji not only a renewed strategy was called for but also reorientation of one's fundamental political values was needed. So Jinnah under the stimulus of Iqbal invented his 'Two-Nation' theory. Within less than a decade, 1940-47, his goal of political action embraced a new state of Pakistan in the Muslim majority areas in the undivided India. His political strategy underwent a fundamental rethinking, for he wanted to pursue his political action in such a way that while the Muslim masses gave it a hospitable reception, the opposition and resentment of the large segment of Hindu minority in the six provinces claimed for the new state of Pakistan were effectively kept at the lowest ebb. Otherwise, it would give the Congress and the Britishers a political axe to grind against the Muslim League Though, in a Speech at Aligarh in March 1944, he asserted that[23] "...Pakistan started the moment the first non-Muslim was converted to Islam in India long before the Muslims established their rule," and Islam figured prominently in most of his writings and speeches, as a part of his new political strategy, he never organized or mobilized the Muslim masses by an appeal to the "Islamic state". The Islamic content of Pakistan had to be downgraded to suit this. So he presented the demand for the state of Pakistan not so much as answering the emotional and politico-cultural needs of the Indian Muslims but as a rational solution to the tangled problem of Indian constitutional settlement arising out of its multinational and multi-linguistic society. This certainly did not make his position indefensible when he declared in the new Constituent Assembly of Pakistan on 11 August 1947:[24]

> "You are free: you are free to go to your temples, you are free to go to your mosques or to any other places of worship in this state of Pakistan. You may belong to any religion or caste or creed that has nothing to do with the business of the State."

This strategy not only brought to fruition his political goal in life - the state of Pakistan but also revealed his political acumen as it yielded rich dividends in the following years. So, it is plausible to view that Jinnah had a clear perception of the risks involved in any political action. As politics is always the art of the possible and the risks therein cannot be eliminated, it is got to be calculated, and minimised through an adroit management and manipulation of political situations for which a sound strategy is called-for. The ends must be related to means and the best must be made up of what is beyond one's power to change. With an unerring instinct he could foresee that the Britishers were ready to quit. Once they depart, the Muslims would be the hewers of wood and the drawers of water in Hindustan. So, in the prevailing constitutional tussle, partition plan would at least concede him the minimum, even if, it was a truncated Pakistan. So, he settled down for the scheme.

Always confident of a predictable future, with a resolute faith in moving and shaping the forces of historical development, he was cautious and compromising and earnestly believed that through a carefully calculated strategy, which minimises political risk, he could pursue his political objectives most effectively. As a result, he was not only flexible and relied upon his royal supporters, sometimes he biased to make complete volte-face of his position in order to put the adversary in an awkward and embarrassing situation and reap maximum political mileage. This exactly happened when he accepted the Cabinet Mission Plan in 1946 after giving the clarion call to the Muslim masses: "Pakistan or Perish". This also revealed another facet of his "choice propensities". He had a masterly sense of timing how to advance one's interest in the face of an all powerful political opponent. His breach with Gandhiji in 1920, though an expression of his revulsion against his methods, was itself a reflection of his belief that the Muslim League could only chalk out their political destiny if they go their separate way, instead of being tied to the apron-strings of the Congress. This very fact also explained his deliberate aloofness from the Khilafat Movement. He never relished the idea of his playing second fiddle to Gandhiji and the Muslim League to that of the Congress. Secondly, this was also evident in his decision to fight the election in 1946 which established his claim to speak on behalf of the Indian Muslims. In conclusion, it can be said that Jinnah was a historic personality fashioned not only by his environment and by the cultural and ideological influences he inherited, but also more importantly also by the way he reacted and reshaped that environment and that tradition by a consciously manipulated strategy of action with a fine sense of timing in application. Speaking of Jinnah, Sarojini Naidu said:[25]

> "But the true criterion of his greatness lies not in the range and variety of his knowledge and experience, but in the faultless perception and flawless refinement of his subtle mind and spirit; not in a diversity of aims and the challenge of a towering personality, but rather in a lofty singleness and sincerity of purpose, and the lasting charm of a character animated by a brave conception of duty and an austere and lovely code of private honour and public integrity."

When Mohammad Ali Jinnah became the Governor-General of independent Pakistan, he was already seventy and slowly dying, though full of euphoric spirit, as he rode to power on the crest of a victory which appeared so uncertain, so elusive for long agonizing years. The nation was in the throes of crisis unparallel in magnitude in human history, thoroughly disorganised and beleagured. With numerous challenges looming large, he came to steer the destiny of the nation pitted against a powerful adversary, the new resurgent India, awake to life and freedom, under the stewardship of a young and dynamic Prime Minister Jawaharlal

Nehru, hardly fifty-seven. With the venerated Gandhiji gone, the old India was dead, marking a watershed in the history of the subcontinent. For Jinnah, the political universe remained a continuing and perpetual strife. It was a conflict between two sovereign independent states minus the British Empire. India, out to dismember and absorb, thus to falsify the 'Two-Nation Theory'—the very basis of Pakistani nationhood. So the new conflict took on the garb of a status conflict in the international system between the two unequal nations hardly distinguishable from the old rivalry of the two unequal partners, the Indian National Congress and the All-India Muslim League. No longer the arena of conflict nor its fall-out remained confined to the subcontinent but in the nature of things got projected to the wider spheres of world politics because the issue was not the determination of the relative status of two communities but of the two nations vying for recongnition and influence in international politics. Political life has become one of acrimony, got new dimension as Mohammad Ali Jinnah had to confront Jawaharlal Nehru, known for his secular democratic outlook and international standing. So the fundamental character of the political opponent changed to a considerable disadvantage and embarrassment of Jinnah tainted with the authorship of the Two-Nation Theory, a derivative from religion. To chalk out a distinct identity for Pakistan in the world, and to prove that it was a going and growing proposition and to make it a great nation became his fundamental values for realisation. But Independent India, under Jawaharlal Nehru, acted as the spanner. Jinnah must take up the gauntlet, but the game was new, the rules of the game were different and the old impartial umpire gone. So, he had to fight alone. It called for new strategy of political action if the adversary was to be outwitted in the changed arena of political battle with changed set of rules. So, it was his cognitive beliefs which impelled him to turn to a new master, for succour and support, of whom he knew little. Having spent his entire energy and time in the freedom struggle in which the Britishers were the key factors, he had never developed any familiarity with the Americans because of absence of direct involvement of the latter in Indian affairs. As he was trained in British legal jurisprudence and had developed over the years some participatory experience in the working of British Parliamentary System, he was unaware of the workings of the American political systems and its decision-making process. Besides, Jinnah had over the years courted many influential Britons in its governmental structure who were sympathetic to his cause and have acted as pro-Pakistani lobby in the British Government during the freedom struggle. In constrast to this, he was almost a foreigner to the key American decision-makers so also his prime advisors, like Liaquat Ali Khan, Zafrullah Khan and others. With these political constraints he faced his new political adversary, Jawaharlal Nehru.

So arguably, he first took the decision to make the United States its leading patron in post-independent era. In this crucial policy preference, it seemed, he had taken the decision all by himself, even if other trusted decision-makers might have been consulted subsequently and communicated to implement his decision. The following evidence stood out in retrospect in support of this line of thinking. In the first place, Jinnah met Raymond A. Hare, Head of the Division of South Asian Affairs, Department of State and Thomas E. Weil, Second Secretary of the United States Embassy in India on 1 May 1947 at his Bombay Residence. In this exclusive interview in which he alone was present, he made no bone of his intention to drive home his point that a new Muslim state was imminent, and it would join other Muslim states to act as a bulwark against the Soviet aggression which would be in conformity with the avowed American objective.[26] He also expressed similar hope that America would assist Pakistan "in its many problems", when Henry F. Grady, the American Ambassador to India met him at the time of his departure to Karachi. When his Excellency enquired to indicate any specific matter, Jinnah bidded for a later date.[27] That he definitely decided this course of action for Pakistan, there was absolutely no iota of doubt, as further progress of his policy was revealed in the records of subsequent periods. Secondly, interestingly enough, he decided such a crucial policy preference when his closest associate Liaquat Ali did not know that he would be picked up by his master to be his Prime Minister, nor Zafrullah Khan ever thought of becoming the Foreign Minister of Pakistan, being a Quaidin. Similarly, Ghulam Mohammad, who was a member of Indian Audits and Accounts service never dreamt of assuming the office of Finance Minister. Stated differently, Jinnah decided his policy towards the United States even before his Cabinet formally assumed the office. With regard to the bureaucracy, it was well-known that there was hardly three Muslim officers of Indian Civil Service with the rank of joint secretaries to the government of India who opted for Pakistan. They were Iskander Mirza in Ministry of Defence and Mian Aminuddin and Mohammad Ikramullah in the Ministry of Commerce. They had had never seen diplomatic service in their career. Similarly, Chaudhuri Mohammad Ali, a member of Indian Audits and Accounts service who was the Financial Advisor to the Government of India before partition, became the Secretary-General and Ikramullah, the Foreign Secretary of independent Pakistan without any stint of diplomatic service.[28] Considering their background, it is futile to assume that they could have ever influenced Jinnah's policy preference which was certainly conceived by him much before these officers opted for the new state, because partition plan was announced on 3 June, 1947, and they became a part of Pakistan's bureaucratic system only after 14 August 1947. Thirdly, M.A.H. Ispahani's correspondence to Jinnah revealed that the Secret mission of Mir Laik Ali, Prime Minister of Hyderabad, to the United States and its detailed progress was directly communicated by Isphani to Jinnah, even Prime Minister Liaquat Ali and the Foreign Minister Zafrullah Khan were not kept posted with detailed information, even if they were in the know of his visit.[29] This showed that the negotiations with the United States were carried on in a thick veil of secrecy which was one of the facets of Jinnah's cognitive beliefs. To posit this is not to say that his prime advisors like Liaquat Ali Khan, Zafrullah 'Khan' and Ghulam Mohammad were not involved. It was Ghulam Mohammad who originated the programme of massive dependence on the United States for meeting the administrative expenses of Pakistan, especially in the field of defence. But true to his cognitive beliefs, it was Jinnah who conceived the idea and like his previous style of functioning during the pre-partition era, he must have presented them as a post-facto approval for working out its details which, as records revealed, was done by Liaquat Ali, Ghulam Mohammad, Chaudhuri Mohammad Ali and Ikramullah and M.A.H. Ispahani. At least, it appeared that they have a shared beliefs about the necessity for Pakistan's reliance on a new master. The very fact that Jinnah bidded for time to specify the requirements of the country during his first meeting with the United States ambassador, Henry G. Gaddy, was a clear indication of the fact that he wanted to work out the details in consultation with his associates, though his policy preference was final. This policy preference led to decision when in October 1947 Jinnah's special emissary, Mir Laik Ali, submitted a memorandum to the officials of the Department of State.

### Section B. The Impact of the Bureaucratic and the Organisational Variables

It is argued that the bureaucratic and the organisational variables have acted as intervening variables between the decision of Jinnah to procure American economic and military assistance and the outcome which resulted in the signing of the Mutual Defence Assistance Agreement on

19 May 1954. There is a strong assumption that had Jinnah been alive, his decision might have resulted in different form of output. In support of this, it is argued, how categorically he declared that Pakistan did not want to be a camp-follower of any Big Power even if he was making all-out effort to impress upon the Americans the desirability of his country's friendship in order to get their assistance for enhancing its capabilities. Besides, it is also said, that given his masterly choice of strategy for political action and his cautious approach of never committing to a step irrevocably which he could not retrace and his careful calculation of the political risk involved in such actions, he could not have carried his policy to this conclusion. While it is very difficult to prove or disprove this, the fact of the matter is that both these variables have dynamics of their own, and they are bound to operate as they are the implementing agencies and they operate independently irrespective of the calculation or the desire of one who makes the policy preference leading to decision. This dynamics take myriad forms and includes not only parochial subcontinency interests of the various implementing agencies like the Defence Ministry, the Foreign Ministry, the Armed Forces but more significantly the personal motivations of those who head them. In case of Pakistan, the record revealed that Ayub Khan, the Command-in-Chief of the armed forces, had played the key role in consummating this decision into the Agreement, assisted by Iskander Mirza, the Defence Secretary at the behest of Ghulam Mohammad, though Chaudhuri Mohammad Ali, and Ikramullah had played marginal role in the initial years. But what is now crucial that is missing in our previous analysis is their motivations that impelled them to distort this decision in terms of a Defence Agreement whose far-reaching implications for the Pakistani society was never understood by them as later events proved.

In the first place, it should be borne in mind that the decision-making in Pakistan came to be monopolized by Punjabi bureaucratic elites with the advent to power of Ghulam Mohammad which spelt the end of the Hindustani domination in Pakistani political life. This was itself a reflection of broader political trends in the country. The Punjabi landed gentry had, over the years, slowly worked their way into the inner portals of power, capturing the central apparatus of government and the Muslim League. Their values and interests were totally incompatible with the outlook and interests of the newly emerging Bengali bourgeoisie who in the provincial election of 1954 destroyed the League in East Pakistan. This nascent bureaucratic military elites, comprising Ghulam Mohammad, Mohammad

Ayub Khan, tortured by its own insecurity vis-a-vis the politicians and goaded by a growing feeling that a vast political change was in offing because of rising vernacular elites in East Bengal, consistently accorded top priority to the involvement of the United States on their side.[30] These dominant leaders, on 30 May 1954, in their efforts to curb the rise of Bengali nationalism, brought about the disintegration of the United Front Ministry headed by the Lion of Bengal, A.K. Fazlul Haq, just to create a favourable impression in Washington.[31] And Ghulam Mohammad sent Iskander Mirza to quell down the Bengali protest against the American alliance which was assailed by all the East Bengali leaders belonging to different political hues. This was preceded by the dismissal of the Bengali Prime Minister Khawaja Nazimuddin by Ghulam Mohammad even though he was commanding a clear majority in the Assembly. In his place, Mohammad Ali Bogra, Pakistan's ambassador to the United States, a man known to be a great votary of the American alliance was installed to eliminate any chances of opposition to the impending agreement. Thus, to preserve the new elite structure with its highly graded social and political hierarchy Ghulam Mohammad took the most unprecedented step of courting Americans in such a way that they would develop a stake in it.

Secondly, the position of this dominant elite could be further strengthened by the creation of a massive war machine. The sub-continental military imbalance and persisting tension with India argued in favour of such a proposition which was skillfully capitalized by them and they knew, the Americans world never settle down for any marginal concessions from their clients unless they become their stooges by entering into a Defence Agreement. The American policy-makers also knew where their support should lie in the tussle of political power in a country. In case of Pakistan, they were well-aware of their henchmen in its highest decision-making structure. The Intelligence Report prepared by the State Department's Office of Intelligence Research made this amply clear:[32]

> "....After 1952, a small group of British-trained administrators and military leaders from West Pakistan centering around the then Governor-General Ghulam Mohammad, gradually assumed political power. In addition to Ghulam Mohammad, this clique included Iskander Mirza and Chaudhury Mohammad Ali, both former civil servants, and General Ayub Khan, Commander-in-Chief of the Army... Ultimate political power in Pakistan continues to rest in the hands of (the clique)..."

Though this position was summed up in 1957, it was a part of the conventional wisdom of Washington since early 1950's. Lastly, the personal motive of Ayub Khan to come to power was one of the decisive factors. His contempt for politicians and greed for political authority were kept shrewdly camouflaged under the thin veneer of his political neutrality. As he wrote in his diary dated 22 May 1958.[33]

> "The elections, of course, are drawing near. The politicians... are trying to get back into power by hook or by crook. And having got there, they know that they will have nothing to show for themselves except working for the disruption of the country further. In that case they will come face to face with the army and me....
>
> ....It seems that we shall have to have a system of government for a generation or so which prepares the country for democracy and solves some of our major problems. Under the present Constitution no one seems to have any power except to destroy discipline and to do harm.

His blue-print for a new political system which he wrote in a London hotel on 4 October 1954 also gave ample testimony of his lewd lust for political power.[34]

> "I was pacing up and down the room when I said to myself: Let me put down my ideas in a military fashion: What is wrong with the country and what can be done to put things right. I approached the question much in the manner of drawing up a military appreciation: What is the problem, what are the factors involved, and what is the solution, if there is a solution.... In a few hours, I had produced a document which contained my thinking and set out my approach to the problems facing the country. I came to the conclusion that the affairs of the country, though in a desperate state, were not beyond redemption."

Over the years he worked with single-minded devotion to fraternise the Americans with the ostensible purpose of enlisting their backing and invoking them in his side for any future contingency. And the Americans also over the years developed their appreciation for Ayub as their strong supporter in Pakistani political system.

> ....He has a reputation for knowing what to look for and insisting on results. He reportedly has great confidence in himself and his forces... The General is reportedly pro-American (...), strongly opposed to Communism; he is a great admirer of the American armed forces... His shortcomings are believed to be over-ambition and a predilection to mix politics with his military career.

In view of all the foregoing facts, it is difficult not to agree that Jinnah's decision was distorted by these bureaucratic and organizational actors to subserve their vested political interests.

In the concluding part of our enquiry, our main objective was to prove that of all the personality traits, the cognitive beliefs is central to the decisional phenomena, while the bureaucratic and organizational variables are not without potency.

It is hypothesized that the foreign-policy decision-making in every political system proceeds in two distinct stages: policy preference leading to decision and action or output. The cognitive beliefs of the decision-makers become weighty on policy preference, while decision that is arrived at is again subject to the vagaries of the bureaucratic and the organizational variables. We have taken Pakistan's decision to conclude the Mutual Security Assistance Agreement with the United States in May 1954 for empirical testing. On exploration, it is found that Jinnah's cognitive traits dominated the policy preference which was reached by himself even before 1947. And it led to a decision when he formally decided to send his special emissary to the United States to present his case before its Government. Jinnah did not live long. So it was left to his successors to implement his decisions. Mohammad Ayub Khan, the Commander-in-Chief of Pakistan armed forces, who enjoyed complete trust of Liaquat Ali and subsequently of Ghulam Mohammad was intimately associated with the task of negotiating with the United States as the agreement had more of military dimensions. In the process, Ayub distorted it to subserve his political ambitions.

## References


1. Nathan Leites, *A Study of Bolshevism* (Illinois, 1953), p. 24.
2. Alexander L. George, "The Operational Code: A Neglected Approach to the Study of Political Leaders and Decision Making", *International Studies Quarterly* (Michigan), Vol.13, no.2, June 1969, pp. 190-222.
3. Gunnar Sjoblom, "Some problems of the Operational Code Approach" in Christer Jonsson, ed., *Cognitive Dynamics and International Politics* (London, 1982), pp. 37-74.
4. Robert Axelrod, ed., *The Structure of Decision: The Cognitive maps of Political Elites* (Princeton, 1976).
5. Ole R. Holsti, "The Operational Code Approach, Problems and Some Solutions" in Christer Jonsson, ed., n-3, pp.75-91.
6. Hector Belitho, *Jinnah, Creator of Pakistan* (Karachi, 1956), p.10.

7. Saleem M.M. Qureshi, "Iqbal and Jinnah: Personalities, Perceptions and Politics" in C.M. Naim, ed., *Iqbal, Jinnah and Pakistan: The Vision and the Reality* (Syracuse, 1978), pp. 11-39.
8. Sharif Al Mujahid, *Quaid-i-Azam Jinnah: Studies in Interpretation* (Karachi, 1981), p.45.
9. *Ibid.*, p.46.
10. Leonard Mosley, *The Last Days of the British Raj* (London, 1961), p.72.
11. *Report of the Proceedings of the Twenty-Second Indian National Congress* held at Calcutta on 26-29 Dec 1906 (Calcutta, 1907), p. 120.
12. Sarojini Naidu, ed., *Mohammad Ali Jinnah: An Ambassador of Unity* (Madras, 1918), p.10.
13. M.H. Saiyid, *Mohammad Ali Jinnah, A Political Biography* (Karachi, 1970), p. 1.
14. See his speech delivered during a debate on the Criminal Law Amendment Bill in the Imperial Legislative Council in 1913, see n.12, p. 228; also Saiyid, n. 13, pp.74-75.
15. S. Sharifuddin Pirzada, ed., *Quaid-I-Azam's Correspondence in India* (Karachi, 1944), p. 81.
16. Mujahid, n. 8, p. 52.
17. Saiyid, n. 13, p. 258.
18. P.D. Kaushik, *The Congress Ideology and Programme, 1920-47* (Bombay, 1964), 92n.
19. Belitho, n. 6, p. 105.
20. Rajni Palme Dutt, *India Today* (Bombay, 1949), rev. ed., pp.435-36.
21. *Autobiography* (Bombay, 1962), p. 72.
22. *Speeches and Writings of M.K. Gandhi* (Madras, 1922), 3rd ed., p. 326.
23. Jamil-ud-Din Ahmad, ed., *Speeches and Writings of Mr. Jinnah* (Lahore, 1964), vol. 2, reprint, p. 2.
24. *Quaid-i-Azam Mohammad Ali Jinnah: Speeches as Governor-General of Pakistan 1947-48* (Karachi, n.9.), pp. 6-11.
25. Quoted in Belitho, n. 6, p. 214.
26. The Charge d'Affairs in New Delhi (George R. Merrell) to the Secretary of State (George C. Marshall), 2 May 1947, *Foreign Relations of the United States 1947* (Washington D.C., 1972), Vol. 3, pp. 154-55.
27. The ambassador in New Delhi (Henry F. Grady) to the Secretary of State (Marshall), *ibid*, pp. 160-61.
28. Ralph Braibanti, "Public Bureaucracy and Judiciary in Pakistan" in Joseph La Palombara, ed., *Bureaucracy and Political Development* (Princeton, 1963), pp.360-441.

29. Z.H. Zaidi, ed., M.A. *Jinnah: Ispahani Correspondence 1936-1948* (Karachi, 1976), pp. 538-41.
30. Sisir Gupta, "Pakistan's Domestic Crisis and Foreign Policy: Problem of Identity and Relations with India", *South Asian Studies* (Jaipur), Vol.7, no.l, January 1972, pp. 114-26.
31. M.S. Venkataramani, *The American Role in Pakistan* (New Delhi, 1982), p. 269.
32. Department of State, *Office of Intelligence Research, Intelligence Reports, No. 7459,* "Prospects and Problems of Pakistan's Ruling Group", 8 March 1957, Diplomatic History Branch, National Archives (Washington D.C. ).
33. Mohammad Ayub Khan, *Friends Not Masters: A Political Autobiography* (London, 1967), p. 61.
34. *Ibid.*, p. 186.
35. The Director of Naval Intellegence to the Chairman of the Joint chief of Staff (Admiral Arthru W. Radford), 23 September 1953, Chairman's File, Records of the Joint Chiefs of Staff.

# Bibliography

**Primary Sources:**

Afzal, M. Rafique, ed., *Speeches* and Statements of *Quaid-i-Millat, Liaquat Ali Khan* (Lahore, Research Society of Pakistan, 1967).

Ahmad, Jamil-ud-Din, ed., *Speeches and Writings of Mr. Jinnah* {Lahore: Mohammad Ashraf, 1960), Vol. 1.

________, ed., *Historic Documents of the Muslim Freedom Movement* (Lahore: Publishers Ltd., 1970).

*American Foreign Policy: Current Documents* (Washington, D.C.: Department of State Publication), for various years from 1947 to 1971.

Azad, Maulana Abul Kalam, *India Wins Freedom: An Autobiographical Narrative* (New York: Longman, Green & Co., 1960).

*Chairman's* File, *Records of the Joint Chief* of *Staff,* Modern Military Records Branch, National Archives, Washington, D.C.

*Foreign Relations of the United States, 1947* (Washington, 1972), Vol. 1, 2 and 3.

*General Assembly, Official Records,* Sessions 2-26, 1947-71.

*Indian Annual Register* (Calcutta, 1941).

*India, Constituent Assembly, Debates*

India, *Lok Sabha, Debates, 1952-71.*

India, *Notes, Memoranda and Letters Exchanged Between the Governments of India and China, October 1962-January 1963, White Paper No. VIII* (New Delhi, 1967).

India, *Rajya Sabha, Debates, 1952-71.*

Iqbal, Mohammad, *The Reconstruction of Religious Thought in Islam* (Lahore: Muhammad Ashraf, 1968, reprint).

Khan, Mohammad Ayub, *Friends Not Masters: A Political Autobiography* (London: Oxford University Press, 1967).

________, *Speeches and Statements* (Karachi: Pakistan Publications, 1958-59), 8 vols.

Malik, Abdullah, ed. *Selected Speeches and Statements of Iftikhar Ud-Din* (Lahore, Nigarishat, 1971).

*National Security Council , Documents (1946-60)* Modern Military Records Branch, National Archives, Washington, D. C.

Nehru, Jawaharlal, *India's Foreign Policy: Speeches, September 1946-April 1961* (New Delhi: Publication Division, Ministry of Information and Broadcasting, Government of India, 1971).

Nixon, Richard M., *.US. Foreign Policy for the 1970s: The Emerging Structure of Peace : A Report to the Congress, 9 February 1972* (Washington D-C , 1972).

Nixon, Richard M., *U.S. Foreign Policy for the 1970s : A New Strategy for Peace: A Report to the Congress, 18 February 1970* (Washington, D.C., 1970).

Noon, Firoz Khan, *From Memory* (Lahore: Ferozsons Ltd., 1969).

Pakistan, *Annual Report for the Year 1947, The Karachi Chamber of Commerce* (Karachi, 1947).

Pakistan, *Constituent Assembly, Debates, 1947-54.*

Pakistan, *Constituent Assembly, Debates, 1947-54 and 1955-56.*

Pakistan, *Economic Survey, 1965-68* (Rawalpindi: Ministry of Finance, The Government of Pakistan, 1969).

________, *Economic Survey 1965-70* (Islamabad: Ministry of Finance, Government of Pakistan, 1979).

Pakistan, *National Assembly, Debates, 1954-68.*

Pakistan, *National Assembly, Debates, 1954-68; 56-68 and 1965-69.*

Pakistan, *Planning Commission; Reports of the Advisory Panel for Fourth Five-Year Plan, 1970-75* (Islamabad: Ministry of Finance, Government of Pakistan, 1971).

________,*Planning Commission; Industrial Policy of the Government of Pakistan* (Karachi: Ministry of Finance, Government of Pakistan, 1961).

*Quaid-i-Azam Mohammad Ali Jinnah, Speeches as Governor-General of Pakistan 1947-48* (Karachi: Pakistan Publication, n.d).

*Records of the Military Advisor to the Office of Near Eastern and African Affairs, Record Group 59*, National Achieves, Washington D.C.

*Security Council, Official Records*, mtgs. 1947-71.

Talbott, S., *Khrushchev Remembers: The Last Testament* (London, 1974).

Truman, Harry S., *Memoirs: Years of Trial and Hope*, Vol. 2 (New York: Doubleday, 1956).

________,Papers, Truman Library, Independence, Missourie.

The United Nations, *National and Per Capita Income of Seventy Countries, Statistical Reports Series*, E. No. 1 (New York: UN Statistical Office, Department of Economic Affairs, 1950).

The United States, *Annual Report on Communist Aid to the Less Developed Countries* (Title Varies); RSB-173, 14 November 1962; RSB-50, 17 June 1966, RSB-80, 21 July 1969, RECS-5, 9 July 1970, RECS-15, 22 September, 1971 (Washington: Bureau of Intelligence, Department of State, 1962-71).

The United States, *Congressional Records*, 1947-71.

The United States, *Department of Defence Documents* (Washington, 1971), vols. 12.

The United States, *Documents of the National Security Council* (Washington, D.C., Modern Military Records Branch, National Archives), for various years.

The United States, *Joint Economic Committee of the Congress Annual Economic Indicators for the USSR* (Washington D.C., United States Government Printing Office, 1964).

Zaidi, N.H., ed., *M.A. Jinnah-Ispahani Correspondence, 1936-48* (Karachi Publication Trust, 1976).

**Books:**

Abbott, Freeland, *Islam and Pakistan* (Ithaca: Cornell University Press, 1968).

Acheson, Dean, *Present at the Creation: My Years in State Department* (New York: W. W. Norton, 1969).

Adams, John and Sabita Iqbal, *Exports , Politics and Economic Development in Pakistan, 1970-82* (Colorado: Westview Press, 1983).

Afzal, M. Rafique, *Speeches and Statements of Quaid-i-Millat Liaquat Ali Khan, 1941-51* (Lahore: Nafees Printers, 1967).

Ahmad, Mohammad, *My Chief* (Lahore: Longman's Green and Co., 1960).

Ahmad, Muneer, *The Civil Servant in Pakistan* (Karachi: Oxford University Press, 1964).

Ahmad, Mushtaq, *The Government and Politics in Pakistan* (Karachi: Space Publishers, 1970).

_______, *Pakistan's Foreign Policy* (Karachi: Space Publishers, 1968).

Ali, Chaudhuri Muhammad, *The Emergence of Pakistan* (New York: Columbia University Press, 1967).

Ali, Tariq, *Pakistan: Military Rule or People's Power* (London: Jonathan Cape Limited, 1970).

_________, *Can Pakistan Survive? The Death of a State* (England: Penguin Books Ltd., 1983).

Allison, Graham T., *Essence of Decision: Explaining Cuban Missile Crisis* (Boston: Little Borwn, 1971).

Almond, Gabriel A. and G. S. Coleman, eds., *The Politics of Developing Areas* (Princeton: Princeton University Press, 1960).

_______and B. Powell, *Comparative Politics* (Toranto: Little Brown & Co., 1966).

Axelrod, Robert, ed., *Structure of Decision: The Cognitive Maps of Political Elites* (Princeton: New Jersey: Princeton University Press, 1976).

Ayoob, Mohammad, *Pakistan's Alliance with the United States 1954-65: A Study in Loads, Capabilities and Responses* (Ann Arbor: Michigan: University of Michigan Press, 1966).

_____,*India, Pakistan and Bangladesh: Search for New Relationship* (New Delhi: Indian Council of World Affairs, 1975).

Aziz, K.K., *Party Politics in Pakistan, 1947-58* (Islamabad: The National Commission on Historical and Cultural Research, 1976).

Barnds, William J., *India, Pakistan and the Great Powers* (New York : Praeger, For Council on Foreign Relations, 1972).

Barnett, A. Doak, *Communist China and Asia: Challenges to American Policy* (New Delhi: Eurasia Publishing House, 1964).

_________, *China Policy: Old Problems and New Challenges* (Washington, D.C.: Brookings Institution, 1977).

_________ , *New U.S. Policy Towards China* (Washington, D.C.: Brookings Institution, 1971).

Bhatia, B.M., *Pakistan's Economic Development 1948-78* (New Delhi: Vikas Publishing House, 1979).

Bhutto, Z.A., *The Myth of Independence* (Lahore: Oxford University Press, 1969).

_______, *Reshaping Foreign Policy* (Karachi: Ferozsons Ltd., 1971).

Binder, Leonard, *Religion and Politics in Pakistan* (Berkeley: University of California Press, 1963).

Birdwood, Lord, *Two Nations and Kashmir* (London: Robert Hale, 1956).

______ , *India and Pakistan: A Continent Decides* (London: Robert Hale, 1953).

Bolitho, Hector, *Jinnah, Creator of Pakistan* (Karachi: Oxford University Press, 1966).

Boulding, K.E., *The Image* (Michigan: Michigan University Press, 1956).

Braybrooke, D. and Charles E. Lindblom, *A Strategy of Decision: Policy Evaluation as a Social Process* (New York: The Free Press, 1963).

Brecher, Michael, *The New States of Asia: A Political Analysis* (London: Oxford University Press, 1968).

________ , *India and World Politics : Krishna Menon's View of the World* (New York: Praeger, 1968).

________, *The Israeli Foreign Policy System* (London: Oxford University Press, 1972).

Brines, Russell, *The Indo-Pakistan Conflict* (London: Pall Mall Press, 1968).

Burgess, Philip M., *Elite Images and Foreign Policy Outcomes* (Columbus: Ohio State University Press, 1967).

Burke, S.M., *Pakistan's Foreign Policy: An Historical Analysis* (London: Oxford University Press, 1973).

_________,*Mainsprings of Indian and Pakistani Foreign Policies* (Minneapolis: University of Minnesota Press, 1974).

Callard, Keith, *Pakistan: A Political Study* (Karachi: Oxford University Press, 1968).

________, *Pakistan's Foreign Policy: An Interpretation*, Revised Edn. (New York: Institute of Pacific Relations, 1960).

Caroe, Olaf, *Wells of Power: The Oilfields of South Western Asia: A. Regional and Global Study* (London: Macmillan, 1951).

________, *The Pathans* (Karachi: Oxford University Press, 1976).

Chaudhury, G. W., *Pakistan's Relations with India, 1947-1966* (London: Pall Mall Press, 1968).

________ , *India, Pakistan, Bangladesh and the Major Powers : Politics of a Divided Subcontinent* (New York: Free Press, 1975).

________ , *Constitutional Development in Pakistan* , rev. Edn. (London: Longman, 1969).

Cohen, Stephen P., *The Pakistan Army* (New Delhi: Himalayan Books, 1984).

Dallin, David J., *Soviet Foreign Policy After Stalin* (Philadelphia, Pa.: Lippincot, 1961).

Deutsch, Karl W., *Analysis of International Relations* (Eaglewood Cliffs: Prentice Hall, 1968).

de Rivera, Joseph H., *The Psychological Dimension of Foreign Policy* (Colombus, Ohio: Merrill, 1968).

Easton, David, *Political System: An Enquiry into the State of Political Science* (Calcutta: Scientific Book Agency, 1971).

________, *Systems Analysis of Political Life* (New York: John Wiley & Sons, 1967).

Falcon, Walter P. and Gustav, P. Papanek, eds., *Development Policy-II — The Pakistan Experience* (Cambridge: Harvard University Press, 1971).

Falkowski, L.S., ed., *Psychological Models in International Politics* (Boulder, Colorado: Westview Press, 1979).

Fieldman, Herbert, *Revolution in Pakistan: A Study of the Martial Law Administration* (London: Oxford University Press, 1967).

Finer, S.E., *Man on the Horseback: The Role of Military in Politics* (Harmondsworth: Penguin, 1975).

Fox, William T.R., ed., *Theoretical Aspects of International Relations* (Notre Dame: 1959).

________, *The Super Powers– The United States, Britain and the Soviet Union: Their Responsibility for Peace* (New York: 1944).

Fraser-Tytler, W.K., *Afghanistan* (London: Oxford University Press, 1967).

Gardezi, Hassan and Jamil Rashid, eds., *Pakistan: The Roots of Dictorship : The Political Economy of a Praetorian State* (New Delhi: Oxford University Press, 1983).

Goldman, Kjell and Gunnar Sjostedt, eds., *Power, Capabilities, Interdependence: Problems in the Study of International Influence* (Beverly Hills: Sage Publications, 1979).

Greenstein, Fred I., *Personality and Politics* (Chicago, Markham, 1969).

Griffin, Keith and Azizur Rahman, eds., *Growth and Inequality in Pakistan* (London: Macmillan, 1972).

Gupta, Sisir, Kashmir, *A study in India-Pakistan Relations* (Bombay: Asia Publishing House, 1967).

Halperin, A.M. ed., *Policies Towards China: Views from Six Continents* (New York: MacGraw Hill, 1965).

Halpern, Morton H., *Bureaucratic Politics and Foreign Policy* (Washington: Brookings Institution, 1974).

Hasan, K. Sarwar, *Pakistan and the United Nations* (New York: Manhattan Publishing Co., 1960).

Hasan, Masuma, ed., *Pakistan in a Changing World* (Karachi: Pakistan Institute of International Affairs, 1978).

Hilsman, Roger, *Strategic Intel ligenee and National Decision* (New York: Free Press Giencoe, 1956).

________, *Politics of Policy-making in Defence and Foreign Affairs* (New York: Harper & Row, 1971).

Hoffmann, Stanley H., ed., *Contemporary Theory in International Relations* (Eaglewood Cliffs, New Jersey: Prentice Hall, 1960).

Holsti, Ole R. and James, N. Rosenau, *American Leadership in World Affairs: Vietnam and the Breakdown of Consensus* (Boston: Allen and Unwin, 1984).

Holt, Robert T. and John E. Turner, eds., *The Methodology of Comparative Research* (New York: The Free Press, 1970).

Hopple, Gerald W., ed., *Biopolitics , Political Psychology and International Politics* (London: France Pinter, 1982).

Hunter, W.W., *The Indian Musalmans* (Lahore: The Premier Book House, 1974).

Huntington, Samuel P., *Political Order in Changing Societies* (New Haven: Yale University Press, 1971).

________, *Changing Patterns of Military Politics* (New York: Free Press of Glencoe, 1962).

Huq, Mahbubul, *The Strategy of Economic Planning: A Case Study of Pakistan* (Lahore: Oxford University Press, 1963).

International Institute of Strategic Studies, *The Military Balance, 1954-64, 1971-72* (London: ISSS, 1971).

Iqbal, Javid, *Ideology of Pakistan* (Karachi: Ferozsons Ltd., 1971).

Ispahani, M.A.H., *Qaid-e-Azam Jinnah as I Knew Him* (Karachi : Ferozsons Ltd., 2nd edn., 1967).

Jafri, Rais Ahmad, *Ayub: Soldier and Statesman* (Lahore: Mohammad Ali Academy, 1966).

Jahan, Rounaq, *Pakistan; Failure in National Inteqration* (New York : Columbia University Press, 1972).

Janowitz, Morris, *The Military in the Political Development of New Nations: An Essay in Comparative Analysis* (Chicago: University of Chicago Press, 1966).

Jonsson, Christer, ed., *Cognitive Dynamics and International Politics* (London: 1982).

Jordan, Amos A. Jr., *Foreign Aid and the Defence of Southeast Asia* (New York: Frederick A. Praeger, 1962).

Kaplan, Morton A., *System and Processes in International Politics* (New York: John Wiley and Sons, 1957).

Khan, Fazal Muqueem, *The Story of the Pakistan Army* (Karachi: Oxford University Press, 1963).

________, *Pakistan's Crisis in Leadership* (Islamabad: National Book Foundation, 1973).

Khan, Liaquat Ali, *Pakistan: The Heart of Asia* (Cambridge, Mass: Harvard University Press, 1950).

Khan, Mohammad Asghar, *Pakistan at the Cross-Roads* (Karachi: Ferozsons, 1969).

________, *The First Round, Indo-Pakistan War, 1965* (New Delhi: Vikas, 1979).

Khan, Chaudhury Zafrullah, *Pakistan's Foreign Relations* (Karachi: Pakistan Institute of International Affairs, 1951).

Kissinger, Henry A., *The White House Years* (New Delhi: Vikas, 1979).

Kizilbash, Hamid H. and Khawar Mumtaz, *Pakistan Foreign Policy and the Legislature : A Preliminary Report* (Lahore: University of Punjab, 1976).

Knorr, Klaus, *The Power of Nations: The Political Economy of International Relations* (New York: Basic Books, 1975).

________ and Sidney Verba, *International System: Theoretical Essays* (Princeton: Princeton University Press, 1961).

Kochanek, Stanley A., *Interest Groups and Development: Business and Politics in Pakistan* (New Delhi: Oxford University Press, 1954).

LaPalombara, J., ed., *Bureaucracy and Political Development* (Princeton: Princeton University Press, 1963).

Laporte, Robert, *Power and Privilege : Influence and Decision-making in Pakistan* (New Delhi: Vikas Publishing House, 1976).

Mason, Edward S., *Foreign Aid and Foreign Policy* (New York: Harper and Row, 1964).

________, *Economic Development in India and Pakistan* (Cambridge: Centre for International Affairs, Harvard University Press, 1966).

Menon, V.P., *The Study of the Integration of Indian States* (Calcutta: Orient Longman, 1956).

________, *The Transfer of Power in India* (Princeton, N.J.: Princeton University Press, 1957).

Misra, K.P., *Studies in Indian Foreign Policy* (New Delhi: Vikas, 1969).

Montgomery, J.D., *Foreign Aid in International Politics* (Bombay: Allied Publishers, 1969).

Morgenthau, Hans J., *Politics Among Nations : The Struggle for Power and Peace* (New York: Alfred A. Knoff, 1948).

Mujahid, Sharif Al, *Quaid-i-Azam Jinnah : Studies in Interpretation* (Karachi: Quaid-i-Azam Academy, 1981).

Mujtaba, Razvi, *The Frontiers of Pakistan: A Study of Frontier Problems in Pakistan's Foreign Policy* (Karachi: National Publishing House, 1971).

Munir, Muhammad, *From Jinnah to Zia* (Delhi: Akbar Publishing House, 1981).

Naim, C.M., ed., *Iqbal, Jinnah and Pakistan: The Vision and the Real ity* (Syracuse: Syracuse University Press, 1979).

Nehru, Jawaharlal, *Soviet Russia: Some Random Sketches and Impressions* (Bombay: Chetna, 1949).

________, *Autobiography: With Musings on Recent Events in India* (London: Bodley Head, 1955).

Noman, Omar, Pakistan: *A Political and Economic History since 1947*, (London, Keganl Paul International Ltd., 1988).

Northedge, F.S. and M.J. Grieve, *A Hundred Years of International Relations* (London: Gerald Duckworth & Co., 1971).

Papanek, Gustav F., *Pakistan's Development: Social Goals and Private Incentives* (Cambridge: Harvard University Press, 1967).

Qureshi, Ishtiaq Husain, *Ulema in Politics* (London: White Lion Publishing Ltd., 1976).

Rab, Abdur, A.K., *Fazlul Hug: Life and Achievement* (Lahore: Ferozsons, 1967).

Rahman, Lt.Gen., M. Attiqur, *Our Defense Cause* (London: White Lion Publishers, 1976).

________, *Leadership: Senior Commanders* (Lahore, Ferozsons, 1973).

Rahman, Seikh Mujibur, *6-Point Formula: Our Right to Live* (Dacca: Pioneer Press, 1966).

Rajan, M.S. and Sivaji Ganguly, eds., *Great Power Re lations, World Order and the Third World* (New Delhi: Vikas Publishing House, 1981).

________ and Sivaji Ganguly, Sisir Gupta*: India and the International System* (New Delhi: Vikas Publishing House, 1981 ).

Rajendra, Prasad, *India Divided* (Bombay: Hind Kitabs, 1947).

Rajput, A.B., *Muslim League : Yesterday and Today* (Lahore: S.M. Ashraf, 1948).

Ranney, Austin, ed., *Essays on the Behavioral Study of Politics* (Urbana: University of Illinois Press, 1962).

Ray, Aswini Kumar, *Domestic Compulsions and Foreign Policy: Pakistan in Indo-Soviet Relations, 1947-58* (New Delhi: Manas Publications, 1975).

Rhodes, Robert, ed., *Imperialism and Underdevelopment: A Reader* (New York: Monthly Review Press, 1970).

Rizvi, Hasan Askari, *The Military and Politics in Pakistan* (Lahore: Progressive Publishers, 1976).

Richards, P.G., *Parliament and Foreign Policy* (London: George Allen and Unwin, 1967).

Rosenau, James N., ed., *in Search of Global Patterns* (New York: The Free Press, 1976).

________,ed.,*Comparing Foreign Policies* (London: Beverly Hills, Sage ,1974).

________, and others, eds., *The Analysis of International Politics* (New York: The Free Press, 1972).

________, *The Study of Global Interdependence Essays on the Transnationalisation of World Affairs* (New York: The Free Press, 1980).

Rosenau, James N., *The Scientific Study of Foreign Policy* (New York: The Free Press, 1971).

________ , ed., *International Policies and Foreign Policy* (New York: The Free Press, rev. ed., 1969).

________, Kenneth W. Thompson and Govin Boyd, eds., *World Politics: An Introduction* (New York: The Free Press, 1976).

Rothstein, Robert C.,, *The weak in the World of the Strong: The Developing Countries in the International system* (New York: 1977).

________, *Alliances and Small Powers* (New York, Columbia University Press, 1968).

Rubinstein, Alvin Z., *Foreign Policy of the Soviet Union* (New York: Random House, 1972).

Saiyid, M.H., Mohammad Ali Jinnah, *A Political Biography* (Karachi: Elite Publishers, 1970).

Sayeed, Khalid B., *Political System of Pakistan* (Boston: Houghton Mifflin, 1967).

Shills, David L., *International Encyclopaedia of the Social Sciences* (New York: The Free Press, 1968).

Siddiqui, Kalim, *Conflict, Crisis and War in Pakistan* (London: Macmillan Press Ltd., 1972).

Singer, J. David, ed., *Quantitative International Politics: Insights and Evidence* (New York: The Free Press, 1968).

Smith, Cantwell W., *Islam in Modern History* (Princeton: Princeton University Press, 1957).

Synder, Richard C., H.W. Bruck and Burton Sapin, eds., *Foreign Policy Decision-Making : An Approach to the Study of International Politics* (New York: Free Press of Glencoe, 1962).

________,and James A. Robinson, *National and International Decision-Making* (New York: Institute for International Order, 1961).

**Articles:**

Adie, W.A.C., "One World Restored? : Sino-American Relations on a New Footing", *Asian Survey* (Berkeley: Calif. ), vol. 12, no.5, May 1972, pp. 365-85.

________, "China, Russia and the Third World", *China Quarterly* (London), Vol.11, July/September 1962, pp.200-13.

Agwani, M.S., "India, Pakistan and West Asia", *International Studies* (New Delhi), Vol.8, no. 1, July 1966-April 1967, pp. 158-67.

Ahmed, Aijas, "Democracy and Dictatorship in Pakistan", *Journal of Contemporary Asia* (Nottingham), Vol. 8, no. 8, 1979, pp. 477-512.

Ahmed, Aziz, "Mawdudi and Orthodox Fundamentalism in Pakistan", *Middle East Journal* (Washington), Vol.21, no.3, LSummer 1967, pp. 369-80.

Allison, Graham, T., "Conceptual Models and the Cuban Missile Crisis", *American Political Science Review* (Wisconsin), vol.63, no.3, September 1969, pp. 689-718.

________, and Morton H. Halperin, "Bureaucratic Politics: A Paradigm and Some Policy Implications", *World Policies* (Princeton), vol. 24, Supplementary, 1972, pp.40-79.

Ayoob, Mohammed, "US Economic Assistance to Pakistan 1954-65: A Case Study in the Politics of Foreign Aid", *India Quarterly* (New Delhi), Vol. XXIII, no. 2, April-June 1967, pp. 127-45.

________, "India as a Factor in Sino-Pakistani Relations", *International Studies* (New Delhi), Vol. 9, no. 1, January 1968, pp. 279-301.

Baloch, A.H., "Pak-Afghan Relations", *Pakistan Review* (Lahore), Vol. 7, no. 5, May 1959, pp. 29-33.

Bandyopadhyaya, Jayantanuja, "Role of External Powers in South Asian Affairs", *India Quarterly* (New Delhi), Vol. XXX, no.4, October-December 1974, pp.276-305.

Banks, M., "Systems Analysis and the Study of Regions", *International Studies Quarterly* (Michigan), Vol.13, no.4, December 1969, pp.335-60.

Barnds, William J., "United States Policy Towards South Asia: Sifting Perceptions and Policy Choices", *Pacific Community* (Tokyo), Vol.8, no.4, July 1977, pp. 645-660.

________, "India in Transition: Friends and Neighbours", *Foreign Affairs* (New York), Vol.46, no.3, April 1968, pp. 548-61.

Barua, B.P., "Jinnah and his Ideas: A Critical Analysis", *Indian Journal of Politics* (Lucknow), Vol. 12, nos. 1 & 2, April-June 1978, pp. 11-16.

Binder, Leonard, "The Middle East as a Subordinate International System", *World Politics* (Princeton), Vol. X., no.3, April 1958, pp. 408-29.

Boorman, Howard L., "The Sino-Soviet Alliance: A New Dimension in World Politics", *Journal of International Affairs* (New York), Vol.11, no.2, 1957, pp. 122-34.

Bowles, Chester, "The China Problem Reconsidered", *Foreign Affairs* (New York), Vol.38, no.3, April 1960, pp. 476-86.

Brecher, Michael, "Elite Images and Foreign Policy Choices", *Pacific Affairs* (Vancouver, B.C.), Vol. XL, Nos. 1 & 2, Summer 1967, pp. 60-93.

________, "Non-Alignment Under Stress: The West and the India-China Border War", *Pacific Affairs,* Vol. 52, no. 4, Winter 1979-80, pp.

Brzezinski, Zbigniew, "How the Cold War was Played", *Foreign Affairs,* Vol. 51, no. 1, October 1972, pp. 181-209.

Burke, S.M., "Sino-Pakistani Relations", *Orbis* (Philadelphia, Pa.), Vol. 8, no. 2, Summer 1964, pp. 391-404.

________, "The Sino-Indian Conflict", *Journal of International Affairs* (New York), Vol. 17, no. 2, 1963, pp. 200-11.

Callard, Keith, "The Political Stability of Pakistan", *Pacific Affairs* (Vancouver, B.C.), Vol. XXIX, no. 1, March 1956, pp. 5-21.

Chao, Kuo-chun, "The Chinese-Indian Controversy", *Current History* (Philadelphia), Vol. 37, no. 220, December 1959, pp. 354-361.

Choudhury, G. W., "The Constitution of Pakistan", *Pacific Affairs*, Vol. XXIX, no. 3, September 1956, pp. 293-53.

________, "The East Pakistan Political Scene 1955-1957", *Pacific Affairs,* Vol. XXX, no. 4, December 1957, pp. 312-321.

________, "Pakistan and the Communist World", *Pacific Community* (Tokyo), Vol. 6, no. 1, October 1974, pp. 107-139.

________, "US Policy Towards the Subcontinent", *Pacific Community,* Vol. 5, no. 1, October 1973, pp.97-113.

Chaudhri, Mohammed Ahsen, "Pakistan's Relations with the Soviet Union", *Asian Survey* (Berkeley, Calif.), Vol. VI, no. 9, September 1966, pp. 492-501.

________,"Pakistan and the Soviet Bloc", *Pakistan Horizon* (Karachi), Vol. 9, no. 2, June 1956, pp. 71-80.

Chen, Y.V., "An Appraisal of America's Current China Policy", *Pacific Community*, Vol. 3, no. 1, October 1971 , pp. 68-86.

"China's Stand on the Sino-Indian Boundary Question", *Peking Review* (Peking), Vol. 27, no. 26, 29 December 1959, pp. 1013-16.

Chun-Ch'uan, Shen, "Triangular Rivalry of Washington, Moscow and Peking in South Asia: A Study in the Light of Relations Between Communist China and Pakistan", *Issues and Studies* (Taipei), Vol. 14, no. 1, January 1978, pp. 11-27.

Dobell, "Ayub Khan as President of Pakistan", *Pacific Affairs,* Vol. XLII, no. 3, Fall 1969, pp. 294-311.

Feldman, Herbert, "The Communal Problem in the Indo-Pakistan Subcontinent: Some Current Implications", *Pacific Affairs,* Vol. XLIII, no. 2, Summer 1969, pp. 145-164.

Goldman, Marshall I., "A Balance Sheet of Soviet Foreign Aid", *Foreign Affairs* (New York), Vol. 43, no. 2, January 1965, pp. 349-360.

Harrison, Seliq S., "Troubled India and Her Neighbours", *Foreign Affairs* (New York), Vol. 43, no. 2, January 1965, pp. 349-360-

________,"India, Pakistan and the United States: Case History of a Mistake", *New Republic* (Washington, D.C.), 141(6/7), 10 August 1959, pp. 10-17; 141(8/9), 24 August 1959, pp. 20-25; 141(10), 7 September 1959, pp. 11-17.

Hasan, K. Sarwar, "The Background of American Arms Aid to Pakistan", *Pakistan Horizon* (Karachi), Vol. XX, no. 2 , April 1967 , pp.

________, "The Foreign Policy of Liaquat Ali Khan", *Pakistan Horizon,* Vol. IV, no. 4, December 1951, pp. 193.

Hasan, Zubeida, "Pakistan's Relations with the USSR in 1960s", *World Today* (London), Vol. 25, no. 1, January 1969, pp. 26-35.

________, "Western Arms Aid to India", *Pakistan Horizon,* Vol. 16, no. 4, 4th Quarter, 1963, pp. 333-43.

Hudson, G.F., "Peking, New Delhi and Moscow", *The New Leader* (New York), Vol. 41, no. 31, 1 September 1958, pp. 9-12.

" Indo-Pakistan Joint Communique on Border Disputes", *Pakistan Horizon,* Vol. 12, no. 4, December 1959, pp. 394-96.

Ispahani, M.A.H., "Pakistan and New Regional Arrangement", *Pakistan Horizon,* Vol. XXII, no. 3, Third Quarter 1969, pp. 199-208.

________, "The Foreign Policy of Pakistan, 1947-64", *Pakistan Horizon*, Vol. XVII, no. 3, 3rd Quarter 1964, pp. 231-52.

________, "Pacts and Aid", *Pakistan Horizon*, Vol. XIX, no. 2, 2nd Quarter 1966, pp. 117-26.

Kennan, George F., "After the Cold War", *Foreign Affairs*, Vol. 51, no. 1, October 1972, pp. 210-227.

Khan, Mohammad Ayub, "Essentials of Pakistan's Foreign Policy", *Pakistan Horizon*, Vol. XIV, no. 4, 4th Quarter, 1961, pp.

Khan, Mohammad Ayub, "Pakistan Perspective", *Foreign Affairs*, Vol. 38, no. l, July 1960, pp. 547-57.

________, "The Pakistan-American Alliance: Stresses and Strains", *Foreign Affairs*, Vol. 42, no. I, January 1964, pp. 195-210.

________, "South Asia: A Perspective", *Pakistan Horizon*, Vol. XVIII, no. 3, Third Quarter 1965, pp.

Khrushchev, Nikita S., "On Peaceful Coexistence", *Foreign Affairs*, Vol. 38, no. 1, October 1959, pp. 1-18.

Kovner, Milton, "Soviet Aid Strategy in Developing Countries", *Orbis*, Vol. 8, no. 3, Fall 1964, pp. 624-40.

Levi, Werner, "Pakistan, the Soviet Union and China", *Pacific Affairs*, Vol. XXXV, no. 2, Fall 1962, pp. 211-22.

Maniruzzaman, Talukdar, "Group Interests in Pakistan Politics, 1947-58", *Pacific Affairs*, Vol. XXXIX, nos. 1 & 2, Spring-Summer 1966, pp. 83-99.

Mansoor, Jafar, "Pakistan and the Baghdad Pact", *Pakistan Review* (Lahore)', Vol. 4, no. 4, April 1956, pp. 7-29.

Mazrui, Ali A., "The Barrel of the Gun and the Barrel of Oil", *Alternatives* (New Delhi), Vol. 3, no. 4, May 1978, p. 474.

Mosley, Philip E., "Communist Policy and the Third World", *Review of Politics* (Notre Dame, Indiana), Vol. 25, no. 2, April 1966, p. 458.

________, "Soviet Policy in the Developing Countries", *Foreign Affairs*, Vol. 43, no. 1, October 1964, pp. 87-98.

________, "The Kremlin and the Third World", *Foreign Affairs*, Vol. 46, no. 1, October 1967, pp. 64-77.

________, "The Chinese-Soviet Rift: Origins and Portents", *Foreign Affairs*, Vol. 42, no. 1, October 1963, pp. 11-24.

Mustafa, Zubeida, "Pakistan and the Middle East", *Pacific Community* (Tokyo), Vol. 7, no. 4, July 1976, pp. 608-20.

________, "China's Policy Towards Pakistan", Vol. 5, no. 1, October 1973, pp. 113-28.

________, "The 1971 Crisis in Pakistan: India, the Soviet Union and China", *Pacific Community,* Vol. 3, no. 1, April 1972, pp. 498-516.

Nairn, Ronald C., "SEATO: A Critique", *Pacific Affairs*, Vol-XLI, no. l, Spring 1968, pp. 5-19.

"Pakistan: The Shadow of Baghdad", *Round Table* (London), Vol. 1949, September 1958, pp. 385-88.

Qureshi, Khalida, "The Soviet Union, Pakistan and India", *Pakistan Horizon,* Vol. 16, no. 4, October 1963, pp. 344-55.

Qureshi, Saleem M.M., "Pakistani Nationalism Reconsidered" *Pacific Affairs*, Vol. 45, no. 4, Winter 1972-73, pp. 556-72.

________, "Pakistan: The Frontier Dispute Between Afghanistan and Pakistan", *Pacific Affairs*, Vol. XXXIX, nos. 1 & 2, Spring-Summer 1966, pp. 99-115.

Rajan, M.S., "India and Pakistan as Factors in Each Other's Foreign Policy and Relations", *International Studies* (New Delhi), Vol. 3, no. 4, April 1962, pp. 349-94.

Rapacki, Adam, "Competition and Cooperation: Peaceful Coexistence", *World Marxist Review* (Toronto), Vol. 2, no. 10, October 1959, pp. 5-10.

Rubinstein, Alvin Z., "Russia and the Uncommitted Nations", *Current History* (Philadelphia), Vol. 43, no. 254, October 1962, pp. 218-23.

Satyapalan, C.N., "The Sino-Indian Border Conflict", *Orbis*, Vol. VIII, No. 2, Summer 1964, pp. 389.

Sayeed, Khalid B., "Religion and Nation-Building in Pakistan", *Middle East Journal* (Washington), Vol. XVII, no. 1, 1963, pp. 279-91.

Sayeed, Khalid B., "Pakistan's Foreign Policy: An Analysis of Pakistan's Fears and Interests", *Asian Survey*, Vol. IV, no. 3, March 1964, pp. 746-756.

________, "Southeast Asia in Pakistan's Foreign Policy", *Pacific Affairs,* Vol. XLI, no. 2, Summer 1968, pp. 230-45.

________, "Jama'at-i-Islami Movement in Pakistan", *Pacific Affairs*, Vol. XXX, no. l, March 1957, pp. 59-68.

________, "The Political Role of Pakistan's Civil Service", *Pacific Affairs,* Vol. XXXI, no. 2, June 1958, pp. 131-47.

________, "Collapse of Parliamentary Democracy in Pakistan, *Middle East Journal*, Vol. 13, no. 4, Autumn 1959, pp. 389-406.

Scalapino, Robert A., "Moscow, Peking and the Communist Parties of Asia", *Foreign Affairs,* Vol. 41, no. 2, October 1962, pp. 323-43.

Seth, S.P., "Russia's Role in Indo-Pak Politics", *Asian Survey,* Vol. IX, no. 8, August 1969, pp. 614-24.

________, "China as a Factor in Indo-Pakistani Politics", *World Today,* Vol. 25, no. l, January 1969, pp. 43.

Siddiqui, Aslam, "US Military Aid to Pakistan", *Pakistan Horizon,* Vol. 12, no. l, March 1959, pp. 45-52.

Sidkey, Mohammad Habib, "Chinese World Strategy and South Asia: The Chinese Factor in Indo-Pakistan Relations", *Asian Survey,* Vol. 16, no. 10, October 1976, pp. 75-80.

Spain, J.W., "Military Assistance for Pakistan", *American Political Science Review* (Washington, D.C.), Vol. XLVIII, no. 3, September 1954, pp. 138-51.

Spector, Ivar, "Russia and Afro-Asian Neutralism", *Current History,* Vol. 37, no. 219, November 1959, pp. 272-83.

________, "Soviet Policy in Asia: A Reappraisal", *Current History,* Vol. 43, no. 255, November 1962, pp. 257-62.

"The foreign Policy of the Chinese People's Republic", *World Today,* Vol. 13, no. 4, April 1957, pp. 162-73.

"The Fundamentals of Pakistan's Foreign Policy", *Pakistan Horizon,* Vol. 9, no. 4, April 1957, pp. 162-73.

Wheeler, R.S., "Governor-General's Role in Pakistan", *Far Eastern Survey* (New York), Vol. XXIV, no. 1, January 1955, pp. 1-8.

Wilcox, Wayne A., "The Pakistan coup d'Etat of 1958", *Pacific Affairs,* Vol. XXXVIII, no. 2, Summer 1965, pp. 142-63.

________, "Political Change in Pakistan: Structures, Functions, Constraints and Goals", *Pacific Affairs,* Vol. XLI, no. 3, Fall 1968, pp. 341-55.

Zagoria, Donald S., "The Widening Gulf Between Mao and Khrushchev", *Reporter,* Vol. 28, no. 9, 25 April 1963, pp. 38-40.

Ziring, Lawrence, "Pakistan and India: Politics, Personalities and Foreign Policy", *Asian Survey,* Vol. 18, no. 7, July 1978, pp. 706-31.

**Newspapers and Periodicals**

*Alternatives* (New Delhi).

*American Political Science Review* (Wisconsin).

*Annals of American Academy of Political and Social Sciences* (Philadelphia, Pa.).

*Asia Quarterly* (Hongkong).

*Asian Survey* (Berkeley, Calif.).

*China Quarterly* (London).
*China Report* (New Delhi).
*Current* (Washington D.C.).
*Current Development in Mainland China* (New Delhi)
*Current History* (Philadelphia, Pa.).
*Dawn* (Karachi ).
*Far Eastern Survey* (New York).
*Financial Times* (London).
*Foreign Affairs* (New York).
*Foreign Policy* (New York).
*Hindustan Times* (New Delhi)
*Indian Express* (New Delhi).
*India Quarterly* (New Delhi).
*International Affairs* (London).
*International Studies* (New Delhi).
*International Studies Quarterly* (Michigan).
*Issue0000000s and Studies* (Taipei).
*Journal of Conflict Resolutions* (New Haven).
*Journal of Contemporary Asia* (Nottingham).
*Journal of International Affairs* (New York).
*Middle East Journal* (Washington D.C.).
*New York Times.*
*New Leader* (New York).
*New Republic* (Washington, D.C.).
*Orbis* (Philadelphia, Pa.).
*Pacific Affairs* (Vancouver, B.C.).
*Pacific Community* (Tokyo).
*Pakistan Horizon* (Karachi).
*Pakistan Review* (Lahore).
*Review of Politics* (Notre Dame, Indiana).
*Round Table* (London).
*The Hindu* (Madras).
*The Statesman* (New Delhi).
*The Times of India* (New Delhi).
*The Times* (London).
*The World Today* (London).
*World Marxist Review* (Toronto).
*World Politics* (Princeton).

# Index

## D

## G



## H



## I

## J



## K